"In the complexity of creating tech solutions for today's ever changing and uncertain environments, design thinking is an invaluable tool. In this book, George delivers the knowledge and resources that will help your team develop human-centered and valuable results quickly."

—*Karen Zeigler, Design Thinking Consultant and Host of "Cultivating Potential" Podcast*

"A terrific practical guide that shows how to navigate unstructured ambiguous situations using proven techniques... 24 hours spent with this book is one of the best investments you will ever make in yourself and for your team."

—*Paul Slater, CEO and Co-Founder, BillionMinds*

"George lays out the path for IT teams to inject Design Thinking across the project lifecycle to more quickly solve key business challenges, noting that Design Thinking methods should not be relegated solely to designers and UX experts but rather used broadly by the whole tech community for velocity and progress."

—*Bruce Gay, PMP, Principal and Founder, Astrevo*

"George understands that the most challenging activity for Design Thinking practitioners is getting other people to adopt their ideas. Hour 23 in particular is a great asset for those trying to make sure their change lands and adoption of their ideas is realized."

—*Luis Solano, Industry Development Manager, Google Cloud*

"The value George brings to the Design Thinking community through *Design Thinking for Tech* is best conveyed in this adaption of a quote from the book: We must capitalize on who we are today, the investments we make in ourselves, and the ability we have to provide value beyond today. Design Thinking gives us that framework for realizing value, and in these pages George walks us through when and how to apply methods within this framework so together we can build the confidence and capabilities necessary to solve the next generation of problems using applied Design Thinking."

—*Sean McGuire, Billboard Design Thinking Founder, Architect, and Author*

George W. Anderson

Design Thinking for Tech:
Solving Problems and Realizing Value
in 24 Hours

 Pearson

Design Thinking for Tech: Solving Problems and Realizing Value in 24 Hours

ISBN-13: 978-0-13-793303-7
ISBN-10: 0-13-793303-7

Library of Congress Control Number: 2022944622

1 2022

Trademarks

All terms mentioned in this book that are known to be trademarks or service marks have been appropriately capitalized. Pearson cannot attest to the accuracy of this information. Use of a term in this book should not be regarded as affecting the validity of any trademark or service mark.

Warning and Disclaimer

Every effort has been made to make this book as complete and as accurate as possible, but no warranty or fitness is implied. The information provided is on an "as is" basis. The author and the publisher shall have neither liability nor responsibility to any person or entity with respect to any loss or damages arising from the information contained in this book.

Special Sales

For information about buying this title in bulk quantities, or for special sales opportunities (which may include electronic versions; custom cover designs; and content particular to your business, training goals, marketing focus, or branding interests), please contact our corporate sales department at corpsales@pearsoned.com or (800) 382-3419.

For government sales inquiries, please contact governmentsales@pearsoned.com.

For questions about sales outside the U.S., please contact intlcs@pearson.com.

Microsoft and/or its respective suppliers make no representations about the suitability of the information contained in the documents and related graphics published as part of the services for any purpose. All such documents and related graphics are provided "as is" without warranty of any kind. Microsoft and/or its respective suppliers hereby disclaim all warranties and conditions with regard to this information, including all warranties and conditions of merchantability, whether express, implied or statutory, fitness for a particular purpose, title and non-infringement. In no event shall Microsoft and/or its respective suppliers be liable for any special, indirect or consequential damages or any damages whatsoever resulting from loss of use, data or profits, whether in an action of contract, negligence or other tortious action, arising out of or in connection with the use or performance of information available from the services.

The documents and related graphics contained herein could include technical inaccuracies or typographical errors. Changes are periodically added to the information herein. Microsoft and/or its respective suppliers may make improvements and/or changes in the product(s) and/or the program(s) described herein at any time. Partial screenshots may be viewed in full within the software version specified.

Microsoft® and Windows® are registered trademarks of the Microsoft Corporation in the U.S.A. and other countries. Screenshots and icons reprinted with permission from the Microsoft Corporation. This book is not sponsored or endorsed by or affiliated with the Microsoft Corporation.

Editor-in-Chief
Mark Taub

Signing Editor
Malobika Chakraborty

Development Editor
Chris Zahn

Managing Editor
Sandra Schroeder

Senior Project Editor
Tonya Simpson

Copy Editor
Chuck Hutchinson

Indexer
Kenneth Johnson

Proofreader
Paula Lowell

Editorial Assistant
Cindy Teeters

Cover Designer
Chuti Prasertsith

Compositor
Tricia Bronkella

Pearson's Commitment to Diversity, Equity, and Inclusion

Pearson is dedicated to creating bias-free content that reflects the diversity of all learners. We embrace the many dimensions of diversity, including but not limited to race, ethnicity, gender, socioeconomic status, ability, age, sexual orientation, and religious or political beliefs.

Education is a powerful force for equity and change in our world. It has the potential to deliver opportunities that improve lives and enable economic mobility. As we work with authors to create content for every product and service, we acknowledge our responsibility to demonstrate inclusivity and incorporate diverse scholarship so that everyone can achieve their potential through learning. As the world's leading learning company, we have a duty to help drive change and live up to our purpose to help more people create a better life for themselves and to create a better world.

Our ambition is to purposefully contribute to a world where

- Everyone has an equitable and lifelong opportunity to succeed through learning

- Our educational products and services are inclusive and represent the rich diversity of learners

- Our educational content accurately reflects the histories and experiences of the learners we serve

- Our educational content prompts deeper discussions with learners and motivates them to expand their own learning (and worldview)

While we work hard to present unbiased content, we want to hear from you about any concerns or needs with this Pearson product so that we can investigate and address them.

Please contact us with concerns about any potential bias at https://www.pearson.com/report-bias.html.

Contents at a Glance

Table of Contents

Figure Credits

Cover

Rarinlada/Shutterstock

Login/Shutterstock

Login/Shutterstock

Chapter

Figure 18.2: Microsoft

Foreword

George Anderson and I first met in 2011, when I became his colleague at Microsoft. It was my first job at Microsoft, and George had only been there a few months longer than I, but it never seemed like it. As I struggled with impostor syndrome and felt almost completely unable to cope with the demands and workload around me, George seemed to be able to calmly get things done. He was, how can I put it? Just in control.

It was hardly surprising that within a few short months he was my manager. As I learned more about him, I could never quite figure out how one person could just DO so much. He and I were close to each other in age, but somehow this guy had managed to squeeze in an MBA and PhD, regularly taught at university, volunteered at his church, *and* had written nearly a dozen books. Oh, and yes, somehow there was a wife and three kids in there as well. How infuriating!

Once I'd got over my inferiority complex, I realized that I had the good fortune to be around someone I could really learn from. As we worked closely together, I was in a sense a "George" apprentice. While I never nailed it quite like him, I could do a pretty good approximation.

Over time, our careers at Microsoft diverged, and we moved from friendly colleagues to friends who would catch up for dinner when he was in town. I never stopped learning from every interaction.

Then around 2019, I realized something I never had realized before about George. Yes, he was remarkable, but remarkable in a different and accessible way. Meet a basketball great, and chances are you know 1) They are superb at what they do, and 2) You will never be as great as them, no matter what you do. But George's particular version of greatness is completely approachable, completely accessible, and even attainable. I may have felt that I could never accomplish what he had, but through his personal interactions with me, his lived example, and through his written work he was literally giving me the roadmap to accomplish what he had accomplished in a practical and step-by-step kind of way. A master of empathy immersion, his written works served as roadmaps that we could all walk together.

This latest book provides you with a roadmap for navigating the complex and the hidden, from someone who has spent a lifetime focusing deeply on how he uses every hour of every day to get the most out of himself and make a difference in the world around him. My advice is to read it, absorb it, learn the techniques, perform the exercises, and expand your career and life. It's written for technology professionals, but just about anyone who is trying to figure out work and life will benefit from the read. It's like George—smart, but deeply approachable and practical.

In 2020, I left Microsoft and formed a company called BillionMinds. Our mission is to help a billion people master tough work environments through behavior change. Every day we work with people to develop a new set of skills, to become in a sense more like George. So, take it from me, it can be done. Change is not only possible but accessible through the kinds of techniques and exercises explained here. Use this book to help master the uncertainty in front of you and the ambiguity surrounding you. Don't let this be the book you get only halfway through and leave on the shelf. Let George help you as he has helped me and so many others, and you will surely be forever changed and, dare I say, grateful.

—Paul Slater, CEO and co-founder, BillionMinds

Preface

There has never been a more appropriate season for thinking and executing differently than the last several years. In that time, we have endured the tragedies and impact of a global pandemic, unforeseen drama around elections and masks and vaccinations, a global recession, the horrors of war and racial inequity, and tremendous changes in the workplace. We've also experienced working from home and sleeping at work, shifting to living life remotely, returning to new normals several times only to go back to remote living, adjusting to massive inflation, and so much more.

In the midst of this chaos and churn, more than ever we are looking for calm and clarity wherever we can find it. And they seem in short supply. Against this backdrop of chaos and change, there are still too many people personally and professionally

- ▶ Adapting by standing still, clinging to what we know and what has worked in the past—even after it's clear that the old norms and ways of thinking will never help us get to a better tomorrow.

- ▶ Pushing back against untried ways of thinking and executing given all the changes we have already been forced to accommodate or work through.

- ▶ Looking in exhaustion for greener grass, often accepting any kind and color of grass as long as it's different from the old grass.

We are fighting harder than ever against further change as we seek to control the little we can actually control. We need a better way to think through challenges and solve our most difficult problems. A better way to navigate uncertainty by taking the next best step. A better way to cut through the ambiguity surrounding us and our situations. We need help, and we need it more than ever. There's never been a better time to think and execute differently, to put Design Thinking to the test in our most cherished and prized circles at home, at work, and in our lives.

Prologue

Have you ever felt as if you were simply not creative or imaginative enough? Do you need to solve tough problems? Are you interested in delivering value throughout a project rather than exclusively at the tail end? If you said yes to any of these questions, then the Design Thinking mindset is actually perfect for you. And no, you don't need to be a designer to use Design Thinking. You just need to be human.

At its core, Design Thinking is about creative problem solving, using trial and error to build and test prototypes targeting the right problem to create the best solution. Design Thinking has been successfully adopted throughout the business, academic, and nonprofit sectors. It helps improve user alignment and understanding across an entire team. And its iterative nature complements other popular practices in the technical field.

In the following pages, George lays out the path for us and for our teams to begin using Design Thinking to solve our company's, our customers', and even our own personal challenges and toughest problems.

It's an interesting and practical approach, too. George doesn't tackle the status quo by turning every meeting into a Design Thinking workshop. On the contrary, George lights up the way to real progress by building the Design Thinking process into *how we already operate, communicate, and get things done*. Rather than bolting on a new way of thinking and executing, he instead thoughtfully injects techniques and exercises into the very fabric of our projects and initiatives.

In this way, Design Thinking becomes another intrinsic enabler for success rather than something we are asked to apply when someone wants to paint a vision, prototype an idea, or deliver a retrospective.

So don't allow Design Thinking to be relegated to designers and user experience experts! And don't simply stand on the sidelines. Everyone in the Tech community, and frankly anyone interested in thinking and doing things smarter, needs it. Jump in and learn how Design Thinking fundamentally changes your own personal and professional playing field!

—Bruce Gay, PMP and Principle/Founder of Astrevo

About the Author

George Anderson is a program director for Microsoft and an adjunct professor and guest lecturer for several universities. George holds Stanford Innovation & Entrepreneurship as well as Innovation Leadership credentials, PMI's Wicked Problem Solving and Prosci's Change Practitioner certifications, an MBA with a focus in Human Resource Management, and a PhD in Applied Management and Decision Sciences.

As a program director, George assembles and leads global tech teams that help organizations transform themselves. George's architects and consultants provide the technology and business skills necessary to design and develop business-enabling technology solutions, and George and his project managers provide the leadership, governance, and communications necessary to deliver those solutions.

In these ways, George's teams solve problems that drive meaningful change and measurable value. George knows first-hand the power of thinking and executing differently to change our world and often shares those learnings and experiences. He has co-led worldwide design thinking communities within Microsoft and has incorporated design thinking techniques and exercises into several of Microsoft's governance methods and project delivery methodologies.

Since 2002, George has also been assembling authoring teams to publish popular technology planning and implementation books, including *Teach Yourself SAP in 24 Hours* (2015) and *SAP Implementation Unleashed* (2009). More recently, he has shared how Design Thinking can be applied to our work and personal lives through *Stuck Happens: 95 Simple Life Hacks for Thinking and Thriving* (2021). And George and his team shared guidance and techniques organized around PMI's Process Groups in *Design Thinking for Program and Project Management* (2019).

Design Thinking for Tech: Solving Problems and Realizing Value in 24 Hours marries George's love of people, high-tech software development, platform-based business solutioning, and Design Thinking. It bridges the real-world intersection of technology and more than 130 Design Thinking techniques and exercises useful in learning, empathizing, and solving difficult problems while providing early and repeatable value along the way. Connect with George on LinkedIn or through email at George.Anderson@Microsoft.com.

Dedication

This book is dedicated to Michelle, the love of my life and a long-time Design Thinker. Her natural ability to effortlessly connect deeply with others, walk beside them, rally around their toughest situations, and work alongside them through solutions to those situations captures the essence of Design Thinking. In these ways, she helps others solve some of the hardest problems imaginable on the journey to leading a richer, valuable, and more fulfilled life.

Her vocation? Pastor, Wife, and Mom.

Acknowledgments

As usual, I have too many people to acknowledge and too little space to do so. Thank you to my fellow Design Thinking colleagues and enthusiasts across Microsoft's Design Thinking communities, LinkedIn's various Design Thinking groups, and my own colleagues and customers spanning several decades of global technology initiatives, programs, and projects.

I want to especially call out Bruce Gay, Sean McGuire, Prashant Mittal, Karen Zeigler, Luis Solano, Brennan Lynch, Amir Naghmi, Jeanette Sjoberg, Darhyl Watkins, Drew Gervino, Rebecca Whitworth, Rick Furino, Paul MacDonald, Mike Carr, Jeffrey Johnson, Michael Pigg, Noopur Hegde, Seema Garg, Charles Lamanna, Suneel Mathur, Michelle Newton, Gregg Barker, Danyal Farooq, Lori Stockton, Jenn Goth, Brent Hawkinson, Jose Mata, Dave Spear, Sharon Long, Jon Greville, Pierre-Frederic Jaffre, James Paley, Ryan Tan, Ming Chao, Puneet Gupta, Bryan McMillan, Laura Martelli, Shaily Nair, Perry Lanaway, Tom Ball, Tim Litton, Rob Standefer, Brian Seitz, Bill Cunnane, Sanjay Lobo, Nita Copley, Phyllis Rhodes, Fazil Osman, Al Rothfuchs, Rick Nye, Don Ballard, Karen Richardson, Paul Mirts, David Driftmier, Bharani Srinivasan, Angelo Cotanidis, Anna MacWilliams, Michael Herold, Adebola Ibironke, Gregory Lisiak, Michael Litman, John Turner, Danny Borden, Sanjay Lobo, Tom Frederick, John Dobbins, Tim Rhodes, Julie Chandler, Andreas Jenzer, Naeem Hashmi, Leonard Glass, Srini Jasti, Brianna Ritter, Teja Immidi, Melanie Putlak, Juergen Imhoff, Marc Ashbrook, Mike Wise, JD Meier, Dave Sanders, Jony Lawrence, Yoav Intrator, Hardy Utley, Jeff Davis, Judson Althoff, Satya Nadella, Uli Homann, and Paul Slater, along with my customers and colleagues around the world. Together, you have helped demonstrate throughout the years how, when, and where it makes sense to apply Design Thinking to Tech. And you have helped me find balance while keeping us grounded in the the real world of delivering value in the toughest situations around the globe.

Thank you also to the team supporting Wicked Problem Solving at the Project Management Institute, the instructors at the LUMA Institute, and the professors and speakers connected to Stanford's d.school for inspiring me by how you embody and demonstrate the best of human-centric thinking. I am grateful for the abilities you have given my teams and me to help others solve tough problems and realize value on our collective journeys to somewhere New, somewhere Better.

And finally, thank you to the One who makes all things possible. I can imagine no better life and no better way to serve than through and with the people you've placed in my path all these years. There is nothing too difficult, nothing impossible, with You by my side.

We Want to Hear from You!

As the reader of this book, *you* are our most important critic and commentator. We value your opinion and want to know what we're doing right, what we could do better, what areas you'd like to see us publish in, and any other words of wisdom you're willing to pass our way.

We welcome your comments. You can email or write to let us know what you did or didn't like about this book—as well as what we can do to make our books better.

Please note that we cannot help you with technical problems related to the topic of this book.

When you write, please be sure to include this book's title and author as well as your name and email address. We will carefully review your comments and share them with the author and editors who worked on the book.

Email: community@informit.com

Why Design Thinking for Technology Professionals?

Let's get to the matter at hand and set the stage for why Design Thinking for technology professionals and those who manage technology projects is so important. The short answer? Because it's needed.

Technology and digital transformation, whether embodied in a six-week tech assessment project or spanning an entire global business transformation, is essential for those organizations that wish to be around in another five years. Technology enables organizations to change how they go to market, how they operate, and how they better serve their customers and communities. We know this stuff. Technology is why these organizations will remain viable as they improve and wholly reimagine their current business capabilities, introduce new AI-enabled capabilities, reduce costs, streamline their technology footprint, enhance their global competitiveness, and more. Technology-enabled change supported with Design Thinking's techniques and exercises will help these same companies solve hard problems, make progress, and deliver value. Let's take a closer look at each of these.

Why Design Thinking? Solving Problems

Design Thinking is a difference maker, helping us solve problems that have lingered and remained unsolved. By replacing our focus on the problem with a focus on the people in the middle of that problem, we have a chance to look, learn, and think differently. We have a chance to humanize the problem. And that's really the key; a human-centric rather than problem-centric perspective helps us make the step-changes we need to solve those tough problems. Design Thinking gives us the ability and permission to pursue the kinds of incremental solutions we can put in place to make progress. Design Thinking helps us let go of long-held beliefs and attitudes and strike out in new ways—ways that might feel as if we're slowing down in the short term but lead to more complete solutions in the long term. Design Thinking connects people and teams, changing our mindset and our abilities, so we can move from trying to deliver perfection to actually incrementally solving some of the toughest problems and situations we face.

Why Design Thinking? More Ideas, More Progress

An important key to solving difficult problems lies in how many ideas we can bring to light; solving problems doesn't happen without the benefit of new thinking and therefore lots of new potential or partial solutions. That's where Design Thinking's myriad of ideation techniques comes into play. With more ways of thinking comes more ideas and with it the ability to try and fail and then learn and ideate—so we can repeat that process again and again, doing so quickly enough to arrive at the "try and succeed" desired outcome that much faster.

Need an example? Consider one of the earliest and most prolific Design Thinkers, Thomas Edison. Edison and his team made 1,000 attempts to solve the problem of creating sustainable and reasonably priced electric-based light. He and his team understood the secret to progress, though. Progress is found in cycling through the "trying and failing and learning and ideating just a bit differently" process. Iterative learning and ideating allowed them to try and try again and again. Combined with great perseverance, Design Thinking paid off.

As we see above, while velocity plays a central role in success, paradoxically so, too, does our failures. It's the rapidly achieved little failures along the way that lead to learning, greater understanding, and ultimately to greater big-picture velocity. In this way, we can finish what others struggled unsuccessfully to achieve, as we see next.

Why Design Thinking? Speedier Value Creation

The best answer to the question "Why Design Thinking for technology?" lies in the power to not only solve problems but to deliver value and do so incrementally and therefore earlier than ever. By dramatically improving time-to-value, even incremental value, organizations benefit on several fronts. First, Design Thinking helps us navigate situations and challenges to ultimately arrive at the finish line faster than we otherwise could (if at all). And second, because we arrive at that finish line faster, we better preserve our budgets. We benefit in terms of the staff and resources that we can reallocate earlier than otherwise possible, because we avoided many of the pitfalls that would have taken us down costly sidetracks, stalls, and dead ends.

Third, by getting to the finish line faster, we also set up an organization to begin more quickly realizing the value of the solutions they've invested so much time in designing, developing, and delivering.

Fourth and even better, Design Thinking helps organizations realize value along the way, too, as we quickly and incrementally deliver something of value to those who desperately need it to simply remain viable. And as our teams intersect with other technology initiatives and projects in flight, Design Thinking techniques and exercises become the difference makers that help anchor others in ways to also make progress and deliver value at velocity.

Why This Book?

The Project Management Institute's Pulse of the Profession Report 2021 tells us that in 2020 approximately 12 percent of all projects failed, 34 percent experienced significant scope creep, only 55 percent completed on time, and only 62 percent completed within budget. And these were improvements over the previous year!

The failure rate is even higher for the most complex and ambiguous projects and initiatives. Experts and our own experiences tell us that between 50 percent and 70 percent of digital transformation projects fail in some kind of fundamental way, and of those that succeed, most still fall far short in achieving their business objectives and key results.

Here's the thing: the problems that these organizations face still remain unsolved. The problems continue to linger, dragging down effectiveness and affecting the organization's employees, customers, and ability to move forward in new and sustainable kinds of ways. These organizations are trapped in a dreadful video game, stuck on level 2 with no hope of beating the monster at the end and advancing to level 3. They don't just need another life or a do-over. They need new weapons.

Instead of new weapons, though, a new project or initiative invariably springs up to address the legacy problems and age-old monsters. New people get involved with vigor and energy but without the benefit of past lessons and experiences. And when they try to tackle those legacy problems, oftentimes in the same way as their predecessors, they also fail. Just like their predecessors. And the cycle repeats itself again and again. Where are the new weapons? What can make the difference to individuals and teams tasked with solving these problems?

This book and, much more importantly, the Design Thinking guidance, techniques, and exercises found here serve as the difference makers. In these ways, problems spanning areas like those listed here may be approached and solved differently, giving organizations not just the hope but the ability to thrive anew:

▶ Understanding and awareness of the landscape and problems today, including how the past has transpired to create today's situation

▶ Connecting with and deeply understanding the right people across an organization to learn and adapt

▶ Building and maintaining healthy and resilient teams

▶ Aligning on incremental approaches to solving tough problems

▶ Creating bite-sized "Agile" plans to tackle what's next versus trying to plan how to solve the entirety of a problem or situation

▶ Establishing a lightweight and tailored governance and communications framework among the minimum bodies, boards, and councils necessary to work effectively

▶ Incorporating a 360-degree view of stakeholder awareness and communications

▶ Setting and managing realistic expectations across internal and external stakeholders, including gaining and retaining executive sponsorship

▶ Understanding and identifying the right problems and priorities for solving them

▶ Driving new ways of iteratively thinking, solutioning, prototyping, demonstrating, and testing as a way of learning and course-correcting fast

▶ Balancing day jobs with technology project realities across an organization's landscape

▶ Blending the right level of business, functional, and technical skills among the various teams

▶ Building smaller and tighter feature teams where fewer people wear more hats and therefore innately benefit from the broader understanding and connections such teaming provides

▶ Identifying blind spots early to iterate or altogether avoid "we didn't know what we didn't know" syndrome

▶ Taking a broader view toward the dependencies surrounding the work we understand, keeping in mind that no new system operates in a silo

▶ Improving and adjusting communications as inevitable issues, challenges, and slippages arise

▶ Thinking through how to land change, how to effectively train users, how to manage adoption, and how to scale our work for the benefit of others

When we initially discussed this book project, we agreed it was important to share lessons learned from years of leading and delivering technology projects and complex business transformations. For this reason, we have included real-world lessons, real-life explanations, and common mistakes to consider. We will help you adopt new ways of thinking and working through uncertainty and ambiguity. We will teach you where and how to sidestep standard practices in favor of different techniques and exercises. We will help you bring people and teams together to create a stronger shared understanding and culture and explain what others have done so you can do the same thing faster and with greater benefit. Finally, we will show you how to gain a competitive edge as you employ Design Thinking techniques and exercises as strategic enablers for delivering value earlier and strategic business outcomes faster.

We also wanted to provide a mechanism for applying what we are reading each hour in a way that really brings it all together. To this end, each hour concludes with an ongoing fictional case study highlighting each hour's material with questions and answers. The questions are not difficult but reinforce the content in a way that should make the learnings "sticky" and memorable.

The final answer to "Why this book?" simply lies in this: Our experiences are real, gleaned from a mix of global programs and complex technology projects across a breadth of industries. The timing is perfect to benefit from Design Thinking in solving tough problems and getting hard things done.

Organizing the Book

This book is organized into five parts that follow the phases of a simple Design Thinking Model for Tech outlined in Hour 1 and detailed in Hour 2 and throughout the book:

- ▶ Part I, "Design Thinking Basics," lays the groundwork for the book and comprises the first five hours. Here, we introduce Design Thinking, explaining the what, how, when, why, and who of Design Thinking. Then we walk through a simple four-phased model for Design Thinking and illustrate how that model applies to individuals as well as teams. We conclude Part I with how to organize and execute a Design Thinking session. With this foundation, we can begin walking through the phases laid out in the next four parts.

- ▶ Part II, "Understanding Broadly," focuses initially on the techniques and exercises we can use to understand the big picture or lay of the land. Then we turn our attention to connecting with, observing, and empathizing with the right people spanning that big picture. In this way, we can identify the right problems that need attention and focus on the techniques and exercises useful for understanding those problems.

- ▶ Part III, "Thinking Differently," considers the need and methods for externalizing the ideas trapped in our heads as a way to explore those ideas more deeply and with others. We look at techniques for thinking divergently, exercises for increasing creativity, and still other exercises for reducing and working through uncertainty. Part II concludes with problem-solving exercises that let us bridge the gap between those problems and the imperfect start of potential solutions to those problems.

- ▶ Part IV, "Delivering Value," introduces us to Design Thinking techniques and exercises that help us find and prioritize the next best steps toward value creation. As we work on solutioning solo and through our small groups and teams, we learn how to unlock the value previously trapped in our problems and situations. Techniques for starting small help us move and deliver with velocity and conclude Part IV, setting the stage for how we continuously improve and scale.

▶ Part V, "Iterating for Progress," is about testing and iterating on feedback from that testing to learn and execute more repeatably. We cover techniques for iterating to refine our understanding of the big picture, the people involved, and the underlying problems, all to help us improve our solutions. As we cut through ambiguity to make progress, we also cover techniques and exercises for scaling our solutions and the way we deploy and support those solutions. The final two hours of Part V conclude with ways of improving how we think about and manage change and operate with velocity as we land solutions.

Like the Design Thinking model we will explore in the pages that follow, we will see how each part walks us stepwise through the model's phases. Each part also reminds us to loop back and learn so we may continuously refine our work. It's through this recursive nature of the Design Thinking process, and the techniques and exercises associated with each phase of the process, that we can together solve the tough problems we face while ultimately delivering measurable value and other benefits along the way.

Audience and Approach

If you wear a technology hat of any kind— if you lead, manage, deliver, equip others, or help support complex technology projects and business-enabled digital transformations— you will find this book useful:

▶ Product owners and product managers

▶ Scrum masters and Agile ceremony leads

▶ Workstream and feature team leads

▶ Program and project managers and other delivery leaders

▶ Enterprise architects, cloud solution architects, and all manner of solution and technology architects

▶ Business, technology, and functional consultants and analysts

▶ DevOps leads and web and application developers

▶ User experience and user interface specialists

- ▶ All manner of system and solution testers

- ▶ System end users, especially those tasked with helping to brainstorm, design, evaluate, and test new technology solutions

- ▶ Network infrastructure specialists

- ▶ Security specialists and privacy experts

- ▶ Data engineers and database administrators

- ▶ Technical integration specialists

- ▶ Cloud automation and deployment engineers

- ▶ Cloud operations engineers and other operations specialists

- ▶ Dashboard and reporting specialists

- ▶ Help desk and call center agents

- ▶ Tech executives, CIOs, CTOs, CDOs, and other IT leaders

- ▶ Executives, sponsors, and other transformation leaders

- ▶ Business managers and analysts

- ▶ IT risk management specialists

- ▶ Innovation and design specialists

- ▶ Change management and new-system adoption specialists

- ▶ Training specialists and other educators

- ▶ Students of Design Thinking, including anyone interested in learning how to apply the Design Thinking process and a host of techniques and exercises useful for problem solving and value creation

In light of the diversity of this audience, it was important to strike a balance in the breadth and depth of the material that yielded another important outcome: Every hour provides some kind of value to every reader, whether a beginner or long-time Design Thinking practitioner.

Thank you again for adding this book to your library!

PART I

Design Thinking Basics

HOUR 1
Design Thinking Explained

What You'll Learn in This Hour:

- ▶ Thinking Slower to Deliver Faster
- ▶ A Process for Progress: Popular Design Thinking Models
- ▶ Our Design Thinking Model for Tech
- ▶ The Battle Between Perfection and Time
- ▶ The What: Techniques and Exercises
- ▶ The How: The Design Thinking Cycle for Progress
- ▶ The When: Ambiguity, Complexity, and Uncertainty
- ▶ The Why: Better Practices and Faster Outcomes
- ▶ The Who: Design Thinking by Technology Role
- ▶ Design Thinking in Action: Real-world Tech Examples
- ▶ What Not to Do: Lessons Learned the Hard Way
- ▶ Summary and Case Study

As we will see, Design Thinking is both a process and a set of techniques and exercises useful for thinking through and solving problems faster than otherwise possible. Hour 1 commences Part I, called "Design Thinking Basics," where we assemble and align around the Design Thinking Cycle for Progress and a Design Thinking Model for Tech (Hours 1–5). Subsequent parts of the book include Part II, "Understanding Broadly" (Hours 6–9), Part III, "Thinking Differently" (Hours 10–14), Part IV, "Delivering Value" (Hours 15–18), and Part V, "Iterating for Progress" (Hours 19–24).

In this first hour, we set the stage for Design Thinking by explaining the process, fundamentals, and structure of popular Design Thinking models. Additional context is provided by covering the what, how, when, why, and who of Design Thinking. A discussion of the natural tension between working fast and thinking slow, along with a view into the kinds of real-world lessons learned to be shared across each hour, concludes Hour 1.

Thinking Slower to Deliver Faster

Design Thinking is about slowing down and taking the time to deeply understand, think, and iterate on solutions to the toughest problems as a way of delivering value. And in cases where there is great complexity, ambiguity, and therefore uncertainty, Design Thinking helps us deliver that value faster than we could ever otherwise do. Consider Design Thinking in terms of Aesop's *Tortoise and the Hare* parable. Design Thinking's process, techniques, and exercises are the tortoise, and the traditional methods of solving problems and delivering outcomes are the hare.

When the path of the race is well marked and the finish line is clear, the hare will nearly always beat the tortoise. Standard practices and proven methodologies will get us to the end of the race pretty consistently and predictably. The hare thrives in the world of simple problems.

But when that world is murky, and the problems are incredibly complex, and the finish line is shrouded in ambiguity, being fast like the hare isn't helpful. Worse, the hare takes us down expensive and time-consuming dead ends. In these cases, the way of the tortoise makes more sense...not because it's slower than the hare but because the tortoise is wiser. Design Thinking encourages us to understand and learn so we identify the right problems, think through making the best next steps, and take the smarter path. Design Thinking gives us the mix of techniques and exercises necessary for thinking and executing in a manner that clears the way for progress.

And here's the thing: The tortoise will actually cross the finish line while the hare is still lost, running around and backtracking and spending a whole lot of time yielding little value. So, to complete the parable, the tortoise will indeed deliver the better time-to-value when it comes to the messiest problems and most complex situations. Slowing down to do the work of Design Thinking will get us to the finish line.

A Process for Progress: Popular Design Thinking Models

Design Thinking is a process for organizing how to make progress, how to get hard stuff done, and how to deliver real value relatively quickly. Though the process looks stepwise, Design Thinking is very much nonlinear: it's full of relearning, circle-backs, and restarts. Interestingly, though, it's not really the Design Thinking *process* that helps us make progress or work through ambiguity and complexity. Instead, we make progress through Design Thinking's *techniques and exercises*.

Design Thinking techniques and exercises help us make progress when we get stuck. More importantly, Design Thinking helps us *avoid* getting completely stuck in the first place. We use Design Thinking proactively—to understand and empathize and think and so on—so we don't wind up sitting around wondering why our technology project has stalled or our business transformation has run off the rails.

Still, there is value in the process. Design Thinking process models help us organize Design Thinking's techniques and exercises; different techniques are called for at different phases in the process. And the process helps us understand a potential precursor or successor that in turn might help us do the work at hand. For example, before we jump in and start thinking and ideating, we probably need to empathize with a situation and the people involved, followed by defining the problem or problems tied to that situation. It doesn't mean we won't go back later and explore other aspects of the situation, its people, and its problems. We likely will! But the stepwise nature of a good Design Thinking process model helps us work left-to-right before we start looping back and looping around. Figure 1.1 reflects some of the most popular Design Thinking process models, and you can see just how similar they are.

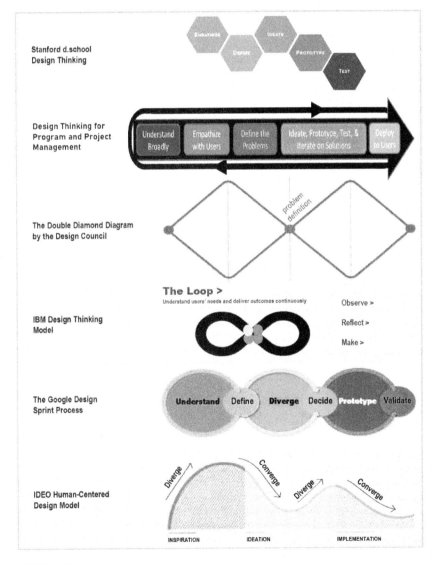

FIGURE 1.1
Popular Design Thinking process models.

You might also notice where they are different. Various Design Thinking models reflect what's important to the creator of that model. Some value thinking, others value connecting with people, and still others value the need for iterative testing and refinement. While these are all good general models, there is still the need for a simpler model for technology professionals.

Our Design Thinking Model for Tech

For our purposes, we need a Design Thinking model that aligns to technology projects, is logically aligned to Design Thinking, and yet is as condensed as we can responsibly condense it. Most importantly, our model needs to consider the importance of iteratively delivering something of *value* throughout the process; we cannot simply conclude our work with a prototype and endless iteration. It's this notion of value that sets our model apart from others. And finally, we need a model that recursively takes us back to improve our understanding, introduce new ways of thinking, deliver value, and so on, as we see in Figure 1.2.

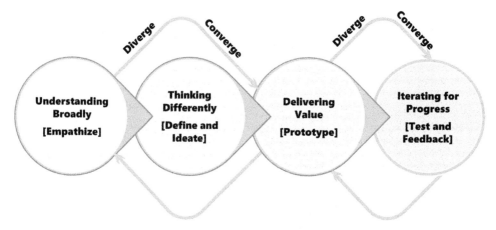

FIGURE 1.2
Our Design Thinking Model for Tech.

Note that we'll explore this model in detail in Hour 2. First, however, we need to set the stage for this model by considering the two enemies of solving difficult problems: the pursuit of perfection and the constraint of time.

The Battle Between Perfection and Time

It's been said that perfection is the enemy of good, but perfection is also the enemy of speed and velocity and of actually getting anything difficult or ambiguous done. So we must battle the urge to create and execute against a perfect plan versus the reality that the pursuit of perfection actually slows us down.

Consider the effect of diminishing returns when introducing something new. Because doing something new means change, new is painful. But change—and therefore pain—is really the only road to long-term longevity; there's no way around it. The key is to get started on the change. We can't possibly change anything without showing up and setting our minds to driving that change. Success lies in starting.

What is really interesting about most success stories, though, is that they are rarely flawless execution stories. Their transformation journeys are littered with false starts, ill-conceived plans, bad ideas, and restarts. But in all of these cases, people tried and failed and yet *learned fast enough* to course-correct. They didn't get everything perfectly right the first time, *but they got enough directionally right fast enough* for their respective work to succeed.

Had they focused on perfection, these success stories would still be works-in-progress. Or long-forgotten and shelved.

So if perfection and time are the real enemies, how might we approach a body of work and complete it faster than our competitors? By drawing from a tool bag of proven Design Thinking techniques and exercises, and in doing so changing the way we execute to solve hard problems and deliver value sooner than later.

The What: Techniques and Exercises

While we've seen that Design Thinking is a recursive process that must result in some kind of value along the way, Design Thinking is made real through the specific techniques we adopt and exercises we practice along the way. The rubber meets the road through Design Thinking techniques and exercises. And there are literally hundreds of each.

- ▶ **Techniques**, also called Design Thinking methods or principles, are ways of learning, thinking, or executing that don't require a bunch of prework or steps to accomplish. The Rule of Threes technique, for example, reminds us that it generally takes at least three iterations of building and testing something to arrive at a usable product. This is a simple axiom. Most techniques align to such axioms or principles and are therefore a bit self-evident. Silent Design, Snaking the Drain, Building to Think, Making Ideas Visible and Visual…these are all examples of Design Thinking techniques that can be understood and applied very quickly.

- ▶ **Exercises**, sometimes called Design Thinking plays, consist of steps and activities. Exercises go well beyond how you might think about a situation, and instead reflect a series of activities executed stepwise, one after the other, to arrive at some kind of understanding or output. Some are easy and require only a few steps. Others, such as a Boats and Anchors exercise, consist of prework and a dozen steps that help us identify factors that affect schedule, which in turn may be used to manage and mitigate schedule risks. Reverse Brainstorming, Running the Swamp, conducting a Premortem, Mesh Networking,

SCAMPER for Brainstorming, Pattern Matching...these are all examples of Design Thinking exercises that take us through a series of steps to arrive at an output or outcome.

▶ **Recipes**, sometimes called playbooks, represent a combination of techniques and exercises that together help us work through a particular phase in the Design Thinking process or part of that process.

As we see in Figure 1.3, each phase in our Design Thinking Model for Tech reflects numerous techniques and exercises. Because there are so many different techniques and exercises, only a few have been shown and mapped to each phase in our Design Thinking process model.

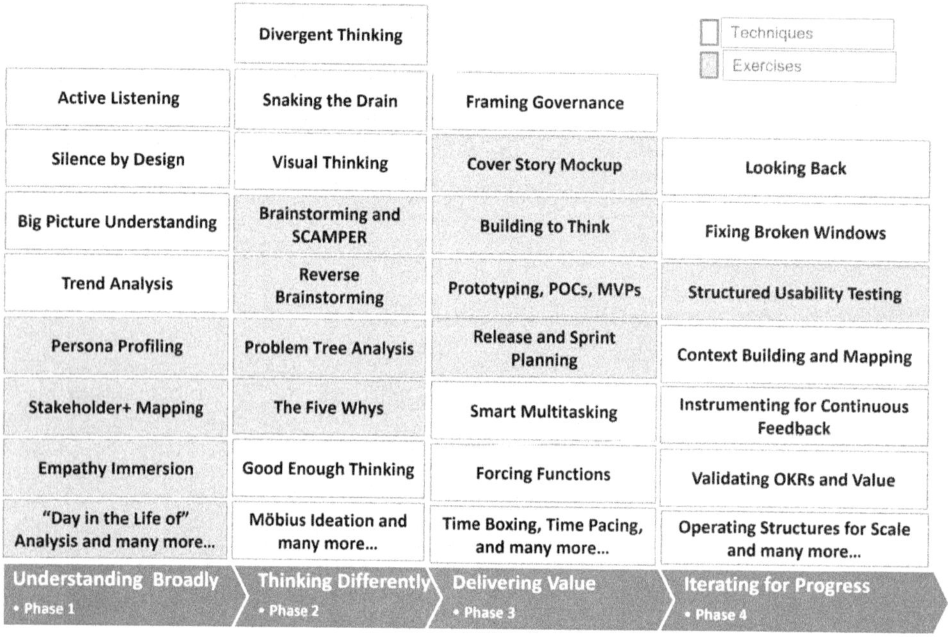

	Divergent Thinking		Techniques
			Exercises
Active Listening	Snaking the Drain	Framing Governance	
Silence by Design	Visual Thinking	Cover Story Mockup	Looking Back
Big Picture Understanding	Brainstorming and SCAMPER	Building to Think	Fixing Broken Windows
Trend Analysis	Reverse Brainstorming	Prototyping, POCs, MVPs	Structured Usability Testing
Persona Profiling	Problem Tree Analysis	Release and Sprint Planning	Context Building and Mapping
Stakeholder+ Mapping	The Five Whys	Smart Multitasking	Instrumenting for Continuous Feedback
Empathy Immersion	Good Enough Thinking	Forcing Functions	Validating OKRs and Value
"Day in the Life of" Analysis and many more...	Möbius Ideation and many more...	Time Boxing, Time Pacing, and many more...	Operating Structures for Scale and many more...
Understanding Broadly • Phase 1	**Thinking Differently** • Phase 2	**Delivering Value** • Phase 3	**Iterating for Progress** • Phase 4

FIGURE 1.3
Mapping techniques and exercises to our Design Thinking Model for Tech.

The How: The Design Thinking Cycle for Progress

Before we identify specific Design Thinking techniques or exercises we might employ, we need to consider which ones will help us along, which ones will bring clarity, and which ones might drive the kinds of outcomes we seek. We need to organize ourselves and plug in our tools (our techniques and exercises) where they make sense to create a recipe for making progress.

Consider how the **Design Thinking Cycle for Progress**, illustrated in Figure 1.4, is used to organize our needs and bring together the techniques or exercises necessary to help us work through the four phases of our Design Thinking Model for Tech.

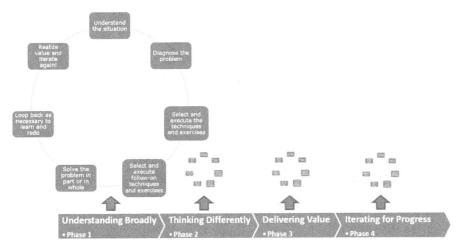

FIGURE 1.4
The Design Thinking Cycle for Progress helps us organize ourselves and our thinking.

The **Design Thinking Cycle for Progress** is recursive and circular. It's circular because we will nearly always need to run through the cycle several times to achieve the outcomes associated with a particular phase (or part of a phase) in our Design Thinking Model for Tech. The cycle helps us create the recipe needed for that particular phase, in the same way we use a recipe for baking a cake. Our chosen Design Thinking techniques and exercises are the ingredients. And like a good baker, we may need to augment a recipe by including additional ingredients or swapping out one ingredient for a slightly different one. We might even need to call on a fellow baker, or connect with an expert baker, to help us think through or consider new or unfamiliar techniques and exercises.

In these ways, the **Design Thinking Cycle for Progress** represents *how* we make progress within each phase of the Design Thinking journey. It's what we use to think through, organize, and run the recipes of techniques and exercises necessary to understand a situation, solve problems, and create value.

The When: Ambiguity, Complexity, and Uncertainty

Conventional software development and project management techniques don't always give us the permission or flexibility we need to creatively solve problems. Conventional techniques may not help us wade through ambiguity, help us figure out the right path to take, help us identify the right problems to solve, or give us the freedom to try and fail and try again.

These conventional techniques often prescribe specific tasks and processes, inject rigid gates and quality checkpoints, and mandate other such practices. And to be clear, these are wonderful practices when a problem is clear, a solution is evident, and the work of solutioning simply needs to be planned and delivered.

But we need something better—a smarter approach—if we expect to overcome the challenges of an ambiguous situation steeped in complexity and a hundred different possible next steps. In these cases, Design Thinking gives us the techniques, exercises, freedom, and flexibility to tackle unknowns as we learn, iterate on those learnings, and deliver value in a way that conserves time.

And that's really the key, right? Time is the most valuable commodity. Completing large-scale unique endeavors takes time. As ambiguity, complexity, and uncertainty increase, the need for more time increases...and so too does the need for techniques and exercises capable of driving deeper understanding, stronger ideation, greater insights, and a clearer path forward. So we can preserve and conserve time. It seems we have a time-to-value crisis, and Design Thinking is our superhero.

As we've said for several years, those who are leading, equipping, managing, and governing our tech teams and the toughest tech projects need to iteratively operate just as their teams must operate. This is a joint exercise where everyone is leaning on Design Thinking to think and learn quickly by doing and failing quickly. Complex problem solving and value creation requires arming our problem solvers as well as those who lead our problem solvers with the techniques and exercises capable of making progress.

So again, if time is our primary enemy, Design Thinking is our response. A human or user-centric way of operating gives the entire team and everyone connected to it—from sponsors and stakeholders to product managers, business leads, architects, feature team leads, developers, and users—the permission, alignment, and guidelines needed to think differently and deliver faster. Design Thinking provides the tools and techniques needed to work through complex problems. It facilitates understanding an environment broadly, empathizing with the people connected to that environment, defining needs and problems, prototyping and testing potential solutions, quickly learning from and iterating on those potential and partial solutions, and delivering and deploying solutions that solve problems and create value.

The Why: Better Practices and Faster Outcomes

Solving difficult and unique problems will always be incredibly hard. Delivering complex technology-enabled solutions and large-scale business transformations will always be hard too. Why? Because their environments and situations are ambiguous and fluid, making problems difficult to define with certainty. Potential next steps and solutions are subsequently unclear and notoriously incomplete as well.

In 1973, Rittel and Webber described these toughest-of-tough endeavors as wicked problems. Such problems are wicked in the sense that they appear insanely difficult to solve. In light of their complexity and challenges, solutions to wicked problems require changes in not only how people think but in how they learn and operate. To paraphrase Einstein, such problems cannot be solved with the same mindset that created them.

Approaching situations and problems with a Design Thinking perspective is helpful in these cases. Why? Because Design Thinking puts people and their needs at the center of our situations and problems, no matter how wickedly complex or ambiguous. And in doing so, we are arming ourselves with ways of working through ambiguity, complexity, and so on as discussed earlier. These ways of working are reflected in best practices, common practices, and Design Thinking practices, covered next.

Best Practices

In most walks of life, we talk of using "best" practices to do or deliver something faster or cheaper or with less risk. Best practices are heralded as the industry's example of the "one best way" and as such are given a lot of attention. But best practices are only "best" for a season, and then they become old. They become stale. And they lose their perch as "best." What we really need is a better way of practicing...something that's a bit more "evergreen" than best.

Common Practices

Sometimes, that better way of practicing is found in the "common" ways we approach a situation or problem. There might be a single best practice today for addressing a particular challenge, but there are surely *many* common ways for addressing that challenge. They might not be best practices, but they're better than most. Common practices strike a more cost-effective balance between what is best and what is acceptable.

To be clear, then, common practices are not as effective as best practices. The classic trade-off cited by those executing common practices over best practices lies in sacrificing capabilities or qualities or even time for the wonderful advantages of *reduced costs*; common practices are nearly always much less expensive than best practices.

We like to say that common practices fall into the bucket of "Good Enough" (a Design Thinking technique in its own right we'll cover later), delivering close to the same capabilities or quality delivered by best practices, but at lower cost. We might also find that common practices can be implemented *faster* than best practices, but again with trade-offs in capabilities, quality, security, and so on.

The key to choosing common practices over best practices is to understand where the appetite for accepting risk lies. Common practices are about diminishing returns. For example, if we can achieve X at the 95th percentile and at half the cost of 96 percent, *and 95 percent is acceptable to our users*, then we have a good case for implementing X using less costly common practices rather than "better" but more costly best practices.

Design Thinking: Beyond Best and Common Practices

There's a third category of practices beyond best practices or common practices. We call this third category Design Thinking practices, and as we might guess, they put people at the center of a problem or situation. More to the point of this discussion, though, Design Thinking practices are used *today* to ultimately uncover what will eventually become best practices *tomorrow* (for a season...).

How might this evolution of Design Thinking practices to best practices to common practices play out? Rather than implementing a standard best practice or an easy-fix common practice, we need to work with the people affected by the problem or situation. We do this to understand the big picture, empathize with those living inside the big picture, define the problems residing within that big picture, and then iteratively prototype and test a solution.

In doing so, we will discover what will become a new set of best and common practices to leverage for that particular situation for a while, at least until those best and common practices grow stale and require another round of Design Thinking, as depicted in Figure 1.5.

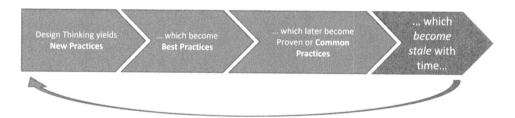

FIGURE 1.5
From Design Thinking practices to best and common practices.

The Who: Design Thinking by Technology Role

In case it's not evident, Design Thinking is for all technology professionals regardless of the role or persona being played. From subject matter experts to various architects and workstream leads, product owners and managers, process experts, managers, executives, and a host of supporting roles, Design Thinking is the glue that brings the Tech family together (see Figure 1.6).

What Is a Persona?

A persona is an amalgamation of similar people with similar interests and needs. Using this technique, we can create fictional characters (such as "finance user," "sales user," "executive stakeholder," and other such amalgamations) to represent types or subsets of a user community who share common needs and will use specific artifacts or features of a solution or deliverable in similar ways.

FIGURE 1.6
Bringing the Tech family together through Design Thinking.

Design Thinking in Action: Real-world Tech Examples

As we walk through each hour, we'll visit real-world step-by-step examples of Design Thinking in action. And we'll apply many of those real-world techniques and exercises in the BigBank Case Study that weaves its way throughout the book. In these ways, Design Thinking will become very real and relevant for every reader, regardless of experience or background.

Rather than provide only a single technique or exercise, we'll cover alternatives that might be a bit easier to execute or lend themselves to exploring a different aspect of a problem or situation. We will also flip things around and cover the hard lessons learned and experiences leaving us wishing for a do-over, covered next.

What Not to Do: Lessons Learned the Hard Way

In the same way that we've included real-world examples during each hour reflecting how to apply Design Thinking techniques or exercises to various technology projects and initiatives, we have also included real-world examples in each hour of lessons learned the hard way: through painful experience. Each of these "What Not to Do" sections is an important part of that hour's learnings as we see how misapplied or ignored Design Thinking distracts, confuses, or lets down the very people who require clarity and progress the most.

Summary

In this first hour, we set the stage for how to think about Design Thinking, including what it is, how it is applied, when it is used, why it makes sense, and who is involved and benefits from it. Design Thinking is a process in and of itself, but the real value of Design Thinking comes in applying Design Thinking techniques and running Design Thinking exercises. It's through techniques and exercises that we solve problems and create value.

We positioned Design Thinking as the answer to the hard problems and most difficult situations. Complexity and ambiguity lead to uncertainty, which in turn magnifies the time required to tackle such problems and situations. Because Design Thinking puts people in the center of problems and situations, it gives us a difference-making lens for making progress when legacy and traditional techniques and exercises fall short. We wrapped up this initial hour by introducing the "What Not to Do" sections, reflecting learnings that are provided at the conclusion of Hours 2 through 24.

Workshop

Case Study

To apply what we've learned, each hour concludes with a case study focused on a fictitious company, BigBank, and its digital transformation. Consider the following situation and questions. You can find the answers to the questions related to this case study in Appendix A, "Case Study Quiz Answers."

Situation

As this case study weaves its way through all 24 hours, it's important to set the stage in this first hour. BigBank is a 100-year-old commercial bank struggling to remain viable as its customers and their needs continue to change. A global financial institution, BigBank has grown through mergers and acquisitions over the last few decades, and its technology infrastructure and standards still reflect that heritage, including significant technical debt and year-over-year costs.

You have been retained by the Executive Committee (EC) of BigBank to assist the bank's decentralized IT teams and various business leadership teams. Your primary sponsor and the Bank's Chief Digital Officer, Satish, has asked you to go deep where you like but to retain a big-picture view of the bank's vision to transform itself around its customers and their needs. Above all, Satish has asked you to keep in mind something he regularly shares with his team, that "digital organizations are more resilient organizations...and we need that resilience to survive another hundred years."

BigBank is organized around several commercial areas and has a presence in 30 countries spanning three continents. Satish sponsors a broad-based global business transformation initiative called OneBank, which in turn consists of a dozen projects and strategic initiatives (you'll learn more about these projects and initiatives in subsequent hours).

The Executive Committee and Satish in particular are counting on you to help the bank reimagine its future, bring people and teams together across business and technology, and partner with OneBank delivery teams on the ground to reinvent how they deliver new business capabilities and outcomes. The goal? To incrementally deliver *value with velocity*.

To help ground the executive committee, Satish has asked you to host a Q&A session to answer several of the committee's questions regarding your early thinking and likely approaches.

Quiz

1. What does it mean to think slower as a means of delivering faster?
2. Simply put, what is the difference between Design Thinking techniques and Design Thinking exercises?
3. What is our primary enemy when it comes to making progress in the midst of the toughest, most ambiguous, and most complex problems?
4. There seems to be a natural stepwise order between common practices, best practices, and Design Thinking practices. What is this order?

A Design Thinking Model for Tech

What You'll Learn in This Hour:

- ▶ Human-Centered Thinking
- ▶ Design Thinking in Four Phases
- ▶ Phase 1: Understanding Broadly
- ▶ Phase 2: Thinking Differently
- ▶ Phase 3: Delivering Value
- ▶ Phase 4: Iterating for Progress
- ▶ What Not to Do: Exclusively Left to Right
- ▶ Summary and Case Study

With the basics of Design Thinking behind us, we turn our attention in Hour 2 to a simple model useful in helping organize the Design Thinking process. We will then review our model's four phases: Understanding Broadly, Thinking Differently, Delivering Value, and Iterating for Progress. A common "What Not to Do" scenario related to poorly set expectations regarding the recursive nature of Design Thinking concludes our second hour.

Human-Centered Thinking

Traditional problem solving focuses on identifying the problem, understanding symptoms or manifestations of the problem, developing solutions, and choosing the best solution. Design Thinking takes a different approach, putting the *people affected by the problem* at the center of the problem or situation. This approach to problem solving is often called Human-Centered (or user-centered) Design Thinking.

Thinking about the people at the center of a problem or situation seems common sense, but it's not as commonplace a practice as we might think. Consider how often we instead put a theme or a project or a need at the center and then try to build around that theme or project or need. Instead of "people who need clean air," we create "air quality projects." And along the way we lose sight of the people who needed the clean air and why it was important for them and their situation.

Human-Centered Design Thinking has taken many forms over the years, but it's generally organized around the following:

▶ Understanding and empathizing with the people facing a particular problem

▶ Defining the problem

▶ Thinking about that problem

▶ Prototyping and testing potential solutions for that problem

▶ Seeking incremental feedback along the way to better understand, empathize, define, think, prototype, test, and improve the solution

As we covered earlier, the process seems stepwise or linear, and it certainly starts that way. In the end, though, it becomes a nonlinear exercise of circling back to refine our understanding of the problem and how we define it; think a bit more; update the prototype and our work-in-progress; and continue testing, iterating, and updating.

Design Thinking in Four Phases

As we briefly introduced in Hour 1, our Design Thinking Model for Tech is composed of four phases, each of which recursively reconnects back to all previous phases, as depicted in Figure 2.1. In this way, the model supports continuous thinking, continuous learning, and continuous improvement. And it enables us to deliver solutions to complex and uniquely wicked problems as outlined in Hour 1.

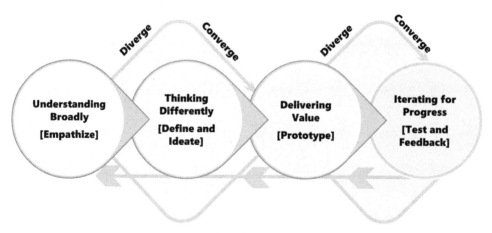

FIGURE 2.1.
Note the step-wise yet recursive nature of our Design Thinking Model for Tech.

How can we use our Design Thinking Model for Tech to solve hard problems in situations where patience may be thin but expectations for solutions only continue to rise? Use our model to

- **Manage expectations.** Mentioned earlier, solving complex problems is not about achieving perfect solutions today, but rather about incrementally learning and using those learnings to improve imperfect solutions over time. If leaders insist on perfect solutions, and users expect the same, nothing will ever get delivered.

- **Broadly understand.** From a big-picture perspective, if the team cannot describe the environment underpinning a problem, they may misunderstand it altogether and solve the wrong problem.

- **Deeply empathize.** If the team does not deeply understand the needs of the people who will be using a solution, including how they will use it, the solution itself might not solve the problem at all.

- **Maximize ideation.** Teams must be designed to be diverse in thought, background, education, experience, and more. Homogeneous teams are limited in their thinking and therefore in their capacity to ideate and innovate.

- **Work through ambiguity.** Understanding the real problem to be solved takes time and a willingness to wade through the unknowns associated with the landscape around and in front of us. Our teams need to be comfortable with "learning and failing and learning and failing" as we work through what we typically cannot control to find greater understanding and clarity.

- **Clarify uncertainty.** Similarly, we must help our teams discover the "best next step" on the journey to clarifying and conquering uncertainty. Complex problem definition and solutioning demands iterative ideating, prototyping, and testing as a way of learning and clarifying.

- **Build to think.** Complex problems cannot be solved exclusively by "thinking and planning." Instead, the team also needs permission and direction to build and try and do on their journey to more deeply understanding and learning.

In these ways, we can evolve the execution and governance techniques that our teams require as we work through situations in search of solutions. Let's take a closer look at how all of this comes together across the four phases of our Design Thinking Model for Tech.

Phase 1: Understanding Broadly

The first phase of our Design Thinking Model for Tech is focused on increasing clarity through listening, understanding, and learning as we connect with the right people and identify the right problems to go after. As we see in Figure 2.2, we therefore need to broadly understand at several different levels or layers:

▶ **The situation.** This includes market conditions, the industry or ecosystem landscape and its challenges, competitor realities and partner expectations, government or regulatory considerations, and the organization and business unit culture and norms.

▶ **The people in the situation.** This includes those who are experiencing the situation and its pain points, and the problems tied to the situation at every layer—those users with whom we need to empathize and understand who live at the center of the situation and its problems.

▶ **The problems associated with the situation.** This includes the specific business challenges and underlying technology constraints and pain points, all with the goal of identifying the right problem or problems that need to be addressed.

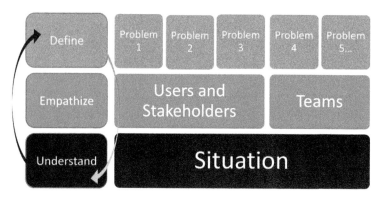

FIGURE 2.2
Gaining a broad understanding spans the general to the specific and includes the various people and problems associated with each situation.

Hours 6 through 9 cover this first phase. With this broad understanding behind us, we can begin thinking through potential solutions to those problems, covered next in Phase 2.

Phase 2: Thinking Differently

In Phase 2 of our Design Thinking Model for Tech, we consider the techniques and exercises that help us think anew, think differently. Why the need to think differently? Because most of us tend to lean on only a couple of ways of thinking, and tough problems demand a new approach. The solution to a tough situation or problem is obviously not that simple; otherwise, someone would have solved it long before we came along. We therefore need more ideas; we need different ways to approach the situation or problem.

And this is where thinking differently comes into play, or more precisely *ideating*. Ideate is a special word for the kind of thinking that is pulled out of the solitude of our mind and in some way made visible. Truth be told, some of us can do the work of ideating pretty well, even when that ideating remains in our heads. We all know someone like this, someone who can pull together mental models and keep a dozen figures and dimensions in their heads. But for most of us, ideating is really done best when we verbalize our ideas, or create from them something physical, or draw our ideas on a whiteboard or scrap of paper. It's in the externalization of our ideas that most of us ideate best. And once demystified and out in the open, externalization allows us to think even more deeply about our ideas. Freed from the confines of a single mind, we can collaborate with other minds to further connect the dots and explore aspects of those ideas. Once outside of our head, we often find that our ideas give birth to even more ideas. This process of building and externalizing is ideation, and it's a powerful difference-maker when it comes to solving problems and creating or realizing value.

Ideation can be performed solo or as part of a broader collaboration with coworkers and others. Reading and research and mentally wading through the work of others can help us ideate as well. For many, the most wonderful of new ideas surface when we ideate with others in small teams. However, experience shows us that real breakthroughs oftentimes arrive when we think solo. And fortunately there are a great number of techniques and exercises that help us:

- ▶ Clear our minds to think differently.

- ▶ Think divergently and then convergently.

- ▶ Establish guardrails for thinking creatively.

- ▶ Push ourselves to think to the extreme.

- ▶ Reduce uncertainty.

- ▶ Think through risks.

- ▶ Work through ambiguity.

- ▶ Build to think.

- ▶ Solve problems incrementally.

Turn to Hours 10 through 14 for the specific techniques and exercises that help us ideate and think differently as we work to understand situations, learn more about those situations, connect with the people living among those situations, wallow through and identify the problems buried in those situations, and in doing so begin to solve those problems.

Phase 3: Delivering Value

It was tempting to title this phase "Delivering Value Early and Often" because the goal of this phase extends well beyond delivering a single shot of value. In complex technology projects and initiatives, the final measure of value is often delivered months or years after kickoff. It's the ability to deliver value in the preceding months and years that sets Design Thinking apart from other ways of thinking about and delivering value.

With Design Thinking driving our mindset, delivering value starts by delivering something small and useful early on. Through building to think and "learning by doing," we discover ways of prototyping to deliver value incrementally. We find that value is created through iterating and teaming with others to deliver partial solutions quickly.

- ▶ Starting small and delivering fast

- ▶ Providing value through proof of concept exercises, MVPs, pilots, and more

- ▶ Applying techniques that help us increase the cadence of value

- ▶ Building on our previous work to deliver more and more value over time

Hours 15 through 18 cover the techniques and exercises we use to deliver value and set the stage for the fourth and final phase 4, Iterating for Progress, which includes the notion of learning and refining our solution.

Phase 4: Iterating for Progress

One of the fundamentals of making progress is to do a bit of work, get some feedback on that work, and use that feedback to make necessary changes as we refine and continue the work. Course-correcting our work based on feedback and iteration loops helps us do the right stuff and do so intentionally. Iteration is about delivering something useful today that is incrementally improved to be better tomorrow. It's in the process and repetition of iteration, feedback, building, and testing that we fine-tune our thinking, improve our understanding of a situation, and ultimately solve some of the toughest problems.

And feedback as we know is really nothing more than what others—particularly the people who will use our work—think about our work. There are several keys to feedback:

- ▶ Ask for feedback early. Don't wait until the end to find out you missed the mark and need to start over!

- ▶ Ask for feedback often. Doing so allows us to iterate or build on our work in the best kind of way as we tweak our work to line up better with what people need from it.

▶ Feedback should flow from the earliest iterations of our drafts and MVPs. We can use that feedback to rethink our problem or situation, rethink how we're tackling the problem or situation, and rethink how to best test and implement our solution.

Where can we get useful feedback? Feedback comes from different people and through different communications channels, including

▶ Testing at the hands of people trying to verify usability

▶ Verbatims or direct quotes from people using the early work we have delivered for the express purpose of gaining feedback

▶ Lessons learned from our own introspection

▶ Silent Design at the hands of people who have made the solution we delivered more useful by changing our solution

Feedback also comes in the form of poking holes at a prototype's or solution's early work-in-progress. It's a form of Building to Think, aimed more at validating what we're doing versus what we're thinking. The idea for poking holes is simple. Share your early draft documents, including "strawman" table of contents, early models, wireframes, rough-and-ready prototypes, and other types of in-progress artifacts with others and ask them:

▶ Am I on the right track?

▶ What am I missing?

▶ What should be removed?

This early feedback helps us understand a problem or potential solution and tweak it before we build it out completely and then ask for feedback. And it's easier for others to poke holes at a half-completed plan or idea than it is to talk about the possibilities inherent to a blank canvas.

Giving people the permission to poke holes at our half-completed ideas and work-in-progress takes courage. But this practice allows everyone to move faster and make progress. Use our draft documents, models, and so on to identify ideas or partial solutions that

▶ Will work for now as-is

▶ Have potential with some minor changes and tweaks

▶ Are weak but might serve as a temporary band-aid for now

▶ Are dead-end, but are useful in the same way that Snaking the Drain helps us restart and rethink

Hours 19 through 24 reflect what it means to test, continuously improve and iterate, operate at scale, and make long-lasting change. As architect Frank Lloyd Wright said, "You can use an eraser on the drafting table or a sledgehammer on the construction site." Iterating through testing and feedback lets us avoid sledgehammers later on down the road.

What Not to Do: Exclusively Left to Right

A large oil company employed a team of consultants to assist the company with a website redesign. The team used a popular Design Thinking model and commenced work empathizing with the customer's user base and its needs. After a brief time, the consultants concluded their empathy exercises and moved on to define the problems.

When this shift in focus from empathizing to problem definition became known, the customer project manager grew irate. In his eyes, there was no way the consultants could have spent enough time talking with users and defining their requirements! The project manager pulled out the statement of work and turned to the image of the Design Thinking model being used, which clearly illustrated that problem definition commenced only after empathizing was concluded.

The lead consultant explained that the model was intended to be iterative and recursive; it looked to be stepwise or left-to-right oriented, but it was not. After wasting a week working through customer escalations and the consultant's own org-internal escalations, the team was able to convince the customer that moving strictly left-to-right would prove much slower than quickly moving between the steps and returning to previous steps as a way to refine understanding and make further progress.

Summary

This hour built upon the foundation established in Hour 1 and fleshed out our Design Thinking Model for Tech. We walked through each of the four Phases: Understanding Broadly, Thinking Differently, Delivering Value, and Iterating for Progress. While the model appears linear and stepwise, we also outlined how Design Thinking in its true form takes us back and around and back again as we iterate and learn to solve problems and deliver value. A "What Not to Do" real-world example showcasing this recursive and "loopy" nature of Design Thinking, including the importance of setting expectations with everyone involved, concluded this hour.

Workshop

Case Study

Consider the following case study and questions. You can find the answers to the questions related to this case study in Appendix A, "Case Study Quiz Answers."

Situation

Satish urgently needs you to begin organizing the dozen initiatives comprising OneBank around a couple of different themes or dimensions. Each initiative is in a different place in terms of initiation status or project lifecycle, for example. And if we look at each initiative through the lens of Design Thinking, each initiative varies in terms of the primary phase it seems to be in. Some are still in the earliest exploratory phases, whereas others seem to be stuck or derailed in various states of solution modeling, prototyping, or testing. Satish believes BigBank can fundamentally change how each initiative's respective teams view its work if each initiative is recast against the Design Thinking phases shared with the Executive Committee.

Help Satish and the Executive Committee reorganize its OneBank initiatives in light of the Design Thinking Model for Tech, answering his questions and those of several OneBank initiative leaders.

Quiz

1. How might we group or organize our OneBank initiatives against the Design Thinking Model for Tech?

2. What does "Understanding Broadly" mean in the context of learning or empathizing?

3. What is the difference between traditional thinking as we most often practice it and the kinds of thinking and ideation that might be necessary to help several of OneBank's initiatives get back on track?

4. From a timing or stepwise perspective, when is value delivered through the Design Thinking process and its techniques and exercises?

5. While it might be useful point-in-time to consider an initiative from a phase perspective, why is a left-to-right orientation of the Design Thinking process fundamentally flawed?

HOUR 3
Design Thinking for Small Audiences

What You'll Learn in This Hour:

- ▶ Design Thinking for Me
- ▶ Learning More Quickly
- ▶ Thinking and Problem Solving
- ▶ Coping with Ambiguity
- ▶ Prioritizing Next Best Steps for Uncertainty
- ▶ Executing More Effectively
- ▶ What Not to Do: This Isn't for Me
- ▶ Summary and Case Study

In our third hour, we take a quick look at more than 20 Design Thinking techniques and light-weight exercises that we can use in small audience situations, including individually, to be more effective. Many of these are covered in detail later as we apply them to drive value within specific Design Thinking phases or across the entirety of a digital transformation journey or major tech initiative. For now, though, it's important to see the breadth of possibilities that Design Thinking's techniques and simple exercises can provide to individuals, teams, and small working groups. We conclude Hour 3 with a real-world "What Not to Do" focused on an architect who concluded Design Thinking was just another "flavor of the day."

Design Thinking for Me

Every one of us faces challenges as we go about our work day. From our daily tasks to our workplace initiatives and across our projects, we are asked to listen and learn, think, problem solve, test our ideas, work through ambiguity, prioritize, and execute effectively. Design Thinking and its various techniques and exercises can help us work through our challenges regardless of the type of problem and regardless of the role or persona we play. That is, if we are a web developer, an IT executive, a product manager, a cloud infrastructure specialist, a systems tester, a security and compliance expert, or a UX designer, there are Design Thinking techniques and exercises that can help us

- ▶ Learn more quickly

- ▶ Think and ideate differently and more deeply

- ▶ Cope with ambiguity

- ▶ Prioritize the next best steps in the face of uncertainty

- ▶ Execute more effectively

Let's take a quick look at each of these areas and the kinds of Design Thinking techniques and exercises that can help us as we go about our day working on individual tasks and in small groups (organized by phase and by area, as we see in Figure 3.1). Again, many of these ways of learning, thinking, and executing will be covered in detail in future hours.

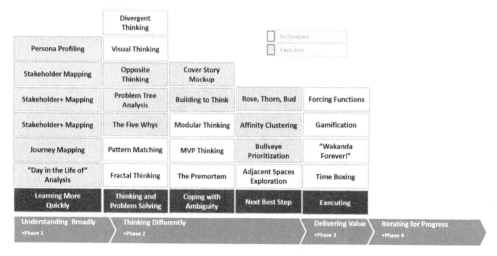

FIGURE 3.1
Note the variety of Design Thinking techniques and exercises we may turn to individually and for our small teams and group initiatives.

Learning More Quickly

The key to solving problems, creating solutions, and delivering value often lies in better understanding the situation, the lay of the land. It's in understanding and learning that we can make progress where we've failed before. The faster we understand and learn, the better.

▶ **Stakeholder Mapping.** Whenever we take on something new, there are other people involved. It's beneficial to identify and "map" these people to the roles they play, the groups they represent, the power and influence they hold, their interests in our work, and their contact information. While a table can be used to capture this information, a graphic representation of this information in the form of a Stakeholder Map lets us see relationships and hierarchy more easily.

▶ **Persona Profiling.** Rather than assessing or documenting specific people, we might wish to aggregate or anonymize personal data by focusing on the role or persona that a person plays in an organization. In this way, we can create a set of fictional characters (such as end user, IT support, help desk technician, and more) to represent groupings of people who share common interests, wants, needs, and behaviors, all of which should influence how we show up, what we design, how we test, who to look to for the best feedback, and so on.

▶ **Stakeholder+ Mapping.** With a Stakeholder Map (and perhaps a set of Persona Profiles or Empathy Maps) in our back pocket, we can create a more insightful version of the traditional Stakeholder Map. A Stakeholder+ Map includes what our stakeholders are saying and what we believe they are thinking. And if we color-code each person's sentiment as red, amber, or green (or through emojis or icons), we can also visually indicate each person's level of satisfaction. Such a visualization helps us prioritize and focus on the right people.

▶ **Journey Mapping.** We can take our visualizations one step further and illustrate *where and how* different people or personas navigate a process as they interact with our product, service, or solution (Kelley & Kelley, 2013). Each touchpoint on the customer journey or stakeholder journey represents an opportunity to satisfy or disappoint that person (the outcome of which may also be captured in a kind of rolled-up Stakeholder+ map or sentiment map).

▶ **"Day in the Life of" Analysis.** Where a Journey Map is tactical to a customer's or stakeholder's specific interaction with a product, service, or solution, a "Day in the Life of" or DILO Analysis seeks to understand *what* a person does—the broader "everything" that a person performs or experiences throughout the day. Observing and recording their activities help us begin to understand more deeply the nature of their work. The more repetitive the work (as seen across multiple hours or perhaps multiple days), the more immediately useful this DILO Analysis; most of us tend to do the same set of activities about 80 to 90 percent day to day.

There is a thread that runs across these techniques and exercises, and that thread is people: understanding who they are, what they think and say, what they do, when they do it, and how they fit into their surrounding problems and situations.

Thinking and Problem Solving

As individuals, we tend to think in only a couple of ways that have worked for us in the past. Design Thinking gives us many more ways, however, which can help us move past the blockers that hold us back. Consider the following:

▶ **Visual Thinking.** Falling under the umbrella of "making ideas and potential solutions visible" by turning words into pictures and figures, this technique has long been used to externalize what's in our heads into something we can see and further think through. In the context of small groups, Visual Thinking is especially powerful given the way that pictures and figures bring clarity and elicit a shared understanding across people and teams.

▶ **Pattern Matching.** A pattern is a repeated blueprint or design, and similarly the notion of Pattern Matching in the context of Design Thinking is about uncovering repeating themes or threads explaining how we behave, think, or execute. We use Pattern Matching to understand the connection between what we've done in the past and what might come to fruition in the future. The power of pattern recognition is realized through insights and knowledge that give us a choice to repeat the pattern or strike out in a new kind of way.

▶ **Fractal Thinking.** A fractal is a special kind of pattern that is self-similar and repeats itself at scale or vertically (explaining why this technique is sometimes called *vertical thinking*). Fractals are all around us. With this fact in mind, use Fractal Thinking to recognize and use the relationship between the small and the large to learn and think differently. Consider how the behaviors and practices in the home are reflected upward in the streets and neighborhoods and cities. And consider how the trends and themes we see at a country level are reflected downward into our economy, industries, businesses, and teams.

▶ **Divergent Thinking.** To ideate more effectively and create many possible solutions or ideas, we need to spend more time diverging and less time converging. Diverging is about gathering ideas, exploring possible solutions, and expanding our options. To diverge is to increase the number of ideas, typically by thinking in different ways. Diverging leads to not only a larger but a more diverse set of options. On the other hand, the goal of converging is to narrow down, whittle, or trim our ideas and choices and solutions to the very few and presumably the very best (based on what we know today). Most people are wired to look at a problem in this latter way, spending 5 or 10 seconds thinking about a problem and the next 5 days implementing the answer. Such convergent thinking normally works quite well most of the time, but in cases of great ambiguity and uncertainty, we need to diverge before we converge.

▶ **Problem Tree Analysis.** As we better understand a person's journey and their "day in the life," we will also see the problems and challenges they face. Perform a Problem Tree Analysis (which is based on Paulo Freire's work in education in the early 1970s) to separate the causes of a problem from the effects or implications of that problem (Freire Institute, 2022). This simple method is based on a tree metaphor. Draw the trunk to represent the problem, the roots below to represent root causes, and the branches above to capture the effects and other outcomes stemming from that problem.

▶ **The Five Whys.** Once we understand a problem or situation on the surface through a Problem Tree Analysis, we might need to further explore the underlying root cause or causes of the problem. The Five Whys, developed by Toyota Motor Corporation in the 1930s, gives us a classic Design Thinking method of working backward to consider the cause-and-effect relationships underpinning a problem or situation today.

▶ **Opposite Thinking or Reverse Brainstorming.** Everyone is familiar with brainstorming where we bring together the minds of several different people to think through a situation or problem. Brainstorming is one of the earliest forms of ideation, and we all naturally tend to use it when a solution isn't obvious. But when traditional brainstorming doesn't generate enough ideas, we should turn to opposite thinking, or Reverse Brainstorming, as outlined by Straker (2012) and conceptualized earlier by others as yet another way to brainstorm. Reverse Brainstorming helps us creatively uncover new risks, find novel solutions, discover new challenges, and grow the size of our ideation funnel. The technique is simple: rather than trying to find a solution to a problem head-on, reverse the problem instead and consider what would make that problem *worse*. This is an easy ideation method because most people are naturally wired to think about why an idea is a bad idea or how a situation could turn for the worse. We are masters at "what if" and "glass half full" thinking. Again, it's pretty easy for us to talk through ways to make a situation or problem worse or to consider all of the things that could go wrong.

Each one of the preceding ideation techniques can be used together to help us think differently and deeply. Each one might be used to conclude a traditional brainstorming session too. If these aren't enough, though, consider the more than 40 ideation techniques and exercises spanning Hours 10 through 14.

Coping with Ambiguity

When the path ahead is clear, it's easy to think about and prioritize the different choices we might make. But what happens when that path is murky or completely hidden? How do we deal with such ambiguity? Design Thinking provides a diverse set of techniques and exercises for driving clarity in a 360-degree kind of way:

▶ **Modular Thinking.** For problem solving, it is often helpful to deconstruct a broad situation into smaller chunks. Such modular thinking lets us think in a more targeted way about a particular aspect of the broader situation.

▶ **Building to Think.** For solutioning, the process of "building to think" is akin to prototyping with our hands. The idea is to create a solution or partial solution to a problem that we can consider and test and iteratively refine. Why? To understand and learn fast, fail fast, iterate on our learnings, and in these ways make meaningful progress as we learn and fail cheaply.

▶ **MVP Thinking.** In the same way we might build something to help us think, we might also drive clarity by considering the attributes of a Minimum Viable Product or solution. Each one of these attributes allows us to think about the big picture while dissecting it into smaller pieces.

▶ **Cover Story Mockup.** Instead of tackling ambiguity head on, we might circumvent the current state of affairs and instead figuratively put ourselves at some point in the future. In our time-traveling future, we're holding the front page of the *New York Times* or our favorite magazine, and our initiative is the cover story. What does that cover story highlight? What did we accomplish? What can our people do better and differently today versus days past? By considering the attributes of success and thinking with the end in mind, we can work backward to consider how to navigate to that cover story future.

▶ **The Premortem.** Better than a postmortem, consider another time-travel technique that involves pretending we are in the future. In this case, the future is bleak, earmarked by complete failure. How did we fail? Who didn't do what was necessary for our project or initiative to be successful? What did we miss along the way that ultimately led to the demise or failure of our project or initiative? Once we capture our thinking and thoughts, like the Cover Story Mockup, we can work backward but in this case *avoid* making these missteps along the way.

In all of these cases, we are approaching our situation in very different ways. In some cases, we focus on problems, whereas in others we think through possible solutions. We might break down our situation into a logical set of components. Or we might avoid today altogether and transport ourselves through time to a bright or dismal future, both alternatives of which give us much to consider and act on today.

Prioritizing Next Best Steps for Uncertainty

Once we arrive at some clarity, once we better understand the lay of the land and its ambiguities, we have a better chance of determining the next best step or two among a breadth of possible choices. Many Design Thinking techniques and exercises can help us distill the next best step.

▶ **Bullseye Prioritization.** This visual exercise helps us organize goals, tasks, and other competing items that are important to us, our team, or our project. It helps us learn through that process of organizing and grouping what is most important, what is least important, and what falls in the middle. By organizing our goals or tasks against a target image subdivided into any number of quadrants, we can also do a certain amount of subgrouping as well.

▶ **Adjacent Spaces Exploration.** The ideal next best step might lie adjacent to what we already consider our core strengths or capabilities. Use this notion of adjacent spaces to assess where change is simpler and risk is lower, with the idea that adjacent options are more easily pursued because they are more similar than not to what we already know, can do, or are skilled at.

▶ **Rose, Thorn, Bud (RTB) Exercise.** When Bullseye Prioritization or an Adjacent Spaces exercise still leaves us with questions, use RTB to narrow down a particular choice in more detail. RTB gives us a simple way to organize the positive, the negative, and the opportunities of each choice so that they may be evaluated individually and against one another. Roses are those aspects of a choice that are positive or healthy or working well. Thorns are those aspects that aren't working well, and buds reflect aspects with potential or areas for improvement (buds can often be the difference makers in choosing one option over another).

▶ **Affinity Clustering.** Sometimes in the midst of a project, an overwhelming amount of information or ambiguity threatens to bog down the pace of progress. Affinity Clustering helps us make smarter near-term choices, which in turn helps us maintain momentum. Whether analyzing research data or considering creative ideas, you can use this method to organize items into logical groups. It is an easy way to bring some order to the chaos. Patterns are revealed when teams sort items based on perceived similarity, defining commonalities that are inherent but not necessarily obvious. In this way, you are able to draw insights and new ideas out of otherwise disparate pieces of information. Discerning patterns among data (or any multitude of items) is also a useful way of taming complexity.

With a short list of "next best steps" or choices, we can turn our attention to techniques and exercises that help us individually, or as a member of a small group, execute more effectively.

Executing More Effectively

Some of the most useful Design Thinking exercises and techniques in our tool bag help us get the work in front of us done more predictably, or faster, or more effectively.

▶ **Forcing Functions.** Use real or artificial deadlines to help us get something done sooner than we otherwise might. Dates can be powerful motivators, after all; missing an artificially early date can help us meet the really important immovable dates too. And consider how upcoming changes in our industry, new competitors in our marketplace, and organizational changes inside our companies can serve as forcing functions as well.

▶ **Time Boxing.** Beyond a deadline imposed through a Forcing Function, we might use a time management technique developed by James Martin called Time Boxing to help us make progress and get a body of work done. A "boxed" amount of time gives us a deadline and thus the maximum amount of time in which we may work on something. This technique drives a sense of urgency and is often used to deliver faster than we otherwise might think prudent or possible.

▶ **Gamification Technique.** Coined in 2002 by Nick Pelling, a computer programmer and inventor, *Gamification* changes our behavior to achieve a desired outcome. It's especially useful incentivizing how quickly we get done the necessary but mundane things of life. The idea is to make a game out of the work using a system that rewards us as we achieve goals along the way. Car manufacturers change driver behavior by lighting up a green dot or other visual when we drive economically. Game makers use badges and scores to keep users engaged and on their platforms. We can use Gamification to reward ourselves when we make progress, check off another item on our list, and so forth.

▶ **"Wakanda Forever!"** If the rallying cry of a military unit or sports team is familiar, it's easy to understand the power of being part of something bigger than just us. With a nod to Marvel's Avengers franchise, the notion of the "Wakanda Forever!" technique is simply to connect an individual to a team, a team with a legacy of purpose and achievement. In doing so, individuals routinely step up and deliver at a higher performance level than they would have been capable of delivering solo. Whether it's healthy pride, greater self-motivation, or the ability to find previously hidden strength that helps us persevere and push forward, "Wakanda Forever!" can make the difference between delivering today and delivering someday.

Most of these techniques and exercises that we have covered here in Hour 3, spanning learning, thinking, coping, prioritizing, and executing, are covered in more detail in later hours. Each method is useful at an individual as well as a group level. Practice each to find ways of naturally using and communicating how they can make a difference in small group settings.

What Not to Do: This Isn't for Me

With anything new comes a choice to adopt or ignore, along with a number of questions. An architect at a legacy automobile manufacturer found himself saying, "Should I try this new thing called Design Thinking? Do I need to try it? Why can't I just stick with what I know works? What's the harm in waiting out this new flavor of the day?"

That architect eventually learned that understanding an ecosystem broadly, empathizing with his end users deeply, defining and solving the right problems, and so on were more than a passing fad. They were instrumental in how he might have worked more effectively regardless of the

Design Thinking label. He wasn't willing to change, however, and eventually was encouraged to retire early.

Don't be the person who says, "This isn't for me." A new way of learning, thinking, coping, prioritizing, and generally working means a change in how we show up and get things done—distracting, awkward, time-consuming, and even unnatural change. And many of the Design Thinking techniques and exercises across this book will definitely feel unnatural if not a little silly or unnecessary. Design Thinking asks us to fundamentally rethink and change how we learn, think, and execute, after all.

But these are good, healthy changes. If everything is going well and our current methods are getting us from Point A to Point B, we might be tempted to shelve this book. But here's the thing: As the pace of external change continues to accelerate around us, and the work we do in tech continues to grow more complex, we must equally accelerate the pace of change inherent to our own methods and tools. We need to add to our tool bag new and incremental ways of getting the job done better and faster. And we need to get comfortable with some of these new techniques and exercises and tools *before* we need them on the job.

When we don't embrace and practice these "for me and my small group" self-focused Design Thinking exercises, we miss the opportunity to develop the confidence necessary to practice these methods more broadly. Learn and refine our skills running Journey Mapping, Problem Tree Analysis, Bullseye Prioritization, and Affinity Clustering exercises *before* our business sponsor or CIO asks us to take on a project that's already run off the rails and requires new ways of understanding and thinking to make progress. Practice Forcing Functions and Time Boxing at home, Gamification with our kids, and Premortems in our small groups at work. Practice these methods and get comfortable using them in small team settings before we really need them in the larger settings.

Summary

In this hour, we looked at Design Thinking techniques and exercises that are easy enough and useful enough to start using personally and in our small groups. In this way, we can start growing accustomed to new ways of learning, thinking, coping, prioritizing, and executing while adding more than 20 new "tools" to our tool bag along the way. Each of these techniques and exercises is covered in more detail in future hours. We concluded Hour 3 with a real-world "What Not to Do" example of an architect unwilling to learn and change and operate in new ways.

Now that we've explored the breadth of possibilities that Design Thinking brings to us as individuals, we're ready in Hour 4 to explore Design Thinking in the context of creating and maintaining resilient and sustainable teams.

Workshop

Case Study

Consider the following case study and questions. You can find the answers to the questions related to this case study in Appendix A, "Case Study Quiz Answers."

Situation

BigBank's OneBank initiative leaders are "sold" on the idea of using Design Thinking to solve problems, make progress, and incrementally deliver value. But the Executive Committee and the Bank's Chief Digital Officer, Satish, have asked you to share a number of lightweight techniques and exercises that the initiative leaders and their teams should be comfortable with and use. They are also hoping you can give the Bank a way of organizing the Design Thinking techniques and exercises useful for individuals and small teams. And they are still a bit confused about the differences between ambiguity and uncertainty.

Quiz

1. How might you organize Design Thinking techniques and exercises for individual use or small team use?

2. How would you explain the difference between ambiguity and uncertainty to the Bank's initiative leaders?

3. What are three Design Thinking techniques or exercises useful for coping with ambiguity?

4. What are three Design Thinking techniques or exercises that can help individuals or small teams think differently?

5. What are three Design Thinking techniques or exercises useful for prioritizing "next best steps" in the face of uncertainty?

HOUR 4
Resilient and Sustainable Teams

While Design Thinking as we covered in Hour 3 is useful for individuals in the workplace, the community, and in small groups, it is also ideal for building, maintaining, and working as a member of a team. In this hour, we cover a number of Design Thinking techniques and exercises useful for building resilient teams, keeping those teams healthy, working in inclusive and effective ways with our fellow team members, creating healthy and intentional connections among and between one another, and more. Hour 4 concludes with an important "What Not to Do" matter related to avoiding the Archipelago Effect.

Design Thinking for Tech Team Alignment

Tech teams may practice a hundred different Design Thinking techniques and exercises in the course of learning faster, empathizing more deeply, identifying problems with greater confidence, ideating smarter, delivering value with velocity, and so on. But none of those techniques may be more personally impactful than the ones they use to help their teams work better and thrive together. In this hour, we'll cover the following:

- ▶ Simple Rules for healthy alignment

- ▶ Guiding Principles for operating consistency

- ▶ "How Might We?" questioning for inclusive teamwork and problem solving

- ▶ Diversity by Design for smarter ideation

- ▶ Growth Mindset for learning and teaming

- ▶ The Rule of Threes for iterating

- ▶ Inclusive and effective meeting techniques

- ▶ Mesh Networking for resiliency

For starters, let's turn our attention to establishing a set of Simple Rules for healthy team alignment.

Design Thinking in Action: Simple Rules for Healthy Alignment

As we're building our teams and establishing norms, it's not too early to think about what it takes to align and preserve that team. A long-term and sustainable approach to faster decisioning, clearer strategy and operational alignment, and therefore team longevity can be realized by creating a set of Simple Rules.

Simple Rules define what the team will be known for, its priorities, what's important and what's not, what the team will create or do, who the team will connect with, and when the team will operate and communicate. Teams develop and apply their own set of team-unique Simple Rules. These rules become the team's guidepost or formula for executing and success. To create clarity and preserve team alignment, document a set of 6 to 10 Simple Rules that answer these questions:

- ▶ Who are we as a team?

- ▶ What do we do; what are our objectives?

- ▶ What will we measure to ensure we meet those objectives?

- ▶ What do we *not* do (so we maintain focus)?

- ▶ When do we do our work; what are our hours?

- ▶ Where do we do our work; what are our boundaries?

- ▶ What will be our legacy; what do we want to be known for?

Adapted from the book *Simple Rules: How to Thrive in a Complex World* by Donald Sull and Kathleen M. Eisenhardt, Simple Rules serve as guidelines to help a group of people stay aligned, stay true to their core values, and make decisions faster. Simple Rules help preserve "who we are" in the wake of other changes happening above, below, and around us and our team. Think of Simple Rules as a North Star (see Figure 4.1).

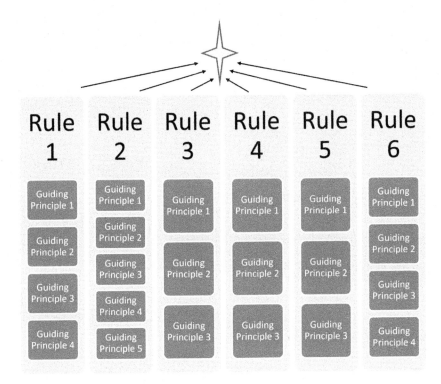

FIGURE 4.1
Simples Rules serve as a North Star for any team or organization regardless of size.

Sometimes a team leader will create a draft set of Simple Rules solo, but for buy-in purposes they're always completed as a team. Simple Rules may be refined over time too, but they're generally pretty durable.

TIME AND PEOPLE: A Simple Rules exercise requires 3–10 people for 30–60 minutes.

To create a set of Simple Rules:

1. Ask the team members a few days in advance to think about the Who and the What and the When that will describe the team.

2. Assemble the team, and one by one ask each team member to write down and reflect individually on the following questions:

   ▶ What does our work look like?

   ▶ What will we be known for?

   ▶ What do we do as a team?

> ▶ What is our primary objective?

> ▶ What is our greatest skill or strength?

> ▶ Where do we work, and what are our boundaries?

> ▶ When do we work to create our outputs?

> ▶ Given the above, who are we as a team?

> ▶ Given the above, what will be our legacy?

3. Work through the preceding answers to draft an initial set of Simple Rules.

4. After a week or so, consolidate and simplify the Simple Rules, addressing gaps to create an improved version of the rules.

5. After another two weeks, prune the list to a top 10 or so.

6. Publish, use, and live by these Simple Rules as a part of the team's culture, pruning and optimizing the words perhaps monthly.

For years, teams around the world have been unknowingly creating Simple Rules to help them stay focused and aligned. The rock band Coldplay created a set of 10 in its early days to drive a consistent artistic process and set of musical outcomes among the band. In their words:

1. Albums must be no longer than 42 minutes or 9 tracks.

2. Production must be amazing, rich but with space; not overlayered, less tracks, more quality, groove, and swing. Drums and rhythm are the most crucial thing to concentrate on.

3. Computers are instruments, not recording aids.

4. Imagery must be classic, colourful, and different....

5. Make sure videos and pictures are great before setting Release Date, and highly original.

6. Always keep mystery. Not many interviews.

7. Groove and swing rhythms and sounds must always be original as possible....

8. Promo/review copies to be on vinyl. Stops copying problem, sounds and looks better.

9. Jaqueline Sabriado, ns p cc, face forward.

10. Think about what to do with charity account. Set up something small but really enabling and constructive.

Through a quarter century of playing together, these Simple Rules have allowed the band Coldplay to remain remarkably consistent in terms of sound, output, and specific audience appeal, all while maintaining a singular sense of self and legacy.

In the small business world, a dental supply company developed a set of Simple Rules to help the company prioritize which potential dentistry customers to pursue. After assessing its own customer database, the company found that 10 percent of its current dental customers accounted for more than half its revenue. The company's Simple Rules served to consolidate the kinds of common characteristics that would help it best grow its base of profitable customers, including

- We will only target dentists who own their own practice.

- The ideal age of our target dentist is 35–55.

- Every dentist we target should be able to commit to $10,000 in products annually.

- The ideal dentist is currently burdened with less than 5 percent financing and thus has bandwidth to work with us.

- The ideal dentist has attended our company-specific training regimen.

After a month of executing against these Simple Rules, the company deleted the first rule as it found this rule didn't really make a difference. The company also reduced the $10,000 commitment value to $5,000 as it proved nearly identical as a predictor. Later, this dental supply company also added the rule "The ideal dentist has a website" based on insights gleaned from current dental customers. A year after executing against this revised set of five Simple Rules, the company was consistently realizing better than 40 percent increases in sales despite a tough market. Its ability to target and align helped the company focus on the right customers consistently.

Design Thinking in Action: Guiding Principles for Operating Consistency

Consistency is important in areas beyond Simple Rules. While a set of Simple Rules defines the Who and What and When, similarly establishing a set of Guiding Principles drives consistency in the How. Guiding Principles outline how a team will operate, how it will think, how it will prioritize, how it will communicate, and more. Guiding Principles give teams the operating guidance necessary to remain sustainable while making smart decisions that align with the team's Simple Rules, its intended legacy, and the organization's overall strategy.

Guiding Principles are therefore the non-negotiable values and parameters that describe how a team shows up for one another and takes care of business and each other day to day. In practical terms, Guiding Principles are the succinct one-liners we draft that serve as universal guardrails for keeping us in our proper lane—just as physical guardrails do for vehicles on the road.

Similar to Simple Rules, Guiding Principles are durable; they should not change much over time. But unlike Simple Rules, we will likely need to draft 5 to 10 Guiding Principles for each area that we decide, as a team, we wish to approach with consistency. We could therefore easily have 50 or more Guiding Principles organized around communications, priorities, operations, and so forth.

To craft an effective Guiding Principle, we combine a core value with a verb that reflects the team's view of its purpose, its mission, or its people. For example, as we consider Guiding Principles for communications, a team might draft

- ▶ We communicate consistently, with one voice.

- ▶ We execute with transparency.

- ▶ We operate with honesty.

- ▶ We practice inclusivity internally and externally.

- ▶ We talk to and treat everyone respectfully.

Teams often start out by creating such a set of principles that describe how they will communicate, by the way. As we know, communications grounds so much about how we operate and what we value. Afterward, teams often draft Guiding Principles focused on how they will support one another, deal with honesty and ethics issues, manage differences and escalations, and so on.

TIME AND PEOPLE: A Guiding Principles exercise requires 3–10 people for 60–120 minutes.

Execute the following steps to help our team create its own set of Guiding Principles, and see Figure 4.2 for a worked example:

1. Pre-work: While not absolutely necessary, first create the team's set of Simple Rules. These rules help teams focus on which areas to rally around and lend themselves to establishing a related set of Guiding Principles.

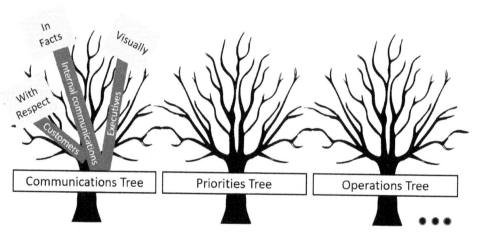

FIGURE 4.2
By organizing Guiding Principles through the metaphor of a tree, we can stay organized as we create new trees and further develop existing ones.

2. Agree on the medium for collaboration. Consider using a physical conference room's whiteboard or an online collaboration tool like Miro or Klaxoon. Or use Zoom or Microsoft Teams to share a virtual desktop or whiteboard. An old-fashioned paper and pen over coffee always works too.

3. Bring the team together to flesh out the first set of these Guiding Principles. Set aside 30 minutes to draft the first set of 5 to 10 Guiding Principles (remember that we want to avoid creating Simple Rules or Guiding Principles solo).

4. List out the various areas for which the team will create Guiding Principles, such as communications, priorities, and operations.

5. To keep this exercise visual, choose a visual metaphor. A tree metaphor with a tree trunk, roots, and branches is especially effective for creating Guiding Principles. Use a different tree for every area (thus, you'll create a communications tree, a priorities tree, an operations tree, and so on).

6. Decide which one of the areas to focus on first and write it down on the trunk of the first tree. For example, the team might decide to start with "We will communicate with respect and integrity."

7. Don't overthink this exercise! Draw a handful of branches coming off the top of the tree trunk (remember that each set of Guiding Principles gets its own tree). Each branch off the trunk should be formed as a question and will represent a dimension of the area (trunk) that we're building out. For example:

   a. Branch #1: "How will we communicate internally within our team?"

   b. Branch #2: "How will we communicate with our business sponsor and other executive stakeholders?"

   c. Branch #3: "How will we communicate inclusively?"

   d. Branch #4: "How will we communicate in a way that is accessible to ensure everyone is in the loop and we leave no one out?"

   e. Branch #5: "How will our team communications respect personal boundaries?"

   f. Branch #6: "How will we communicate escalations among ourselves when we disagree or aren't aligned?"

8. Round-robin through each team member to add additional tree branches one by one. Add and label these tree branches as needed. It's fine to have many branches! We can consolidate later.

9. Round-robin through each team member asking "how" the team will fulfill what is written on Branch #1, then Branch #2, and so on. Note that the answer to each "how" question is a Guiding Principle, and it should be documented in a leaf. Each branch will likely have many such leaves or Guiding Principles.

10. By way of example, for Branch #2, "How will we communicate with our business sponsor and other executive stakeholders?" we might create the following set of leaves or Guiding Principles:

   a. Branch #2, Leaf #1: Cover the urgent first; do not bury bad news or build up to bad news through a story.

   b. Branch #2, Leaf #2: Communicate with facts, dates, and risk mitigations.

   c. Branch #2, Leaf #3: Communicate visually in pictures and dashboards.

   d. Branch #2, Leaf #4: Communicate in a way that reflects executive expectations.

   e. Branch #2, Leaf #5: Spell out acronyms until sure they are part of our shared vocabulary.

11. Continue building out each branch and its leaves, and the tree will take shape.

12. Later, the team might wish to group the leaves by theme or priority using some of the techniques we covered briefly in Hour 3 and cover in more detail in future hours (such as Pattern Matching and Affinity Clustering).

Repeat the entire process for the team's other 5 to 9 Simple Rules or focus areas, and in the end the team will have assembled a tiny forest of 6 to 10 trees, each with maybe 5 to 10 branches and maybe 5 or so leaves or Guiding Principles per branch. Note how a single Simple Rule or focus area therefore drives 20 to 40 or more Guiding Principles.

After the exercise is done, consolidate and share these Guiding Principles. They need to be seen and used by the team! Follow them, reinforce them, prune them over time, and add to them through regular team follow-ups.

Design Thinking in Action: "How Might We?" for Inclusive Teamwork

"How Might We?" is a Socratic-inspired Design Thinking staple that has proven itself useful in many contexts for many years. "How might we?" questioning reflects the kind of positive can-do attitude necessary to bring together a group of individuals and create a team. "How might we?" creates a safe place for team ideation, team problem solving, and therefore good collaboration and teamwork. It implies that many solutions are possible, and that the team will tackle this problem or situation together, as a team. It's optimistic and inclusive thinking at its best. And like other techniques that establish a positive environment for thinking and executing, "How might we?" is perfect for gathering perspectives, driving ideation, solving problems, and ultimately making progress.

Design Thinking for Sustainable Teams

Beyond basic alignment, sustainable teams need to push themselves to practice self-care and team-care to be healthy. If we are not going to take care of something we have so carefully built, why build it at all? Five important techniques and practices include

- ▶ Diversity by Design for smarter ideation
- ▶ Growth Mindset for learning and teaming
- ▶ The Rule of Three for iterating
- ▶ Inclusive and effective meeting techniques
- ▶ Mesh Networking for resiliency

Let's take a closer look at these five Design Thinking techniques and practices useful for building teams that play well and stay together.

Design Thinking in Action: Diversity by Design for Smarter Ideation

Experience and more than two decades of research tell us that diverse teams accelerate innovation (Forbes, 2011). This does not mean that diversity in thought, experience, culture, education, and so forth is easy, nor does it mean that we won't face other challenges tied to communications style and cultural norms. But it does mean that if we are looking for ways to think differently and solve really hard problems, we are much better positioned to do so by pulling together a diverse or cross-boundary team.

A cross-boundary team is just another word for a diverse team, one whose team members reflect diversity in geography, gender, background, culture, education, abilities, ethnicity, organizations, disciplines, skills, qualifications, and more. Cross-boundary teams merge people to work together, bringing their unique experiences and perspectives to bear. Through this innate diversity, the greatest benefits of cross-boundary teaming are found in improved ideation and the end results that these kinds of teams deliver. Apply cross-boundary teaming across the Design Thinking process for maximum effect.

NOTE

Diversity by Design

Diversity by Design is surely the first technique we ever used individually for problem solving. Think about it. When we were children and had a problem or got stuck, what did we do? We probably asked our older brother what to do, or cried out our sorrows in our dad's arms, or whined to our mom— leaning on someone older, with a completely different background, a rich set of diverse experiences, and maybe even a different gender. When we were kids, our family members were about as diverse as we could imagine, different from us in most every way. They had unique and unusual ways of thinking and executing, and more often than not, they got us out of trouble. Diversity to the rescue!

Diversity helps us dig our way out when we get stalled and helps us avoid getting stalled in the first place. Not only do our diverse colleagues give us different perspectives than our own, but by virtue of their gender, background, experiences, culture, race, abilities, and other differences, they naturally help us think and execute differently.

On the flip side, homogeneous same-same teams and v-teams are naturally limited in their thinking and therefore in their capacity to ideate and innovate. If you look around and see a bunch of people who look just like you, the first step toward thinking smarter is as easy as bringing some new people into that team.

Keep in mind that Diversity by Design does not mean everything gets easier. The *Diversity Paradox* reminds us that diverse teams are not an all-encompassing cure for inclusion and innovation. After all, people are still people, and greater team diversity naturally introduces new biases and default patterns to work through.

But experience also tells us that diverse teams accelerate innovation and problem solving. We'll ideate and prototype faster. So again, if we're looking for ways to think differently and solve hard problems, we're better off pulling together a diverse team than trying to think and solve and create solo.

Diversity helps us see the world and our problems from new angles. Literally. Think about the perspectives of a cylinder. The person who views a cylinder from above naturally will be convinced they see a circle. Another person with a side view will be naturally convinced they are looking at a rectangle. And neither person would be wrong, as illustrated in Figure 4.3. A third person can walk in, though, and through their experiences and differences see a different view, perhaps even the cylinder. We need people who see things differently than we do to help us look at our problems or situations in different ways.

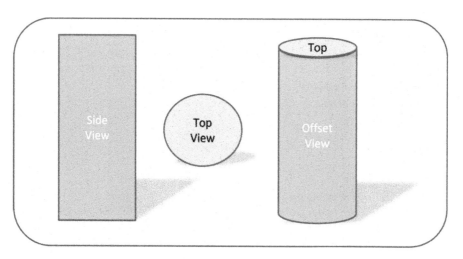

FIGURE 4.3
A situation may look very different from different perspectives.

Sure, we can teach the people we have on our teams to think differently and embrace new perspectives. But the example here reminds us why difficult problems are rarely solved singularly. Ideation is more often than not a team sport as we will see in future hours. And common sense tells us it's better to have 10 team members and therefore potentially 10 different perspectives of a situation than a single view and one shot at solving a problem.

Design Thinking in Action: Growth Mindset for Learning and Teaming

As we walk through life, we can choose an attitude that is resigned to staying put and sticking to what we know today. We call this a fixed mindset, and it's the de facto operating model for most people most of the time. Or we can choose an attitude that reflects the ability to learn and fail and ultimately grow, also called a Growth Mindset. Guess which one helps you solve more problems and create value faster? Created by Dr. Carol Dweck and outlined in her book *Mindset: The New Psychology of Success*, operating and thinking with a Growth Mindset is predicated on the notion that

▶ People are capable of learning regardless of age, experience, education, or area of expertise.

▶ People want to be successful and naturally dislike failing.

▶ Failure therefore needs to become a healthy part of trying and doing, as it's a crucial step on the journey to achievement.

▶ Failure provides a unique way of learning and is the ultimate form of feedback.

▶ Persistence is another key ingredient to success as people fail and learn while practicing a Growth Mindset.

▶ Grace is the final ingredient to success; it must be practiced across and within team members for a Growth Mindset to become a sticky and durable part of a team's culture or workplace climate.

These final points can't be repeated enough. Having a Growth Mindset requires individuals and teams alike to view failure in a healthy light. We must ask of others the grace to try and fail and learn, and likewise we must extend that grace to them as *they* try and fail and learn.

A Growth Mindset is incomplete without that two-way street of grace.

If we find ourselves with a fixed mindset today, choose to change it. Choose to believe that we are able to move beyond where we are today and learn, grow, fail, and ultimately succeed *because* of those failures. Recast failure as learning! And believe that the best is yet to come.

And in the same way, don't allow our team members with fixed mindsets to change *our* mindset for the worse! We cannot change other people, but through our own actions, we can show them another way. Model a Growth Mindset across the team. Be that person who extends the grace of a Growth Mindset to fellow team members, and watch it returned and reflected across the team over time.

Design Thinking in Action: The Rule of Threes for Iterating

Experience and common sense tell us that we rarely get anything right the first time we do something new. It's for this reason that we iterate and refine our work. Iteration is how we make progress.

So it follows that perfection is nearly impossible if we're expected to deliver that perfection the first time around, out of the gate. We cannot achieve perfection and do so with velocity. So as we set out to quickly deliver something of value, we must

- ► Set expectations with our users and other stakeholders that perfection is not the primary goal.

- ► Choose instead to iterate and build on a first release or prototype or an MVP...something that is directionally good enough to warrant an initial round of feedback from the community that will use that first release.

- ► Consider the role that other forms of thinking and ideating (beyond Good Enough Thinking) might play in delivering something of value sooner rather than later.

- ► And finally, communicate broadly that we're following the Rule of Threes, which says we will likely need three iterations (and some say up to five iterations) to get our first release directionally sound enough to share with our user community

The Rule of Threes tells us that our prototype, new design, solution, deliverable, or other work product will take three iterations to meet minimum requirements. The Rule of Threes gives us a way of thinking with confidence, building on and learning from our first two iterations, and getting more done faster than would otherwise have been possible. The key is to set realistic expectations and extend grace throughout the iterating process as we improve our work and move from Good to Better to First Release.

Design Thinking in Action: Inclusive and Effective Meeting Techniques

In the workplace, life often feels like a series of meetings, one after the other. Some occur regularly, others ad hoc, some face to face, others through remote means. Regardless of the time and place and format of the meeting, these interactions with fellow humans require a safe place for thinking and collaborating. Inclusive and effective meeting techniques help provide this safe place.

Consider this list of techniques and Guiding Principles for how to run inclusive, effective, and therefore healthy meetings:

- Invite the right people to show up in the right place at the right time with the right amount of advance notice.

- Demonstrate positive intent and a focus on positive outcomes.

- Lay out a meeting agenda or schedule for all meetings, even if it's one of a series. People have the right to forget what we want to chat about; the agenda serves as our reminder and our vehicle for helping others come prepared.

- When canceling or rescheduling meetings, provide as much advance notice as possible to give attendees the opportunity to tend to other work or priorities.

- If we expect a difficult meeting, think about what we can do to set the stage and deliver the message well.

- Let attendees know if they're optional and allow them to "opt out" of attending a particular meeting (and let them also know to expect meeting notes sometime quickly after the meeting concludes).

- Identify a meeting note taker as the first order of business when the meeting commences; human memory is no substitute for written or recorded words.

- As remote meetings start, encourage attendees to turn on video at least for the first few minutes (with the goal of making meetings visual and people visible). To preserve privacy and maintain a safe place to collaborate, *never* require video; make it optional. But model the behavior we wish to see, and more often than not we will see it.

- For recurring meetings, make sure we rotate or share the workload of taking notes (and above all remember that note taking is not a gender-specific task).

- For meetings that include remote attendees, when it's time to discuss or ideate, drive inclusion by asking remote attendees to share their thoughts and ideas first.

- Use technology to drive inclusive meetings too, including IM threads, "raise hand" features, and emoji and other such feedback features that help people connect, ask questions, share sentiment, and participate.

- Know when to tell stories and when to be concise (and gently help others in these areas as well).

▶ Remember to draw out the quietest attendees and ask them what they think too. Everyone needs to know that they will have a chance to speak or share their thoughts before a meeting concludes.

▶ Before too many people disengage as a meeting comes to a close, discuss if a follow-up meeting is needed and try to schedule it then and there rather than later.

▶ Identify and agree on the communication channel for follow-up (and use that channel to share the meeting notes and next steps).

Send those meeting notes and next steps out before the day ends, or worst case within 24 hours. Don't let the fear of a couple of typos or grammar issues keep people from publishing meeting notes immediately after a meeting concludes. The trade-off in terms of rapid post-meeting follow-ups and actions is worth the occasional typo.

Design Thinking in Action: Mesh Networking for Resiliency

Sometimes called *Archipelago Networking* in light of the need to connect islands of people and teams, Mesh Networking is about the caring and feeding of teams through intentional connections and a mesh of informal and formal communications. Through an overlay of these connections, we can increase belonging, community, social capital, and social cohesion across our teams, which in turn will positively affect the team's culture and work climate.

QUOTE: "The axis on which all successful cultures sit is the feeling of belonging" —Karen Zeiglcr

During the first year of the pandemic, our informal ties to one another dropped 30 percent compared to what was observed in 2019. We were quickly becoming islands, and our workplace and communications reflected this growing disconnect, as shown in Figure 4.4.

And there was no way of getting around this island or archipelago effect. It was real, and we needed a new way of connecting people, of connecting islands, and of reestablishing belonging. Effective teamwork demanded that these islands be connected in new and diverse ways through a mesh of formal networks and communications links. Later we realized we needed to do the same informally as people lost the informal bridges they once had with colleagues and workplace friends and other teams potentially spanning the world.

Use Mesh Networking to keep a team connected, especially if the people involved are distributed over distance or time zones. Actively link islands of individuals, and larger islands of small teams, to one another to drive broader awareness, more effective communications, and deeper collaboration. Maximize connectedness to keep our people and teams healthy and less likely to mentally check out or do the other kinds of things that people do when they feel isolated, ignored, and alone.

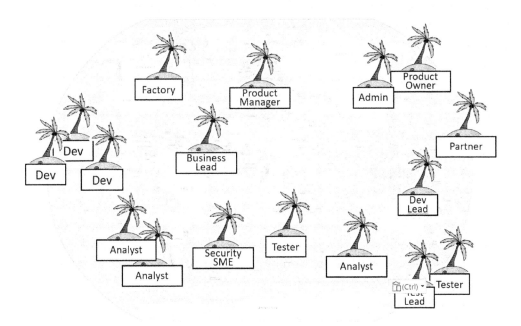

FIGURE 4.4
Consider how from afar many organizations look simply like a collection of islands rather than a cohesive team.

Good island-to-island connections are facilitated through both Inclusive Communications and Concentric Communications (detailed in Hour 15) and include peer-to-peer and peer-to-mentor relationships. Connecting in these ways lets us make progress and achieve outcomes that would be difficult alone too. As we have seen through Diversity by Design and the ideation-related techniques and exercises we will cover in Hours 10 through 14, difficult problems become even more difficult to think through and solve when that thinking and solving are attempted solo.

What does a good mesh network look like? As we see in Figure 4.5, it comprises

▶ Multiple point-to-point connections, which together create an overlapping mesh of relationship, connection, and belonging

▶ Short but frequent point-to-point communications cadences between people and teams and communities of practice, which again reinforces belonging

▶ Regular formal and informal connections with others through simple actions such as *checking in* (where we pointedly ask another how they are feeling, what they are feeling, and what is distracting or pulling at them today or this week)

▶ Lightweight bridges established to other less-traveled islands including people who aren't directly connected to our daily life or work (it's important to mesh across and between people outside of our core circles of connection)

▶ Big-picture geographic groupings and connections to people and resources who know something about what's going on broadly in our projects, initiatives, or other areas we care about

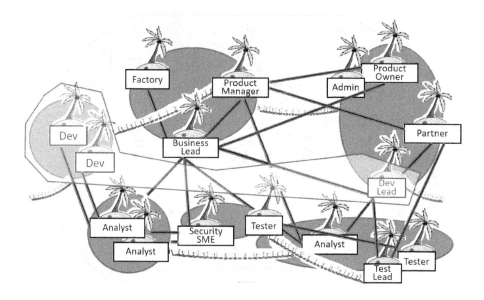

FIGURE 4.5
A healthy Mesh Network consists of multiple points of connection and relationship spanning not only the workplace but well beyond.

Reinforce the mesh network by introducing relationship-building methods found in the Increasing Shared Identity technique. This might include

▶ This is Me profiles

▶ Remote team building

▶ Other informal relationship building methods

▶ Informal Happy Hours or ChitChat sessions (virtual/online as well as face-to-face, depending on what's possible)

Finally, extend the mesh network to others who share a common fence, a shared set of goals or interests, or might become part of our team one day. Consider both remote and physical means of connecting:

▶ Traditions or team rituals such as fantasy football or softball leagues, Aloha Wednesday half-day celebrations, Friday night virtual barbeques, Saturday morning virtual brunches, Monday night football parties, 5K walks, fishing and hunting weekends, camping and bowling nights, date night or movie watch parties, card and domino and pool tournaments, and so on

▶ Service projects sponsored by the local community, churches, schools, or neighborhoods

▶ Charity and disaster relief events that naturally bind people together to help others (none of whom would likely even know one another otherwise)

In the easy times and in the most difficult of times, connect and mesh with those who give you energy, purpose, an outlet, a voice, or a valuable perspective. Use Mesh Networking to grow our own networks intentionally, a person and a team and an event at a time. After all, none of us can afford to operate as an island or archipelago for long.

Responsibly Operating at Speed

Beyond roles and clarity and connections, we need to operate our teams in a way that equips them to move quickly to improve Time-to-Value while promoting healthy collaboration and teaming. Practices that embody many of the Design Thinking techniques and exercises outlined this hour include the following:

▶ **Exercise and model trust.** Teams survive longer, move faster, experiment smarter, practice a Growth Mindset, and therefore take smarter risks when individuals transparently believe in and trust one another.

▶ **Require alignment.** Reserve the time for teams to establish a set of Simple Rules and Guiding Principles that help them better align and more quickly turn around decisions.

▶ **Enforce accountability.** To preserve trust, we need to ensure that when our teams say they are going to do something that they are held to that promise. Consequences are a natural part of life; do not shy away from them but rather use consequences as a way to reinforce what is important and non-negotiable.

▶ **Practice transparency.** To reinforce both accountability and trust, deploy real-time team dashboards and other means of making team progress "visual and visible." Such dashboards provide visibility into bottlenecks and blockades that will naturally occur over the life of a tech initiative or project as well, giving the team and its leaders more time to work the issues.

▶ **Validate inclusion.** Audit and check in with teams to ensure that everyone's voice is indeed being heard, that people are working in healthy ways, and that teams are truly diverse as intended (that is, by design).

▶ **Mandate low overhead.** Create flatter organizations with fewer levels of management and hierarchy to naturally increase visibility, simplify accountability, and accelerate decision-making.

▶ **Institute fewer gates.** Minimize the number of forced "stops" or gates and other checkpoints that people and teams often insert into processes; ensure teams work together as they create deliverables or artifacts to minimize or eliminate the time tied to a gate or checkpoint.

In these ways, practice many of the techniques and exercises outlined in this hour to balance a team's speed with its ability and track record to create value and deliver business outcomes.

What Not to Do: The Archipelago Effect

When we fail to take the time to do the hard work of connecting people and teams, we risk falling into a trap called the Archipelago Effect. Thousands of organizations fell victim to this trap during the pandemic, especially late in Year 1 when no one really envisioned the pandemic lasting more than 6 to 12 months.

By the end of 2020, much of the global workforce became isolated islands, pushing decisions and choices ad infinitum or making them solo and uninformed. People started "checking out" from boredom and feeling disconnected, whereas others become apathetic. Workers started retiring and quitting the workforce in droves, while in other cases work took a back seat to taking care of loved ones, helping children with remote school, and engaging in impromptu video game tournaments, half-day cigarette breaks, and out-of-control day drinking.

People aren't meant to do life in isolation. Many of the people who still showed up for work found themselves overburdened, stuck, and unhappy, feeling like a part of nothing worthwhile. This lack of connectedness explained in part why so many sought out new jobs and new ways to spend the day. In the wake of the Great Reshuffle, the grass might not have been greener, but at least it was different grass.

Despite what some of us tell ourselves, everyone needs a broad mesh of peers, friends, and family to stay healthy, engaged, and motivated. Mesh Networking is about inclusiveness and connection, about leaving no one out. Expand our Mesh Network across work, family, neighbors, clubs, our church family, and our broader neighborhoods and community. Make sure others we care about do the same, too. Healthy people and strong connections will help us avoid the Archipelago Effect.

Summary

Hour 4 expanded on the broad foundation laid in Hour 3. In this hour, we introduced eight new Design Thinking techniques and exercises for building and maintaining resilient and sustainable teams. We explored drafting Simple Rules and Guiding Principles for healthy alignment and operating consistency, and then layered in "How Might We?" questioning for inclusive team-work. Next, we covered Diversity by Design for smarter ideation, Growth Mindset for learning and teaming, and the Rule of Threes for iterating and setting expectations. We walked through a series of techniques and Guiding Principles to help us hold inclusive and effective meetings, and we covered how to execute Mesh Networking as a way of connecting otherwise isolated people and teams to one another. Hour 4 concluded with what it means to bring these techniques and exercises together to operate at speed, along with a "What Not to Do" section focused on avoiding the Archipelago Effect.

Workshop

Case Study

Consider the following case study and questions. You can find the answers to the questions related to this case study in Appendix A, "Case Study Quiz Answers."

Situation

Satish is concerned about several of his OneBank initiative leaders. It seems that several of the Bank's initiatives are failing at a fundamental level to make decisions or remain strategically and operationally aligned. Two of the most homogeneous initiative teams are stalled in ideating and problem solving too. Finally, there are also reports of numerous incidents related to what seems to be noninclusive behavior in meetings and workshops. Satish has a few questions and needs your initial thoughts before you chat with the initiative leaders.

Quiz

1. What type of Design Thinking technique or exercise might help some of these teams make decisions more quickly and stay aligned from a strategy and operational perspective?

2. In what way might "How Might We?" questioning help these indecisive and unaligned teams too?

3. What kind of Design Thinking technique might improve a team's ability to ideate and problem solve?

4. What kind of Design Thinking techniques might help the teams that are suffering from non-inclusive behavior in meetings and workshops?

5. How would you briefly explain the Archipelago Effect?

HOUR 5
Visible and Visual Teamwork

In this hour, we explore not only how to use Design Thinking principles for teamwork and collaboration, but how to execute a Design Thinking exercise in the form of a workshop or session. After covering the importance of Visual Thinking and listing more than two dozen exercises for visual collaboration, we highlight several online Design Thinking collaboration tools. Then we walk through a simple three-stage process for successfully executing any Design Thinking exercise: preparing for the exercise, running the exercise, and concluding the exercise. By keeping the process streamlined and open for exercise-specific additions, and including key steps within each stage, we set the stage for remote as well as face-to-face collaboration. A "What Not to Do" highlighting the importance of gaining a shared understanding between team members concludes Hour 5.

Making Teamwork Visible and Visual

If we are thinking solo, we might not absolutely need to get our initial thoughts down on paper, a whiteboard, or into some kind of a digital format. Though our chances are slim, we might get lucky and remember enough of the factors and implications surrounding our thoughts to actually arrive at a solution. It's not the smartest approach, but sometimes it works.

However, if we are working in a team, we absolutely need to get what's in our heads *out* of our heads. Mere words are rarely adequate if only because it's too easy to misuse and misinterpret words. The best way to get what's in our heads out of our heads is to do so visually. We call this general technique *Making Ideas Visible and Visual*. And it's nothing more than creating and together refining pictures, figures, charts, models, and so on to help us create a shared understanding between our team members and others we might invite to help us think through and solve problems. Two methods for making our work visible and visual include Visual Thinking and visually based Design Thinking exercises for visual collaboration.

Design Thinking in Action: Visual Thinking for Understanding

For our purposes, Visual Thinking is about intentionally augmenting or even replacing words with pictures and figures. As we've heard countless times, a picture is worth a thousand words. While we might argue the word count, as we see in Figure 5.1, a picture can indeed create a shared understanding more effectively than pages of words.

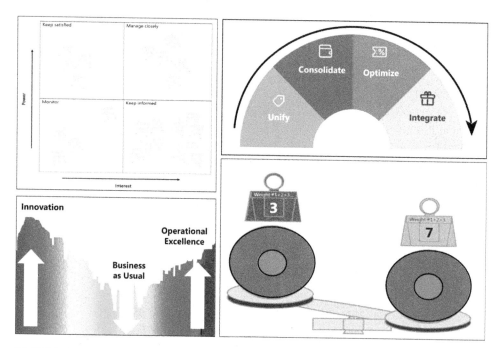

FIGURE 5.1
Note how the visuals here help anyone, regardless of their previous involvement, begin to understand the problem or challenge that a team may be facing.

Design Thinking in Action: Exercises for Visual Collaboration

As we have already seen, fundamental to Design Thinking is the notion of making ideas visible and visual. It's in these ways that we can pull our thinking out of our heads and share it with others to empathize, ideate, communicate, empathize, prototype, test, operationalize, execute, and more. Throughout the book, we cover more than three dozen exercises for collaborating visually and visibly. Some of these include

▶ Stakeholder Mapping for learning about people more quickly

▶ The Power/Interest Grid for prioritizing stakeholders

▶ Journey Mapping to learn more about people and their work

▶ Empathy Mapping for learning more about users and personas

▶ Problem Tree Analysis for separating causes from effects

▶ Boats and Anchors for thinking through schedules

▶ Metaphor and Analogy Thinking for simplifying the complex

▶ Mission Impossible thinking for ideation

▶ Möbius Ideation for "efficiency thinking"

▶ Pattern Matching and Fractal Thinking for identifying themes

▶ Affinity Clustering for finding patterns and themes

▶ Running the Swamp for ideation and empathy

▶ The Culture Cube for understanding broadly

▶ Golden Ratio Analysis for validating the fit of natural patterns

▶ Bullseye Prioritization to understand what's first, second, third

▶ Force Field Analysis for visualizing forces for and against change

▶ Mind Mapping for visual problem solving

▶ Concentric Communications for right person, right time

▶ Structured Text for rapid comprehension

▶ 2×2 Matrix Thinking for focus and prioritization

▶ Adjacent Space Exploration for low-risk next steps

▶ Cover Story Mockup to align and excite

- ▶ RTB for smarter next steps

- ▶ Process Flows for shared understanding

- ▶ Mockups for learning and feedback

- ▶ The Inverse Power Law for responsibly accommodating change

Let us now turn our attention to a set of tools that facilitate visual and visible collaboration and give us ways for geographically disbursed teams to run through Design Thinking exercises together.

Tools for Visual Collaboration

All of us are accustomed to collaborating with others face to face. We use whiteboards, take a look at figures and plans across a desk or table from one another, and communicate in meeting rooms and conference spaces.

But as we know, collaboration cannot always be done face to face. As our teams span further distances and geographies, and a myriad of local and worldwide conditions make travel difficult or expensive, the need to collaborate virtually has become more important than ever.

For Design Thinking exercises and other such real-time interactions, consider using popular tools such as the following:

- ▶ Klaxoon boards and its workshop platform for running interactive meetings and Design Thinking workshops, reviewing and marking up pre-prepared content created in Microsoft PowerPoint or Visio or Adobe's collaboration tools, running live exercises using Klaxoon's multicolored smart and resizable sticky notes, and more. In cases where a team cannot physically meet to run a Design Thinking exercise, Klaxoon and Microsoft Whiteboard (covered next) are easy to use. See https://klaxoon.com/ to create an account and start using Klaxoon's workshop platform.

- ▶ Microsoft Whiteboard and its prepopulated problem-solving, design, strategy, retrospective, and empathy map templates and more for live sketching, working out concepts, marking up content to drop into a Klaxoon board, and so on. Whiteboard is included in Windows 11, is available in a limited Web version, and can be downloaded for other Windows platforms, Apple iPhone, and iPads. See the online Microsoft store for the app.

- ▶ Figma for wireframing, marking up sticky notes, and sharing ideas quickly with others including using custom libraries to host and iterate on prototypes for our projects and initiatives. And use Figma's FigJam for online whiteboarding, ideating, and exploring ideas together. See https://www.figma.com to set up an account and use this tool.

▶ Microsoft Teams and Zoom Video Communications for communicating and collaborating through video, sharing figures and other data, and communicating both real time and asynchronously. Download Zoom at www.zoom.us/download and download Microsoft Teams at www.microsoft.com/en-us/microsoft-teams/download-app.

Of course, many other tools are available, too. Use Miro for collaboration, Canva for prototyping, Mural for Design Thinking templates and canvases, the Billboard Design Thinking group on LinkedIn for templates, and others similar to the ones listed here for running real-time collaboration and video sessions on platforms such as Linux and various mobile platforms.

Executing a Design Thinking Exercise

There are entire books and courses dedicated to delivering Design Thinking workshops and facilitating exercises. For our purposes, we have simplified "running a Design Thinking exercise" into three stages, as noted here and illustrated in Figure 5.2.

▶ Stage One: Prepare for the Exercise

▶ Stage Two: Run the Exercise

▶ Stage Three: Conclude the Exercise

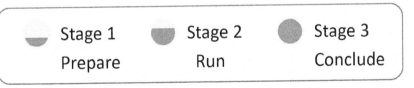

FIGURE 5.2
Use this simple three-stage process for thinking through and executing a Design Thinking exercise.

Use these three stages and the steps contained within each stage to execute any of the Design Thinking exercises outlined in this book. Each stage is detailed next.

NOTE

Just a Bit of Clarity...

Though another term might have been ideal, we settled on the term *stage* to avoid confusion with the *phases* associated with the Design Thinking Model for Tech and the *steps* associated with running Design Thinking exercises.

Stage One: Prepare for the Exercise

There are entire courses dedicated to preparing for and delivering Design Thinking workshops, sessions, or exercises (terms that are generally interchangeable). For our purposes, we want to keep any overhead as light as we responsibly can to create as simple a process as possible.

We need to consider the "people aspect" of an exercise too; not only the community of users who must be central to our work, but our team members and other stakeholders we will ask to join us in a Design Thinking exercise.

Finally, if we keep in mind that our exercises are generally intended to broadly learn, deeply empathize, define problems to ideate and problem solve, or prototype and test, and we understand where our Design Thinking exercise sits on this continuum, then we should know more about *what* to gather, *how* to plan, and *who* to invite and prepare.

Prepare and plan for running a Design Thinking exercise by performing the following:

1. Select an owner to determine the need for a particular Design Thinking exercise and prepare for it. Oftentimes the owner will also serve as the exercise facilitator (or coach), but we should not make that assumption just yet.

2. Pull together all of the logistics including how the exercise will be facilitated (in a physical location or through a tool such as Klaxoon).

3. Arrange for the tools and materials necessary to facilitate the exercise (ranging from physical whiteboards, tables, markers, and sticky notes to virtual equivalents of the same).

4. Establish the key challenge to be tackled, a brief set of exercise objectives, and a simple agenda.

5. Based on the objectives, ensure that the planned Design Thinking exercise is still appropriate. Adjust or add additional exercises and update the agenda as needed.

6. Consider how much time is needed to run the exercise (refer to the *Exercise Notes* for that exercise). Identify the number and makeup of the necessary attendees and the actual calendar date and timing for the exercise based on attendee and presumed facilitator or coach availability.

7. Send out the meeting invitations early enough to lock in the attendees. Include the agenda and objectives in this meeting invitation, and make it clear that the exercise will not only be fun and a great use of time, but also an important step toward together achieving our goals.

8. Based on what we've learned through this process, identify and prepare our Design Thinking exercise facilitator or coach. Ensure that the facilitator runs through a mock set of the exercises to familiarize themselves. The facilitator needs to be ready and excited to engage the attendees and drive our exercise's outcomes.

This simple and repeatable process may be modified, of course, but it should serve as a good starting point or template for any exercise.

Stage Two: Run the Exercise

If we have prepared well, then we should have a physical or virtual room full of attendees ready and excited to work together. Commence and execute the Design Thinking exercise by performing the following:

1. Be the first to (physically or virtually) arrive and welcome everyone. Round-robin through brief 30-second introductions. Include a simple icebreaker as each attendee introduces themselves (see the note here for a list of popular and favorite icebreakers).

2. Share any logistics or housekeeping rules related to facilities, scheduled breaks, practices for reducing distractions, expectations for participation, protocols for participating, and so on. Keep these lighthearted and optimistic, creating a safe space for collaboration and open communication.

3. Introduce the topic and objectives of the meeting, the agenda, what we should all know about the problem or situation or lay of the land, and our ultimate goal today: the outcome we wish to achieve (which might include understanding more about a situation, modeling or defining a problem, ideating to learn or potentially solve a problem, building a prototype, and so on).

4. Prior to commencing the actual Design Thinking exercise, it may be useful to start with a warm-up intended to help people think creatively. See Hour 10 for warm-ups, including activities such as drawing what's in our heads, building a skyscraper with toy blocks or LEGO blocks, building a pasta noodle or paper bridge with a neighbor, creating the most accurate or best-distance paper airplane, designing a four-cup holder with only paper and tape, drawing a house without lifting the pen or retracing a line, and so on.

5. Introduce the Design Thinking exercise, the challenge we face, the materials we will use, and the outcomes we are seeking. Remind the attendees of the key user communities we need to stay focused on, including those users and edge cases at risk of being ignored or marginalized.

6. Run the actual Design Thinking exercise following the steps outlined here or in other sources.

7. If the attendees stall or get stuck or distracted, consider introducing a set of guardrails for thinking differently (as outlined in Hour 11) or running a quick check-in to see how everyone is doing. Provide clarity or help as needed.

NOTE

Important Icebreaker Guidance

Some of our favorite icebreakers include having an attendee share their dream job, favorite sports team, first car, proudest accomplishment, the item at the top of their bucket list, the music or podcast they're currently listening to, the last book they read, how they spent last weekend, or to share something that few people probably know about them. Be careful to create an inclusive and encouraging environment, however, while walking through each attendee's answers!

This process looks easy on paper, but challenges will arise. Be prepared to optimistically navigate those challenges, keeping in mind the outcomes we need to achieve and the fact that we all need to cross the finish line together.

Stage Three: Conclude the Exercise

While the conclusion of a particular exercise may yield very different outputs and outcomes, there are still several common steps to execute to conclude our time together.

1. Perform a simple retrospective on the exercise and how it was delivered and received, including where it sits in the Design Thinking continuum and what was accomplished.

2. Collect or record or otherwise save all of the completed templates, worked examples, problem statements and framing outputs, models, lists of ideas, prioritized choices or decisions, prototypes and drawings, test plans and outputs, and all of the visuals that were likely created along the way.

3. Agree with the attendees about what next steps and follow-up look like, including the next set of decisions, techniques, and exercises.

4. Prior to dismissing anyone, ask for attendee feedback regarding the usefulness of the exercise, tools, and materials, the effectiveness of the facilitator or coach, and what should be done differently next time.

5. Wrap up the exercise and thank everyone for coming and participating.

6. Run a leadership-internal debrief to share outcomes and outputs and to discuss with this smaller audience what should be done differently next time.

Afterward, share in digital format the outputs, conclusions, next steps, and so forth with the attendees and relevant stakeholders so they're not lost in the aftermath of the exercise.

What Not to Do: Keeping It All Inside

A regional retailer was in the middle of a business transformation and found its people working incredible hours but making little progress, as evidenced in the slow development cycles and poor test results. Someone eventually suggested that the team was too entrenched in the details and weeds; team members needed a North Star and a way of aligning their work to that North Star.

Cursory ideas were tossed about, but no one thought to drive the team's thinking in a way that pulled ideas out of their heads and into the open so that others could "see" and consider them. The team was keeping everything inside, trapped in their heads…one person's perspective slightly different than another's. The team needed to make their ideas and their work visible and visual. They needed to arrive at some kind of shared understanding and use a shared vocabulary regarding their interim and final outputs.

Instead, they were told to get back to work. After another year of slogging through their business transformation, the company decided the broader change just wasn't worth the effort and halted the project.

Summary

In Hour 5, we explored Design Thinking principles for visible and visual teamwork and collaboration. We outlined Visual Thinking for creating a shared understanding between people, followed by an extensive list of visual exercises for visual collaboration. After walking through a set of simple tools to facilitate this collaboration among remote and geographically dispersed teammates, we then turned to the three stages for running any of the more than three dozen Design Thinking exercises spanning this book: Phase 1 for preparing for an exercise, Phase 2 for running an exercise, and Phase 3 for concluding the exercise. By keeping the process for running exercises simple, and including key steps within each stage, we created a simple and repeatable process. A "What Not to Do" reiterating the importance of gaining a shared understanding among team members concludes Hour 5.

Workbook

Case Study

Consider the following case study and questions. You can find the answers to the questions related to this case study in Appendix A, "Case Study Quiz Answers."

Situation

Satish has noted numerous communications issues recently and has concluded that several of the OneBank initiative teams are using common words and phrases in ways that mean one thing to them but something completely different to others. As he's tackling that shared vocabulary issue, he has asked you to also share with those teams your perspectives on making teamwork visible and visual. The teams have passed on a few questions for you to answer first.

Quiz

1. What is Visual Thinking in the simplest terms?

2. What are some examples of Design Thinking exercises for Visual Collaboration?

3. In cases where a team cannot physically meet to run a Design Thinking exercise or session, what alternatives might be most useful?

4. What kind of stepwise process might be used to organize and execute a Design Thinking exercise or session?

PART II

Understanding Broadly

HOUR 6
Understanding the Lay of the Land

What You'll Learn in This Hour:

▶ Listening and Understanding

▶ Assessing the Broader Environment

▶ Understanding and Articulating Value

▶ What Not to Do: Ignore the Culture Fractals

▶ Summary and Case Study

Hour 6 commences Part II, "Understanding Broadly," where we focus on Phase 2 of our Design Thinking Model for Tech (see Figure 6.1). These next four hours take us on a journey to understand the lay of the land, connect with the right people peppered across this landscape, and learn more about those people as a way to empathize, successfully problem solve, and ultimately create value together. Here in Hour 6 we focus on three areas: listening, understanding, and learning. We do this work of listening, understanding, and learning in the context of a situation or problem. After all, we should understand the lay of the land—the ecosystem, the industry, and the organization and its culture—before we start more deeply connecting and empathizing with the specific people who will make a difference for us. All of this work is embodied in Phase 1 of our Design Thinking Model for Tech, and we pursue it to help us figure out what it's going to take to successfully solve problems and deliver value. A "What Not to Do" case study focused on the implications of ignoring culture-derived fractals concludes this hour.

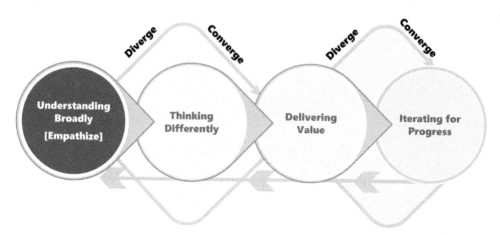

FIGURE 6.1
Phase 1 of our Design Thinking Model for Tech.

Listening and Understanding

Listening is a skill. But it's also a process, and good listening benefits from a bit of preplanning. Before we can be really good listeners, we need to think ahead and intentionally

- ▶ **Know what we need.** Think about the information you need and who might be in a position to share that information. More importantly, think deeply about whether we are seeking "a ha" revelations, lessons learned, a history or debrief, feedback on recent events, thoughts on future ideas, or something else.

- ▶ **Choose those who know what we need.** Consider the balance between purposefully finding and sitting down with an audience versus also being open to having our audience find us and sit us down. Nuggets of wisdom and insight come from everywhere.

- ▶ **Be present.** There is nothing worse than a presumed listener failing to actually listen. All of us know this from experience…it is far too easy to tell when our audience is distracted and therefore not fully present. If we are there to listen, then listen! Put away the phone, shut the lid to our laptop, find a good place without distractions, and *be present.* Listen and learn and take notes afterward to ensure we do not forget what we just heard, learned, and felt.

- ▶ **Be self-aware.** Listening also means responding in real time to show we are engaged, thinking, and learning. Nodding our head subtly can be useful, as are the occasional simple words of affirmation, but do not overuse these techniques! We all know people who pretend to listen when in fact they are not, and we all know people who listen in such distracting ways that we cannot help but wonder if they are really listening at all. Know ourselves.

NOTE

Need to Listen Better?

Become a better self-aware listener by practicing Active Listening, Silence by Design, and other listening and learning techniques outlined here. In doing so, we can begin to master the art of *situational fluency*.

Long-time MIT academic Kurt Lewin once said that the best way to understand a situation was to try to change it. Why? Because people will flock to help us understand why change is unnecessary and everything is just fine as it is. Conversely, others will also flock to help explain why a particular change fails to meet their needs or solve their problems. Still others will flock to give their perspectives on how to go about change, what to change, and when to do so.

Through all of the "help" of all of these people, we can grow in our understanding of the situation. But such ad hoc growth does not build the broad understanding we might require or drive the kind of head knowledge and heart empathy necessary for sustainable change. Instead, we should start practicing Active Listening, covered next.

Design Thinking in Action: Active Listening

People are usually quick to say that they are good listeners. But it's more difficult than we think. It's a skill that needs to be honed, just like any other skill. To actively listen is to show up and

▶ Be fully engaged, without distractions.

▶ Continually fight the urge to interrupt, until it is time to do so.

▶ Rather than interrupting to share our own thoughts, choose instead to reflect what we just heard.

▶ Reflect our understanding of what we are hearing too, through verbal cues, a smile, a nod of the head, and so on.

▶ Paraphrase when it makes sense to do so, as a way to clarify and condense key themes or learnings.

▶ Do our part to stay focused on the subject at hand, recognizing that others might take the conversation in other directions.

▶ Ask questions as needed, remembering to minimize interruptions along the way.

Remember that Active Listening is about putting away our phones, our laptops, our biases, and everything we *think* we know. Be present, listen like we are wrong, and learn (see Figure 6.2). There is arguably no better way to learn and empathize than through listening to another's experiences, their stories, and their unsolicited challenges and pain.

FIGURE 6.2
Active Listening reflects how we show up and stay focused on others. (Pressmaster/Shutterstock)

Design Thinking in Action: Silence by Design

Create and use awkward silence and other healthy discomforts as a way to learn about what's going on in other people's minds. Silence by Design is a method for gaining understanding by not filling in the pauses or gaps in a discussion when having a conversation with another person. Instead, let the silence stand...let it sit...and wait. Wait patiently for the other person to finally restart the conversation, all while observing body language and other nonverbal communications.

The idea is simple. When we are quiet, when we choose to listen rather than fill in the blanks with our own ramblings, we give others a gift. We give them the ability to fill in awkward silences with their own insights and with what is really on their mind. Regardless of whether we are having a positive conversation or an argument, Silence by Design can give us a targeted view into what another person is thinking. And what they are feeling. And these insights are like gold.

And during those awkward silences, because we are not struggling to find our own words, we have the opportunity to pay attention more. We have a chance to consider all of the nonverbal reactions and body language surrounding the discussion. Learn from these nonverbal communications—a raise of the eyebrows, folding of the arms, rolling of the eyes, or exasperated shake of the head—to help us figure out where to take the conversation once we have allowed Silence by Design to run its course.

Larry King once observed, "Nothing I say this day will teach me anything. So, if I'm going to learn, I must do it by listening." Listening takes a number of forms. Initially, we want and need to listen across a wide spectrum to those stakeholders willing to talk. Eventually we will learn to filter the nuggets from the noise, but it's important to give everyone a fair shot at being heard; don't exclude people too early from being heard. The most vocal are often the most affected or interested, after all, even if they might be the most difficult or irritating.

And we must listen across a breadth of audiences too, from the top to the bottom, from the bosses to the workers…from the masses in the middle of everything to the people on the "edge" or on the outside who may have valuable learnings and perspectives for us (see Figure 6.3).

FIGURE 6.3
Silence by Design can yield greater insights as we watch and listen across the breath of our stakeholders, potential users, and more.

NOTE

Shhhhhhh…

When we are quiet—when we choose to listen rather than fill in conversation gaps with our own ramblings—we will eventually find that others fill in those awkward silences with their unique insights and what's really on their minds.

Design Thinking in Action: Supervillain Monologuing

In the same way that the movies often feature villains who take the time to "reveal their evil plans," we might need to get the people who have the history with our situation and the landscape as it stands today to monologue about their perspectives...like an evil supervillain! We need to know what's on their minds, and we need to know how the situation came to evolve to where it is today.

How might we learn what's on another's mind? For starters, try inviting a response to open-ended questions that affect their future, such as

- ▶ "With so many changes taking place around here, what do you think is going to happen next to us?"
- ▶ "What are your plans if this situation plays out like you probably think it will?"
- ▶ "What does the future here hold for people like me and you?"

Or state something provocative about the current situation or organization as a way to elicit a response:

- ▶ "How do you think these industry changes will affect us in the long term?"
- ▶ "What do you think about half the leadership team leaving these last six months?"
- ▶ "How did Allison not get that promotion to managing director?"
- ▶ "When was the last time you saw something like that happen!?"

Supervillain Monologuing is useful for engaging with others and understanding what we've gotten ourselves into, as we see in Figure 6.4. Through this technique we may discover what the future holds, the ambiguity and other challenges we may face, and the decisions we may need to take. And it's really easy to do with people who are naturally chatty or prone to oversharing. Find them, engage them, and learn!

It's not difficult to lead unhappy or disgruntled people to talk either. If we are not up for the hard questions, find a willing colleague and tag-team the situation. Together, lead that other person right where they want to go, and sit back and listen and learn. And just remember that no one in these situations is truly an evil supervillain; we are simply using a common engagement technique to learn more.

"... the system today is just really slow.... I get so frustrated when I try to log on every morning or run my weekly reports before I leave Monday, gosh, and our cloud DevOps team is great, but Nancy is leaving and one of the guys is so checked out or maybe doesn't have a clue!"

FIGURE 6.4
Encouraging others to talk and share their perspectives a la Supervillain Monologuing can lead to even greater insights than Active Listening and Silence by Design.

Design Thinking in Action: Probing for Better Understanding

With a reasonable understanding of a situation or problem, we can finally start drilling or "mining" for details. We do this by asking the kinds of questions that cannot be answered without some thought. In this way, we can achieve the goal of Probing for Understanding, which is to bring clarity to a situation to not only learn more but to avoid mistakes that have been made before.

Probing questions go beyond questions that clarify too. Good probing questions open the back doors as well as the front doors to situations, so we can explore those situations in a 360-degree kind of way. How? By asking open-ended "Why...?" questions and pursuing similar lines of questioning. When we probe and ask deep questions to understand a situation, we are

▶ Looking back into the past, as a way to explain how we got here

▶ Assessing the present day, to understand why things are the way they are

▶ Peering into the future, to think through what might happen when change is introduced

We probe by asking questions that cannot be answered without some thought. The goal is to bring more clarity to a situation, whether current or potential, to avoid mistakes that have been made before and to find a way through the ambiguity ahead of us.

Probing questions must go beyond questions that only clarify, though; probing questions are used to seek and understand the edges of a situation. For this reason, they are open-ended and often preceded with "Why...?"

Importantly, probing questions are not intended to eliminate ambiguity! Complex situations typically reflect a degree of ambiguity, and the investment in time and energy to eliminate all ambiguity is futile. Our goal is to simply cut through the first few "layers" of ambiguity so we can be smarter as we pursue a broader understanding of the lay of the land.

As we strive for greater understanding around why we or others are stuck, we may need to ask deep and probing questions, the kind that really help us unlock the mindset of another person. If we don't probe to understand why another person thinks a particular way or values a particular thing, or we fail to learn how the current situation came to be, we may never quite understand the nuances that capture that person's struggles, thinking, and behaviors.

There are several ways to tactfully inquire and truth-seek, but open-ended questions and funnel questions are typically the easiest and most useful. Open-ended questions cannot be answered with a yes or no. They are exploratory in nature, the kind of question that really makes a person avoid automatic responses and actually think about the question. Consider the following examples:

▶ "What was on your mind when you designed this interface?"

▶ "How did you intend to uncover the requirements?"

▶ "Why did you think that was a good way to manage a backlog?"

▶ "Tell me more about..."

Funnel questions start with easy questions (ask for names, how things are going, what the person has been doing lately), and once the person being questioned is comfortable, the questions turn more pointed or thoughtful:

▶ "Why haven't you been more successful in...?"

▶ "What problems have you overcome during...?"

▶ "When was the last time you looked at...?"

▶ "Who told you about...?"

Despite the way probing (and funnel questions in particular) can feel, the goal of probing is to bring clarity and honesty to a situation. Probing provides understanding, which in turn helps us avoid mistakes and understand more about what's in front of us.

Probing for Understanding clears a path through the uncertainty ahead of us. To deliver a good Probing for Understanding exercise or line of questioning, keep in mind the following:

▶ Give freedom, space, and time to think to the person being questioned.

▶ Do not prematurely answer our own questions or lead our audience down a path of our own making; practice good Silence by Design!

Allow questions to sit and sink in and be answered in their own time. Be patient. Chances are we will be rewarded with something we did not already know.

▶ Use provocative or highly emotional questions sparingly.

▶ Avoid bombarding a person with too many tough questions at once.

▶ Balance the need to perform basic fact finding with the need to be led down unexpected learning paths (where the real rewards are).

▶ Avoid jumping to conclusions; jumping interrupts the flow of information and implies that we think we already have all the answers!

▶ Use our listening skills to identify the right clarifying questions. Clarification will improve both understanding and empathy.

▶ Show engagement throughout the communications process.

▶ Provide thoughtful and authentic feedback to the answers to our questions to show we are listening. Echo especially important aspects of a response or experience or story as a way to reinforce the communicator's message or invite further detail.

▶ Pay attention to our own body language and facial expressions. Nothing shuts down a hard conversation faster than uncontrolled body language.

Probing lets us cut through the slanted viewpoints, the ambiguity, and the little bits of information that people choose to share so that we can learn and see the bigger picture and grow a bit wiser in the process.

NOTE

Know It All? No Thank You.

Remember that as we Probe for Understanding we need to avoid looking like a know-it-all! Instead, seek to be known as a great listener, to be thought of as a listen-to-it-all.

Assessing the Broader Environment

Once we have listened and probed for understanding, we need to do a bit of research to fill in the gaps. Specifically, we're looking at gaining a Big Picture Understanding followed by understanding the organization's culture, workplace climate, and biases.

Design Thinking in Action: Big Picture Understanding

As we briefly covered in Hour 2, gaining a Big Picture Understanding boils down to researching and understanding a number of environmental dimensions that start with a broad pursuit and drive deeper and deeper to better understand

▶ The macroeconomic environment and industry

▶ The company or entity within its industry and environment

▶ The organization or business unit within the company or entity

For example, as we see in Figure 6.5, we might first explore the broader industry, economic or regulatory environment, and other macro or big picture matters to learn the answers to questions such as

1. What is the status and health of the overall industry or landscape (economics, problems, and current trends)?

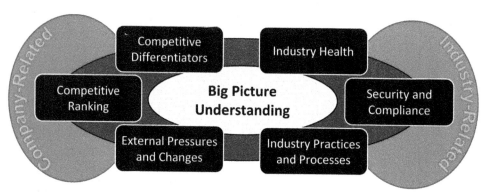

FIGURE 6.5
By exploring macro and other high-level matters surrounding an organization, we can gain a broad and Big Picture Understanding of that organization.

2. Which security and compliance mandates are top of mind?

3. Are there specific industry practices, processes, and quality bars to be considered?

4. What are the most relevant external pressures and changes (such as competitive pressures, economic changes, or regulatory issues)?

5. Where does the company or entity rank in its industry and among its competitors?

6. What differentiates the company from otherwise similar companies? How are they different, and why?

Then we might explore more about the company, its culture and standards, and its specific business and technology problems:

7. What is the overall vision of the company or entity? Who does it aspire to be, and what is the time frame for that to-be vision?

8. How well does the company's current culture reflect who it aspires to be? Where are the gaps?

9. What is the general state of the company from a financial, customer, partner, employee work/life balance, and employee morale perspective?

10. How is the company handling external business pressures and changes?

11. What are the company's top business or operational pain points and challenges? How are these affected by technology constraints or limitations?

12. What about its top strategic business or operational strategies or initiatives? Is technology hindering or helping?

13. With regard to these strategies and initiatives, is the company protecting technology or other sacred cows and the status quo?

14. Is the company and its leadership team running from something rather than running toward a unifying vision or mission?

15. How has the company's business and technology strategy fared lately, and what is changing or could potentially change?

We might then fill in gaps reflecting the company's specific organization or business unit and its people who are affected by the business and technology situations and problems:

16. What changes in the business unit's functional strategies and capabilities are needed?

17. How well are current functional capabilities delivered? How mature are these delivery capabilities? Where are the key gaps?

18. For any given business-enabling technology, is there a track record of identifying and rallying around business-specific or technology-specific change drivers?

19. To what extent is the business unit and its people capable of changing? How has this been demonstrated in previous projects or initiatives?

20. To what extent does the business unit's culture enable or prohibit change?

21. How positively is the business unit perceived internally?

22. What does "value" mean to the business unit and its people?

23. Who defines this notion of "value" and how it's measured?

24. How stable is the business unit from a leadership and management perspective?

25. What do the people working in the business unit think about their work, their leaders, their own team, and their all-up organization?

With all of this broad understanding and context in place, we can work through the organization's situations and problems as we identify the right people and right problems to focus on. Then we need to do some more work and research surrounding culture and the pace of change surrounding the situation and its problems.

Design Thinking in Action: The Culture Snail for Pace of Change

Understanding the big picture and an organization's broad lay of the land is one thing. Understanding how well a company or business unit can change is another. In any IT project or tech initiative, there's a natural intersection of technology teams and the business teams who will benefit from the final tech-enabled business solution. At this intersection sits a number of cultural attributes that inform and shape each team, each business unit, the company, and perhaps even the broader industry and macro-economic environment.

In this multilevel kind of way, we can see culture morph and change a little bit here, a little bit there. This shaping takes time. And the changes come about slowly, a person at a time and a day at a time, moving like a snail making its way on a journey. Like a snail, culture change is organic and alive, slow to move and change, and sometimes amorphous and messy (see Figure 6.6).

Map this journey! Draw it out with the help of others and consider what you see. An organization's culture journey tells us about the organization's ability to change and what that pace of change looks like. It shows us how well the organization can absorb change. Do you see inflection points where change was rapid and adopted well? Do you see other times where change was avoided and stalled the organization? How does this culture journey reflect projects, initiatives, mergers and acquisitions, divestitures, changes in strategy, product launches and product failures, economic downturns, industry changes, and so forth?

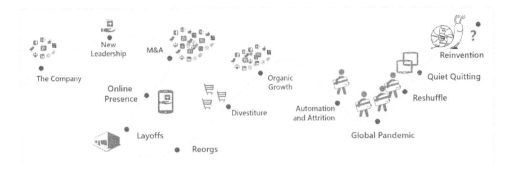

FIGURE 6.6
Culture reflects the countless changes reflected by people over time as they join and leave a team and broader organization.

Beyond its slow-moving nature, culture is also multidimensional and complex. Consider how our external partners, training organizations, cloud and application vendors, hardware and network providers, and so many others have influenced the status quo culture and ways of working. And turn to the Culture Cube to think more deeply about the dimensions of culture and how they work together to better describe a business unit's or company's culture and work climate today.

Design Thinking in Action: The Culture Cube for Understanding

Common sense and experience tell us that we cannot change culture by "changing culture." Culture initiatives take time and therefore change takes time. Culture is changed or shaped a person at a time and a behavior at a time—and it takes time. Instead, we should seek to first take the following broad-based steps:

1. **Draw on the current culture.** The idea here is to meet our people and our teams where they are, just as we do when it comes to developing our people's capabilities or our organization's maturity. In this way, we can immediately use and build upon the most valuable existing aspects of our team's or organization's culture as we learn to work through existing patterns and biases and start rebuilding momentum for progress.

2. **Intentionally evolve and shape culture.** Next, in parallel to drawing on the current culture to make initial progress, we need to shape and redefine over time what it means to be an effective team or a supportive organization. We need to promote specific attitudes, behaviors, and healthy biases, and squash others. And in doing so, we must consider how the current culture will react and evolve across the three dimensions of environment, work climate, and work style.

Our goal here is to gently push the culture to a place where differences are intentionally leveraged for good and take a back seat to achieving a program's or project's goals and objectives. We want to take steps to bring teams together, to reward work well done, and to embrace the perspective that the right person for a particular assignment has nothing to do with differences but rather with capabilities, maturity, and attitude.

We must be careful not to inadvertently segregate or separate particular teams or departments from one another. The goal and the right thing to do is to drive inclusion. There are no outsiders on a team, regardless of geographical boundaries or experiences.

And in cases where someone has infringed upon another's rights or created a less than safe work environment, we must take swift steps to address the problem and set a positive example—not just leaders, but everyone.

Helping one another bring the best that we can bring to work every day is not just a job for leadership; it is everyone's job and everyone's responsibility to look out for one another.

How and where do we start? The easiest way to assess our team's or organization's culture is to simply look around. What do people do? What seems to be the team's default and perhaps unwritten Simple Rules and Guiding Principles? How do people act? Which behaviors are tolerated, and which are not? What does the team prioritize and value? What is their track record for getting hard things done? Look and listen!

And pay attention to what other people say about the team—our team—and our organization here and now. These nuggets of solicited and unsolicited feedback and insight reveal an important point-in-time perspective. Such perspectives give us a baseline against which we can later measure our culture's evolution. For our purposes here as we consider what it means to apply Design Thinking to technology, let us condense culture into a three-dimensional cube reflecting three dimensions and eight perspectives (see Figure 6.7).

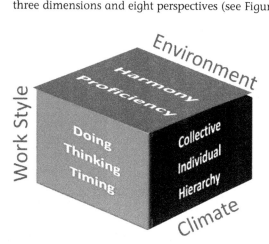

FIGURE 6.7
The Culture Cube and its dimensions and perspectives.

As we see from the figure, the culture cube reflects three dimensions: the business unit's or company's environment, its work climate, and its work style. Each dimension includes two or more perspectives. To assess an organization's culture or team's workplace climate, assess the following:

TIME AND PEOPLE: A Culture Cube exercise requires 3–10 people for 30–120 minutes.

1. **Environment.** Consider how people think about their overall workplace.

   ▶ Harmony, or the ability to work and relate with one another effectively in the workplace.

   ▶ Proficiency, or the desire to continually improve at something that matters and is therefore meaningful (Pink, 2009).

2. **Work Climate.** Consider how people work with and relate to one another.

   ▶ Collective, or the extent to which a team works effectively together, values people and/or the work being done, and shares similar ideas of goals and success.

   ▶ Individual, or what each team member personally brings to a team in terms of background, experience, biases, values (and respect, initiative, leadership "follow-ship" styles, empathy, conflict management skills, and more).

   ▶ Hierarchy, or the "vertical differences between team members" (Greer, 2018) spanning teams and the overall organization.

3. **Work Style.** Consider how and when people get things done.

   ▶ Doing, or how and why work is executed and the extent to which the work is strictly structured and governed (or not).

   ▶ Thinking, or the planning performed before work is executed.

   ▶ Timing, or when work is executed.

As we know from the Culture Snail, culture moves slowly and in subtle ways, reflecting incremental changes with every new hire brought to a team and every gap left when someone leaves. These individual changes slowly affect and in their small ways change an organization's culture in terms of the overall environment, the more tactical work climates of each team, and the observed work styles both within and between each team.

Design Thinking in Action: Recognizing and Validating Bias

Another important technique for assessing the broader environment lies in recognizing and validating cross-team and business unit biases. Everyone is biased; we all have our preferences and default ways of thinking and responding. These biases float "up" into our teams, business units, and so on.

For our purposes, biases are akin to really bad mental shortcuts. They're bad only because they circumvent deep thinking and instead dump our thoughts and automatic responses into the world of assumptions. The key is therefore to *see* our own biases and recognize biases in others and across our teams. In this way, we can break free from behaviors and patterns that might be keeping us tied to old ways of thinking and executing.

Biases come from what we have experienced and seen in the past, and those biases can be manifested in the present as we unconsciously apply those past experiences to how we work, communicate, collaborate, and make decisions. Because unintentional and unconscious biases hurt people and relationships (and teams and their reputations) just as intentional biases do, it's important to identify and validate them early.

There are many forms of bias, but when it comes to interacting in healthy ways with other people, several forms of biases easily go overlooked:

▶ Bandwagon bias, or the notion that an idea already adopted by others is the right one for us, too (rather than debating it or setting it aside while we seek additional ideas).

▶ Confirmation bias, which occurs because people want to believe something that confirms what we think we already know.

▶ Framing bias, which occurs when a poor idea is adopted simply because it was presented or "framed" really well.

▶ Action bias, or the notion that it is better to do something than nothing even in the absence of information supporting that "something," which in turn can keep us stuck while we work on the wrong things or head in the wrong direction.

▶ Information bias, where people demand more information to make the best decision (keeping us stuck in the meantime).

▶ Pro-innovation bias, where new ideas are adopted simply because they are new and therefore presumed innovative.

▶ In-group bias, or the practice of dismissing out of hand the ideas that come from groups of people who differ from you in culture, background, experience, education, skin color, height, weight, and infinite other attributes.

Biases show up in teams and organizations in the same way they do at an individual level: one person at a time. And biases show up in products and services too. Consider the stories of so many people of color who have to turn over their hands to the "lighter side" to get hands-free sensors to dispense soap and water. Why? Because those sensors were designed for a particular skin tone.

Biases exclude people, shut down innovation, shortcut assumptions, and negatively affect data gathering and feedback sessions. For example, in-group bias will drive teams to favor their own ideas or thinking over other teams' ideas or thinking. Framing bias will drive a team or an individual to perceive a well-presented idea as perhaps the best idea. Teams, especially those expected to be innovative, will err on the side of action bias rather than risking the perception that they are "thinking (too much) to build." These biases have zero merit, yet they all too often influence our actions and those of our teams.

So be on the alert for these biases. When you hear phrases such as "that will never get approved by the board" or "we tried that and it failed" or "nobody would want that," gently call out these statements as perceptions worthy of consideration but reflective of the past. Remind the team that we must learn from our mistakes but remain focused on the future. Find ways of connecting empathy for what we have seen and heard with the desire to hear all perspectives—old and new alike.

We need to keep communications open and flowing. After all, today's problems are never identical to yesterday's problems, nor can they always be solved by yesterday's solutions. And as we will see next, we have a much better chance at solving today's problems if we can draw on a broader and more diverse cross section of potential ideas.

Design Thinking in Action: Trend Analysis

Our final technique for assessing the broader environment lies in a long-time observation, research, and analysis technique called Trend Analysis. This technique is usually associated with end user and user community trends, but it can be applied more broadly to teams, business units, companies, industries, and other sources.

Trend Analysis requires collecting and analyzing data from the source in question to determine if there is a correlation or relationship present in the data over time. You might assess similarities and differences based on groups of users or other sources and correlate these similarities or differences (deltas) based on the time or day (or week, month, or season), geography, industry, organization, education, language, age, gender, effectiveness, performance, number of errors, choices offered, default decisions made, and so on.

Use Trend Analysis to draw high-level conclusions about a situation's big picture, an organization's culture, and a team's work climate and biases. Take special care to *avoid* introducing biases in the process. Analyzing trends is error prone and far from foolproof, so for our purposes draw only the broadest of conclusions (and ensure those conclusions are caveated appropriately). The larger the sample size (numbers of users or groups, for example), the better the conclusions and outcomes.

Understanding and Articulating Value

Before we get too far along in our initiatives, projects, and the Design Thinking process, we need to answer a few questions that will one day be critical to our success. For our team, organization, product, solution, and leaders, consider the following:

- ▶ Do we have a sense of our organization's and our team's vision and mission?

- ▶ What are our broad-based objectives to fulfill our vision and mission?

- ▶ What does value look like when those objectives are met?

- ▶ Who among a myriad of stakeholders defines this value?

- ▶ How quickly does value need to be delivered?

- ▶ Through what key results will value be measured?

The sooner we understand the attributes of value expected to be delivered through technology, the better chance we have of preserving that focus over time. Later, as we work through connecting and empathizing, ideating, prototyping and testing, and so on, we will naturally return to this notion of value again and again. As we're solutioning and planning for the delivery of value and other benefits, we'll identify specific objectives for our work. And we will identify key results useful in measuring the success of that work. For now, though, we simply need a Big Picture Understanding of value as seen through the lens of various stakeholders.

What Not to Do: Ignore the Culture Fractals

Earlier in Hour 3, we briefly looked at Fractal Thinking as a way of considering patterns at scale for thinking differently and deeply. Fractals are all around us, culturally and otherwise. And for a large healthcare company, failing to capitalize on trends seen at scale at a worldwide level and reflected at the industry level and across their competitive landscape cost the organization not only first-mover advantage but a year of stalled work. Had the company recognized the fractal and exercised the courage to push ahead in its vision of instrumenting homes and people for remote care, the company would have been a full year ahead of competitors when COVID shut down much of the world in March of 2020. The fractal eventually played out in a way that fundamentally changed the culture of the health-care industry globally along with many of its key players. This particular fractal echoed downward into companies, public entities, joint partnerships, business units, and teams.

Summary

Throughout Hour 6 we covered techniques and exercises to help us listen better and understand more deeply, including Active Listening, Silence by Design, Supervillain Monologuing, and Probing for Understanding. Next, we outlined techniques and exercises useful in assessing a company's or business unit's culture, biases, and other big picture insights. Then we introduced the importance of gaining early visibility into what value looks like, who defines it, and when it needs to be delivered, all of which will be critical in future hours as we ideate, problem solve, prototype, iterate, and start solutioning. A "What Not to Do" real-world example surrounding the implications of ignoring culture fractals concluded this hour.

Workshop

Case Study

Consider the following case study and questions. You can find the answers to the questions related to this case study in Appendix A, "Case Study Quiz Answers."

Situation

BigBank's dozen projects and initiatives under the umbrella of the OneBank global business transformation have been taking a toll on the organization's limited support staff. Satish and the Executive Committee are curious to hear about any techniques that might help each initiative's leadership team more quickly learn and understand how its respective parts of the business "got to where they are today." And Satish is personally interested in any technique that can help drive some of the business stakeholders to talk more freely about their own thoughts and perspectives.

Quiz

1. Beyond good active listening skills, what are three "listening and understanding" techniques that might help Satish encourage the organization's business stakeholders to talk more freely and openly?

2. How might the Culture Snail for Pace of Change help explain how various parts of the business got to where they are today?

3. Which Design Thinking technique helps us view our team's culture in terms of dimensions and perspectives?

4. When it comes to researching and arriving at a Big Picture Understanding of a company or organization, what are the environmental dimensions that start broad but help us narrow down and understand the organization more deeply?

HOUR 7
Connecting with the Right People

What You'll Learn in This Hour:

▶ A Framework for Finding and Prioritizing People
▶ Exercises for Stakeholder Mapping and Prioritization
▶ Techniques and Exercises for Engaging Stakeholders
▶ What Not to Do: Stick to the Happy Path
▶ Summary and Case Study

In Hour 7 we build on what it means to understand the situation we find ourselves in and in particular the people who share that situation with us. In the context of IT projects or initiatives, there are people called stakeholders who have a vested interest in our work or who have the power to affect that work. We must identify these people, connect with them, learn more about them, prioritize how we engage with them, and actively manage the relationships and expectations of those people most critical to our work. To help us along, this hour we explore a framework that reflects these activities, and we step through several Design Thinking exercises to assist us. Doing so sets the stage for Hour 8, where we will cover what it means to empathize and more deeply connect with an important subset of these stakeholders. We conclude this hour with a "What Not to Do" related to thinking beyond the "happy path" of customer relationships and ensuring we connect with those important people who are perhaps anything but happy.

A Framework for Finding and Prioritizing People

While we were busy listening, understanding, and assessing the broader environment in Hour 6, we naturally found and connected with people. Many of them were in supporting roles—partners, industry experts, people familiar with the company or entity, and so on. Others might have been people who will eventually be more directly involved in the work we're taking on. Perhaps you chatted with end users or business managers and tech leaders.

Regardless of their role, we need to begin making sense of their position in the overall organization and how connected we need to be. And we need to figure out the gaps. Who is missing? Who do we need to connect with and hear from?

The key is to identify those people, connect with them, learn a bit about them (knowing that deeper learning and relationship building come with time, covered in Hour 8), prioritize how we stay connected to them, and actively manage relationships and expectations of those people most important or influential. We call the first half of this process *Stakeholder Mapping* and the second half *Stakeholder Engagement and Expectation Management*. Together, they are critical activities underpinning our work (see Figure 7.1).

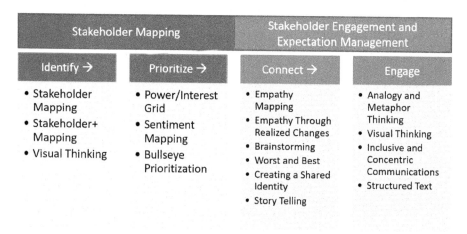

Stakeholder Mapping		Stakeholder Engagement and Expectation Management	
Identify →	Prioritize →	Connect →	Engage
• Stakeholder Mapping • Stakeholder+ Mapping • Visual Thinking	• Power/Interest Grid • Sentiment Mapping • Bullseye Prioritization	• Empathy Mapping • Empathy Through Realized Changes • Brainstorming • Worst and Best • Creating a Shared Identity • Story Telling	• Analogy and Metaphor Thinking • Visual Thinking • Inclusive and Concentric Communications • Structured Text

FIGURE 7.1
A framework for connecting and engaging with the right people.

Let's take a closer look at common Design Thinking exercises for mapping, connecting, and engaging with our stakeholders.

Exercises for Stakeholder Mapping and Prioritization

Our framework for finding and prioritizing people reflects a natural left-to-right timewise progression. That is, we need to identify stakeholders before we can begin organizing and mapping them, followed by activities to connect, engage, and prioritize their engagement. The next set of four design thinking exercises walks us through this framework.

Design Thinking in Action: Identifying and Mapping Stakeholders

The word *stakeholder* might not be familiar, but it's just another word for people who have a vested interest in the same thing. If we are running a business, our business partners and employees and vendors and customers are all stakeholders of the business. And we actually need to understand and know these people better than we may think. Hidden in the maze of daily connections we make with people are some of the reasons why our projects derail or how people are manipulated in ways that affect our work.

Identifying, visualizing, and connecting the dots between all of the stakeholders tied to our initiative or situation helps us understand who to pay attention to. More importantly, the process of doing so helps us see gaps in the picture too. Traditional Stakeholder Mapping starts with creating a simple picture, or "map," of the people connected to our project, initiative, or work (and probably to one another; see Figure 7.2). These maps are powerful reminders of the lay of the land, and they form the foundation for additional insights around who to stay connected with, who to consider, and who to be careful with. This is why Stakeholder Mapping is so common in business. It's a Design Thinking exercise that's been performed for years despite the other labels it might have been given.

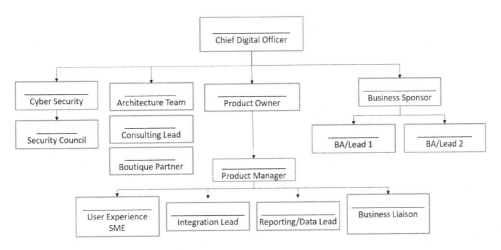

FIGURE 7.2
A typical Stakeholder Map reflects key stakeholders and their hierarchy within an organization.

Design Thinking in Action: Stakeholder+ Mapping

The **Stakeholder+ Mapping** exercise adds a useful Design Thinking element to a traditional Stakeholder Map by including thought bubbles and speech bubbles to each stakeholder identified on the map. Thought bubbles reflect what we think each stakeholder is thinking, and speech bubbles reflect what each stakeholder is telling us or sharing with others. Thus, this expanded version of the traditional Stakeholder Map takes on some pretty powerful attributes associated with an Empathy Map, which we will look at in the next hour.

TIME AND PEOPLE: A Stakeholder+ Mapping exercise requires 1–10 people for 30–120 minutes, depending on the level of completeness we aspire to.

Let's create a Stakeholder+ Map for a sample work project, starting with a blank sheet of paper and a pen:

1. Create a box in the middle of the paper and call this our project or product team. This is the start of our Stakeholder Map.

2. Surrounding our team, add to this another set of boxes that reflect the various teams or departments outside of our team that you work with.

3. Think about our team's business partners, contractors, vendors, and so on, and add those boxes to the map too.

4. As the map comes together, organize and assign relationships or roles to each box.

5. In a speech bubble above each box, write down what we know each stakeholder is "saying" about us or the team.

6. In a thought bubble below each box, write what we think each stakeholder is worried or excited about or has on their mind.

7. If it's useful and doesn't affect the accessibility of our work, consider using different colors for different sets of stakeholders, or for negative bubbles and positive bubbles (that is, color-coding).

8. We might want to redo the map now, based on how messy the whole thing has become. Clean it up and circle the groups most important to the team's success, apply more color-coding as we like, color-code similar roles (make all of our managers red, all of our business stakeholders blue, all of our key partners green, and so on), and organize problems and challenges.

9. Draw color-coded arrows connecting like-for-like roles within distinct groups and label those arrows with "relationships."

Need an example? Refer to the Stakeholder+ Map illustrated in Figure 7.3.

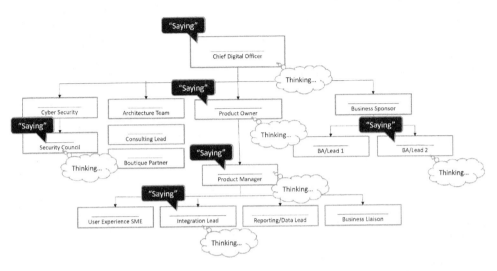

FIGURE 7.3
A sample Stakeholder+ Map adds speech and thought bubbles to a traditional Stakeholder Map.

With our **Stakeholder+ Mapping** concluded and a completed map in front of us, sit back and consider what we are seeing:

▶ Who is most important? Who is most influential? Who is missing?

▶ Who do we need to pay more attention to?

▶ Who do we need to be careful with?

▶ Who do we need to communicate more (or perhaps less) with?

▶ Who is important to our day-to-day life?

▶ Who is important to our future?

We will use the Stakeholder Power/Interest Grid (covered next) to explore some of these questions in an easy kind of way. But for now remember to revisit this Stakeholder+ Map every month or so to help you reflect on who and what has changed. Who has come and gone? Who has changed roles? What do we and our team need to be doing differently given these changes? Think about

▶ What problems are we (still) trying to solve?

▶ What is our (updated?) strategy for solving those problems?

▶ What does success look like, and how will we measure it?

▶ How will we be different tomorrow than we are today, and why is that difference important?

▶ Do we have new stakeholders to add to the Stakeholder+ Map? Others we need to remove?

▶ Is there an opportunity to increase shared identity (covered later) between us and our stakeholders?

Let's turn our attention now to another exercise where we map stakeholders in terms of the power they hold and the interest they have in our work. With this information, we'll be able to create and use the Stakeholder Power/Interest Grid.

Design Thinking in Action: The Power/Interest Grid for Prioritizing

Once we know the "who," we need to think about who really needs the most attention. The outcome of this prioritization exercise is a Stakeholder Power/Interest Grid (or map). The Power/Interest Grid is a visual representation of stakeholders that reflects the power (or influence) and interest that each stakeholder holds in our IT project or initiative. It is a common but powerful and more thoughtful form of a traditional Stakeholder Map. Use it to think through

▶ The people who hold the most power or influence over decision-making

▶ The people who have the highest interest in our work and therefore need to be informed so as to maintain their advocacy for our work

▶ The people who just need to be kept satisfied

▶ The people who simply need to be monitored

The following exercise guides us in making an initial determination of who belongs on this particular Stakeholder Map and how to map those people in terms of their power and interest. The Stakeholder Map we create will help us plan our ongoing engagement with individuals to maximize strategic impact and alignment around achieving business outcomes.

NOTE

Keep It Alive!

Remember that any map of stakeholders is a dynamic, living document that will naturally change over time. Stakeholder Maps change not only as our relationships with stakeholders evolve but also as new people are introduced, move in and out of roles, get promoted, take on new projects and responsibilities, develop new interests, or simply leave.

TIME AND PEOPLE: A Stakeholder Power/Interest Grid exercise requires 1–10 people for 30–120 minutes, depending on the level of completeness we aspire to.

The following steps help us build a Stakeholder Power/Interest Grid.

1. Run a Brainstorming session to identify the list of individuals involved in or affected by our solution, project, or initiative.

2. Run a Reverse Brainstorming session as well, asking ourselves and our team "Who would really be upset if we forgot to include them?" to further identify the breadth of stakeholders across our solution, project, or initiative.

3. Begin populating a simple table with names and roles, taking care to include

    ▶ Our own team members connected to the solution, project, or initiative

    ▶ Our partners and subcontractors we have brought into the team or are asked to include

    ▶ Key customer contacts, including business sponsors and leads, tech sponsors and leads, customer workstream leads and SMEs, change management SMEs, training leads, persons with special interests, customer-internal IT, procurement and contracting people, and so on who will use or interface with our solution, project, or initiative

    ▶ Various company-internal personnel who in some way support or are connected to the solution, project, or initiative

4. Rank each individual, and determine separately the levels of power and interest each person has. Ask ourselves

    ▶ Who has the power to advance or block the work?

    ▶ What is each individual's level of interest in our project or initiative?

Assign each individual a rating for both power and interest on a scale of 1 to 4, with 4 being the highest or greatest value, using an expanded table like the following:

Power Rating Scale (from little power to great power):

    ▶ Little or no power

    ▶ Some power either over the work itself or other stakeholders

    ▶ Significant power over the work itself or other stakeholders

    ▶ Much power to advance or block the work

Interest Rating Scale (from little interest to high interest):

    ▶ Little or no interest in the work or its outcomes

    ▶ Some interest or peripheral investment in the outcome

▶ Significant interest or investment in the outcome

▶ Highly interested and invested in the outcome

Stakeholder Name	Role or Title	Power (from 1 to 4, where 4 is high)	Interest (from 1 to 4, where 4 is high)

Add additional lines as needed. Something in the range of 15 to 50 stakeholders is probably appropriate for most engagements (and large programs can easily exceed 100 stakeholders).

5. Finally, place our stakeholders in the Stakeholder Power/Interest Grid using a simple template like the one in Figure 7.4. Use the list and rankings we created to place each individual on one of the four Power/Interest Stakeholder Grid squares according to their power and interest.

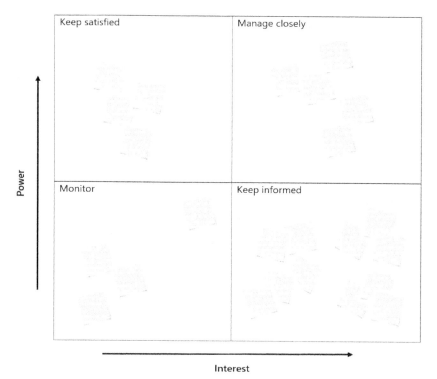

FIGURE 7.4
A template for creating a Power/Interest Grid.

With the grid fully populated, how might we now *use* this grid?

▶ Top-right quadrant = Manage Closely. This is our "proactive engagement" quadrant, and it contains the individuals we want to manage and work with most closely. Meet with them regularly through our Governance Framework's various boards (covered later in Hour 15). Be disciplined about taking notes and following up. Be aware of their schedules and make them aware of ours. Above all, prioritize these stakeholders in our communications.

▶ Top-left quadrant = Keep Satisfied. This is our "reactive engagement" quadrant. Keep these individuals satisfied and keep them in the loop. Share news, invite them to events, and reactively respond to their communications in a timely manner. Stay connected through regular communications, copy them in important emails and IM threads, and tag them in relevant posts.

▶ Bottom-right quadrant = Keep Informed. These stakeholders are interested but not necessarily influential or powerful. Keep them informed and consult with them to glean insights that may improve and advance the project's goals or business outcomes.

▶ Bottom-left quadrant = Monitor. These stakeholders require only a minimum of effort. Monitor their activity, including them in an appropriate cadence of communications, and be sure to keep track of role changes that may affect their position on our Stakeholder Power/Interest Grid.

Use the Stakeholder Power/Interest Grid to define our rhythm of engagement with the customer, our partners, and our company-internal stakeholders. Rhythms include how often we need to communicate with each stakeholder, in what format, and why (all of which needs to be reflected in the project's or initiative's communication management plan, perhaps organized into a Concentric Communications format as we will cover in Hour 15). Consider the following guidance as well (see Figure 7.5).

For stakeholders with high power and high interest, make sure to have documented conditions of satisfaction that we discuss regularly to maintain their position in the top-right quadrant.

Strategically engage with stakeholders who have high power but low interest, with the goal of raising their level of interest and moving them from the top-left quadrant to the top-right quadrant. Build a "power plan" by finding common objectives or offering something of value.

For stakeholders with low power but high interest, try to raise their profile within their organization or our project or initiative. Leverage these individuals to increase others' interest, helping them increase their power within their organization to move them into the top-right quadrant.

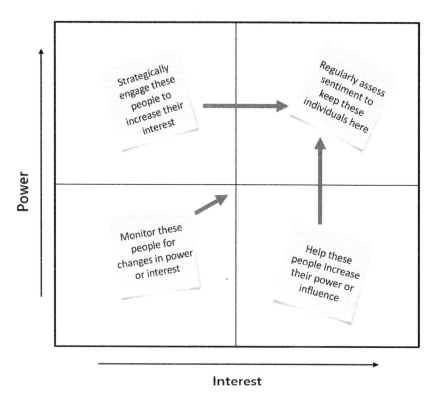

FIGURE 7.5
Regularly use the Power/Interest Grid to strategically manage and even shift stakeholder power and interest over time.

Also keep an eye on the stakeholders who fall in the bottom-left quadrant. A promotion or role change might move them into the top-left or bottom-right quadrant. If so, be sure to adjust our level of engagement with them quickly and accordingly.

Pay special attention to stakeholders who can help accelerate or might slow down our work. Be especially cautious with stakeholders who have a *negative interest* too, as they can become road-blocks to progress. Two strategies to bring along stakeholders with negative interest include:

▶ **Benchmarking.** Use a comparison against industry standards to demonstrate that our solution has been successful in other organizations for achieving that organization's planned business outcomes.

▶ **Reciprocation.** Provide the stakeholder with something of value to increase the likelihood that they will return the favor, assuming doing so still aligns to good ethical practices.

Old-fashioned peer pressure can be useful too. Make it clear to the stakeholder that others are on board, especially if they are the only holdout, and ask them what might be necessary to get them on board.

Exercises and Techniques for Engaging Stakeholders

While we have a couple of very specific exercises for mapping and prioritizing stakeholders, when it comes to engaging and managing expectations, we also have many tools at our disposal. The key is to understand the need so we can select the right tool, the right technique, or the right exercise.

Design Thinking in Action: Techniques for Engaging Stakeholders

Once we have identified, mapped, and begun to understand our stakeholders, we need to actively and consistently engage them (Furino, 2016). It's through engagement that relationships are cemented and the necessary contributions of our stakeholders may be realized.

NOTE

Managing Our Stakeholders?

Somewhere between publishing the sixth edition of the PMBOK (2017) and the fourth edition of the Standard for Program Management (2017), the Project Management Institute (PMI) changed its stance on stakeholders from *managing them* to *engaging them and managing their expectations*. To be sure, there are still cases where we need to actually manage our stakeholders, but we rarely "manage" executive stakeholders and sponsors, seeking instead to manage their engagement and expectations.

After we run our Design Thinking exercises and exhaust other traditional stakeholder engagement methods, turn to this list of Design Thinking techniques and exercises for identifying, planning, managing, or monitoring stakeholder engagement and their expectations:

▸ Empathy Mapping covered in Hour 8

▸ Analogy and Metaphor Thinking covered in Hour 11

▸ Brainstorming, Worst and Best, and Reverse Brainstorming covered in Hour 3 and in more detail in Hour 14

▸ Various visual techniques outlined in Hours 5 and 12

▸ Creating or Increasing a Shared Identity covered in Hour 15

▸ Inclusive and Concentric Communications, Story Telling, Structured Text, and other communications techniques, also covered in Hour 15

▸ Empathy through Realized Changes

With regard to the final bullet, in practicing Design Thinking, teams usually spend their time empathizing with users. However, when users or stakeholders empathize with the team seeking to help the users or stakeholders, we might witness empathy through realized changes. This type of empathy comes as a result of realized changes and seeing real progress (no matter how small that progress might be). Thus, empathy through realized changes flips the user/team source/target relationship and flow of empathy from team-to-users to users-to-team.

As time goes by and we consider changes to our Stakeholder Maps, consider also tracking the changing sentiment of those stakeholders using various visualization techniques, covered next.

Design Thinking in Action: Stakeholder Sentiment Mapping

With any Stakeholder+ Map, Power/Interest Grid, or other people-centric tool or template, consider how color or icons can also be used to visually communicate stakeholder sentiment. We call this technique Stakeholder Sentiment Mapping or Visualizing Stakeholder Sentiment. And it's incredibly easy to add this technique to our current work.

For example, we might use the popular RAG (red, amber, green) taxonomy to color-code if our stakeholders are unhappy (red), neutral (amber or yellow), or generally satisfied (green). In cases where color differentiation is impractical for accessibility or other reasons, use happy/neutral/ unhappy emojis to communicate RAG status (see Figure 7.6).

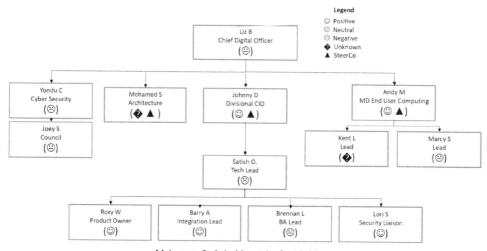

Make your Stakeholder attitudes Visible

FIGURE 7.6
Note how a Stakeholder Sentiment Map builds on the traditional map to reflect stakeholder attitudes or satisfaction.

What Not to Do: Stick to the Happy Path

In the world of testing, there's this notion that we must test beyond the typical and natural processes that our users will execute—the Happy Path—and also carefully test for all of the unexpected crazy stuff that users also do with our solutions and products.

In the same way, when we're connecting with people across our IT projects and initiatives, we need to connect well beyond the happy and satisfied people. We have to connect with the less satisfied, the less friendly, and frankly the grumpy and irritating people too.

At a global insurance provider, nearly every team asked to interface with a particular stakeholder avoided doing so simply because he was a terrible human being who treated others disrespectfully and worse. People actively and naturally avoided this important stakeholder. But in the end, the solution and its user community were the ones that really suffered the most out of this avoidance strategy; key use cases and other insights that could have been uncovered early were missed and had to be baked in after the solution was in the hands of its users.

We must connect and engage with our satisfied and positive sentiment stakeholders *as well as* the neutral and negative stakeholders to properly understand, define, prototype, and solution. We do this to ultimately create satisfied stakeholders. Remember, no one ever said customer satisfaction equals customer happiness! Find a way to engage and work with *every* key stakeholder, keeping in mind that an important community of people who need to use our solution or product or service—and the reputation of a project team and every stakeholder surrounding that project team—hang in the balance. Everyone has something to contribute to solving problems and realizing value, including the people we might prefer to avoid.

Summary

This hour explored techniques and exercises for connecting and engaging with stakeholders, the people important or influential to our project or initiative. To quickly see the steps involved in the overall process, we started this hour with a framework for identifying, connecting, engaging, and prioritizing stakeholders. Then we walked through Design Thinking exercises for identifying and mapping stakeholders, followed by using the Power/Interest Grid to identify the people holding the most influence or power. A list of various techniques and exercises for engaging stakeholders, a Stakeholder Mapping exercise reflecting and managing stakeholder sentiment, and a "What Not to Do" section focused on connecting with the breadth of stakeholders, satisfied and otherwise, concluded this hour.

Workbook

Case Study

Consider the following case study and questions. You can find the answers to the questions related to this case study in Appendix A, "Case Study Quiz Answers."

Situation

The dozen initiatives underpinning the OneBank global business transformation reflect numerous stakeholders spanning different business teams, technology teams, partnerships, executive influencers, and more. Satish has asked you to help the initiative leaders capture the breadth of these stakeholders and organize them in ways that reflect hierarchy, power or influence, and stakeholders' sentiment. He is also looking for techniques that might help him engage with some of the most important or influential stakeholders.

Quiz

1. What exercise should each of the initiative leaders perform to map the breadth of stakeholders across their respective initiatives?

2. Once a Stakeholder Map is created, what is an easy way to reflect stakeholder sentiment?

3. What are the two dimensions of the Power/Interest Grid, and which quadrants are probably most important for Satish and his leads to pay attention to?

4. What are some of the techniques and exercises that Satish might use to help him engage more deeply with his most important or influential stakeholders?

HOUR 8
Learning and Empathizing

In this hour, we get to what many call the heart of Design Thinking: empathizing with the people in the center of problems and situations we're seeking to improve. Empathy is a journey that starts with observing and questioning and concludes with learning through exercises that can help us empathize in three distinct ways. We also take a look at what it means to empathize with our edge case users, including a "What Not to Do" that illustrates how understanding this 20 percent is necessary to help the whole of the user community.

From Stakeholders to Personas

As we strive for greater understanding on the journey toward empathy and understanding, we need to focus less on specific people and more on the roles or personas that those people play. Remember that personas are amalgamations of fictional characters (such as "finance user," "sales user," "executives," and so on) of a community who share common needs and will use specific artifacts or features of a solution or deliverables in similar ways.

▶ Our Stakeholder Maps from Hour 7 can help us make sense of the various roles that people hold.

▶ We need to organize these roles into groups that can later become abstracted personas.

▶ Then we can create a profile for the personas that we need to understand better.

▶ With a collection of relevant personas in hand, we can turn to various types of empathy-related exercises to understand those personas better.

▶ To better understand these personas, we can also map their micro journeys as they interact with systems and other people today.

▶ And finally we can take a macro view of these personas and explore a full "day in the life" of individuals or personas, the ultimate way of understanding the breadth of activities, decisions, and connections that people make day in and day out.

Interestingly, we might practice different types of empathy for different people or groups of personas. Before we organize our personas into a 360-degree model for empathizing, let's first take a look at three types of empathy.

Three Types of Empathy

As mentioned, empathizing is central to Design Thinking, and there is no one-size-fits-all single way to empathize with others. But there are proven ways to connect and empathize with others using a related set of Design Thinking techniques and exercises.

Consider the following three types of empathy. While each type may build on its predecessor, each one may also be practiced independently. Consider also how empathy manifests itself differently in each type in terms of how the empathizer "shows up," how the empathizer connects and learns, and finally how the empathizer serves the other person and that person's community.

▶ **Cognitive Empathy.** The simplest form of empathy is cognitive empathy, which is "connecting at a head level" to understand intellectually what another person or team thinks and feels. To empathize at a cognitive level, we typically lean on Persona Profiling, Journey Mapping, and general precursors such as traditional Stakeholder Mapping.

Cognitive empathy *says*: "I see that you have fallen into a deep hole and can't seem to escape. That can't be any fun."

▶ **Emotional Empathy.** The next form of empathy connects two people at an emotional level. Emotional empathy lets us share or experience the feelings of another person in the moment. Design Thinking techniques to empathize emotionally include Empathy Immersion, Day-in-the-Life, and other forms of one-on-one connection that allow emotional connections to be made.

Emotional empathy *acknowledges and asks*: "That hole you are in looks pretty bad, and I can see it's taking a toll on you. How can I help you help yourself?"

▶ **Compassionate Empathy.** The final form of empathy drives a person to take action. Compassionate empathy is not satisfied with simply acknowledging a situation or helping someone help themselves. Compassionate empathy draws on relationships to compel action. Such Design Thinking exercises might include Empathy Immersion, Journey Mapping, Day-in-the-Life, Building to Think, and getting our hands dirty through iterative prototyping and testing. As we can see, compassionate empathy goes beyond understanding and traditional empathizing.

Compassionate empathy *acts and serves in a side-by-side kind of way* with another: "Now that I've climbed into this hole with you, together we will figure out how to escape here and never return."

Emotions and empathy go hand in hand for two of the three types of empathy. As Dev Patnaik (2022) tells us, "[T]he more emotionally charged an event is, the more vivid it feels to our amygdala, which then helps our hippocampus to hold on to the event for the long haul. That's why our most emotional memories are also our most vivid ones: Our brains literally encode them more forcefully than they do other data." Use these realities of the human mind to better respond to emotional events and create emotionally sticky experiences. See Figure 8.1 for a light-hearted but accurate perspective on the three types of empathy.

FIGURE 8.1
Empathizing looks very different based on the type of empathy being practiced.

We can see how these three types of empathy build on one another as we move from head empathy to heart empathy to empathy steeped in action. Viewing the hole from a distance (cognitive) is a good start, but it is quite different from acknowledging that the hole exists and is painful (emotional), which in turn is quite different from jumping in alongside a person and helping them escape the hole altogether (compassionate).

With these three types of empathy in mind, let's turn our attention to a comprehensive model for empathizing effectively. Afterward, with a host of Design Thinking exercises at our disposal, we will walk through a recipe for empathizing effectively.

A 360-Degree Model for Empathizing

A good way to build empathy is to walk through the three types of empathy, understanding and connecting more deeply along the way. As we know, the first step for empathizing is to focus on the people who are in the midst of the problem we are solving and therefore users of the solution we will build and the business outcomes that will be delivered. This initial focus is central to everything else we'll do; it provides the problem and outcomes-based focus we need to better connect and empathize with people.

With the "middle" well understood, we next need to take a 360-degree view of the people and teams around the middle (see Figure 8.2). We need to consider our Stakeholder Maps and Power/Interest Grids to identify everyone who will come together to solve the problem, prototype and test potential solutions, and deliver the solution and its business outcomes. Thus, we need to consider the following:

- ▶ The central end user community and collection of personas for whom we're solving a problem and providing a solution

- ▶ The business and operations people, teams, and personas who also benefit from the problem solving and solutioning executed on behalf of their user communities

- ▶ The sponsors, executives, and other key stakeholders and personas who hold the political, budgetary, and sponsorship influence necessary to be successful

- ▶ The Design Thinking specialists, team members, and partners who, together, will help others understand and solve problems, design and iterate on the interim and final solution, and ultimately help create value and enable business outcomes on behalf of the user community

- ▶ The IT and PMO teams and people who will manage, design, build, and deploy the interim MVPs and Pilots and other valuable outcomes, including ultimately supporting the final solution and its user communities

With this 360-degree view in mind, we can turn our attention to the exercises and overall recipe for empathizing.

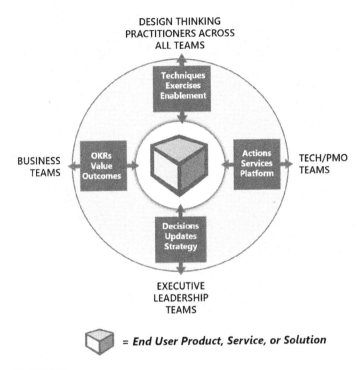

DESIGN THINKING PRACTITIONERS ACROSS ALL TEAMS

Techniques
Exercises
Enablement

BUSINESS
TEAMS

OKRs
Value
Outcomes

Actions
Services
Platform

TECH/PMO
TEAMS

Decisions
Updates
Strategy

EXECUTIVE LEADERSHIP TEAMS

= *End User Product, Service, or Solution*

FIGURE 8.2
The 360-Degree Empathy Model for organizing stakeholders.

A Recipe for Empathizing

With our understanding of the three types of empathy and the kinds of exercises most useful for each, we can build a simple recipe for empathizing. And using our 360-degree empathy model, we would apply this recipe—or parts of the recipe—to each group of personas or stakeholders.

Design Thinking in Action: Persona Profiling

Also called Persona Mapping or Persona Analysis, this exercise is intended to help us document, group, and learn more about what our key personas are thinking, feeling, doing, saying, and more. Remember that a persona is a fictional character reflecting an amalgamation of similar people with similar interests and needs. A useful set of personas helps guide our decisions as we consider problems, design and prototype solutions to those problems, and test and iterate on those solutions.

Even though personas are fictional characters, it's useful to assign a face or emoji to the persona as a way to make the persona "real." A face makes the persona easier to remember and use as teams consider the people for whom they are solving problems and designing solutions.

TIME AND PEOPLE: A Persona Profile exercise requires 1–5 people for 10–15 minutes per persona.

To create a Persona Profile:

1. Assemble the Stakeholder Maps and other artifacts that reflect the breadth of people.

2. Organize the people and personas to be profiled into the five groups described in the 360-degree empathy model (end user community, other business stakeholders, executives and sponsors, the Design Thinkers across the various teams or tied to the initiative, and the tech and PMO teams).

3. Further deconstruct these groups into sets of fictional characters (such as "sales users" or "security team" or "executives" and so on). These are our draft personas.

4. Assign a description to each persona.

5. Subdivide personas as necessary to create our final list of personas (and assign a description to any new persona).

6. With these descriptions in mind, give each persona an easy-to-remember name.

7. Assign a fictional face or emoji to each persona as a way to make that persona "sticky" in the minds of the team.

8. For each persona:

    a. Define their (future) end goals.

    b. Define their (tactical) needs today.

    c. Describe up to three distinguishing attributes.

    d. Assign a verbatim or other memorable quote.

    e. Include any other summary information, pictures, or figures that give this persona life and further cement each persona in the minds of the team.

By way of example, consider the sample Persona Profile illustrated in Figure 8.3.

If we consider the breadth of stakeholders beyond "end users" connected to a large project or initiative, it's not unusual to create tens and tens of Persona Profiles. Fight the urge to get too granular, though. And remember to accommodate edge cases and consider accessibility and sensitive design needs. Finally, be careful to avoid biases and stereotypes as we pull together the faces and images that represent the breadth of our project's or initiative's personas.

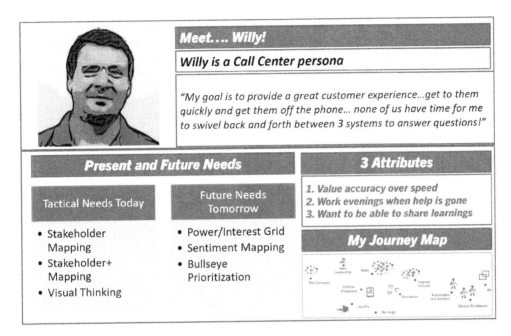

FIGURE 8.3
A worked example of a Persona Profile.

Design Thinking in Action: Empathy Mapping

Empathizing with others, including where they have been and what they are experiencing today, is key to learning about people. As we have said before, empathy is how we see the world through another's eyes, or walk in another's shoes, or wear another's hat. Empathy is about learning. And remember that learning is not just about observing and gathering information. Learning is also about listening, understanding, and connecting at a cognitive, emotional, and compassionate level to understand what others are going through and what they need.

A long-standing and visual way of doing just this is through Empathy Mapping. If we have the information we need, we can do this exercise from the safety of our desk. The simple template we use to document this information is called an *Empathy Map*. Create an Empathy Map, one for each persona, to capture and learn more about that specific persona in terms of what that persona is:

▶ Likely thinking and probably feeling

▶ Likely seeing and hearing

▶ Actually saying and doing

▶ Experiencing in terms of their biggest pain points, hurts, or needs

▶ Seeking or looking for, including their top goals, gains, or objectives

Consider the sample Empathy Map template illustrated in Figure 8.4.

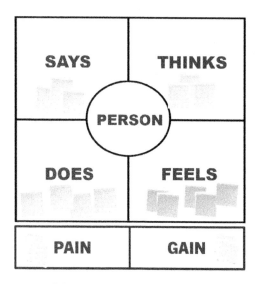

FIGURE 8.4
An easy-to-use Empathy Map template.

To practice, choose a problem in our own life and perform this Empathy Mapping exercise on ourselves. And then try applying this exercise to another person such as our manager at work, keeping in mind that we will never know with 100 percent certainty *all* of the answers to all the sections in the template:

TIME AND PEOPLE: An Empathy Mapping exercise requires 2–5 people for 10–15 minutes per person or persona.

1. **See.** What does their environment look like? What kind of things are they surrounded by and constantly seeing?

2. **Hear.** What are they hearing from their own management team, direct reports, and peers? What are company-internal announcements, industry trends, and the media saying about the company or industry?

3. **Think and Feel.** What do they think and feel about their work or their role? What concerns them or makes them happy? What frustrates them?

4. **Say and Do.** What do they say they want to accomplish? What are they *actually* doing and achieving? What motivates them? What is getting in the way of their achievements or progress? Can we capture any verbatims or direct quotes to support this section?

5. **Pains (or Hurts).** What might haunt them from the past or represent a pain point today? What challenges are they facing? What might really worry them underneath the façade they might put up, and what might they fear will happen to them? What do they seem to want or need?

6. **Gains or (Goals).** Regardless of what they might say or do, what are their true goals? Is there parity between what they say or do and what they say or seem to want? What do they need to achieve those goals? What does success look like for them?

Once we have gained a bit of practice using Empathy Mapping, we may apply the Empathy Mapping process to each of the personas identified earlier. We can also apply Empathy Mapping to individuals too, or any group of people who are pretty consistent in how or what they are thinking, feeling, seeing, hearing, saying, doing, and so on.

As we perform more Empathy Mapping for our project or initiative, we will begin to realize another level of value out of this work. Empathy Mapping helps us uncover themes, and it helps us uncover inconsistencies or gaps as well. For example, if our people and personas are saying one thing but doing something counter to that one thing, there's an inconsistency that needs to be explored. Inconsistencies are red flags. And if many people across a group or set of personas are expressing the same pain points or gripes, this theme needs to be explored. It's in these themes and inconsistencies that Empathy Mapping can help us identify root causes to problems, opportunities for solutioning, and much more.

Design Thinking in Action: Empathy Immersion

Empathy Immersion or "Walk-a-Mile" (in another's shoes) takes Empathy Mapping to a deeper level as we personally take a person's journey and experience their joys, conflicts, and weariness along the way. When we allow ourselves to be truly immersed, we not only see but also feel what it is like to live in the world as another person.

Practically speaking, this could mean any number of things: donning the equipment someone uses and performing a task, artificially altering one or more of our senses, forgoing (or perhaps experiencing) some of life's luxuries, or even living among people of a different culture or society.

Whatever the extent, the idea is to deepen our empathy for others and to use that experience to better inform our decision-making. Once we understand people's motivations, we can better understand their needs.

TIME AND PEOPLE: An Empathy Immersion exercise requires 1–5 people for at least several hours per experience, preferably repeated at different times.

To plan and prepare for an Empathy Immersion exercise:

1. Set the stage regarding the industry, team, and role or person:

   ▶ Research and learn enough to identify the role or person.

   ▶ Connect with the role or person to discuss the relevant situation or experiences to replicate.

   ▶ Work with that role or person to identify the specific tasks and activities to be performed.

2. Identify the best time and place to walk in the role's or person's shoes.

3. Identify and obtain any special permissions or access needed.

4. Consider alternatives such as shadowing the role or person or taking part in a simulated "walk-through" if safety, security, or other factors make the exercise personally untenable.

5. Complete any other necessary preparations, including special items, safety equipment, clothing, or tools needed.

Once prepared, to execute an Empathy Immersion exercise, simply

1. Show up!

2. Document our perspectives on the experiences, capturing visuals and taking photos if allowed.

3. Document the flow or journey associated with the specific tasks and activities we are performing, including feedback from others.

4. As we uncover challenges or opportunities with processes, tools, and information, document them.

Be sure to perform the tasks and activities as realistically as possible. Don't take shortcuts, but instead walk in the shoes of, wear the hat of, and live in the skin of the person who does this work day in and day out. Be sure to capture visuals and take pictures too. Doing so will help us remember and help others "see" the situation for themselves. And later, with these special insights and experiences, the team will be better able to assist with needs analysis, brainstorming, problem solving, prototyping, solutioning, and more.

Design Thinking in Action: Journey Mapping

Journey Mapping is the process of illustrating the various touchpoints from beginning to end that together describe how a customer or a stakeholder walks or flows through their interaction with a product, process, or service (Kelley & Kelley, 2013). Each customer or stakeholder touch-point represents an opportunity to satisfy or disappoint that person.

For our purposes, Journey Mapping is about the "stuff" of our day-to-day life—the places our users go and the things they do in those places, including how long those interactions take. Sometimes the easiest way to understand the challenges we face every day is to draw a map.

With a board, blank sheet of paper, drawing app, or chalk on the sidewalk, draw a box to represent what our users do at the start of a typical day at work. Or we might wish to analyze a specific time-boxed set of interactions with another team or with an application, for example. Either way, illustrate each step in the journey with another box, and then another, and then another. Or simply create a time-oriented table or list. Do what's easiest for us at the time; the key is to understand all of the "what" of the day that we are assessing and the person who is experiencing that day.

We might group those boxes or items on our list in ways that combine similar aspects of work. Perhaps our user logs in or physically walks into work at 7 a.m. and checks emails and IMs for 30 minutes and then spends another 30 minutes in a scheduling app followed by a 15-minute stand-up meeting, 30 minutes reporting, an hour to work on various tasks, another hour in the weekly product council meeting, 30 minutes for lunch, 30 minutes planning for next week's business review, another hour dealing with emails and IMs again, and so on. Afterward, we might box up or cluster this detail into time spent in asynchronous communications (emails and IMs), time spent in synchronous communications (live meetings and conference calls), time spent working in applications, time spent planning, and time spent executing. Just be sure to include how many minutes or hours each item or step in the journey takes out of the day. In the end, we will have a time-oriented map of the day that reflects the what and the when.

And this is a wonderful outcome! Why? Because we will then begin to understand the situation our user faces and the reasons why they are caught in the middle of certain problems or challenges somewhere in the busyness of their day. And because we see the tasks, applications, and people they're spending their time with in ways they may not even realize, we will see the complexity more objectively. We will see opportunities where they can recover some of that valuable time back for themselves. Or time that they can choose to invest in other areas.

And we will recognize areas that are frustrating and need to be smoothed out. We will see opportunities to redesign processes and interfaces and organizational structures. And see the potential for introducing partial quick-win solutions and perhaps new ways of working. By way of example, consider the sample Journey Map illustrated in Figure 8.5 (keeping in mind that Journey Maps can take many different forms).

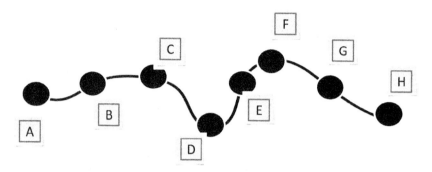

FIGURE 8.5
A worked example of one type of Journey Map.

We might choose to map in more detail a time-consuming process our user repeats each day (such as all of the steps they take performing an hours-long financial management and reporting function twice a week). The idea here is to understand their overall daily journey and its complexity so we can see where and more about why they are struggling with the status quo and where there are opportunities to partner together very tactically near term or more strategically longer term.

If all of this Journey Map information isn't enough, we may wish to build more detail into the Journey Map using another empathy technique called a "Day in the Life of" Analysis, or DILO, covered next.

Design Thinking in Action: A "Day in the Life of" Analysis

Our final exercise for empathizing takes the broadest view of a person, persona, or role and considers the richness of a full day's activities. In this way, it is much broader than a Journey Map where we learned about and connected the "stuff" a user does during a subset of the day into a journey that helps us understand what they do, how much time they spend doing it, the problems they face along the way, and the opportunities we have in front of us to make improvements. With a "Day in the Life of" analysis, we take our knowledge and understanding of our user to the next level, building on the Journey Map or "journey list" previously created by adding three items.

TIME AND PEOPLE: A "Day in the Life of" Analysis exercise requires 1–5 people for half a day to several days depending on the level of detail we aspire to.

1. We extend the "journey" to consider the full day versus a portion of the day.

2. We add context about how our user *feels* as they navigate their daily journey.

3. We include their thoughts and weigh in with our own thoughts as to how effectively or efficiently the time is being spent and tasks are being completed.

Don't short-change this exercise! It might seem unusual or strange at first, but connecting how a person feels to what they do and the effectiveness of that "doing" gives us great insight. It paints a much better picture of what may need to change to help the user navigate their situation, solve their problem, or begin crafting potential solutions.

So, let's return to the Journey Map we created earlier. For each stop along our daily journey, draw a *sentiment bubble* or *feelings bubble* that reflects how the user feels as they move from one task to another. And rate that stop from an effectiveness or efficiency perspective. Was it a good use of time? Could it be automated? Could it be reduced, handed off to others, or removed altogether?

When we bring all of these insights together, we have a sentiment-infused map of the user's day. Do we see any patterns or themes (does the user hate how long it takes to check email)? Do we see consistent places of frustration or irritation (does every meeting seem to start late and end even later)? Do we see a need to change the what, the when, or the who?

We might add other dimensions to each stop along the journey too, in the form of other bubbles that reflect what a user is thinking or saying:

▶ Add a *why bubble* and inside of it explain why the user missed lunch again or why the user enjoyed working on that particular task so much.

▶ Add a *who bubble* to represent all of the people the user interacted with on each stop of the journey. Note the people who seemed to give the user energy and those who seemed to sap the joy out of their joint encounter.

▶ Add a *wish bubble* to track what the user expressed they wish could be different about their day. Tie the wishes to the tasks or stops along the way and provide any relevant details (perhaps related to the people or activities related to that stop).

Consider assessing different days for our most important users or personas too, to get a better picture of how their DILO seems to change based on the day of the week or month, or the time of year, or the timing within a particular season. By way of example, review the DILO illustrated in Figure 8.6 (noting again that, like a Journey Map, a DILO can take many different forms).

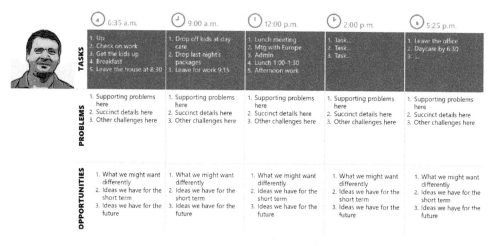

FIGURE 8.6
A worked example of a sample "Day in the Life of" Analysis exercise.

In the end, a pattern will emerge that reflects what a person actually *likes* about their day, along with what and who they dislike or avoid. Use these nuggets of understanding to help shape what's next for them in terms of tasks, experiences, or processes.

▶ Consider the time they spend inside and between the stops of their journey across their full DILO, perhaps even including commute hours.

▶ Where do they really spend the most time? By task, where does their energy come from, and where is it spent?

▶ Where would they *like* to spend more time? Capture any verbatims.

▶ Similarly, where are they wasting time? Capture these verbatims as well.

▶ How does each stop on the journey represent an opportunity to bring joy, frustration, confusion, or disappointment to them or to others who are also a part of that stop? Consider marking each stop with a red/amber/green sentiment designation or emoji (such as a positive or negative sign or happy or sad face).

▶ Who are the people they interact with, and what's the nature of that interaction? Try to find one or two words to describe the nature of those interactions. Are they positive? Optimistic? Negative? Something else? Include this detail next to their names in the *who bubbles* for each stop.

▶ We may wish to note the nature of these interactions in other ways too. Again, consider using color or emojis to assign sentiment to a relationship (where red might indicate poor interactions and green might indicate healthy interactions).

▶ How are the burdens across the DILO distributed? Is our user carrying nearly all of the "weight" associated with a particular task or activity? Could another person or helper make a difference? Reflect this insight.

▶ Does the user have the tools and resources necessary for their daily tasks? What's missing? And who might help think through what can be done to change this situation?

Ask about how the person's DILO has stayed the same over the years and how it's changed too. What needs to change? Who needs to change? What can be easily changed or controlled in the short term? And, finally, where are the long-term opportunities for change?

What Not to Do: Ignore the 20 Percent

Because 80 percent of a user's tasks tend to be the same day after day, and 80 percent of users for a given capability or feature tend to do the same thing, it's easy and seemingly logical to assess that 80 percent and then start designing and prototyping systems and solutions. But there is real value and real cost savings in at least lightly assessing the remaining 20 percent of tasks and 20 percent of users prior to making design decisions.

A household retailer assessed 80 percent of its user community and got to work designing a set of interfaces for traditional desktop users along with portal users and mobile users. The retailer applied good Design Thinking techniques throughout the process and rapidly iterated, collected feedback, deployed valuable updates every 2 weeks, collected Silent Design changes made at the hands of production users, and more. And then the retailer finally decided to think more deeply about the remaining 20 percent of its users and use cases, many of which reflected the requests of users with special needs and accessibility requirements.

The retailer assessed the remaining 20 percent of edge cases and users with special needs and ran an Accessibility Checker on the design work that had already been completed. It found several months and $400,000 of rework were necessary to update the existing user interfaces and underlying code, work that could have been pretty easily completed while the 80 percent was in flight. More damaging, the retailer found that many of these ignored users had already written off the project as "not for them," leading to major adoption issues well after the code and interface changes were deployed. In the end, while saving time and budget would have made earlier attention to the 20 percent worthwhile, a focus on serving the broader user community more fully would have better positioned the project and better served the retailer and its full breadth of users.

Summary

In this hour, we covered methods of deeply observing, connecting, and empathizing with stakeholders, users, and amalgamations of users called personas. We discussed cognitive, emotional, and compassionate empathy including how each one resonates at a different level with users and with those practicing that particular type of empathy. Then we laid out a simple model for empathizing with others and connected five Design Thinking empathy exercises to this model. We concluded Hour 8 with a "What Not to Do" focused on the dangers of excluding the 20 percent of users and use cases "on the edge" of our project or initiative, noting that more quickly considering edge cases and empathizing with users with different needs beyond the 80 percent not only saves time and money but assists with adoption while serving the broader user community more fully.

Workshop

Case Study

Consider the following case study and questions. You can find the answers to the questions related to this case study in Appendix A, "Case Study Quiz Answers."

Situation

One of BigBank's most critical and ambitious initiatives, Project Moonshot, has been tasked with reinventing the retail side of the banking business. Satish has asked you to get personally involved with understanding, empathizing, and organizing the types of users who bank with BigBank today, along with users who choose to bank elsewhere. Satish knows a bit about user personas and connecting with users to understand their requirements, but he needs your expertise.

Quiz

1. How would you explain what a persona is to the Moonshot team?

2. What Design Thinking exercise might be useful for organizing personas?

3. What are the three types of empathy, and which of the three might be most useful in understanding why consumers choose to bank elsewhere?

4. In what ways does Empathy Immersion differ from Empathy Mapping?

5. What three additional dimensions set "Day in the Life of" Analysis apart from Journey Mapping?

HOUR 9
Identifying the Right Problem

What You'll Learn in This Hour:

- ▶ Identifying and Understanding a Problem
- ▶ Three Exercises for Problem Identification
- ▶ Techniques and Exercises for Problem Validation
- ▶ What Not to Do: Jump In! (to the Wrong Problem)
- ▶ Summary and Case Study

The focus of this hour is problem identification. Not problem solving, but rather making sure we've worked through the various causes and effects and surrounding symptoms and identified the right problem to solve. In this hour we will work through seven exercises for identifying and better understanding a problem, setting the stage for the next several hours where we ideate and think differently to create potential solutions for that problem. And we conclude with a "What Not to Do" example focused on jumping in (normally a wonderful Design Thinking practice in other circumstances) to work on the wrong problem.

Identifying and Understanding a Problem

After we've spent time understanding the lay of the land, connecting with and listening to the right people, and empathizing with their situations at several levels, we might feel as though we have a good handle on the underlying problems. And indeed we might. But for complex situations, the danger in *assuming* we know which problem to solve too often leads to false starts and wasted time. So an important interim step between empathizing and problem solving lies in identifying the problem followed by better understanding and validating it.

Three Exercises for Problem Identification

Several good methods exist for exploring, identifying, and understanding problems. But Problem Tree Analysis and Problem Framing are two of the simplest exercises that can quickly help a team find and focus on the right problem. And with that understanding and insight we can use a third exercise, Problem Stating, to create a problem statement reflecting our evolved understanding.

Design Thinking in Action: Problem Tree Analysis for Clarity

When the causes and the effects of a particular situation or problem are getting jumbled in our minds, it can be helpful to get the jumbled stuff out of our minds and down on paper. One method of assessing the causes and effects of a problem or situation is to execute a Problem Tree Analysis. This exercise, credited to Paulo Freire's work in education in the early 1970s (Freire Institute, 2022), uses the visual of a tree as a metaphor, as previously outlined in Hour 3.

How do we start? Draw a simple tree like the one illustrated in Figure 9.1. We will use this simple visual to help us see a relationship between our problem (as we understand it today) and the problem's causes and effects. To run a Problem Tree Analysis solo or with a group:

TIME AND PEOPLE: A Problem Tree Analysis exercise requires 1–5 people for 30–60 minutes per problem (and can extend much broader and longer depending on the nature and complexity of the problem).

▶ Draw a simple tree on a whiteboard like the one illustrated in Figure 9.1.

▶ Label the tree trunk with the overall problem or situation we are seeking to understand and define.

▶ Label 5 to 10 of the tree's roots with the systemic or other "root" causes of the problem as we understand that problem today (and consider how the Five Whys covered later in this hour can help us further explore these roots now or shortly after this exercise concludes).

▶ Label the 5 to 10 branches shooting off the tree trunk. Each branch is a unique realized or possible effect or consequence of the problem being analyzed.

Round-robin through a team to focus first on causes (roots) and then later on effects (branches), giving everyone the chance to participate and draw on the tree. After adding a root or a branch, focus back again on the tree trunk to recenter the team on the problem.

Don't be afraid to re-create the tree based on a new understanding of the problem. Similarly, don't be afraid to add branches to other branches, or smaller roots connected to larger roots. The value of this exercise lies in the visual nature of the outcome, the tree. Working through a Problem Tree Analysis is like creating a situation-specific Mind Map or cause-and-effect diagram useful for exploring what has happened, why it might be happening, and what might happen next.

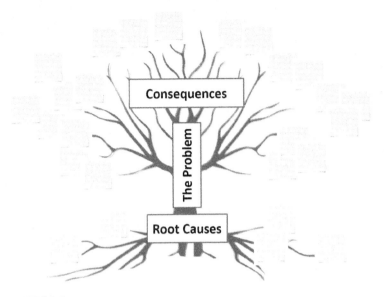

FIGURE 9.1
A Problem Tree Analysis uses a simple tree metaphor to help us identify and separate a problem from its causes and effects.

But if we are having problems fundamentally understanding a problem (or agreeing on and prioritizing that problem), turn to a Problem Framing exercise, described next.

Design Thinking in Action: Problem Framing

When a simple visual approach like Problem Tree Analysis fails to bring together a team in agreement on a problem or its prioritization among many problems, consider another exercise called Problem Framing. Derived from the research that Getzels and Csikszentmihalyi performed in 1976 on the need to understand problems as a precursor to creativity, Problem Framing helps us understand and prioritize a particular problem over a set of other potential problems. And it gives us much-needed context.

The value of a Problem Framing exercise is its ability to

- ▶ Force a discussion.

- ▶ Arrive at a shared understanding.

- ▶ Drive unity and buy-in around that shared understanding.

- ▶ Connect the past and present context with future goals or hopeful outcomes.

- ▶ Explore if the problem is indeed the right problem to tackle.

- ▶ Determine if the problem is even worth tackling.

▶ Validate that the team has the right skills or abilities to actually tackle the problem.

▶ Create clarity around a potential set of next steps.

▶ Define the problem as it is understood today and create a draft *problem statement*.

The steps of a Problem Framing exercise help frame a problem, hence the name. And through the outcomes outlined here, Problem Framing helps establish the "next best steps" in a team-oriented kind of way. The exercise therefore brings people together in important ways at exactly the time they probably need to be brought together.

To run a lightweight Problem Framing exercise with a group, follow these steps:

TIME AND PEOPLE: A Problem Framing exercise requires 2–5 people for 30–60 minutes per problem (and can extend much broader and longer depending on the nature and complexity of the problem).

1. Review the proposed problem. Give everyone the opportunity to weigh in with what they know about the problem, including background and assumptions.

2. Link the problem to its source. Identify other connected or related problems and discuss their relationships to this problem.

3. Consider the ideal outcome. Identify what the team wishes to see happen and discuss the broader future in question or broader goals at play.

4. Consider the users, stakeholders, and other people surrounding the problem and situation. Revisit what is known about the broader environment, the people involved, and how they're involved. Turn to Stakeholder and Empathy Maps, Journey Maps, "Day in the Life of" findings, and so forth to put people (back) at the center of this problem.

5. Ask and agree if the problem as identified is truly worth thinking about and solving. Through consensus, the team needs to decide whether this is the right problem to tackle, whether this is the right time to tackle it, and whether the problem is even worth trying to tackle.

6. Agree whether to proceed or stop. With the problem now framed and better understood in several different ways, and the team aligned, it should be possible to make a next-step decision.

As a result of this exercise, a team can better identify and subsequently tackle the problem, if indeed that's the next step. Problem Framing makes it clearer if an expert needs to be brought in next too, or if other problems need to be solved first. Problem Framing importantly gives us the ability to create a definitive problem statement too, covered next and used across Hours 10 through 14 as we ideate and explore problems to find potential solutions.

Design Thinking in Action: Problem Stating

One of the outcomes of Problem Framing is the ability to create a draft problem statement. With a reasonably good understanding and framing of the potential problem and how it differs from its causes or effects or other aspects of an ambiguous environment, we can now identify the likely problem. And this is a really big win.

Sure, our understanding of the problem will mature as we work through additional problem-related exercises (and later, thinking and solutioning-related exercises). But being able to turn a potential problem around and over a bit to help ensure it's indeed the *right* problem is critical to creating our problem statement. Why is this important? Our problem statement provides a crisp shared understanding, which in turn helps rally others around what's needed to solve that problem.

Attributes of a good problem statement include

▶ It is formed as a statement and a single sentence.

▶ This single sentence addresses the "what," "for whom," and the "need."

▶ It is written in simple, crisp, and understandable terms.

▶ It therefore precisely informs our understanding of the problem (knowing that our understanding will be clarified further through this and other exercises shared this hour).

▶ It sets the stage and serves as input for "How Might We?" questioning and other ideation and solutioning techniques we will turn to later.

To run a simple Problem Stating exercise with a group, follow these steps:

TIME AND PEOPLE: A Problem Stating exercise requires 2–5 people for 15–30 minutes per problem (and can extend much broader and longer depending on the nature and complexity of the problem).

1. Share the outcomes of previous problem identification exercises including Problem Tree visuals and draft problem statements coming out of Problem Framing exercises.

2. Ask the team to answer these questions:

   ▶ What is the primary problem?

   ▶ Why is this a problem?

   ▶ Who has this problem?

   ▶ When does this problem occur?

   ▶ What seems to be missing or needed?

   ▶ How is this problem worked around or addressed today, if at all?

3. As a team, review the answers and vote on which ones (the "top answers") are most true or valid given what the team has previously learned and is seeing now.

4. Copy or rewrite the draft problem statements that best define the gap between the current state of affairs and the desired outcome, constructing a single sentence in the form "<the what> for <the who> does(do) not satisfy <the need>."

Thus, a good and simple problem statement might look like these examples:

▶ The portal interface for our users with visual impairment does not satisfy their need to enter sales orders.

▶ Our team communications methods for our remote employees do not satisfy their need to be heard and represented.

▶ Our end-to-end warehouse management system for users working from home does not satisfy their real-time performance expectations.

To directionally validate a problem statement, we might flip it into a "How Might We?" question. Begin combining these top answers to construct a mirror to the problem statement in the form "How might we change <the what> for <the who> to better satisfy <the need>."

After we've worked through the details together, a "How Might We?" mirror response to a good problem statement might look like these examples:

▶ How might we change the portal interface for our users with visual impairment to better satisfy their ability to enter sales orders?

▶ How might we change our team communications for our remote employees to better satisfy their need to be heard and represented?

▶ How might we change our end-to-end warehouse management system for our home-based users to better satisfy their real-time performance needs?

And with our problem statement in hand, if needed we can turn to one or more problem validation methods before we earnestly start thinking, problem solving, and solutioning. Four of these techniques or exercises are covered next.

Techniques and Exercises for Problem Validation

As a final step before seeking to solve problems and create solutions, consider running one or more Design Thinking techniques or exercises that let us quickly validate our understanding of the problem and potentially refine our problem statement. The following four techniques or exercises represent a good cross section of lightweight Design Thinking methods:

▶ Verbatim Mapping

▶ AEIOU for Rapid Review

▶ The Five Whys for Root Cause Analysis

▶ Pattern Matching for Themes

Each of these problem-oriented Design Thinking techniques or exercises is useful in other areas as well but are covered in a problem validation–related context next.

Design Thinking in Action: Verbatim Mapping

Useful in many different ways, a smart first step for validating the problems underpinning a situation is to listen to people and document what they say. Called Verbatim Mapping, this technique is a staple of interviewing and represents a great way to listen while we compile a set of beliefs or statements useful for later providing context.

Verbatims, like the word implies, are the word-for-word direct quotes, stories, and other feedback spoken by a person that describes or documents that person's perspectives. When we think of verbatims, we usually think about negative feedback, challenges, or pain points. But verbatims include good news, insights, and positive feedback too. Buried in these verbatims are the underlying themes that might explain why, when, where, how, and with whom we have a problem.

Pull verbatims out of meetings, stories, and what you hear through Supervillain Monologuing and Silence by Design listening sessions. And if you have access to history (old stories or meeting notes, for example), use previously documented verbatims to help understand how a problem or situation has evolved over time.

With all of this information, run a Verbatim Mapping exercise by following these steps:

TIME AND PEOPLE: A Verbatim Mapping exercise requires 1–3 people for 15–30 minutes per person or meeting being assessed (and can extend longer depending on the availability of source documents).

1. For privacy reasons, ensure that the person or team is informed beforehand that we are conducting such an exercise.

2. Pay attention to the repeated words/phrases you hear and see and document these verbatim (word for word).

3. If the event is real time (versus researching past events using meeting notes and meeting minutes), consider clustering trends or themes as the exercise progresses.

4. After the meeting or event concludes, group the repeated words and phrases into logical groups or themes (using Affinity Clustering, for example, covered briefly in Hour 3 and in more detail in Hour 13).

5. Create a personal hypothesis explaining what we think explains each cluster.

6. Identify a set of "next best steps" and specifically call out what needs to be further explored, what needs to be learned or further understood, and where we have enough information to begin taking preliminary or remediating actions.

7. Plug these verbatim clusters into our Stakeholder+ Maps and Empathy Maps as *speech bubbles*, mapping each verbatim cluster to the appropriate people or teams as a way to enrich our existing maps.

In the end, as we see in Figure 9.2, verbatims help us learn something new and perhaps even corroborate our understanding of a situation and its underlying problems. And verbatims give us a rich and more complete picture of our users and other stakeholders, helping us learn more about the people as well as the problem or situation at hand.

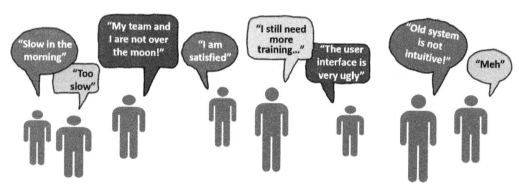

FIGURE 9.2
Verbatim Mapping helps us learn more and validate what we think we know.

Design Thinking in Action: AEIOU Questioning for Rapid Review

Sometimes a simple set of questions can help ensure we are thinking about the right things or focusing on the relevant dimensions of a problem. Created by Rick E. Robinson (2015), use the AEIOU Questioning exercise to rapidly review a situation and mentally tick off a set of key dimensions as we validate a problem, question and interview others, run a meeting, perform

DILO exercises, execute Journey Mapping, conduct an Empathy Mapping exercise, engage with users in Empathy Immersion, and more.

AEIOU stands for Activities, Environment, Interaction, Objects, and Users. The simple AEIOU acronym and five-step exercise can be injected into other exercises to quickly structure a situation or validate a problem. And because it's a mnemonic, AEIOU is easy to remember and therefore easy to follow.

If we are exploring and validating a problem around effectively prioritizing a backlog, for example, we might run an exercise where we think about and explore this backlog prioritization problem in terms of the following:

TIME AND PEOPLE: An AEIOU Questioning exercise requires 2–5 people for 5–15 minutes per problem.

1. **Set the Stage.** Share the problem statement or issue.

2. **Activities.** Are we doing the right things and executing the proper Agile ceremonies (or other methodology-specific tasks) at the right time?

3. **Environment.** Do we have the right forum or space for effectively doing this work of backlog prioritization?

4. **Interaction.** Do we understand the steps necessary to prioritize the backlog? Are we executing them properly and in the right sequence?

5. **Objects.** Do we have the right tools for collaborating in-person or remotely? Do we have an effective DevOps tool for documentation, transparency, and accountability? Are we using the right tool and processes to map epics to features to user stories?

6. **Users.** Do we have the right people involved? Do we understand the personas at stake? Are we engaging early enough or at the right time? Who are we missing? Who is being inadvertently or otherwise marginalized?

7. **Warnings or Patterns.** Do we need to return to a particular area and further explore it?

The AEIOU Questioning process is circular, as we see in Figure 9.3. The idea is to validate our understanding of the problem and identify those areas or themes that might need further exploration and iteration. Iterating might explain what we're missing or inadvertently ignoring.

FIGURE 9.3
The AEIOU Questioning exercise reflects a circular or iterative process for validating our understanding.

Design Thinking in Action: The Five Whys for Root Cause Analysis

Highlighted briefly in Hour 3 and developed years ago by Sakichi Toyoda, the Five Whys are used for discovering the root cause or reason behind a particular situation, line of thinking, decision, and problems in general. This technique helps us understand a person's or team's motivations, values, and biases as well.

The technique is deceptively simple, but it's usually organized around an exercise rather than the simple technique of asking "why" again and again, five times. The key is to pivot the questioning based on the previous response, going beyond the obvious to explore the hidden.

The Five Whys is akin to following a rabbit trail to discover what lies around the corner or beneath what's visible. In the end, you should arrive at the root cause. No, addressing the root cause will not always solve the problem in and of itself, but understanding the root cause is a good start toward better understanding the problem itself. As we saw in the Problem Tree Analysis exercise, simply separating the causes from the effects provides clarity and therefore great value. This exercise should help us better define the true problem statement while thinking in new ways.

TIME AND PEOPLE: A Five Whys exercise requires 2–5 people for 5–15 minutes per problem (and can extend much broader and longer depending on the nature and complexity of the problem).

To run a Five Whys exercise:

1. Share the problem statement.

2. Ask "Why?" five times, taking care to evaluate the previous answer before asking more about it. Consider the following example:

    a. Why did we miss our deployment date? ("Because we completed development and testing late.")

    b. Why did we complete development and testing late? ("Because the business process was more complex than we estimated.")

    c. Why was the business process more complex than we estimated? ("Because our DevOps T-shirt estimation technique maxes out at Extra Large, or XL, and this particular business process was actually Extra *Extra* Large, or XXL.")

    d. Why did we characterize this business process inaccurately in our DevOps system as XL rather than XXL? ("Because our DevOps estimation system does not accommodate anything beyond XL—we can enter in only four sizes, and XXL is not one of those sizes.")

    e. Why is our DevOps estimation system limited to only four sizes? ("Because the current DevOps template is hard-coded for four sizes.")

In the example here, as illustrated in Figure 9.4, the root cause started becoming evident at the *third* Why, but we might never have known of the DevOps template limitation had we not finally gotten to the *fifth—and clearly very important*—Why.

The Five Whys is by no means foolproof, though. This exercise takes us down a pretty narrow path and doesn't really give us the latitude to explore other problems that might surround the one we're seeking to validate. Thus, it's up to the questioner to discern that proper path (or run a series of Five Whys exercises to explore multiple paths).

Also, this exercise itself can stir up other issues along the way. For example, the process of asking why, why, and why again and again can put people on the defensive, leading to people shutting down or seeking a target to blame. Alternatively, try the Probing for Understanding or Supervillain Monologuing techniques to help us drive out more clarity and validate a problem. And consider a final exercise for problem validation, Pattern Matching, covered next.

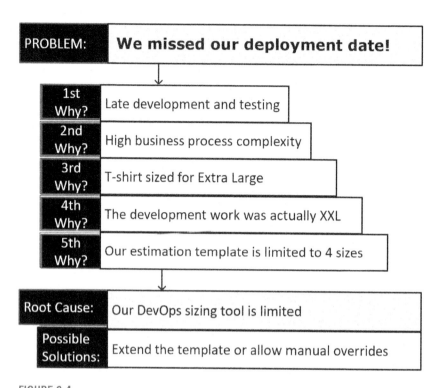

FIGURE 9.4
While the root cause became evident in the third Why, it wasn't until the fifth Why in this Five Whys exercise that we finally arrived at the root cause.

Design Thinking in Action: Pattern Matching for Themes

Looking for recurring patterns to learn something new is an age-old technique used in every part of life. For our purposes here, though, Pattern Matching can help us uncover repeating themes or threads of meaning that validate our problem or tell us something about how we are thinking or executing. For the purpose of validating a particular problem statement, consider these questions:

▶ Does the way we tend to see something contribute to how we react, which in turn leads to the same problems over and over? Do we have a perspective problem getting in the way of understanding the real problem at hand?

▶ Does our problem reflect a singular pattern (our deployment cycles are always late for one reason or another) or a stepwise pattern (our use cases are more complex than we expected, leading to longer development times, longer test cycles, and therefore late deployment cycles)?

TIME AND PEOPLE: A Pattern Matching exercise requires 1–5 people for 15–60 minutes per problem (and can extend much broader and longer depending on the nature and complexity of the problem).

To execute a simple Pattern Matching exercise:

1. Remember that pattern matching is difficult without good data. Gather together the data from which the patterns and themes will be derived. Data can come from documented issues, previously completed interviews and Verbatim Mapping exercises, observations, listening exercises, risk reviews, meeting notes, and so on.

2. Group like items together. Start with big groupings (such as positives and negatives, or input and outputs, or symptoms and outcomes, or causes and effects—whatever makes sense).

3. Further sort these groups by themes. If you don't see obvious patterns related to actions or consequences, start by looking for the nouns (*time, deadlines, work, confidence, self-esteem, turnover, retention, meetings, communications, names, education, image, day, night, money, schedule, bills, security, escalations, activities,* and so on) or verbs (*stressed, depressed, hate, rushed, drive, think, spent, talked,* and so on), and go from there.

4. Now we should start seeing patterns and themes emerge. Label each group by its theme.

5. Identify the outcomes associated with each group (positive, negative, uncertainty, budget overruns, high quality, schedule implications, team attitude, group performance, poor focus, unhealthy peer pressure, healthy competition, high stress, and so on).

6. Work as a team to further consolidate and refine these outcomes. You might wish to prioritize these as well, creating a top-five list of patterns and themes, for example.

For each theme or pattern, be sure to include separate data points that reflect positive sentiment as well as negative sentiment (such as good quality and poor quality or coming in ahead of schedule and delivering behind schedule). It's through these polar extremes that we might identify patterns that provide special insight or help us drill down further into specific groupings.

What Not to Do: Jump In! (to the Wrong Problem)

When a regional home builder began using Design Thinking methods to change how the company interacted with prospective home buyers, the owners missed the importance of validating its particular set of problems prior to making process and procedure changes. Instead, the builder jumped in to learn along the way. The company misunderstood the value of validating and corroborating what it learned in Problem Framing and creating its problem statement. And it wasted months "fixing" problem areas that weren't problems at all, while ignoring other areas that indeed needed fixing.

Jumping in is an important part of the Design Thinking process. We typically want to jump in and get busy learning and building and doing. But this practice of jumping in usually applies to ideating and prototyping and solutioning. When it comes to understanding our situation and its problems, we need to spend the time and resources in validating what we think we know before we go about spending precious time and budget working on the wrong problem.

Summary

Hour 9 closed out an important aspect of Design Thinking related to identifying, understanding, and validating problems before we invest time and effort in thinking and problem solving and solutioning. In this hour, we covered three exercises useful for identifying the problem: Problem Tree Analysis, Problem Framing, and Problem Stating (creating the problem statement). Then we turned our attention to validating our view of the problem through Verbatim Mapping, AEIOU Questioning, and running Five Whys and Pattern Matching exercises. We concluded this hour with a "What Not to Do" story of a home builder who misunderstood the power of jumping in to learn; instead, the company jumped in to solve the wrong problem, committing an expensive mistake and expending a tremendous amount of time and effort in the misstep.

Workshop

Case Study

Consider the following case study and questions. You can find the answers to the questions related to this case study in Appendix A, "Case Study Quiz Answers."

Situation

The Executive Committee (EC) at BigBank is convinced that their star initiative leaders have a handle on the company's most pressing problems. The EC is putting pressure on several initiative leaders to commence the work of ideating, problem solving, and solutioning. Satish is concerned about the budget and schedule implications of starting fast to solve the wrong problems, though, and he needs your assistance to guide the organization more responsibly. In the meantime, the EC keeps reiterating that Design Thinking is about starting fast, failing fast, and learning fast, and they don't understand Satish's hesitancy to apply this same logic to identifying the right problem to solve.

Quiz

1. What are two different Design Thinking exercises known to be useful in creating problem statements?

2. How does a Problem Tree Analysis provide clarity?

3. What are four different Design Thinking techniques or exercises useful in validating a particular problem?

4. How is the Executive Committee misunderstanding the power of Design Thinking for starting and learning fast?

PART III

Thinking Differently

HOUR 10
Introduction to Thinking Differently

What You'll Learn in This Hour:

▶ Ideation and Thinking for Problem Solving

▶ Divergent and Convergent Thinking

▶ Warm-ups for Thinking Differently

▶ Techniques for Clearing the Mind

▶ What Not to Do: Stay Convergent!

▶ Summary and Case Study

Hour 10 commences Part III, "Thinking Differently," where we focus on Phase 2 of our Design Thinking Model for Tech (see Figure 10.1). In these next five hours, we explore techniques and exercises for thinking differently and more deeply on the journey to solving the problems we identified and validated in Hour 9. Hour 10 sets the stage for what many consider to be the core of Design Thinking: the need to think divergently and broadly before we narrow or converge that thinking to arrive at a short list of "best" ideas. Once we have converged on the right problem to solve, and that problem is presumably something we can't solve quickly, we need to alternate between divergent and convergent thinking, perhaps engage in a set of thinking warm-ups to loosen the mind, and probably work through a couple of exercises to help us clear and unclog the mind. We conclude this hour with a real-world "What Not to Do" related to remaining convergent when the situation calls for us to do just the opposite to break free from the mental chains holding us back.

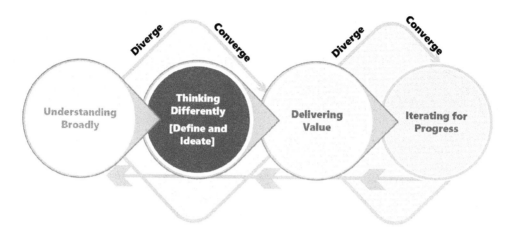

FIGURE 10.1
Phase 2 of our Design Thinking Model for Tech.

Ideation and Thinking for Problem Solving

Why would we ever need to think differently? The short answer is in cases where our usual ways of thinking still leave us at a loss for what to do next. In those cases, we need a place to turn for new ideas on how to come up with new ideas! After all, if the solution to our problem or situation was simple enough to solve with our current tool bag or techniques and exercises, *it would have already been solved.*

And this is where the power of thinking and ideating differently comes into play. We outlined the notion of ideating in the first two hours. Ideating is a word for a special kind of thinking, the kind that has been pulled out of the quiet of our minds and moved out into the open. It has been shared verbally, transferred to a picture or model, drawn on a whiteboard, or written down and mulled over on a tablet or sheet of paper. Ideation is thought that has been externalized.

As we know, ideation can be performed solo or as part of a broader discussion with our coworkers or broader teams and others. When we ideate solo, we can sometimes arrive at brilliant ideas on our own. With the help of others, though, ideating can help us work through those brilliant ideas and identify more ideas for solving complex problems. In this way we can create and fill up an *Ideation Funnel* composed of lots of potential ideas, as we see in Figure 10.2.

Let us explore the Ideation Funnel in the context of how our thinking needs to move from convergent (to fill up the funnel) to divergent (to identify and use the best ideas) and possibly back and forth several times as needed.

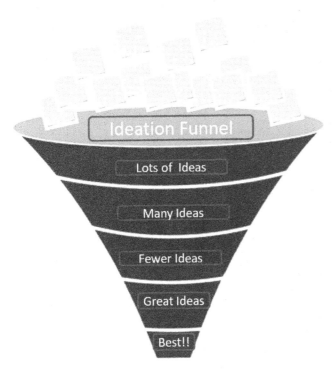

FIGURE 10.2
The Ideation Funnel is a simple and effective metaphor for collecting ideas.

Divergent and Convergent Thinking

To create and fill up our Ideation Funnel, we need to spend more time diverging and less time converging. As we covered in Hour 3, diverging is about gathering ideas, exploring possible solutions, and expanding our options. To diverge is to grow our ideation pool larger and more diverse. It is precisely the opposite of converging, which is about narrowing down and whittling and trimming our ideas and choices and solutions to very few (and presumably the very best, at least based on what we know today about the problems and situation).

Most of us are naturally wired to look at a problem in a convergent kind of way. We spend very little time diverging (in our heads, typically), and a tremendous amount of time implementing an idea that took us maybe a few seconds to decide upon. But convergent thinking works well for us most of the time because most of our situations and problems are not incredibly complex.

NOTE

The 55 and the 5

Albert Einstein is famous for his little quips related to thinking. Einstein had the Design Thinker's hat on when he said, "If I had an hour to solve a problem, I'd spend 55 minutes thinking about the problem and 5 minutes thinking about solutions" (Debevoise, 2021).

But what about when our situations and problems are indeed complicated? And full of expensive and risky options and implications for making a poor initial choice? What if we need more ideas? Better ideas? The key to more ideas and better ideas lies in the ability to diverge, to fundamentally change how we think. Rather than trying to find the single "right" answer to a problem, we need to focus instead on creating a strong list of potential answers or ideas with which to fill up our funnel. The more ideas, the better. That's the goal! The more, the better. And our funnel of ideas needs to challenge our current thinking as a way to explore our problem or situation through new eyes. There are no bad ideas.

Einstein's quote on having an hour to spend on a problem captures the essence of Divergent Thinking. The informal goal is twofold:

1. Come up with lots of ideas.

2. Avoid jumping into solving the problem too quickly.

Divergent thinking helps us twist around and reframe our problem through many ideas so we can attack the problem with the one or two or three best potential solutions. Thus, we diverge as we think broadly and then converge as we target the potential "best" solution (see Figure 10.3).

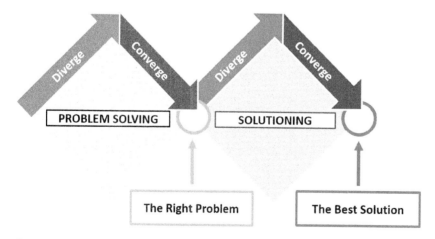

FIGURE 10.3
Consider how divergent thinking increases the number of ideas and potential solutions we have while convergent thinking helps us arrive at the right problem and the best solution.

The process of diverging and converging sounds easy. But it is not. It's hard work. As Einstein also famously said, "Thinking is hard work; that's why so few do it."

How can we make thinking, especially thinking creatively, differently, and divergently, easier? Warm-ups can help us, as we cover next.

Warm-ups for Thinking Differently

Research and our own experience bear this out: There are steps we can take to help us get into a more creative mindset. Some might be considered Design Thinking techniques in their own right, but many are simply little tips to help us think afresh.

Design Thinking in Action: Taxonomy Kick-starters

In the same way that guardrails (which we'll cover next hour) help us ideate more richly, sometimes a bit of structure can help kickstart our thinking processes. Taxonomies can give us a much-needed mental boost when our minds are too tired or too cluttered to think in new ways:

▶ SCAMPER's 7-step process gives us new ways of brainstorming and filling up our Ideation Funnel.

▶ The Agile Manifesto gives us 4 values and 12 principles by which to evaluate and think.

▶ UX Design leverages Heuristic Analysis for ideation and its 10 usability heuristics.

▶ The Possible Futures exercise uses the STEEP acronym to help us think across 5 or more dimensions.

▶ A Boats and Anchors exercise can benefit from a standard risk register taxonomy as a way to think more broadly.

▶ The AEIOU exercise for problem validations uses 5 steps organized around the AEIOU mnemonic to help us easily remember to validate activities, the environment, interactions, necessary objects, and users.

Taxonomies are like cheat cards for our brains! They're fair game and super useful when we need a set of thinking and creativity kick-starters.

Design Thinking in Action: Solo Tips for Divergent Thinking

Steps and tips we take as individuals can help us get into a mindset for thinking differently and divergently. Thinking in a divergent rather than traditional convergent manner takes practice, and we walk through many of these in the next few hours. From common Brainstorming to

Running the Swamp, MVP Thinking, Worst and Best Exercise, Backporting into the Past, Fractal Thinking, Force Field and Golden Ratio Analyses, Möbius Ideation, Finding the Wormhole, and so many others, there are plenty of techniques and exercises for thinking differently and filling up our Ideation Funnel.

And there are practical activities or simple tips that can help us more quickly get into a divergent or creative mindset. Consider how our own experience with some of these tips might have given us some of our own best ideas over the years as we see in the following list and in Figure 10.4:

- Dreaming about what the future could hold
- Drawing what's in our head
- Building a skyscraper with toy blocks or LEGOs
- Building a pasta noodle or paper bridge with a neighbor
- Creating the most accurate or best-distance paper airplane
- Designing a four-cup holder with only paper and tape
- Drawing a house without lifting the pen or retracing a line
- Considering which car we've owned that we should have kept
- Listening to a podcast or music
- Taking a relaxing bath or shower
- Meditating and praying in a quiet place
- Getting a massage or spa treatment
- Taking a walk or going for a run

Of course, there are many other useful activities for thinking differently. Biking, mowing the lawn, yoga, swimming, surfing, lifting weights, and performing other repetitive activities give our minds space and time to wander. With space and time and repetition comes mental freedom.

FIGURE 10.4
Tips and techniques for thinking divergently are at our fingertips.

Design Thinking in Action: Teaming Up for Divergent Thinking

Once we have completed our solo act for warming up, it'll eventually make sense to get back together with others and practice Divergent Thinking in a team setting. For starters, make sure we actually include others to help us think. The key to thinking differently is as much about Diversity by Design (covered in Hour 4 and throughout) as it is about techniques and exercises that help us think differently. For example:

▶ Practice mindfulness exercises together before we think together.

▶ Build (something, anything!) together to think together.

▶ Explore the more than 40 different kinds of thinking and ideation covered here and across the next four hours.

With our creative juices flowing and a divergent mindset to match, it's time to actually think differently. But thinking differently doesn't mean giving ourselves a blank sheet of paper. As we will soon see, thinking differently thrives within the constraints, boundaries, lenses, perspectives, or guardrails that we give ourselves. Turn to Hour 11 to learn more, and more importantly to practice and use these techniques and exercises.

Techniques for Clearing the Mind

Sometimes our minds are so full of our own ideas and self-reinforcing biases that we need to clean things out before we get down to thinking. Consider how the next two simple techniques help us work through the stuff in our heads and clear the path for thinking differently and freshly.

Design Thinking in Action: Snaking the Drain to Work Through Clogs

When problems arise, all of us tend to fall back on what's known and comfortable. Low-stress answers help us deal with high-stress situations. So we naturally look for the quick fix that's always worked before. But what if the quick fix isn't quick or isn't the right fix? What if it's just clogging up our thinking? What if that's why we are unable to think differently?

When the quick fix is not enough, we need to reset our minds and our teams and our colleagues to think differently. We need to clean out the muck and mess in our heads. And it can be hard! We cannot just ignore what's stuck in our heads, after all; the simple and known quick fixes tend to creep back, keeping us from thinking differently.

When the muck or clutter of old ideas remains stuck in our heads, we often cannot help but stay stuck in that mindset. To free our minds to think differently, consider Snaking the Drain. Try talking through how the quick fix maps to today's realities:

- ▶ What do we like about the quick fix?

- ▶ Why is the quick fix not a good fit this time?

- ▶ What will the quick fix lead to?

- ▶ Why is it time to bury it, at least for this particular situation?

With as little emotion as possible, talk through its advantages and disadvantages to rule out that quick fix for the last time so we can restart our thinking with a clean slate. Snake the Drain to refresh, reset, and rethink (see Figure 10.5).

And if we still find that old idea creeping up and crowding out new ideas, turn to Sacrificing the Calf instead, covered next.

FIGURE 10.5
Snaking the Drain helps us refresh, reset, and rethink.

Design Thinking in Action: Sacrificing the Calf to Kill Dead-End Ideas

We've all been in situations where we try to think of new ideas, but the same old tired solutions or quick fixes keep pushing themselves back into our heads. These dead-end ideas might even make sense too. But what if there's a better way? More to the point, what are the *many* ways, the many possibilities? How can we think anew to identify these possibilities?

One way to do so is to simply take the dead-end ideas off the table and call them what they are for us at this particular time and with this particular problem: dead. These dead ideas truly need to be killed (or some may prefer "retired"). Killing off our dead-end thinking can help us see a new path for solving a tough problem or making progress again. We use their death as a *Forcing Function* (a powerful technique we'll cover in more detail in Hour 16) for trying new ideas or learning new skills.

Examples of dead-end thinking might include

▶ Leaning exclusively on what we know today versus discovering something new to carry us into the future

▶ Leveraging our current skills and competencies rather than modernizing them

- ▶ Defending our ideas or positions simply because they were *ours* (and leaning on any other biases as well)

- ▶ Protecting our sacred cows rather than reinventing those cows in a way that's more relevant to today's markets, realities, or economics

- ▶ Failing to toss out traditional strategies in favor of new thinking

- ▶ Panicking by choosing to stand still

Use this technique in conjunction with others such as Snaking the Drain, covered previously, to reset and think anew. Venturing into the unknown will surely pay dividends compared to staying in the same past, unsuccessfully navigating the same problems again and again.

What Not to Do: Stay Convergent!

If we don't change our mindset or respark our creativity, how will we ever break free from the mental chains holding us back? In a large high-tech company stuck in a slow ERP transformation process, the team on the ground kept falling back on the same techniques and ideas that failed previously to make a difference. They battled schedule and staffing issues with traditional IT project management techniques, battled mis-set expectations with band-aids, and essentially relegated themselves to reacting at the whim of an executive team who was, by design, never really close enough to the details to drive real progress.

The project team spent little time thinking and lots of time doing. Instead of thinking through problems deeply and differently, the team quickly arrived at a perceived next best step and then invested tremendous time and energy executing what was typically *not* the next best step. Further, they wasted even more time dealing with executive escalations and unhappy stakeholders. They didn't know what they didn't know, however, and didn't see another way until a fresh set of minds flipped this ongoing cycle.

Instead of spending a brief time thinking through their myriad of challenges, with new eyes and new techniques they worked through each challenge together. Design Thinking slowed the team down at just the point where the executive team was escalating and screaming to go faster, go faster. But Design Thinking eventually made that velocity possible as a period of divergent thinking paid dividends that convergent thinking was incapable of delivering. Listening to Einstein and spending more time thinking and less time doing helped this team and this critical business transformation program break free of its well-camouflaged chains. And it helped the executive team and a broad base of stakeholders regain confidence in the team on the ground and their ability to make real progress again.

Summary

In this hour, we explored the critical need for both convergent and divergent thinking. Together, these foundational techniques form the core for ideating and thinking differently. Then we turned to three warm-ups for helping us loosen our minds, including Taxonomy Kick-starters, tips for thinking divergently solo, and additional tips for thinking divergently as a team. Another two exercises—Snaking the Drain and Sacrificing the Calf—helped us unclog our minds. And we concluded Hour 10 with a real-world example of "What Not to Do" when we're stuck and the same old kinds of thinking lead to the same old outcomes and no progress. We saw how the power of slowing down and thinking divergently can help us restore confidence and velocity by breaking free from the mental chains that hold back our teams and ourselves.

Workshop

Case Study

Consider the following case study and questions. You can find the answers to the questions related to this case study in Appendix A, "Case Study Quiz Answers."

Situation

The Executive Committee at BigBank is losing faith in the ability of the team executing one of the dozen initiatives underneath the OneBank umbrella. Satish himself has stepped in at different times over the last year to help, but no real difference in velocity has materialized. Team members are executing in the same ways they have previously executed, and unsurprisingly they're getting the same results and little progress. The initiative's key stakeholders are nervous they'll need to move go-live yet again, and a few of them have started questioning if BigBank needs to disband the team or the initiative altogether.

Satish needs your help again, and he's willing to fight whatever battles need to be fought—based on your advice—to restore confidence in this team and in the value of this initiative.

Quiz

1. Is this initiative's team fundamentally flawed in how they have been executing?

2. How might the team flip their execution model in the short term?

3. What is the danger in changing how the team thinks and executes in the short term?

4. What kinds of warm-ups or simple exercises might the team find helpful in thinking differently?

5. Some of the team members seem stuck in their way of thinking, and they need help clearing or unclogging their minds so they can think with a fresh perspective. What do you suggest?

HOUR 11
Guardrails for Thinking Creatively

What You'll Learn in This Hour:

▶ Constraints and Guardrails
▶ Simple Guardrails for Thinking Differently
▶ Exercises for Thinking Through Risks
▶ Crazy Techniques for Extreme Thinking
▶ What Not to Do: Avoid the Silly-Sounding Stuff
▶ Summary and Case Study

In this hour, we build on what we learned about thinking divergently. Hour 11 introduces us to five more techniques or guardrails for thinking differently, two exercises for thinking through risks, and two techniques for extreme thinking. Together, these methods can form a powerful set of recipes for thinking differently. Some of the names are a bit crazy or silly sounding, but these techniques and exercises take us to a new level of thinking and ideating. Appropriately so, we close out the hour with a "What Not to Do" focused on not letting silly-sounding Design Thinking labels and names scare us away from using them (including how to avoid or remedy such situations).

Constraints and Guardrails

Have you ever considered that truly creative thinking thrives within constraints, within boundaries? Not limitless possibilities, not a blank sheet of paper, but a set of guardrails or lenses or perspectives that help us focus our thinking. These guardrails, lenses, and perspectives help us think and ideate in new ways. Consider when we were back in middle school and the teacher said we could write a paper about anything. Was the result not our best work? Consider other times when the teacher gave us a topic for that paper or created a set of boundary conditions. Perhaps the teacher asked the class to write about their summer break, or write about an unexpected gift we might have received over the holidays, or tell about a time that a stranger helped us or someone in our family. How much better were those papers?

The teacher's boundary conditions created guardrails that helped our mind more tightly focus. With less time needed to artificially craft a storyline from trillions of options, we had more time to think deeply and meaningfully about the important stuff—what we would actually write about.

This same kind of logic, guardrail logic, applies to any situation where we are asked to be creative or to find creative solutions. Though it seems counterintuitive, giving ourselves a set of guardrails or a specific lens through which to think helps us do so more deeply and more completely. Let's take a look at a number of these simple guardrails for thinking differently.

Simple Guardrails for Thinking Differently

While Divergent Thinking is the uber technique for thinking differently, there are hundreds of simple techniques or guardrails that can help people and teams think just a little bit differently, a little outside the norm. How might we create our own set of thought-provoking guardrails? Consider the following guardrails:

▶ **Analogy or Metaphor.** Can we use an analogy or a cause-and-effect relationship to think differently? Can a simple metaphor help us get our heads around a complex situation?

▶ **Adequacy or "Good Enough."** Where is the boundary between adequate and excess? How might a "good enough" perspective inform what and how we think and plan and execute?

▶ **Edge Case.** What do we need to consider on the edge of what we know about our product or solution? How might someone use or adapt our product or solution in ways we didn't intend or simply never planned for?

▶ **Inclusiveness and Accessibility.** How might our user community's accessibility needs and special abilities inform our data gathering, thinking, prototyping, or solutioning?

▶ **Decomposition or Modularity.** How might our problem or solution be deconstructed into smaller, more manageable chunks?

▶ **Time Travel.** If we could time travel to the future and look back, what missteps and poor assumptions might we find, and how might this information help us today?

▶ **Schedule.** If we look ahead into the future, what might slow us down or stop us in our tracks? Where are the dangers, and how might we prepare for and alleviate their potential impact?

▶ **Moon Shot.** How might we use a nearly impossible goal to help us think differently, with the goal of achieving more than we otherwise probably would have without the benefit of the pressure of an impossible goal?

▶ **Resourcing or Efficiency.** Is there a sufficient albeit less-than-perfect idea that gets us to the finish line? How might the need for stretching our limited resources inform our thinking?

▶ **Visualization.** Is there a picture or figure that could drive a shared understanding more easily or more quickly than words alone?

▶ **Volume.** Do we have an adequate number or volume of ideas to explore? Is our Ideation Funnel full of ideas for consideration, or is it nearly empty? How might we further stock that funnel?

▶ **Time Pressure.** How might our thinking change under duress or tremendous time pressure to find a solution in the next five minutes? Or faster?

▶ **Fractal.** Similar to seeking out traditional patterns at play as we covered in Hour 9, is there a vertical pattern at play? A pattern that presents itself at a smaller or larger scale?

▶ **X to Y Validation.** How might a natural relationship become distorted over time? How might we open our eyes to abnormal or dysfunctional conditions that have somehow become normal?

▶ **Reverse Logic.** Rather than solving our problem, what would make our problem or situation *worse*? Can we use that kind of reverse thinking to find new solutions to our original problem or situation?

Let's begin by taking a look at the first five of these guardrails and the ideation or thinking techniques represented by them. In subsequent hours we'll cover the remainder of these guardrails.

Design Thinking in Action: Analogy and Metaphor Thinking

Imagine we need to travel a complex journey from Point A to Point B with a group of co-travelers, and the group is unclear about why or how. Sharing an analogy or metaphor can help! Why? Because analogies and metaphors help us understand complex ideas by equating them to known or simpler ideas. People naturally gravitate to analogies and metaphors because they help us quickly align, get people on the same page, and get ourselves moving together and in the same direction. Consider how the common analogies and metaphors here can help us simplify the complex:

▶ **Animals.** We might ask how a crocodile or a hippo or collection of animals in a zoo would solve a problem. Similarly, we might use the old "eating an elephant a bite at a time" analogy to describe a long-running project or complex design, or describe a legacy system as a dinosaur.

▶ **Everyday items.** We might view an initiative as a boat on a journey, a set of choices as points on a dart board or radar, a problem as a speedbump rather than a roadblock, and a day of battling situations as a rollercoaster. Future options may be considered through the lens and analogy of a wheel, and we may consider prototypes as clay to be molded and shaped.

▶ **Nature.** We might use a lake as an obstacle to cross or a tree as a way to break down a situation (where a tree trunk is a problem, the tree's roots reflect the problem's causes, and the tree's branches are the effects or consequences, a la the Problem Tree Analysis exercise). Tree analogies can also be useful when creating Guiding Principles, and they serve as another example of fractals a la Fractal Thinking.

▶ **The waterfall.** We might bring together several analogies to construct a richer situation with many different outcomes. Consider how a group of people can survive together on a boat in the middle of a lake, for example. Change the size and type of boat to reflect the team's size, position, limitations, and so on. Add a finish line on one end of the lake and a waterfall at the other end. We might further explain how each person or role has a job to do on the boat to help the team reach the finish line. We might plan for the inertia that will naturally pull the people and the boat toward the waterfall, including storms and currents and even dysfunctional relationships (see Figure 11.1).

FIGURE 11.1
Consider how the Waterfall Analogy brings together several analogies and metaphors to describe a project or initiative, its people, and its situation.

- ▶ **Fictional characters.** We might ask how a fictional cartoon character or superhero with a set of super powers or gifts might tackle a situation. Or how that cartoon character might avoid the situation altogether.

- ▶ **Historical events.** We might compare a pointless activity to "rearranging the deck chairs" on the Titanic, or an antiquated way of thinking or operating to "horse and buggy."

- ▶ **Popular movies.** We might consider how Lieutenant Caffe coaxed the truth from Colonel Nathan R. Jessup in *A Few Good Men*, or how Jack Dawson gave his everything to ensure his fictional love, Rose, would survive the sinking of the *Titanic*.

- ▶ **Sporting events.** We can use an endless supply of sports analogies to help explain how we might work together or achieve the goals ahead of us. Consider how golf and motocross, or a soccer game or rugby game, or American Baseball's World Series or the National Football League's playoff process can help us explain the need to work together to realize our mission, or how our individual performance or the team's collaboration will be measured, will help us get to the finish line, and so on.

Such exercises help us think through complex and difficult matters in less-stressful and more easily comprehended kinds of ways, opening the door to buy-in and deeper understanding.

Design Thinking in Action: Good Enough Thinking

Imagine if we need to get from Point A to a far-off land called Point B, and we've only been given $50 and two days. We don't need a perfect experience or a luxurious yacht or personal jet. We simply need a way to arrive at Point B alive and healthy. What mode of transportation would be adequate or good enough to get the job done? How might we recast the need and replace transportation with another solution, such as a telephone call or virtual meeting?

Long ago, the French philosopher Voltaire said, "Don't let perfect be the enemy of good." That is, don't spend so much time and energy seeking perfection that we ignore good enough and instead find ourselves wasting time, money, energy, and more for no real reason. Perfection costs dearly, and it's just another reason why budgets get drained unnecessarily.

Perfection versus Good Enough scenarios are all too common in tech, particularly when we are reacting to urgent demands or new needs. Good Enough Thinking gives us the mindset to consider the bare minimums and the point of diminishing returns. When we know our boundaries in terms of scope, schedule, and budget, we can use these guardrails to drive solutioning within those needs and constraints.

Good Enough therefore saves time, optimizes budgets, and preserves other resources. Trade-offs might include experience, quality, long-term supportability, and more, so it's important to weigh these trade-offs carefully. But when "better" simply wastes time and resources, Good Enough is, well, good enough. Consider the following Good Enough dimensions:

▶ **Acceptable Quality.** The longer we refine a product, the exponentially more expensive that product becomes. Why? Because increases in effort and time are often synonymous with exponential expense. Increasing a product's quality 1 percent, from 95 percent to 96 percent, for example, could actually double the product's cost or double the schedule needed to achieve 96 percent. Ask ourselves and confirm with one another what "good" looks like so we know when to stop.

▶ **Acceptable Time.** If we have been working on an assignment and met its requirements, then any additional time we spend on that assignment is beyond good enough. Unless there's a really good reason to do more (implying we didn't fully understand the requirements), doing more is a waste of everyone's time. Know when to say we are done, and truly finish.

▶ **Acceptable Risks.** Risk taking is a part of life. Don't get stuck weighing the pros and cons for too long. Instead, quickly evaluate the situation and make the next best step or decision to start on that journey.

▶ **Acceptable Downstream Impact.** Decisions and trade-offs we make today have lasting impact. Ensure that impact is acceptable for now or create a plan to address less-than-favorable impact that might be realized as we work to make progress today.

Good Enough Thinking is therefore about acknowledging diminishing returns and trade-offs. Reach a shared understanding about what "good" looks like; know the boundaries of scope, quality, schedule, budget, and other resources; and don't go beyond those boundaries without good reason. When we do the work and meet its requirements, we need to call the work done. And be done, knowing we can always iterate later against a fresh set of requirements and good enough quality bar.

NOTE

The "Good Enough" Quality Bar
Detractors might say "good enough" lowers the bar for acceptable quality. It doesn't. Instead, Good Enough Thinking helps us discover whether our original plan or the work we're focused on today exceeds the necessary quality. Thus, Good Enough Thinking seeks to precisely meet the necessary quality bar and nothing more.

Design Thinking in Action: Edge Case Thinking

Imagine if we must change a large community's experience between Point A and Point B and ensure the final experience encompasses the needs of the full community. We probably know generally *what* the community wants in the final experience in terms of capabilities, but what if we don't know everything they want? What if our understanding only represents 80 percent of their wants? How might we think about the 20 percent of the edge cases we don't know today, edge cases that might derail us once we arrive at Point A?

Edge Case Thinking is a Design Thinking technique for inclusion through empathy for the "edge" (see Figure 11.2). The term *edge case* is just another way to describe the needs of people on the fringes of our situation or solution, people who have additional needs or expectations beyond what we already know and intend to solve.

FIGURE 11.2
Note how the edge of a situation or problem may represent 20 percent or more of a potential solution's needs.

People on the edge help us think and see and deliver differently. If we hope to cover all of our bases, then we need to consider and include this 20 percent who reflect more about what our solution is missing as we understand it today. Ensure we don't inadvertently marginalize the needs of those who sit on the boundaries or edges.

▶ How might they act or respond in a way that's different from what we are thinking or planning?

▶ How can their needs be helpful to the broader community?

▶ How can we bring all of these needs together to serve the whole of the community?

Such insights help us understand the breadth of our problems and situations more deeply, so we can create smarter designs and solutions in the long run.

Design Thinking in Action: Inclusive and Accessible Thinking

While Edge Case Thinking represents the missing 20 percent in terms of product needs or solution capabilities, Inclusive and Accessible Thinking represents the even greater percentage of our community with special usability and accessibility needs. Consider how any community is made up of people with vision and hearing impairments, people with technology and band-width limitations, people with unseen and invisible disabilities, and people with other needs who are inadvertently excluded from using our product or solution. As we see in Figure 11.3, these are the people who typically do not have the same homogeneous background, education, experiences, capabilities, and needs embodied in the core community. We might think we have a shared understanding of a need, but when we avoid or skip Inclusive and Accessible Thinking, we overlook a tremendous cross section of our community. Some have suggested that ignoring accessibility and inclusion can marginalize nearly half of a user community!

FIGURE 11.3
In contrast to Edge Case Thinking, where we focus on capturing needs at the edge of our situation or problem, Inclusive and Accessible Thinking focuses on people and their needs to access and use a solution.

Imagine we are on a journey from Point A to Point B and we cannot afford to exclude anyone. Getting the whole user community from Point A to Point B requires Inclusive and Accessible Thinking as early in the journey as possible, including before we even leave Point A. Inclusive and Accessible Thinking helps us think holistically early enough to avoid usability and accessibility missteps so we solve for the whole community's needs.

Inclusive and Accessible Thinking is about finding and taking care of the people that we too often marginalize or forget about altogether. It's about giving a voice to the customer, especially the voiceless and ignored. How do we make vocal the voice of those not generally heard? The answer lies in intentionality and by asking ourselves:

- ▶ Who is missing in our discussions and discovery as we seek to broadly learn and understand?

- ▶ Who are we intentionally excluding today and why? Who can we help climb out of the abyss that the organization has accidentally or otherwise created or reinforced over time?

- ▶ Who is missing in our problem solving as we consider solution and product capabilities and how to release them?

- ▶ Who needs an ally when it comes to designing our solution? How might we serve in that capacity?

- ▶ Who can we help make a place for, so we all cross the finish line together?

▶ Who requires a unique way to participate in what we are doing, and how might we include those colleagues with differing abilities in our journey?

▶ Who else needs to be included even when it's not convenient or not part of our plan?

Consider the whole of each person, including their obvious and less obvious abilities and disabilities. Consider how each person likes to work, think, communicate, interact, and be treated. What are their distinct cultural, language, ethnic, and other distinctive dimensions? Consider what connects the community to one another, too. Where are the common threads and themes that can unify a community fragmented and isolated over time?

Finally, when it comes to our community's accessibility challenges, abilities, voice, and coping strategies:

▶ Learn how accessibility affects communications and inclusion and use language that builds up rather than tears down as a way to set the bar for inclusive and respectful communications across the board.

▶ Create inclusive boards and councils to drive greater awareness and inclusion.

▶ Discuss and agree as a team and community how to quickly resolve disagreements and conflicts.

▶ Use analogies and metaphors that are also inclusive, so they bring people together rather than alienating a subset.

▶ Consider how people may be intentionally hiding or muting what makes them unique; work to give people the freedom to be themselves.

▶ Proactively consider the overlap between edge cases and the need for greater inclusion and attention to accessibility

▶ Drive awareness campaigns to drive greater inclusion and enhance a team's ability to work and communicate together; awareness in this case is about respecting differences rather than driving uniformity.

▶ Finally, promote allyship across the problem-solving and solutioning spectrum. Attention to Inclusive and Accessible Thinking means that everyone has a friend and ally. Allies speak up to correct oversights and preserve healthy relationships across teams and the community being served, playing a key role in course-correcting along the journey from Point A to B.

Beyond a community's accessibility challenges, abilities, and coping strategies, consider culture, values, lifestyle, and more, as covered previously. Allow this knowledge of the community's cultural diversity to influence how everyone shows up, thinks together, and solves together.

Design Thinking in Action: Modular Thinking and Building

Let's say we have a tremendous number of people to get from Point A to Point B as we develop a new solution to their problems and challenges, but their needs differ from one another today and will probably continue to differ when we arrive at Point B. How might we make this journey in a way that lets us develop the solution and onboard different groups of people to that solution over time? How can we think in a way that lets those making the journey increase in numbers over time as our solution accommodates their unique needs? Can we accommodate such needs in a parallel kind of way, or should we pursue them in more of a linear kind of way?

We need options. We need ways of decomposing the problem and its solution into modules so we can deliver that solution over time (stepwise or horizontally), including to larger groups of users at a time (horizontal with a vertical aspect).

Modularity is about interchangeable components too, so we can work on the whole by working in parallel on the parts. Designing for modularity creates opportunities to improve and upgrade the whole by incrementally improving and upgrading the solution's parts. It's why modularity is so popular in automobiles, homes, computers, and literally millions of other products and services. Modularity gives us freedom and options. Imagine having to buy a new computer because we could not replace the hard drive or upgrade the memory or make the system perform better by upgrading the operating system and its applications.

A popular take on Modular Thinking is captured in another technique called Regenerating through Combining. Consider how we can combine the old with the new in a modular way, the outcome of which is naturally "less new" and therefore easier to realize and highly consumable to our users (compared to something completely new). Being modular is about small wins through incremental add-ons and plug-ins that introduce a new or better set of capabilities to take us another step closer to our goal. As we think ahead and work to bring a complex group of people on a complex journey, consider how to build the new foundation in a modular way so we can bring everyone along.

Exercises for Thinking Through Risks

Design Thinking is ripe with techniques and exercises for identifying, thinking through, managing, and mitigating risks. As we step into the uncertain and unclear, a useful first step includes assessing the situation in these ways. Next, we take a look at two exercises that not only let us explore the entirety of a situation but also let us visually view that situation through a couple of different lenses.

Design Thinking in Action: The Premortem for Thinking Ahead

Consider bringing a group of people from Point A to B on a journey where the entire trip is fraught with danger. Before taking the first step, wouldn't it make sense to run through that journey mentally and consider the dangers and perils along the way? This is where running a Premortem exercise can be valuable. Most of us know what a postmortem is: it's taking a look at something after that something has died. And the learnings in the wake of a postmortem can be useful for sure, but in the end the thing is still dead. There's gotta be a smarter way to think and learn. The Premortem gives us that way, to take a look at something while the initiative or project is still viable and alive.

This "pre" version of the postmortem was coined by Gary Klein and published in the *Harvard Business Review* in 2007. It calls for a detailed assessment before death as a way to hopefully avoid death in the first place.

The idea is simple, too. We need to purposely think ahead about what might fail in our project, or what might happen externally to cause death, or who might fail to deliver key aspects of the project. We do this thinking ahead of time *before* such failure or death occurs. As Gary Klein explains, "In a premortem, team members assume that the project they are planning has just failed—as so many do—and then generate plausible reasons for its demise. Those with reservations may speak freely at the outset, so that the project can be improved rather than autopsied" (2007).

Premortems include building in mitigations or additional user involvement to avoid these failure scenarios. Such mitigations and involvement can help us identify and avoid the kinds of fantastic failures that otherwise surprise and shut down projects, initiatives, and more.

A Premortem also gives people the ability to call out potential issues in a "here is what happened" looking-back kind of way that's less politically sensitive than "What if Marcy in our integrations group fails to deliver the system integrations on time?" The Premortem is therefore another way to brainstorm by looking back rather than looking ahead. Premortem exercises are useful to help teams

- ▶ Identify potential issues.

- ▶ Prioritize those issues in terms of impact.

- ▶ Design mitigations in advance to avoid those unwanted issues.

- ▶ Identify potential biases and missteps we might encounter along the way, including mitigations or next steps.

- ▶ Think ahead about how potential risks might become actual issues in light of our plans, up-and-coming industry trends, and other events we might be tracking or planning.

Running a Premortem exercise is easy, and because it's performed prior to failing, it's generally low stress if not fun. Consider the steps here:

TIME AND PEOPLE: A Premortem exercise requires 3–10 people for 60–120 minutes per project or initiative (and can extend much broader and longer depending on the nature and complexity of the project or initiative).

1. Identify the project or initiative on which to execute a Premortem. Remember we are doing this exercise early in the project or initiative's lifecycle, well before anything might have failed.

2. Bring the team together and set the stage: we've traveled into the future, and our project turned out to be a disaster!

3. Ask each person to imagine what caused the disaster and share these ideas one by one on physical or virtual sticky notes. Note duplicate answers as a way to later prioritize the riskiest areas, and push the team for fresh ideas as well.

4. If ideation has stalled, introduce a risk or project methodology taxonomy to help the team think anew.

5. Revisit and note the ideas with the most votes.

6. Identify and group the ideas and answers into Affinity Clusters or themes.

7. Identify the ideas' most critical clusters or themes through a risk management lens.

8. Brainstorm and potentially run SCAMPER exercises to consider early focus areas and preventive steps and discuss these together.

9. Document, prioritize, and introduce mitigations and decisions in a formal risk register.

Once we've executed a Premortem, it can make sense to dig deeper into the single most troublesome area for any complex endeavor: schedule. Let's take a look next at a popular Design Thinking exercise for assessing schedule challenges.

Design Thinking in Action: Boats and Anchors for Schedule Risks

Imagine we are on a journey and simply need to get from Point A to Point B. It's a simple enough premise. More to the point, though, what might slow us down or stop us completely on our journey? What do we need to be watchful of? How might we run aground or stray off course? Use Boats and Anchors, a fun and helpful exercise, to think about schedule challenges. Identify the obstacles or "anchors" that might slow down our boat and assess these anchors to consider how to minimize their drag on the boat or cut the anchors off completely.

Expand the exercise by identifying more than just the anchors. Consider the rocks and shoals along the way too. What about the sharks in the water? Hurricanes and other storms on the horizon? Pirates seeking to plunder and pillage? How might these factors affect the people on the journey and the project or initiatives (the boat) making the journey? For each of these factors or obstacles to progress, use visuals and stick or draw them atop a visual of our boat. And then—the most important part—once we've identified the factors, consider how each might slow us down and determine how to cut those anchors, avoid those storms, and navigate around the sharks. And we might consider how to at least *minimize* anchor drag if we can't free ourselves completely from their hold. Even more interesting, we might also consider how anchors could be transformed into speed enablers!

And we can break up our journey into phases to assess each phase more deeply. For example, what might slow down our project as we mobilize our teams, understand the lay of the land, ideate and problem solve, prototype and develop solutions, test and iterate on those solutions, and so on?

Running a Boats and Anchors exercise requires a team and a bit of imagination. Imagine we have onboarded the group onto our boat, and we are on our way to a beautiful island called Point B. We need to protect and preserve our schedule for arriving at this beautiful island. Now consider this: the water surrounding our boat is our situation. How will we navigate the water to avoid getting stuck along the way? How can we be sure we will arrive at the island on schedule?

Use a whiteboard or poster board to draw the boat, the island, our journey, and so on. Use sticky notes to represent anchors and other factors. Let the team add potential anchors, one per sticky note, and stick those to the board. Will we run out of gas (budget) before we arrive? Do we have the right skills or right people on the team to navigate the boat? Do we need special help during certain parts of the journey? Use this Boats and Anchors analogy to think ahead about other kinds of schedule-related threats that could affect our journey to the island too. Again, we might identify ill-intentioned or dangerous sharks in the water, detour-forcing rocks and shoals between us and our destination, pirates who want to steal our resources or commandeer our boat, and storms or hurricanes on the horizon that might change our course entirely. Consider Figure 11.4 here. Be creative!

How will each one of these anchors and rocks and so on slow us down, or divert us, or in some other way get between where we are today and arriving at the island? What additional resources or help might provide us with speed enablers? With the help of others, now consider how to keep on track or get back on schedule.

FIGURE 11.4
Running a Boats and Anchors exercise helps us think creatively about schedule challenges.

Run a Boats and Anchors exercise by following the steps here:

TIME AND PEOPLE: A Boats and Anchors exercise requires 3–10 people for 60 minutes per schedule dilemma or challenge.

1. Establish and share the challenge or situation today.

2. Initialize the shared collaboration space (whiteboard, Klaxoon, and so on). with a picture of the boat (our project or initiative), where we are today (Point A), and the Island (Point B, our destination).

3. Develop a list of potentials obstacles (anchors, rocks, shoals, pirates, and so on) to be explored with the team.

4. Give everyone virtual or physical sticky notes.

5. Round-robin through each team member, one phase at a time, and identify an anchor for that phase. What would slow down our boat? Or stop it completely? Where are the shoals? The sharks? Who might be our pirates to be wary of?

6. If ideation is stalling, introduce a risk or project methodology taxonomy to help people think anew.

7. After completing all phases, review and consolidate the learnings.

8. Populate the project's Risk Register with these new risks.

9. Begin a new exercise to explore and mitigate each new risk.

A Boats and Anchors exercise therefore combines the analogy of a boat and various forms of Brainstorming and Reverse Brainstorming to view a problem or situation from a schedule perspective, including the challenges and risks we are likely to face on our boat journey.

Crazy Techniques for Extreme Thinking

As we will cover here and throughout the next several hours, we can draw on quite a few simple but crazy-sounding techniques to help us think creatively and differently. Two of these techniques include Mission Impossible Thinking and Möbius Ideation, covered next.

Design Thinking in Action: Mission Impossible Thinking

Sometimes when we face a very important journey, we might choose to give ourselves an impossible goal as a way to help us achieve as close to that goal as possible. A super-extreme scenario or "moon shot" can help us think and decide differently than we might by default. This extreme way of thinking can unblock how we approach situations that are hard if not impossible. Credited to James Macanufo and discussed by Dave Gray in *Gamestorming: A Playbook for Innovators, Rulebreakers, and Changemakers* (2010), Mission Impossible Thinking forces us to think beyond the obvious and easy answers.

For example, if we must get from Point A to Point B with a healthy budget and plenty of time, we can do so pretty easily. But what if we have only $20 and 24 hours, and Points A and B are San Francisco and New Orleans? Now we have a challenge that requires tremendous resourcefulness and creativity.

In the end, we may not find a way to actually complete the impossible mission. We may fall short. But with options in front of us, we will have choices to make that might not have been evident otherwise. And that's really the point; with more ideas to help us along the way, we set up ourselves and our teams and our communities for a greater chance at success, even if our final journey requires a bit more expense or time-consuming path than we aimed for in our Mission Impossible quest.

Design Thinking in Action: Möbius Ideation

In other cases, we might need to move a whole lot of people from Point A to Point B but need to do so in a way that maximizes our resources most effectively and efficiently. This technique is akin to Good Enough Thinking but with a twist: how might we rethink or reassemble our resources to draw maximum usefulness?

Consider how a Möbius strip may be fully used, front and back, to provide potentially twice the value we might see on the surface (as we see in Figure 11.5). How might we optimize our resourcing model to fully utilize our resources? How might we use our equipment and tools differently? How might we employ our people and teams in fresh ways to deliver more value? Möbius Ideation helps us answer these questions by doing more with the resources we have on hand.

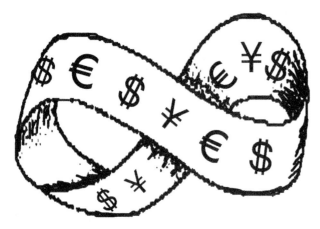

FIGURE 11.5
Consider how a Möbius Strip provides twice the resource or capability of a traditional loop, and use this notion to ideate with a guardrail or lens of efficiency.

NOTE

Möbius in Action!

Unclear about how a Möbius strip functions? Open up a web browser, search on "animated Möbius strip" and take a look at the images resulting from that search. If we walked a classic Möbius strip, we would travel its length not once but twice before we got back to our original starting point. We would fully use both sides of that strip, doubling its lifespan. We would see half the wear and tear and get twice the value out of that strip than if the strip were looped in the classic way.

When resources are scarce and efficiency is most important, Möbius Ideation can help us innovate. Consider how some conveyor belts, old typewriter ribbons, and moving sidewalks might use a Möbius approach to double the life of those assets. What can we learn and apply to our own problems and potential solutions? Examples might include redeploying our people to wear more hats or take on more roles, giving us greater efficiency when it comes to onboarding, communications, management, stakeholder connections, and so on.

But we're not here to twist what we have into a Möbius shape. The Möbius analogy is just to help us view our resources in a new way. The real goal here is to think differently about how we can use what we already have in a way that's more efficient than today. It's not about taking away obligations or finding a new budget but rather about maximizing the usefulness of the resources at our disposal as we go about our journey.

To perform a Möbius Ideation exercise:

TIME AND PEOPLE: A Möbius Ideation exercise requires 2–5 people for 60 minutes per problem (and can extend much broader and longer depending on the nature and complexity of the problem and early fit of potential solutions).

1. Bring the team together, identify the project or initiative, and identify the challenge, problem, or situation.

2. Create a list of the human resources available to the team today, organized by people or role and their skillsets, capabilities, experiences, and qualifications.

3. Identify the project's constraints or boundary conditions, such as a fixed budget or schedule.

4. Identify the project team's constraints, such as the inability to travel or limited bandwidth.

5. For each constraint, identify why changing the problem or situation is difficult if not impossible.

6. For each constraint, identify what the project or project team is lacking.

7. Finally, consider each person and each resource connected to this situation, and discuss within the constraints today:

    a. What can be changed?

    b. What or who can be stretched?

    c. What or who can fulfill unaddressed needs?

    d. How might the team tackle any remaining unaddressed needs?

    e. What are the trade-offs, and how might they be managed (including burnout, role complexity, and responsibility or accountability misalignment)?

When resources are scarce and we need to "play with the team we have on the field," look for the Möbius opportunities in our situations. Consider how we might investigate how to use more fully *who and what we already have* to provide more value at the same cost. Look for those ways to fully maximize how our resources are being used, from people and teams to equipment and tools and more. Reassemble resources differently, look for options to uncover more value from the same people, and benefit from the efficiencies of Möbius Ideation.

What Not to Do: Avoid the Silly-Sounding Stuff

When we are faced with failure and need to think in dramatically new kinds of ways, we need to enlist the help of new kinds of thinking. A small health-care company found itself in the cross-hairs of a privacy and compliance nightmare and would have benefited from news ways of understanding and thinking. The IT team on the hook for this nightmare ignored the ideas prof- fered by the legal team and a small staff of external change management and ideation consul- tants, though. The IT team instead chose to brainstorm internally with the same team that got itself into the mess in the first place. And matters only grew worse until the IT team was let go or replaced and a new team was introduced to navigate the privacy fallout.

Why did the health-care company's IT team ignore its own experts? Because one of the external consultants too eagerly jumped into a preliminary conference call talking about Opposite Think- ing, using creative analogies or metaphors to create a shared understanding about the situation, and running through a Boats and Anchors exercise to think through the next several months of navigating shark-infested waters. The team was scared away by what seemed like crazy tech- niques and silly-sounding waste-of-time "stuff."

In retrospect, the eager change management and ideation consultant didn't do their job either. Rather than sharing the names of these Design Thinking techniques and exercises with people who have never even heard of them, they could have simply talked about the process or its out- comes. For example, the consultant might have shared more generally how the IT team would benefit from thinking a bit differently to extricate itself from the mess. The consultant could have mentioned the need to align the broader team around the situation. The consultant might have even suggested thinking more deeply about the challenges on the immediate horizon. Alienating the very team needing help wasn't useful for anyone. But in the end, *not* doing the crazy or silly- sounding "stuff" cost people their jobs and prolonged working through a critical privacy and compliance incident.

Summary

Hour 11 built on the ideation warmup and divergent techniques we covered in Hour 10 and introduced five more techniques or guardrails for thinking differently: Analogy and Metaphor Thinking, Good Enough Thinking, Edge Case Thinking, Inclusive and Accessible Thinking, and Modular Thinking. Then we explored the Premortem and Boats and Anchors exercises for thinking through risks, followed by two extreme thinking techniques including Mission Impossible Thinking and Möbius Ideation. While some of the names of these techniques sound a bit crazy or silly, they take us to a new level of ideating. Appropriately so, we closed out the hour with a "What Not to Do" focused on better handling situations and people who might be scared away from using "silly-sounding stuff" simply because of the names or labels of certain Design Thinking techniques and exercises.

Workshop

Case Study

Consider the following case study and questions. You can find the answers to the questions related to this case study in Appendix A, "Case Study Quiz Answers."

Situation

Satish and you have restored confidence in the work of several OneBank initiatives, and happily the Executive Team has turned its attention to other matters. But you have gotten wind of a recent blowup related to a key OneBank initiative. You are curious how such a seemingly well-planned initiative failed so abruptly and spectacularly. The initiative's goal was to upgrade the merged set of systems sitting atop a well-known customer relationship management platform. The overall system was cobbled together in the wake of a merger three years ago. Everyone knew the technology infrastructure was frail, so expectations were set that the platform project would be tough but was nonetheless absolutely achievable as soon as an extensive and expensive end user downtime window could be organized.

After months of planning and successfully testing the upgrade, the team arranged a full weekend of downtime to do the work of the upgrade. Within an hour of commencing, the first attempt at upgrading the system failed spectacularly. And several days later, stakeholder confidence was still shattered as no one really understood what had happened.

Satish has now formally asked you to get involved to understand what might need to be done differently. He needs you to share techniques or exercises useful in succeeding after failing, the kinds of "difference makers" that would lead to a new outcome. Satish's goal is simple: help the team arrive at a less-risky upgrade process and predictable schedule with an aspirational goal of zero mistakes or defects.

Quiz

1. While a postmortem would be useful, what else might the team do as it seeks to identify another round of risks and plan for the next upgrade attempt?

2. What exercise might the team employ to aspirationally target zero downtime so as to minimize the required downtime as much as possible?

3. The team seemed to spend extra energy and resources on aspects of the plan that exceeded the required quality goals. What kind of thinking might be useful in this case?

4. How might the team more deeply think about schedule risks as it lays out the next multiweek upgrade plan?

5. Which Design Thinking technique asks us to view a problem or situation through the lens of efficiency?

HOUR 12
Exercises for Increasing Creativity

What You'll Learn in This Hour:

▶ Creativity and Thinking
▶ Exercises for Creative Thinking
▶ What Not to Do: Concluding Thinking Too Early
▶ Summary and Case Study

In this hour, we continue to build on Hours 10 and 11 and outline techniques and exercises for thinking differently, in this case to build on or increase creativity. From the basics around Visual and Divergent Thinking, we then turn to unique methods for pushing ourselves to ideate in fresh new ways. Exercises such as Running the Swamp, Fractal Thinking, Golden Ratio Analysis, and Reverse Brainstorming broadly push the notion of guardrails and give us the kinds of "bolt-ons" useful for pushing our thinking beyond the ideation we've already completed. We conclude Hour 12 with a "What Not to Do" example focused on real-world missed opportunities when we fail to think through the opportunities in front of us.

Creativity and Thinking

In Hour 11 we discovered techniques and exercises useful for creative thinking, and we organized these methods around the notion of "guardrails" for thinking differently. From Analogy and Metaphor Thinking to Good Enough, Edge Case, Inclusive and Accessible, and Modular Thinking, we outlined new ways of approaching a problem or situation. We then applied creativity to risk management and outlined techniques for extreme thinking.

But what if thinking creatively is simply not adequate? What if we need to not just think creatively but *increase our creativity*? How might we overlay additional techniques or exercises atop our foundation for thinking to push ourselves in different ways? What are the ideation bolt-ons and recipes that we can use to increase creativity?

In this hour, we take a look at six ways of rethinking what we've already thought through to take us in new directions, from Visual and Divergent Thinking to Running the Swamp, Fractal

Thinking, Golden Ratio Analysis, and Reverse Brainstorming. Armed with these methods used in conjunction with other methods, we just might find new ways to conquer long-standing problems.

Techniques and Exercises for Creative Thinking

Beyond the guardrails for thinking differently that we've already covered, a number of additional exercises can take our brains to new places. Think of these as "bolt-ons" to other ways of thinking. Visual Thinking, for example, is a long-time technique we can add to our tool bag and apply to most any problem or situation regardless of the ways we might have thought about that problem or situation previously.

Design Thinking in Action: Visual Thinking for Understanding

As outlined in Hour 5, the more we can turn our ideas and plans and solutions into pictures and figures—thus making them visible and visual—the faster we will arrive at a shared understanding. Much of this book is organized around techniques and exercises that enable Visual Thinking or the simple process of imaging, showing, looking, and seeing. When we can transform the shapeless and invisible thoughts in our heads into figures and maps and images, we can better think and communicate that thinking and understanding with others. We all know that complex ideas and processes are often best communicated visually, which is why it's been said that "a picture is worth a thousand words." A picture can supply exactly what is needed to understand or solve a problem, as we see in Figure 12.1.

When our ideation and thinking processes leave us unable to make more progress or communicate clearly, and when our words fail us, draw a picture. If you are overwhelmed by the complexity of a situation, think about the two or three key parts of that situation—and draw. Pictures help us see relationships and dependencies, and they help us simplify conditions and arrive at a shared understanding faster and more clearly than words.

Beyond pictures, figures, graphs, models, and heatmaps (see the following note), consider active and animated content (videos, for example) to communicate complex processes effectively and with repeatable consistency. For example, viewing one of the hundreds of animated Möbius strips on the Internet (as we discussed in Hour 11) is much better at communicating resource efficiency than these words are.

FIGURE 12.1
As all of us know first-hand, figures and pictures can transform the complex into the understandable, in this case explaining why someone appears to be quickly driving away from a situation.

NOTE
_____

Heatmapping!

Red/yellow/green *heatmaps* are wonderful for visualizing data or concepts through the use of color coding (or other identifying marks to accommodate accessibility realities). The variety and gradation of color or other markings help illustrate status or changes, and therefore help draw attention to that status or those changes.
_____

NOTE
_____

Structured Text

When words are still the best method for communication, consider using Structured Text, outlined later in Hour 15 to communicate crisply and economically.
_____

Design Thinking in Action: Divergent Thinking

As we saw in Hour 10, helping ourselves think more divergently opens the floodgates to new ideas. It's about generating a range of possibilities rather than discovering the single best or right idea. And with many ideas to further explore, we can create a virtuous cycle where new ideas create more ideas, giving us the volume, depth, and breadth necessary to make progress. Don't fear mistakes or being "wrong." Instead, put on our Divergent Hat, enlist the aid of the following Divergent Thinking warm-ups, and bask in new levels of creativity.

▶ Take a walk or go for a run.

▶ Get a massage.

▶ Dream about what the future could hold.

▶ Draw what is in our head.

▶ Play blocks or LEGO with our kids.

▶ Build something with our hands.

▶ Listen to a podcast or music.

▶ Take a relaxing bath or shower.

▶ Meditate and pray in a quiet place.

And remember what Albert Einstein said about the importance of ideas: "The only sure way to avoid making mistakes is to have no new ideas." Lean on Divergent Thinking tips and techniques to fill up our ideation funnel.

Design Thinking in Action: Running the Swamp

Once we have spent some time thinking deeply through a problem or situation, we might want to turn the tables and instead think rapidly. Without overthinking it, what is our first response to a situation? Without getting buried in potential consequences or root causes, what should be done? Now? It's this kind of time pressure that can generate the ideas necessary to make progress or survive.

Like earlier techniques and exercises, we can view this exercise through the lens of a group of people. Imagine we need to get ourselves and our community from Point A to Point B, and there is a swamp between the two points. How can we cross the swamp fast enough to avoid sinking into it? How might we cross the swamp in a special kind of way or with a special type of gear? How might we circumvent the swamp? Can we fly over it or run across it like a green basilisk lizard? Time pressure can help us break through logic barriers.

Running the Swamp is a timed Divergent Thinking exercise at its core. The exercise combines various forms of Brainstorming, Analogy and Metaphor Thinking, Visual Thinking, and so on—anything to drive creative ideation. Use this exercise to surface big and bold ideas that would probably not otherwise surface without the time constraint. Hidden in the big and bold are the nuggets of insight that could help us navigate the swamp.

This exercise is best done visually. Obtain a photograph of the community who are at risk of sinking into a swamp and superimpose that photograph over an image of a swamp (see Figure 12.2). For starters, ensure there is plenty of space between the people and the swamp. Throughout this timed exercise, we will watch those people sink into the swamp minute after minute as we fail to come up with ideas and solutions that can help them survive.

FIGURE 12.2
Running the Swamp puts us and our team in a time-crunch situation to ideate rapidly with less thought to common sense or consequences.

Here's an example of how to Run the Swamp:

TIME AND PEOPLE: A Run the Swamp exercise requires 5–10 people for 5–10-minute blocks of time (though postexercise discussion could take us to 30–45 minutes).

1. Start the exercise by bringing our group together, sharing the situation and challenge we are facing, and placing the photo of the people affected by the situation atop a larger image of a swamp. Physical and virtual whiteboards are perfect for this exercise.

2. With the photo mounted well above the image of the swamp, pose the problem or situation again to the team and explain that this is a timed exercise with no bad ideas.

3. Start the 10-minute timer and commence thinking and brainstorming. How will the community and team traverse the swamp? Capture potential and partial solutions on physical or virtual sticky notes or on the whiteboard.

4. As each minute elapses, make a show of pushing the photo of the people affected by the situation deeper into the swamp. You might cut off the bottom of the photo if that's easier. Snip it off! Again, make a show of it to increase the tension in the room or on the call. The community is sinking; the team is failing to rescue the community…

5. Repeat Step 4 again and again, after each minute elapses.

6. When the team stalls, introduce different ways of brainstorming. For example, consider running a super-condensed version of a Worst and Best exercise or a Reverse Brainstorming exercise (both covered in Hour 14) as a way to think differently. Rather than fixing the problem, how might this situation turn even worse? (worse than dying in a swamp? Yes.)

7. Continue updating the visual each minute as the community and team continue to sink deeper. Push the team to consider any kind of solution. Again, capture the proposed solutions on sticky notes or the whiteboard. Show them the impending doom to drive our team to think even more deeply beyond the easy and obvious.

8. Show the photo of the affected people sinking up to their waist…their chest…their neck… their chin…and feel the pressure increase as the primordial ooze reaches their mouths. There are no crazy ideas. Save them!

Consider how time pressure should have helped the team think of seemingly crazy solutions as failure and death became more and more imminent. Running the Swamp gives people the freedom to share potential solutions that they normally would not be inclined to share, ideas that aren't constrained by overthinking and citing all of the "that will never work" excuses. We will come up with a mix of solutions, some untenable and others more practical. Still others will be difficult but potentially workable.

Another unexpected outcome of Running the Swamp includes the empathy it builds for the community that must traverse the swamp. Why? Because we're not watching a project or initiative, or a product or solution, sink into the swamp. Instead, we're watching the *people* we've been asked to shepherd through a situation get swallowed up. And in this way we find the reason and the courage to think in dramatically new ways.

NOTE

What Is a Swamp?

Different parts of the world reflect different kinds of danger. Consider renaming Running the Swamp to something more geo-relevant. For example, this exercise is also known as Beating the Train, Crossing the Quicksand, Crossing the Bridge, Wading the Lake, Zombie Crossing, and similar time-sensitive danger-based analogies. Use the one that fits the situation, the geography, the people, or the problem best.

Design Thinking in Action: Fractal Thinking

In Hour 9, we covered the Pattern Matching exercise for identifying problems and themes and then briefly touched on a special kind of pattern called a fractal. A fractal is "never-ending, infinitely complex and self-similar like a repetitious feedback loop" (Sheedy, 2021). Fractal Thinking, or "vertical" thinking, gives us another unique lens through which to see problems or situations: the *self-similar* patterns that exist at smaller or larger scale, such as similar patterns that really just differ in size. A fractal might be smaller than our problem or larger than our problem, but mathematically speaking it's where X is similar to Y (X ~ Y).

NOTE

Self-Similar Patterns

Remember that when two geometric objects have exactly the same shape (although not necessarily the same size), then they are said to be similar. When a self-similar pattern exists at different scales, they are said to be fractals of one another.

Fractal Thinking, then, is about recognizing and using the relationship between the small and the large to learn and to think differently. Look for a recursive pattern found over and over again in a particular environment or problem set, and then use this at-scale pattern as a high-level blueprint, design, or guide for influencing change. We might actually hypothesize that what is true at one scale is true at a smaller or a larger scale.

Fractals are seen throughout nature, both here on earth and out across the cosmos. In their similarity there may be something that can be learned and applied, as we see in Figure 12.3.

Fractals help us think through and think differently about a situation in the context of change, where the smallest patterns play out in bigger and bigger circles or in smaller and smaller circles. Consider how patterns seen at home play out in the neighborhood and again across the city. Similarly, consider how patterns in a national government party echo at the state and local levels and are repeated in companies, workplaces, teams, and individual perceptions and actions. Fractals are all around us. Understanding them can help us see with fresh eyes and anticipate what might be coming next.

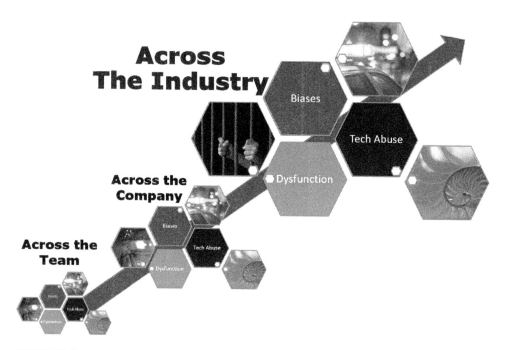

FIGURE 12.3
Fractal Thinking can help us further ideate on a problem as we move beyond traditional patterns and themes and think vertically.

Fractal Thinking helps us find patterns that help us better understand and fill in the gaps of our own pattern of problems. Need examples? Consider these common fractals seen in nature:

▶ The patterns observed in atoms, solar systems, and galaxies

▶ Tree branches subdividing to smaller self-similar tree branches

▶ Circulatory systems giving way to smaller and smaller yet self-similar blood vessels and capillaries

▶ River systems being fed by a repeating set of smaller rivers and tributaries and streams

▶ Sponges and seashells, pinecones, pineapples, and even broccoli

Fractals allow us to predict and plan for the whole puzzle, even when we see only a piece of the puzzle. Conversely, fractals also help us simplify what might first look to be an incredibly complex landscape, problem, or situation. Apply Fractal Thinking atop other forms of thinking and ideation.

Design Thinking in Action: Golden Ratio Analysis

When we look around at the world surrounding us, there are an astonishing number of examples of items that seem to be proportioned just right. From the largest galaxies above to the smallest of plants in the ground, the world is full of examples that just seem to be sized and proportioned in a way that's pleasing. They make sense; they have a certain natural symmetry. But there's nothing obvious that explains why they're pleasing.

In these cases, our observations may be rooted in the fact that the world around us—from galaxies and our solar system to hurricanes and sea shells to strands of DNA and more—reflects a symmetry based on how things naturally grow as captured in the Fibonacci Sequence (which starts 1, 2, 3, 5, 8, 13, 21, 34, 55, 89 and grows ad infinitum).

When we take a closer look at the numbers in the sequence, we observe a simple pattern. For example, 5+8=13 and 8+13=21. Simply add two adjacent numbers, and we arrive at the next number in the sequence. Cells, flowers, storms, and more grow in very specific ways that often map back to this pattern, explaining, for example, why so many flowers have 5 or 8 or 13 or 21 petals, including why the daisy typically has 34 or 55 petals.

Beyond the pattern, there's another number at play that sets the stage for a unique and creative thinking technique: the ratio between the two numbers adjacent to one another. The ratio is 1.6 to 1, and we call this the Golden Ratio. This ratio helps explain why fetuses naturally grow the way they do, why faces are pleasing to the eye, why the iPhone just looks right, and why Microsoft's Azure logo is proportioned just so. Each of these examples reflects the Fibonacci Sequence and more to the point the Golden Ratio. In fact, as we see in Figure 12.4, the world around us has reflected this ratio since the beginning of time. Smart product designers and thinkers realize and use this knowledge. We should too.

Let's say that we need to move a community from Point A to Point B, and a cursory review of the lay of the land just doesn't seem right. Something seems out of whack or doesn't quite look or feel right. We might see issues with the

- ▶ Dimensions of our journey
- ▶ Makeup of our staffing model
- ▶ Sizing of our sprint work items
- ▶ Structure of our team
- ▶ Look and feel of our prototype or user interface
- ▶ Makeup of our communications cadences
- ▶ Profiles of our team from a diversity or experience perspective
- ▶ Specific mix of test cases within our test plans
- ▶ Progression or growth in our risk register

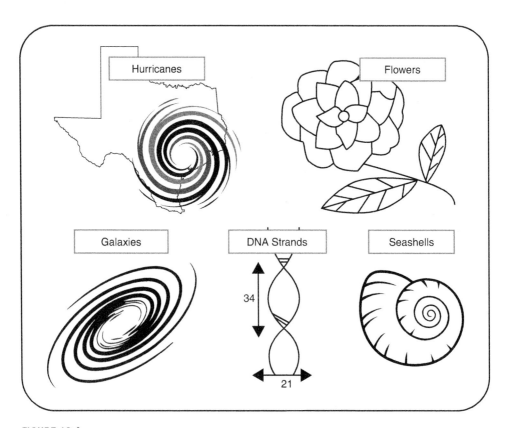

FIGURE 12.4
Use the Golden Ratio as a special lens for uncovering unnatural or less-than-optimized relationships within the dimensions of a problem or situation.

Perhaps we need to consider how the dimensions of the situation or the problem or a potential solution reflect or stray from the Golden Ratio. Perhaps the Golden Ratio can help us validate the natural fit or dimensions of the work in front of us.

In the end, the Fibonacci Sequence does indeed turn out to be the most efficient or practical way for certain organisms or systems of nature to grow and change. Look within our environment, our team, and the processes surrounding us for the natural symmetry reflected in the Golden Ratio. Can we see that ratio at work? Chances are good that if something just feels "off" that the fix might hinge on recognizing and realigning to the Golden Ratio.

Design Thinking in Action: Reverse Brainstorming

Though we cover this technique in more detail later in Hour 14, Reverse Brainstorming and other thinking-in-reverse techniques and exercises are really smart "bolt-ons" for thinking differently, as we see in Figure 12.5. Before we complete any ideation or thinking exercise, we should conclude with a brainstorming-in-reverse exercise and create a new list of ideas reflecting the problem or situation from a completely different perspective: what would make our problem or situation *worse*?

Reverse Brainstorm
1. How could I make this problem worse?
2. How might I have caused this problem?
3. Who might I ignore to make matters worse?

Now Flip our Questions Above
1. How could I make this problem better?
2. How might I solve this problem?
3. Who should I include to help?

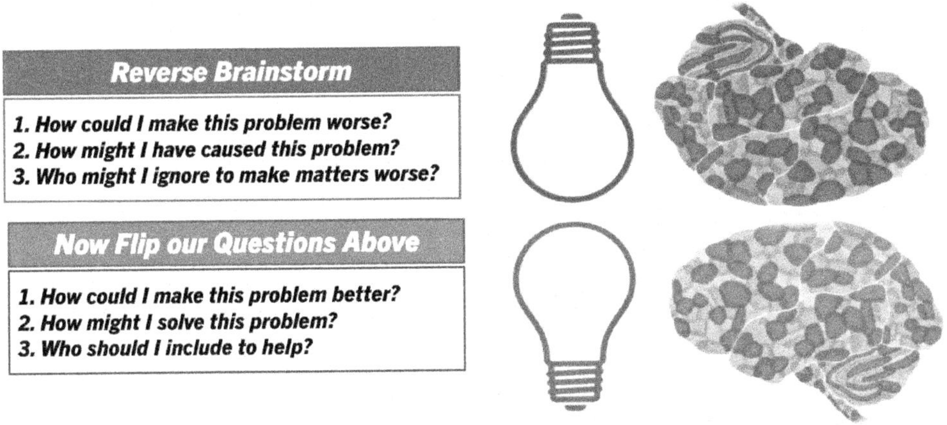

FIGURE 12.5
Consider how flipping our logic and running a Reverse Brainstorming session should conclude traditional brainstorming and most any other ideation or thinking exercise.

And such lists are easy to compile. Why? Because most people are naturally wired to think about what could go wrong. It's one of the few techniques we all use in an almost de facto kind of way. Employed with intention, though, Reverse Brainstorming can give us exactly what we need to think our way out of tough situations: an enormous list of what-not-to-do ideas. With our list in hand of ideas that would make our problem or situation worse, we can then work one by one down the list, flipping each item to transform a what-not-to-do into a possible solution.

For example, if we are faced with a budget shortfall problem, instead of trying to fix this budget problem, we might instead consider what we could do to make our budget problem even worse!

▶ Continue spending more despite already being over budget.

▶ Access next year's budget early.

▶ Take out a short-term loan.

▶ Borrow from other departments.

▶ Steal from other departments.

- ▶ Ignore the problem.

- ▶ Keep the problem to ourselves.

- ▶ Hide the problem using credit cards.

- ▶ Blame the problem on someone else.

- ▶ Creatively adjust the accounting records to remove the problem.

- ▶ Destroy the accounting records.

- ▶ Burn down the building and its records.

- ▶ Find a new job before the shortfall is realized.

With this strong list of what-not-to-do actions, we can turn each action around to compile a list of positive actions that we may have missed in traditional brainstorming.

What Not to Do: Concluding Thinking Too Early

A large systems integrator (SI) found itself in dire straits. Its cash cows had dried up, the sales team had failed to replace those dying revenue streams with new sources of income, and a resulting mass exodus of talent left the SI looking like a shell of its former self. The SI's leadership team employed an outside consultancy to consider and discuss new market prospects, new branding opportunities, and ideas for reinventing the company. Ultimately, an acquisition was orchestrated, the SI was acquired, and a strong legacy of innovation and accomplishment disappeared inside another dying company.

In retrospect, the SI's leaders realized later that the outside consultancy failed to deeply understand and ideate on its behalf. The consultancy missed the fact that the SI was sitting on a gold mine of assets and IP that in several years would be popularly called "cloud computing." It missed the fractals echoing across industry, data center technology, and shared-nothing compute platforms. The outside consultancy never pushed beyond what amounted to surface-level brainstorming to really consider the SI's potential. It failed to fill up an ideation funnel with ideas through divergent thinking techniques. It quit thinking too early, and many paid the price. In the end, the consultancy let down countless shareholders and thousands of people affected by the acquisition, layoffs, and missed market opportunities.

Summary

In Hour 12, we built on the techniques and exercises shared in earlier hours and explored six bolt-on methods for increasing creativity. From Visual and Divergent Thinking to Running the Swamp, Fractal Thinking, Golden Ratio Analysis, and Reverse Brainstorming, we outlined the kinds of thinking and next steps we can use to top off our ideation funnel. Hour 12 concluded with a "What Not to Do" related to missing key opportunities to think divergently and quitting our thinking too early.

Workshop

Case Study

Consider the following case study and questions. You can find the answers to the questions related to this case study in Appendix A, "Case Study Quiz Answers."

Situation

BigBank's Chief Digital Officer, Satish, is seeing too many missed opportunities in the way that the various OneBank initiative leaders ideate and execute. He has asked you to host an ideation workshop to explore different ways of improving the team's creativity and ideation processes.

Quiz

1. Which of the six techniques and exercises is really focused on getting thoughts out of the head and onto paper or a whiteboard as a way to increase shared understanding among a group?

2. Which technique actually consists of many tips and techniques useful for thinking differently?

3. How does a timed exercise such as Running the Swamp drive greater empathy in addition to new ideas?

4. Which technique has us consider patterns playing out at scale below us or beyond us?

5. Which technique asks us to consider how Fibonacci's Sequence might be affecting the natural fit or dimensions of a particular solution?

6. How might the workshop's participants collectively view the six creative thinking techniques and exercises, and in particular how classic brainstorming might be naturally augmented?

Exercises for Reducing Uncertainty

What You'll Learn in This Hour:

▶ Next-Step Thinking for Uncertain Situations

▶ Reducing Uncertainty and Ambiguity

▶ Working Through Uncertainty and What's Next

▶ What Not to Do: The Brute-Force Path

▶ Summary and Case Study

In this hour, we explore a special subset of Design Thinking techniques and exercises useful for reducing uncertainty. After working through Next-Step Thinking and establishing the differences between ambiguity and uncertainty, we learn four ways to move forward with greater certainty than otherwise possible. Then we explore seven techniques or exercises for determining the "next best step" when the path ahead is unclear. Hour 13 concludes with a "What Not to Do" focused on avoiding brute force in the face of ambiguity.

Next-Step Thinking for Uncertain Situations

Like fog, ambiguity hides the path in front of us. When there's really no way to illuminate the whole path, use the exercises in this hour to at least light up the portion of the path just ahead of us. Called Next-Step Thinking, this technique is essentially an "umbrella technique" for a whole collection of tips and exercises that have been used for years to make progress one step at a time.

That's really the goal: to move with intention through the journey, from one step to the next, acknowledging that not every step will be perfect, but every step will add learnings and therefore value. And with our roadmap of short-term, mid-term, and long-term horizons laid out, we can use other techniques covered this hour, such as Buy a Feature and MVP Thinking to build some consensus and make some strong initial progress. But then what? How do we get to that mid-term or next horizon?

To be clear, we probably need to first "control the controllable." And then we need to turn to Next-Step Thinking to think through how to make the jumps between our short-term, mid-term, and long-term horizons. Start with the thought that in between the various horizons or phases of our projects and initiatives lies the opportunity to think through how to

- Preserve and reuse what we (now) know

- Leverage our experiences and what we have accomplished

- Lean on the relationships we have built over time

- Acknowledge and fill in our gaps

- Recognize patterns and opportunities to help others

- Bring the whole of ourselves to a new problem or situation

Next-Step Thinking helps us conceptualize the broader situation, our team's skills, and what's probably needed as a stepping-stone to achieving what's next. Think about what our teams have done, and where, with whom, and how successfully, along with our track record of delivery.

In a more personal context, Next-Step Thinking is also an important part of capitalizing on who we are today, the investments we've made in ourselves, and the ability we have to provide value beyond today.

- Can we earn a promotion in-role by using today's success as an exemplar for why a promotion is merited?

- Can we extend our current success by growing the community we serve?

- Can we work with others to explore and tackle Adjacent Spaces (discussed later this hour) or seek out new ways of creating value?

- Can we grow our skills and reduce our gaps to take our manager's role? Or another leadership role?

- Should we take everything we've learned and accomplished to another organization that needs the kind of help we provide?

Consider the following principles for Next-Step Thinking:

- Become an expert at delivering value with what we have on hand; find success with what we have, who we have, and where we have it.

- The Important is more critical than the Urgent; ensure that the Important is delivered, even as a fast-follower to the Urgent.

- Meet people's needs where they are, and then figure out their next set of needs.

▶ Before moving to the next step or next challenge, take the actions necessary to ensure that solved problems don't devolve back into the old problems.

Most every exercise this hour represents a form of Next-Step Thinking. Let's start with four exercises that can help us take a smart step forward by minimizing the uncertainty, ambiguity, and risks that lay just ahead.

Reducing Uncertainty and Ambiguity

Thinking through less-risky and more-risky outcomes helps us expose areas of uncertainty and ambiguity, which in turn can help us make a smarter next best step. When we're faced with uncertainty, *reduce* that uncertainty the best we can through exercises including Possible Futures Thinking, Aligning Strategy to Time Horizons, Backporting into the Past, and Adjacent Space Exploration. Consider running two or more of these exercises sequentially too, essentially creating a custom recipe for reducing uncertainty.

Design Thinking in Action: Possible Futures Thinking

Jerome C. Glenn created the *Futures Wheel* in 1971, and today a wheel analogy is still a powerful and simple tool for thinking. The wheel and its various forms helps us organize our thoughts around a central idea or event. And as a method of Visual Thinking, this visually oriented Possible Futures Thinking exercise helps us model different versions of the future based on current-day trends or events and the possible consequences of those trends or events.

A Possible Futures Thinking exercise is easily done solo or with a group of people (on a physical or virtual whiteboard or through a tool like Miro or Klaxoon, for example). Use the wheel analogy to view a situation through the lenses of six categories or sections of the wheel. The original version of the *Futures Wheel* aligned these categories or sections to the acronym STEEP (which is another useful taxonomy for thinking in its own right, regardless of the method or tool):

▶ Social

▶ Technology

▶ Economic

▶ Environmental

▶ Political

▶ <and an empty sixth section of our own choosing>

The sixth "insert yours here" section of the wheel is a custom section available to us to categorize based on another dimension, emerging change, or a pattern we wish to think through. If we see more than just one emerging change or pattern, such as an industry trend or a set of cultural realities we wish to consider, we may divide our wheel into eight sections or more. A classic six-section wheel is illustrated in Figure 13.1.

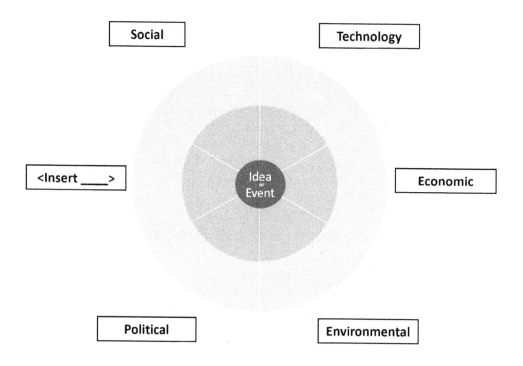

FIGURE 13.1
Use a simple wheel analogy to identify and explore a situation through the lenses of a number of sections or categories.

Now map out the future possibilities and what-ifs related to the intersection of our central idea with each of these dimensions or sections. As we work through the wheel, we should find ourselves thinking about opportunities, identifying risks and constraints, considering how to build consensus, thinking strategically about possible changes and their effects on those possible futures, and more.

Design Thinking in Action: Aligning Strategy to Time Horizons

When the next best step is apparent, the importance of the second and third steps might become more important more quickly than we're prepared to think through. Some say that this leap from the short-term to the mid-term horizon might be the most important too. The midterm is the bridge, after all, connecting what we know and do today (which is probably pretty comfortable for us simply because it's known) to our long-term future that we can plan for and dream about but, frankly, cannot see.

Thus, Aligning Strategy to Time Horizons can become an important tool for thinking ahead by thinking backward (from the future to the present) organized around three steps:

▶ Create the overall Horizon Plan (which is necessarily high level and strategic but subject to the unknowns and therefore a bit aspirational as we look far out into the future).

▶ Create an initiative roadmap or project roadmap to provide more clarity near term (thus creating a mid-level and mid-strategic plan).

▶ Create a Release Plan with an underlying Sprint Plan, and the necessary project plan useful in navigating day-to-day tasks and near-term milestones (keeping details in our DevOps tool so we can keep our project plan as lightweight as possible, ideally focused on high-level milestones and dependencies with other work in flight).

Aligning Strategy to Time Horizons is a visual exercise, using bubbles that we place atop a time horizons template similar to the one displayed in Figure 13.2. Lay out these horizons and plans visually to help consider priorities, what might need to be executed as a prerequisite, what may be executed in parallel, and so on.

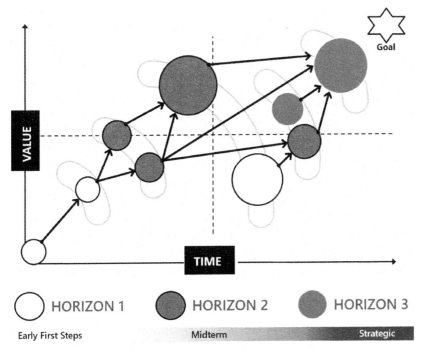

FIGURE 13.2
Use this worked example template to Align Strategy to Time Horizons.

Draw the first bubble in the long-term horizon and label that first bubble with something that describes what needs to be achieved long term. We might label it "Reinvent Our Team" or "Complete the Company's Business Transformation" or "Retire in Ten Years." The time frame—1 year, 4 years, 20 years—isn't as important as dividing the journey into the three big steps or milestones necessary to arrive at the final destination. And if it seems that the exercise highlights four or five steps, so be it! Just add a few more horizons to the template.

The second bubble reflects where we are today; now we have an end-to-end view that simply needs to be fleshed out. Do some thinking to create the third short-term bubble and fourth mid-term bubble. We might realize, for example, that we need to get a particular promotion or role or complete some education before we can pursue our mid-term goal.

If possible, lean on a colleague or friend who has successfully navigated most or all of this journey to help identify the various steps (bubbles) typically taken on this journey. As we identify those bubbles, place them in their respective short-term, mid-term, and long-term locations. Then connect the dots between the bubbles to visually depict stepwise priorities (Step 1, Step 2, Step 3) and dependencies (Step 1 and Step 2 might both need to be completed before we can arrive at Step 3, for example).

Once we finish mapping out the really large milestones on our journey, we might want to revisit those and flesh out the little stepping-stones in between the horizons. Go as deep and detailed as we need, but at some point employ a bit of Good Enough Thinking (Hour 11) and get started taking that important first step!

Combine this exercise with Possible Futures Thinking to consider three or four possible futures to get a better idea of which are the most achievable, most time-consuming, most expensive, most risky, and so on.

Design Thinking in Action: Backporting into the Past

In software development, backporting is "when a software patch or update is taken from a recent software version and applied to an older version of the same software" (CrowdStrike, 2022). We can use this approach to navigate the near term and breathe new life into how we view what's around us and unchangeable. In the name of playing the cards we have been dealt, or putting the team we have on the field, or working with what we know and who we have been given, Backporting into the Past can be exactly the kind of approach we need to reduce uncertainty.

Consider this: Rarely does a tech team have the opportunity to build a solution greenfield, or leverage a new set of platforms and tools, or just start fresh with a clean slate. More often than not we are faced with a massive amount of technical debt, legacy systems, and processes that we need to understand, adapt to in some areas, work around in other areas, and eventually transform.

As a Design Thinking technique, Backporting into the Past is about recognizing today's reality and limited set of choices, and then working within those choices and constraints to make something new happen. It helps us deal with uncertainty because we are not walking into a new situation to change it. Instead, we use what we have in front of us, the team we have to work with, and the skills and experience that we have in this present day—all of which is super valuable—to create options.

How? Let's start with a list:

- Identify the situation. What's unchangeable? What might be changed? Give this some thought and consider Snaking the Drain to clean out old ideas that just aren't viable or waste the time of others trapped by and thinking about them.

- Identify who we are as a subject matter expert. What are we really good at? What are our superpowers? Think through this and document it as a way to further think.

- Do the same with our team. What special set of skills can we collectively claim, what industries do we span, and where are the gaps? Identify the work that we have completed over the years. These experiences do not define who we are, but they are still our basis for credibility and experience spanning people, technology, business, and more. Dig deep and document these items.

- Identify what we love. What are we as individuals and as a team passionate about? What kind of job or role wouldn't even feel like work if we got to do it together 40 hours a week?

- Identify where we can quickly learn something new and where diminishing returns influence that kind of investment in time and energy and cost.

Finally, now comes the creative uncertainty-fighting value of this technique. Consider how we can backport ourselves and our teams into roles or projects similar to those that we have held before and (with our most recent experience and skills) give those new roles or projects fresh life. This Design Thinking technique is not just about narrowing down our choices and options, but about creatively adapting and reusing who and what we are in novel ways (Mittal, 2022). Accelerate to the future faster by injecting our current-day selves into new roles and projects that mirror old roles and projects.

Combine people and teams to create hybrid opportunities and new options. Write down these options! Think on these options solo and together. Brainstorm and Reverse Brainstorm with others to work through the unseen or unspoken. In the end, we should have a strong list of real options, crazy options, and a number of other opportunities in the middle.

Design Thinking in Action: Adjacent Space Exploration for Lower Risks

Can a neighboring future or similar-to-what-we-know option help us find a low-risk next step? Can such a next step serve as a time saver and choice maker? Yes! Instead of striking out in a brand-new direction, we might instead take a few steps down a lower-risk path that's adjacent to what we already know. Pursuing adjacent options or exploring adjacent spaces may not transform our future, but these methods can help us make meaningful progress in the short term.

Oftentimes we apply this method in our careers, building on what we know by moving into new but adjacent spaces; doing so allows us to use what we know, learn the "new" in the adjacent space, and become experts in an even broader surface area, as we see in Figure 13.3.

FIGURE 13.3
Consider how we might navigate Adjacent Spaces throughout our careers as a way to incrementally transform ourselves in a low-risk kind of way.

Companies and organizations do the same thing as they explore incremental markets or make minor progress on the fringe of what they already know and do. This strategy is fine for a while...but eventually what we've focused on and known for years becomes obsolete in some kind of way. Or we grow bored with the known or simply see more opportunity around the known than remaining inside the known.

How might we apply this same "adjacent spaces" mindset to the next release of our application platform or software drops? What can we do to keep our users relatively comfortable while we introduce new capabilities or interface changes?

Loosely based on Stuart Kauffman's perspectives on growth in his book *Investigations* (2002), Adjacent Space Exploration can help us identify areas where we can incrementally grow and iterate on (at least some of) what we already know. Walking out into the unchartered waters or white space *surrounding* what we already know and do today helps us think and take the next steps toward a new but likely familiar future. It's easy because of what remains the same; what we know and what surrounds what we know are more similar than they are different.

Working Through Uncertainty and What's Next

Sometimes we have no choice but to live with and work through the uncertainty in front of us and the ambiguity surrounding us—and we need to figure out and take the Next Best Step. We have covered how Pattern Matching and Fractal Thinking can help us envision what's next, how Adjacent Spaces can reduce the risk of that next step, and how mapping Possible Futures and Aligning Strategies to long-term, mid-term, and short-term Time Horizons can be helpful. But we've only scratched the surface when it comes to techniques and exercises useful for working through uncertainty. In the next several pages, we will cover seven more ways of creating clarity while we take the best step forward.

Design Thinking in Action: "What, So What, Now What?"

Without wallowing in the past, it can be useful to consider what happened, its consequences, and what to do next in light of those consequences. This might not be the best strategic next step, but it helps us navigate the road ahead while we consider other options in parallel.

Sometimes playing a game is the easiest way to work through a problem, especially if we need to make some quick forward progress to get unstuck or just don't have the appetite to get bogged down in petty details. An easy such game is the "What, So What, Now What?" exercise, which can help us learn enough to break free of indecision and move forward.

Management scientists Chris Argyris and Peter Senge, in their *Ladder of Inference* model published in 1990, introduced this approach. The idea is to work through a recent event and view it through the questions and lenses of

1. What? We need to discuss the *what* (that happened) associated with an event.

2. So what? We need to discuss the implications or consequences of the event.

3. And now what? We need to conclude with next steps and possible do-overs.

This simple three-step process is a great exercise for new tech teams, executive committees, and initiative leaders to explore a current problem or situation. "What, So What, Now What?" teaches an uncomplicated way to approach potentially difficult problems or situations. It also opens the door to determining the next best step while having healthy conversations about how to tackle these same situations more effectively in the future.

Design Thinking in Action: MVP Thinking

Many of us are familiar with the term *Minimum Viable Product*, or MVP. An MVP is that earliest version of a capability or product that meets the minimum needs of a person or community. An MVP isn't the best in terms of functions or features, but it's sufficient (and perhaps Good Enough, as we discussed in Hour 11).

Exercising MVP Thinking is nothing more than thinking through what a Minimum Viable Product or capability is in the hands of another. It is also "seed thinking" in the sense that an MVP, like a seed, will become much more when it is cared for, watered, and nurtured.

When we are faced with identifying the next best step, use MVP Thinking to determine if we can either create a simple MVP or elaborate on an existing MVP; either strategy can safely take us to the next step. By way of example, we might feel overwhelmed with a goal such as "get a doctorate" or "start a business" or "reinvent my team." Rather than setting out to achieve that long-term goal, though, consider instead what the MVP looks like for each of these goals. What's the first or next best step to take on each respective journey? By tackling the smaller goal, we are steps closer to achieving the larger and more difficult goal.

How? Carve out the minimum level of achievement, capability, or functionality that gets us to our goal. Call that minimum bar a Minimum Viable Product or MVP and take the first baby step:

▶ Do we want to pursue a doctorate? Use MVP Thinking and start with a one-year or two-year degree.

▶ Do we want to open our own business? Use MVP Thinking and start with a simple Schedule C sole proprietorship.

▶ Do we wish to learn more about e-commerce and websites? Use MVP Thinking and start by volunteering or helping others build a website, or by taking an online or Linked Learning course.

▶ Are we thinking about a career in project management and need some real experience before we can get hired for such a role? Again, use MVP Thinking! Start by running small projects at home, for the church, or for the neighborhood or community. Take some low-cost training from ExpertRating.com and in the process earn a basic project management certification. Call this basic certification our MVP, but don't stop there. Build on this MVP by completing a PMI CAPM certification. And once we meet the required project management experience necessary for certification, study for and pass the PMI PMP certification.

As we see in Figure 13.4, MVP Thinking helps us build on what we know. And MVP Thinking helps us validate along the way that the larger goal is indeed still worth pursuing.

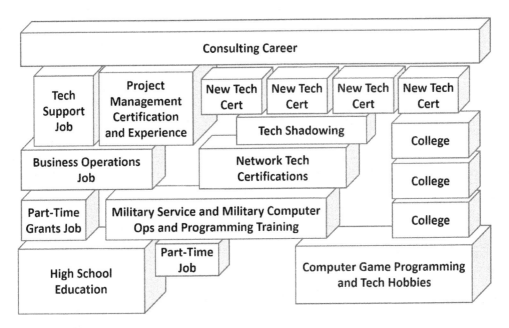

FIGURE 13.4
Use MVP Thinking to build on what we know in a low-risk way while validating along the way that our direction is still worth pursuing.

Design Thinking in Action: 2×2 Matrix Thinking for What's Next

When we need to know which way to go, sometimes it's helpful to dissect two dimensions of a situation such as effort versus time, difficulty versus importance, cost versus effort, and so on. Credited to Alex Lowy and Phil Hood in their 2004 book *The Power of the 2×2 Matrix: Using 2×2 Thinking to Solve Business Problems and Make Better Decisions*, the simple 2×2 matrix has been used for years to help people and teams evaluate a number of options across two dimensions. Considering options in this way can help us uncover the best choice or the ideal path forward. Sometimes called 2×2 Matrix Thinking, this method helps us get moving again with confidence.

Some of the most common uses of 2×2 Matrix Thinking include

▶ Urgency versus Importance (tasks or goals)

▶ Importance versus Difficulty (tasks or goals)

▶ Effort versus Value (tasks or goals)

▶ Cost versus Value (tasks or goals)

▶ Simplicity versus Outcome (tasks or goals)

▶ Power versus Interest (stakeholders)

Starting to use the 2×2 matrix is easy. For example, draw a horizontal line and label this "Importance" (we will call this the horizontal or x-axis), and then draw a vertical line and label this one "Difficulty" (let's call this the vertical or y-axis). Use these two lines as the bottom and left side, respectively, of a box. Divide that box into four smaller boxes like the example in Figure 13.5, and we now have a 2×2 matrix.

FIGURE 13.5
It is easy to draw and use a 2×2 matrix for thinking about two dimensions of a problem or situation. (raywoo/123RF)

Alternatively, simply draw a large plus sign to create a set of four open-ended boxes. And then add an x-axis and a y-axis and label those with the dimension that each axis represents.

While the process of creating and populating the matrix is useful in itself, the real value comes once the matrix is populated. For example, once an Importance versus Difficulty 2×2 matrix is populated, we can see which tasks or goals are the most important *and* the least difficult, and we would probably prioritize those items (and that entire quadrant). Conversely, we would be able to see the tasks and goals that are least important and yet the most difficult to achieve, and we would probably deprioritize those items and that quadrant. And in this way, we would gain more clarity in terms of next steps.

Design Thinking in Action: Bullseye Prioritization

When our team is stuck and we are unable to see a path forward, a special adaptation of 2×2 matrix thinking can prove useful. Called Bullseye Prioritization, this visual method combines a 2×2 matrix overlaid with a bullseye or radar image. Combined, the two images together help us make the next best choice or decision when we are presented with many possible choices or decisions.

The key to this exercise is organization. Bullseye Prioritization helps us organize the choices in front of us into the four quadrants of the matrix, and then within each quadrant organize what's most important, what's second most important, and so on to the team (see Figure 13.6, keeping in mind that each sticky note would include the actual written choice). Visualizing each choice makes this exercise quite intuitive; the closer to the bullseye, the more important the team agrees is the choice or decision.

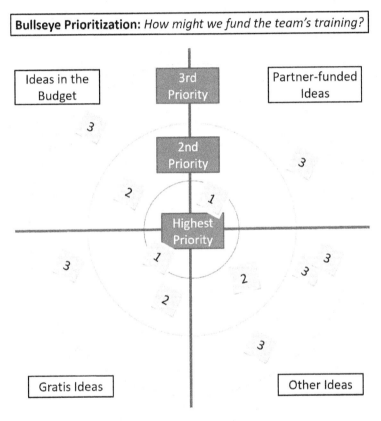

Bullseye Prioritization: *How might we fund the team's training?*

FIGURE 13.6
A quadrant-based bullseye provides two distinct dimensions for insights—one for organizing groups and another for prioritizing the items within those groups.

To execute a Bullseye Prioritization exercise for organizing and prioritizing options, invite our team or an ideation group together and then do the following:

TIME AND PEOPLE: A Bullseye Prioritization exercise requires 5–10 people for 60–120 minutes.

1. Write out the problem or situation on a virtual or physical whiteboard.

2. Off to the side on the whiteboard, round-robin through the team to create a list of options or choices related to the problem or situation. We don't want to start grouping or prioritizing yet! Simply populate this list.

3. Once the list is off to a good start, begin identifying the emerging themes and groupings. Ideally, identify three or four groupings. More is fine, but generally three to four is ideal.

4. Ask the team to label these groupings with a theme. The act of talking through labeling will help drive a shared understanding of each group (and probably help the team identify several more choices or options or list items).

5. Now draw an image of a bullseye (or radar screen or dart board) on the whiteboard and divide the image into four quadrants. Label each quadrant with a theme. Again, it's okay for starters if we have only a couple of themes.

6. Write each option or choice from our list onto a sticky note. We will place these sticky notes on the bullseye or radar screen or dart board image next.

7. Starting with the first sticky note, read it aloud to the team. Together, think about where it belongs on the image in terms of the appropriate quadrant. Place the sticky note in that quadrant and don't worry about its placement relative to the middle of the image (the bullseye) or the outer edge of the image. Simply place it into the appropriate quadrant.

8. Work through the next set of sticky notes, placing them in the appropriate quadrant.

9. As a quadrant becomes a bit crowded, the team might be inclined to start prioritizing the placement of each sticky note relative to the bullseye or center of the image. Fight the urge!

10. When all of the sticky notes are placed, now we can think about each one's importance relative to the other sticky notes in the same quadrant. Adjust how far each is from the center of the radar based on the options near it. If one option is better or more important than another, "promote" the better option closer to the center of the bullseye.

11. As the team discusses and determines one option is worse or less valuable than another, move it out toward the edge of the image. Allow room for the best options to take center stage.

12. Agree on and place the most important options at the center of the image, one sticky note per quadrant.

13. Continue prioritizing, pushing the less important options out further and further from the middle of the radar screen; the further from the middle, the less important the option.

That's it! We may wish to use different forms of democratic voting if too few voices tend to drive the prioritization effort. We need everyone weighing in with their opinions and experiences.

Similarly, if we are faced with ties or choices that are too close to call, we may wish to use another Design Thinking exercise to solve for tiebreakers. Examples of easy tiebreaker exercises include

▶ Use Rose, Thorn, Bud (covered next) to learn more about each option in terms of its positives, negatives, and possibilities.

▶ Use the Five Whys (covered in Hour 9) to better understand each option, starting by asking the team or group "Why is this option the best option in this quadrant?"

▶ Use "How Might We" Questioning (covered generally already and in more detail in Hour 14) to optimistically set the stage for why one option is more achievable or healthier than another option. Use this discussion to reprioritize the options.

Alternatively, if we find ourselves comparing options that sit across only two quadrants (rather than four like we can easily do with the bullseye image-based approach), consider using 2×2 Matrix Thinking. A 2×2 matrix is good for comparing a set of options against two dimensions such as cost versus value, or cost versus difficulty, or importance versus urgency. And to think about a single dimension, such as how the difficulty in implementing or executing a particular option might be reflected in the changes for and changes against that option, look to Force Field Analysis. Both of these exercises are found in Hour 14.

Design Thinking in Action: RTB for Smarter Next Steps

Created by the LUMA Institute in 2012, we use a "Rose, Thorn, Bud," or RTB, exercise to explore a particular choice in detail. The idea here is to organize together the positive, the negative, and the opportunities associated with an option or choice. Each dimension forms a group. We view our option or choice in terms of the roses, thorns, and buds it produces. In doing so, we will find aspects of a situation or choice that are good, others that are holding us back, and still others that might offer an opportunity or way out. More specifically:

▶ Roses are those aspects of an option or choice that are positive, healthy, or working well.

▶ Thorns are those outcomes or consequences that are not positive or healthy.

▶ Buds are the areas of potential; they represent insights and opportunities or areas for improvement. Buds are often the difference makers in choosing one option over another.

To run a simple RTB exercise, follow the steps here:

TIME AND PEOPLE: An RTB exercise requires 3–5 people for 30 minutes or longer depending on the complexity of the situation or landscape.

1. Bring together our team or group, determine whether a physical or virtual whiteboard is appropriate, and explain the situation or problem and the goal: to identify options or choices.

2. Discuss and agree on three unique types of sticky notes (including the use of an icon or emoji) for identifying the positives, negatives, and opportunities. Each unique sticky note will represent one of the three RTB dimensions.

3. Give each person a set of all three sticky notes.

4. Use something similar to the template in Figure 13.7 and ask each person to identify their first rose, thorn, and bud.

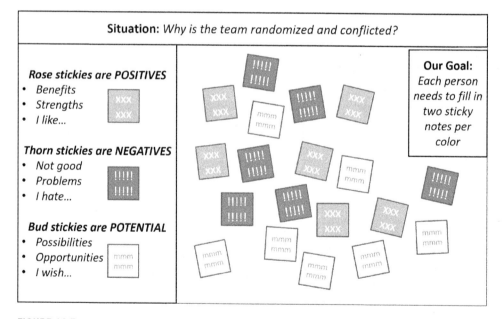

FIGURE 13.7
Use RTB to organize the dimensions of an option or choice along the lines of those that are positive, negative, or represent opportunities.

5. Round-robin through the team or group, giving each person the chance to participate.

6. When everyone has had a chance, repeat the exercise and do so through several loops. The more, the better.

NOTE

Roses Are Red, Right?

Be careful using color in an RTB exercise. Of course, we know that color isn't always the best choice for visualizing because it can exclude people with color and other visual impairments. But in the case of an RTB exercise, the most commonly used colors can cause confusion. For example, the color red often means stop or danger, but in an RTB exercise a red rose reflects something "positive." Similarly, green often means go or progress or something healthy, but in an RTB exercise, green reflects the color of stems and thorns, which are a "negative." One solution? Stick with icons and emojis instead!

Several themes will emerge in an RTB exercise, and a quick look at these themes may be enough to guide a team or group to make a choice. But in cases where multiple themes emerge, we might go back and run a Bullseye Prioritization exercise or turn instead to our next exercise, Affinity Clustering.

Design Thinking in Action: Affinity Clustering for Pattern Finding

Sometimes we are faced with so much data and so many possibilities for next steps that we just don't know how to go about sorting through and understanding what is in front of us. And doing nothing obviously doesn't help us make progress. Fortunately, we have several techniques available to provide more clarity, including the LUMA Institute's Affinity Clustering approach (LUMA, 2012).

Affinity Clustering helps us see the logical groups or clusters of options in front of us, which can help us make some initial choices and smarter next best steps. And through the exercise itself, Affinity Clustering naturally reduces some of the uncertainty surrounding seemingly complex situations.

How does Affinity Clustering work? Let's say we have recently graduated college and have dozens of options available to pursue now. Use an Affinity Clustering exercise to first sort through the options based on similarity (rather than getting bogged down looking at each option individually). For example, we might determine we have options related to the military, joining one of several small start-ups, joining one of several more established firms, striking out on our own, helping with one of the family businesses, pursuing a graduate degree, taking some time off to travel before diving into the workplace, or settling down and raising a family. We might combine several of these options as well and introduce hybrids such as working part time or pursuing a graduate degree part time or raising a family and working on our career full time.

Regardless of the myriad of choices, organize them into clusters or groups, as we see in Figure 13.8. We might organize our options around three clusters; for example, based on work, education, and personal themes.

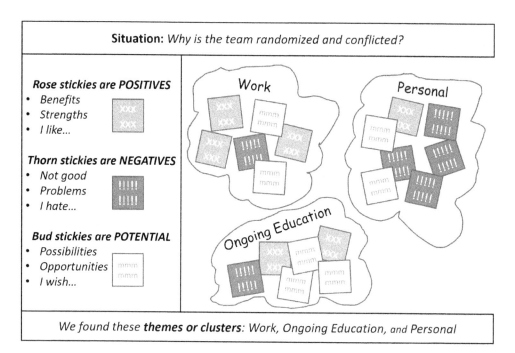

Situation: *Why is the team randomized and conflicted?*

Rose stickies are POSITIVES
- *Benefits*
- *Strengths*
- *I like...*

Thorn stickies are NEGATIVES
- *Not good*
- *Problems*
- *I hate...*

Bud stickies are POTENTIAL
- *Possibilities*
- *Opportunities*
- *I wish...*

Work

Personal

Ongoing Education

*We found these **themes or clusters**: Work, Ongoing Education, and Personal*

FIGURE 13.8
We may find the next best step after we organize and cluster the options in front of us.

Conversely, we might use our Pattern Matching skills to find other, less-obvious connections between our options. For example, we might create clusters or groups that are aligned by geography (options that keep us near our family, others that keep us in the state or region, and still others that are travel-based or international). We might create clusters or groups that are organized around the notion of family too (such as family-friendly options, family-neutral options, and anti-family-friendly options).

Design Thinking in Action: Buy a Feature for Consensus

When all else fails and we don't have a clear next step ahead of us, we still probably need to do *something*—some kind of next step. In this case, it's smart to gain a certain amount of consensus to move in some kind of direction with some level of unity. Use LUMA Institute's Buy a Feature exercise to prioritize and drive this consensus.

The premise for Buy a Feature is simple: The team needs to pull together a list of features, or next best steps, or options, and then align on the priority of the items in this list. They align not by words, though, but with imaginary money a la "put your money where your mouth is." If a feature or next step or option is important to many people, it will probably be given the most budget, and they come out as the clear winner. In this way, Buy a Feature draws out what each team member truly values rather than what they might *say* they value. The money does the talking.

Note that Buy a Feature typically requires that all team members are equal and are given an imaginary $100 budget (we can change the rules, of course, and give our product manager or VP of Sales more money and hence more voter "weighting," but it's generally a good idea to keep everyone equal). Each team member is asked to allocate their imaginary money across the compiled list (of different features, or next best steps, or options). In some cases, it's better to allocate these budgets anonymously, whereas in other cases the exercise leader might wish for all participants to see one another's choices.

Whether they are passionate or on the fence about an item, a person may choose to drop their whole wad of faux cash on a single item in the list, or they may choose to spread their money around. And they may be swayed as we mentioned earlier. The choice is theirs.

And just like in the real world, unless budgets are allocated anonymously, this method creates a certain amount of tension. People tend to pair up or group up to use their influence, power, and budget to drive a choice. We need to take these kinds of actions into consideration, and further we need to take the steps necessary to drive unity again after such an exercise! It's only consensus if everyone agrees to abide by the outcome after all.

What Not to Do: The Brute-Force Path

The most difficult circumstances often lead to the most brash decisions. Sometimes these decisions are exactly what an organization needs to avoid analysis paralysis. But consider the example of a national wholesaler faced with several different "next best steps." Instead of working through these and prioritizing them with her experienced team using Bullseye Prioritization or Affinity Clustering, or gaining some level of consensus through exercises such as "What, So What, Now What?" or Buy a Feature, a fairly new mid-level executive decided the fate of the company unilaterally. She decided that the path through personal uncertainty and broader companywide and industry ambiguity was to charge ahead in a brute-force kind of "get out of the way and follow me" manner.

The executive believed in making decisions quickly but did so without the benefit of others' hard-earned experiences, expertise, and insight. She took her team down a brute-force path hoping that the journey would lift the fog and clear away the uncertainty. Instead, she lost her key leaders and six months later found herself explaining her strategy in an exit interview. "Just Do It" might be great for advertising slogans, but it is rarely the right approach when the next step is shrouded in uncertainty.

Summary

In Hour 13, we explored eleven techniques and exercises helpful in reducing uncertainty and clarifying the "Next Best Step." Along the way we explored the differences between ambiguity and uncertainty as we applied Possible Futures, Aligning Strategy to Time Horizons, Backporting into the Past, and Adjacent Spaces. Then we reviewed a collection of methods for prioritization, grouping patterns and themes, gaining consensus, and more. The hour concluded with a "What Not to Do" focused on traveling the unknown path through sheer brute force.

Workshop

Case Study

Consider the following case study and questions. You can find the answers to the questions related to this case study in Appendix A, "Case Study Quiz Answers."

Situation

While BigBank seems to be making progress across many fronts around the world, there are still key OneBank initiatives fumbling with restarts, replanning, and poorly executed next steps. Satish heard you talking about several techniques and exercises for navigating uncertainty and ambiguity. He would like you to chat with and answer the questions of several OneBank initiative leaders.

Quiz

1. How would you explain the difference between uncertainty and ambiguity in a single short sentence?

2. What technique or exercise might help a team look into the future and assess that future against a broad taxonomy of areas such as technology or economic factors?

3. If an organization wants to capitalize on what it already knows and what it already does but still transform itself incrementally, what technique covered this hour would be appropriate?

4. In what two ways does Bullseye Prioritization help a team figure out next steps?

5. Of the three horizons, which is said to be the most difficult to envision or achieve?

6. Which technique covered this hour might be useful for creating consensus when the next best step is elusive, and the team seems wishy-washy in what option they truly support?

HOUR 14
Thinking for Problem Solving

Over the last several hours, we have covered more than 20 Design Thinking techniques and exercises useful for thinking differently. To be clear, the eight techniques and exercises covered in this hour will also help us think and ideate. But with our Ideation Funnel brimming with ideas, we can turn the corner from thinking divergently to thinking a bit more convergently—that is, with an eye toward narrowing down and refining and potentially solving the problem in front of us. Hour 14 concludes with a "What Not to Do" story and implications when we skimp on Brainstorming.

From Ideas to Potential Solutions

The techniques and exercises across this hour will help us bridge the gap from divergent thinking to problem solving and exploring potential solutions. In subsequent hours, we will refine these potential solutions into partial or full solutions. For starters, let's take a look at the first five methods for problem solving.

Design Thinking in Action: "How Might We?" for Problem Solving

As highlighted briefly in Hour 4, "How Might We?" for problem solving has been used for years to create a safe place for ideation and problem solving. This technique reflects an optimistic attitude useful for bringing together people and teams to ideate and solve problems.

▶ **How.** This opening word opens the door to problem solving, suggesting that a solution is indeed possible.

▶ **Might.** This simple word tells the team that any idea is worthy of consideration. It opens the door for exploration without forcing people to consider only ideas that will solve the problem.

▶ **We.** This final word sets the stage for collaboration. It says that this problem-solving exercise is not unilateral but rather to be done together, as a team.

▶ **?.** By formatting this Design Thinking technique into an interrogative sentence, we let people know that the question has yet to be answered. This approach encourages people to think creatively, to explore the situation, and to consider what might not otherwise be considered.

"How Might We?" is optimistic and inclusive thinking. It reflects the true spirit of Design Thinking. And as we shared in Hour 4, "How Might We?" is perfect for gathering perspectives, driving ideation, solving problems, and ultimately making progress.

Design Thinking in Action: Brainstorming

Often considered the father of thinking differently, exploring problems, and solving problems, Alex Osborn popularized brainstorming in 1953 (Besant, 2016). Brainstorming is an interesting ideation approach in that it results in divergent thinking as well as convergent thinking. We could therefore have included it much earlier in Hours 10 or 11, but as a method for converging and problem solving, it also made sense to save it for this hour.

We have all brainstormed at one time or another. At face value it seems like a simple way to think deeply about a problem or situation. But Brainstorming is not easy to do well. IDEO (2022) has shared a stepwise process for running an effective brainstorming exercise, the core of which is reflected here alongside methods for augmenting and improving the session through participant preparation, guardrails for thinking differently and deeply, and more. Note that we should be building on the work we completed to identify the right problem (Hour 9) so that we're sure we are not getting together to solve the wrong problem.

To run an effective Brainstorming session, execute the following steps:

TIME AND PEOPLE: A Brainstorming exercise requires 5–10 people for 15–120 minutes depending on the complexity of the issues or areas being explored. We may choose to run several Brainstorming sessions sequentially.

1. Pull together a diverse team of people to brainstorm, using Diversity by Design principles outlined in Hour 4 to maximize the team's variety in how it thinks and ideates. Diversity of thought, experience, education, culture, time with the organization, type of role, perspective in terms of stakeholder representation, and more are all important to facilitating a good Brainstorming session.

2. Prior to meeting, share the Problem Statement and situation to be brainstormed. The team would have likely been involved earlier in Problem Identification exercises such as Problem Tree Analysis or Problem Framing (all of which are covered in Hour 9); ensure the team has this background.

3. It may be useful to share in advance with the team what the most current research or our organization's most recent experiences reveal about this problem or situation.

4. Alternatively, consider *not* sharing the problem or situation earlier. Traditional Brainstorming benefits from advance notice, but too much advance notice can create a situation where people walk in "with the answers."

5. Upon meeting, state aloud to the team that curiosity is the goal; no idea is too crazy, and nothing is off the table.

6. Before starting the actual Brainstorming exercise, consider running a creative warm-up to get people thinking (turn to Hour 10 for warm-up ideas, including taxonomies, divergent thinking tips and techniques, and more).

7. Commence the actual Brainstorming exercise using the "How Might We?" technique. For example, we might start the session with "How might we improve our software development factory in ways that improve code quality?"

8. As we facilitate the Brainstorming exercise, consider the following:

   ▶ If the team seems to already have preconceived ideas and solutions, consider clearing or unclogging the mind with a Snaking the Drain or Sacrificing the Calf exercise.

   ▶ Transition to solo Brainstorming, where each person individually considers ideas and potential solutions. It can be useful to ask each participant to document their ideas using sticky notes.

   ▶ It may be necessary to remind the team every so often that there is no bad idea when it comes to Brainstorming.

   ▶ After solo Brainstorming for 10 minutes or another agreed-upon period of time, create a number of diverse groups to consider their individual ideas. Group ideation can up-level the solo Brainstorming outcomes.

   ▶ Make sure the groups are sharing their ideas and building on one another's ideas within the group, taking care to ensure that all voices are being heard and considered.

9. Using sticky notes, document and share the ideas that came out of the group Brainstorming sessions. Consider adding to this collection of sticky notes the individual Brainstorming outcomes as well (to get *all* of the ideas on a virtual or physical whiteboard, for example).

10. Consolidate the ideas using Affinity Clustering (outlined in Hour 13) to create clusters or groups of similar ideas.

11. Discuss the ideas, organizing them further into potential solutions, partial solutions, and perhaps other groups to be explored further.

12. Schedule and run follow-up Brainstorming sessions as needed, gathering feedback along the way while incorporating new ideas through virtual team and community Brainstorming.

There are dozens of additional techniques we might employ to make our time spent Brainstorming even more productive. For example:

▶ We might wish to use a *keyword* as a lens through which to see the problem or situation. If we are thinking through a code quality situation with our team, for example, we might say, "Let's think about this situation through the lens of velocity." Adding a keyword adds a bit of complexity, but like the guardrails for thinking that we covered across Hour 11, a keyword can also help people think differently and more deeply.

▶ We might wish to approach this session as an initial learning session and say, "Let's think about this problem or situation in terms of what we first need to learn or know before we think through it more deeply and decide together what to do about it."

▶ We need to be prepared with additional mini-exercises when the team hits a dead-end in its thinking. One of the many guardrails for thinking covered in Hour 11, for example, can help us refocus or reinvigorate our Brainstorming session.

▶ We should also build in a mini-exercise where we look at the problem or situation (or even potential solutions) through the lens of "opposite thinking." Two types of these exercises, Worst and Best and Reverse Brainstorming, are covered later this hour.

▶ Mission Impossible, Visual, Fractal, Good Enough, and other forms of thinking differently covered in the last several hours, including SCAMPER, covered next, can add a thoughtful dimension to our Brainstorming sessions and help reinvigorate a session that has stalled or gone off the rails.

Remember that perfect or complete solutions are not all that likely during Brainstorming, and they are frankly not the goal. Any ideas that yield potential solutions are typically the best we can do in the short term. But it's these new ideas and potential solutions that give us our starting point. Combined, these Brainstorming outcomes give us a foundation for prototyping and solutioning covered in the next hour.

Design Thinking in Action: SCAMPER for Better Brainstorming

SCAMPER is another exercise that's been around for years, and it is often underrated in terms of its usefulness to help solve difficult problems. Bob Eberle (2008) created SCAMPER as a way to spark greater creativity during brainstorming sessions. This method provides participants with a stepwise way for improving how we brainstorm.

SCAMPER is an acronym for the following seven activities: (S) substitute, (C) combine, (A) adapt, (M) modify (or sometimes magnify), (P) purpose or put to another use, (E) eliminate or minimize, and (R) reverse or rearrange. Each keyword represents a question we can ask as we run through a Brainstorming session, as we see in Figure 14.1. We may also use SCAMPER as a lighthearted problem-specific precursor technique before running an actual Brainstorming session.

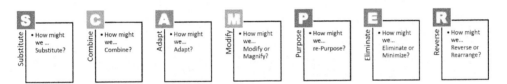

FIGURE 14.1
Use SCAMPER as a useful taxonomy for Brainstorming in a prescribed yet time-proven way.

To run a SCAMPER exercise, walk a team through the following seven activities using the keyword in the form of a question. Phrase each question along the lines of "How Might We?" to create an optimistic and creative ideation exercise.

In the following example, we walk through the code quality issue outlined previously this hour:

▶ **Substitute.** How might we substitute one part or aspect of our code development service or solution with another? Consider how we could substitute a part of the process without affecting the entire development lifecycle, or inject a smarter alternative, or simplify the process. Perhaps we could outsource the code review process, for example, or replace one development team with a partner development team.

▶ **Combine.** How might we combine or merge parts of our code development process together? Should we partner with another organization to yield higher-quality outcomes? Perhaps we could combine manual and automated testing to create better code or combine our development team with our business analysts to drive greater functional understanding before a piece of code is ever even developed.

▶ **Adapt.** How might we adapt our process or the components of our process to yield a better outcome? What should we change or adjust to drive greater predictability or process transparency? For example, perhaps we could improve our DevOps processes to give us a real-time window into the code development process.

▶ **Modify.** How might we modify the code development process to drive greater throughput, higher quality, and improved transparency? Would there be an opportunity to innovate or improve our code quality if our team doubled in size or the market for our code doubled in size?

▶ **Purpose (or Put to another use).** How might we use our code development process in other parts of our organization or with our partners and customers? Should we pursue a co-innovation (see the following note) or co-development strategy? Perhaps we could borrow the quality and compliance processes used in other parts of our business and apply them to our code development factory.

▶ **Eliminate or Minimize.** What aspects of our code development process could we eliminate entirely? Are we running redundant processes? What if we lost half our team or half our market? For example, we might replace most of our manual code testing with automated testing.

▶ **Rearrange or Reverse.** How might we rearrange the steps in our current process to yield a better outcome? Should we left-shift or move a portion of our testing to somewhere earlier in the development cycle? If we worked backward from the end result to when the team received the request to develop a set of code, is there an opportunity to do something smarter? For example, should our developers be more engaged with predevelopment requirements gathering before they ever even see a functional specification?

NOTE

Co-Innovation

One way of delivering business value faster is through co-innovation. The idea is to develop solutions and deliverables together with our partners, users, team members, or others in real time side by side, rather than going back and forth between iterative defining, ideating, prototyping, demonstrating and testing, ideating again, eventually building the solution or deliverable, and so on. Co-innovation breaks down the walls and seams between people and organizations, illustrating yet another example where joint design can drive faster business value (Gay, 2016).

SCAMPER provides a team with several benefits:

▶ It naturally helps us find the gaps and holes within the Problem Statement of the situation being explored.

▶ It serves as another useful taxonomy (as outlined in Hour 10) that we can use in our Brainstorming process, especially if the team is stalled or unable to think differently enough.

▶ It gives us another strong way of improving our Brainstorming process and its outcomes.

We might even consider our Brainstorming incomplete without running a brief SCAMPER mini-exercise before concluding a Brainstorming session. Similarly, we should consider the next two Design Thinking exercises in the same way, as a natural extension to Brainstorming. Both of these next two methods build on the "R" in SCAMPER and help us think more deeply about a situation by considering it "in reverse."

Design Thinking in Action: Worst and Best Ideation

The Worst and Best thinking-in-reverse ideation exercise is effective and quite simple. The method is one of several opposite thinking exercises. It is more lighthearted than the others, though, and is intended to drive initial discussions with groups and people who are unfamiliar with one another and may be uncomfortable thinking so "differently."

Worst and Best is drawn from the *Worst Possible Idea* method shared by Interaction-Design.org (2022). Instead of putting people on the spot to spout forth brilliant idea after brilliant idea, each participant is given a situation or problem and simply asked to share what would make this situation or problem even worse. That's it! A single "worst idea" from each participant is all we need, as we see in Figure 14.2.

Problem: <u>Missing Users in Design Sessions!</u>

Worst Ideas:
1. Forget who they are
2. Intentionally ignore them
3. Only invite their manager
4. Design without anyone
5. Randomly select users
   from the overall team

New Best Ideas:
1. _____
2. _____
3. _____
4. _____
5. _____

FIGURE 14.2
For simple thinking-in-reverse, run a Worst and Best exercise with a team and start with the "worst ideas," as illustrated here.

Direct the participants to avoid overthinking this exercise. This should be easy: share the worst idea that comes to mind and enjoy listening to others' horrible ideas. Goofy and crazy ideas are gold, as they help get the participants more comfortable thinking outside of the norms, which will yield more interesting and better ideas later in this exercise.

We might visually organize these worst ideas into a continuum of bad to really bad ideas. Alternatively, we might also create a simple 2×2 matrix, as we covered last hour, and place these worst ideas in one of the four quadrants. Think about dimensions such as ease of implementation versus cost, or viability versus practicability, or importance versus difficulty (remember that in a "worst" exercise, the worst quadrant will likely be overflowing while the others are fairly empty).

Once we have had everyone share their worst ideas and placed them on the continuum or a 2×2 matrix, we are ready for the really useful part of this exercise. Like we do in Reverse Brainstorming, "flip" each worst idea on its head to create a "best" idea, document these best ideas, and populate the 2×2 grid with these best ideas, as we see in Figure 14.3. If we find that a "worst" idea yields two or three best ideas, that is even better.

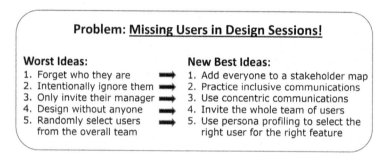

Problem: <u>Missing Users in Design Sessions!</u>

Worst Ideas:
1. Forget who they are ➡
2. Intentionally ignore them ➡
3. Only invite their manager ➡
4. Design without anyone ➡
5. Randomly select users ➡
   from the overall team

New Best Ideas:
1. Add everyone to a stakeholder map
2. Practice inclusive communications
3. Use concentric communications
4. Invite the whole team of users
5. Use persona profiling to select the
   right user for the right feature

FIGURE 14.3
For simple thinking-in-reverse, now opposite-flip each Worst idea into a Best idea.

With the team comfortable thinking in reverse, we may wish to repeat the exercise a la Reverse Brainstorming covered next.

Design Thinking in Action: Reverse Brainstorming

As we mentioned in previous hours and covered at length in Hour 12, Reverse Brainstorming, or brainstorming in reverse, gives us another creative way to brainstorm and think differently. This method was outlined by D. Straker in 2012 and conceptualized earlier by others. Reverse Brainstorming helps us uncover new ideas, identify new risks and stakeholders, find novel solutions and challenges, and turn problems into potential solutions.

When our Brainstorming sessions just don't seem to be adequate, consider appending those sessions with a Reverse Brainstorming exercise. Like Worst and Best, this exercise helps us solve problems by ideating and connecting the problem-to-potential-solution dots in new kinds of ways. It fills up our Ideation Funnel, giving us not only more ideas but more potential solutions.

As we have already seen, the premise of Reverse Brainstorming is simple: What would make things worse rather than better? Consider what would make our problem or situation worse. We might even ask ourselves what might make our potential *solution* worse. Then flip our answers to identify a list of new ideas that might actually make things better.

Noted previously, this approach is sometimes called Opposite Thinking. And it's easy to do because, as we shared in Hour 12, it is easy to create a long list of things that could go wrong or make a problem or situation worse. Why? Because many people are naturally wired to think deeply about how things can get worse rather than get better. And that's the beauty of Reverse

Brainstorming. Like our Worst and Best exercise, it's easy to think of the bad and the worst in a situation.

Of course, the value in this exercise isn't in finding those bad ideas. After thinking through what would make a problem or situation worse, we need to flip those answers to think anew about how to make things better. Cycle through this process of uncovering bad ideas and converting them into good ideas and potential solutions until we have the basis for several potential solutions. And consider the visual exercises next to bring further clarity to our problem solving.

Visual Exercises for Problem Solving

While the previous five techniques and exercises are great tools for problem solving, there's nothing quite like a visual exercise to help us conceptualize and literally "see" a partial solution or an area worth exploring further.

Design Thinking in Action: Building to Consider and Converge

As we have outlined in previous hours, creating a model or building a mock-up or prototype on paper or a whiteboard can help us think in new ways. Using our hands can also help us converge on one or a few best ideas as we transfer our thoughts and potential solutions from our minds out into the open where we and others can consider those thoughts and potential solutions.

The idea? Building to Consider and Converge is easy: draw, outline, build, organize, consider, and discuss, in any order and recursively as the need arises. These are the kinds of steps that allow us to move from divergent thinking to convergent solutioning and perhaps back and forth as we crystallize our problem solving around a potential solution. And when this free-form kind of convergent ideation and partial solutioning is inadequate, consider two other visualization techniques for problem solving: Force Field Analysis and Mind Mapping, covered next.

Design Thinking in Action: Force Field Analysis for Visualizing

Sometimes visually laying out the forces for a change and the forces against a change can help us see a problem differently. Created by Kurt Lewin in 1951 as a tool for the social sciences, a Force Field Analysis, or FFA, helps us visualize a situation and the pressure for and against changing that situation.

Reasons surrounding uncertainty or priorities can come to light through an FFA. A Force Field Analysis helps us see the forces in action around a proposed change, the pushing against and pulling away. And because this analysis is visual, as we see in Figure 14.4, it is easier to create a shared understanding with others than by simply using words alone.

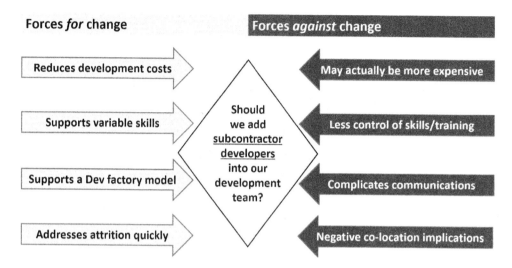

FIGURE 14.4
Visualizing the forces for a proposed change and the forces against a proposed change can help us think more deeply about that change.

A Force Field Analysis is more than just a pros/cons list. The idea is that we are organizing a view of the forces for change and the forces against change (or for maintaining the status quo). Forces could be financial, political, social, strategic, and more. We might also think of this exercise in terms of "why a change should take place" versus "why a change should be avoided." Use a popular taxonomy like those used in SCAMPER, AEIOU, STEEP used in the Futures Wheel, or a risk taxonomy used in a Boats and Anchors exercise if we find a team struggling to think deeply enough.

Pull together materials including data, verbatims, and information we have collected through research, listening to others, the experiences of others, and our own observations to create this list of forces for change and forces against change. Lean on the techniques and exercises covered throughout our earlier hours, using their outputs as inputs to this exercise.

To show the relative strength or priorities of the forces for and the forces against a proposed change, we might size or number or color-code the forces differently. If there are many forces to consider, we might even rank or order the most powerful positive and negative forces using an Affinity Clustering or other prioritizing exercise outlined previously in Hour 13.

Design Thinking in Action: Mind Mapping

Mind Mapping is another common technique used across business and elsewhere to brainstorm, think, drive clarity, and eventually create a shared understanding of a problem or idea. Created by Tony Buzan (2017) in the 1970s, the resulting Mind Map from a Mind Mapping exercise gives us a visual representation as we explore and better understand a problem or idea.

Mind Mapping functions by linking a central problem, idea, or solution to another tier of ideas or dimensions, dependencies, people, and so on, followed by linking a third set of ideas or dimensions to the previous tier, and so on. As we branch out from the central idea or core problem, the process of Mind Mapping to create a Mind Map gives us an increasingly better understanding of our central problem or idea. The process externalizes not only the "lay of the land" for us in detail, but it helps us think and problem solve in ways we could never do if our thinking remained internalized inside our heads.

For example, if we have a problem with managing our team's time, we might create a time management Mind Map to arrive at a set of ideas, one of which might include delegation (as we see in Figure 14.5). As we further flesh out this delegation idea, we might think about what and where and to whom we could actually delegate. These areas might in turn drive us to explore the 50 tasks associated with items our team has been asked to work on. And this set of tasks could further drive our thinking about which ones we could indeed hand off to others, which ones we should keep within the team, and so on. Finally, as we consider tasks that we could delegate and to whom, we might consider how we assign those tasks, whether or not we need to pay someone to do them, how we will manage the completion of those tasks, and more.

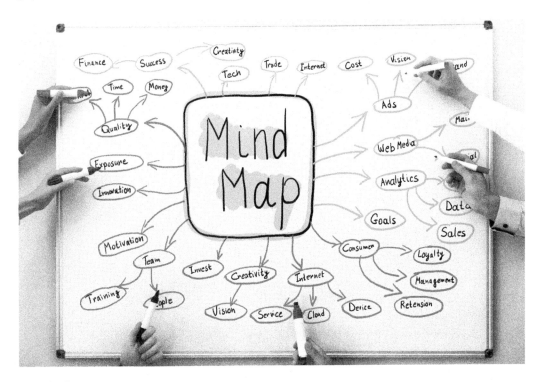

FIGURE 14.5
Creating a simple Mind Map can give us problem solving insights difficult to achieve nonvisually.
(andreypopov/123RF)

What Not to Do: Skimp on Brainstorming

When a small defense contractor ran into problems, the innovation team did what it always did: gave lip service to Brainstorming and afterward set out on a premature path that only made sense at a surface level. The defense contractor's list of misses was impressive in a disappointing kind of way. They gave little advance warning of the session to its participants, didn't actually think more than 15 minutes about the problem despite scheduling an hour, didn't consider diversity of thought or experience in terms of those who participated, didn't use SCAMPER or another taxonomy to brainstorm deeply and differently, didn't consider warm-ups or guardrails to facilitate thinking beforehand or during the session, and didn't conclude their Brainstorming session with any kind of opposite or Reverse Brainstorming. The team simply showed up, discussed the problem, arrived at several cursory conclusions, and chose a path forward. Today, it's no wonder the organization and its people have dispersed to the four winds. The defense contractor is only a memory, a footnote in the pages of history now.

Summary

This hour concluded a series of five hours dedicated to thinking differently, driving creativity, working through risks, reducing uncertainty and ambiguity, working through uncertainty to determine the next best step, and problem solving. Hour 14 in particular featured seven techniques and exercises useful for helping us move along from problem statements to ideas and potential solutions. We covered "How Might We?" questioning and classic Brainstorming in detail, SCAMPER-informed Brainstorming, Worst and Best and Reverse Brainstorming for opposite thinking, Building to Consider and Converge, and then Force Field Analysis and Mind Mapping for visual problem solving. We concluded this hour with a "What Not to Do" focused on a real-world outcome of thinly covered and poorly executed Brainstorming.

Workshop

Case Study

Consider the following case study and questions. You can find the answers to the questions related to this case study in Appendix A, "Case Study Quiz Answers."

Situation

The Executive Committee (EC) of BigBank has for many years considered itself effective in considering and solving problems. The committee learned of your detailed approach to Brainstorming, though, and has asked if you would entertain questions related to how to run more effective Brainstorming sessions. To help facilitate the EC's request, Satish has arranged a Q&A session for you to answer the committee's questions.

Quiz

1. How would you recommend the Executive Committee select and prepare participants for Brainstorming?

2. How should each Brainstorming session begin?

3. When a Brainstorming session seems stalled or derailed, how do you recommend the Executive Committee reinvigorate the team's ability to focus or think?

4. What does SCAMPER mean, and how is it useful?

5. How should the Executive Committee conclude its Brainstorming sessions in a way that helps ensure every rock has been turned over and considered?

PART IV

Delivering Value

HOUR 15

Cross-Teaming and Communicating for Outcomes

What You'll Learn in This Hour:

▸ Cross-Boundary Teaming for Collaboration

▸ Techniques for Working Across Teams

▸ Techniques for Communications Challenges

▸ What Not to Do: Using Words When a Picture Is Needed

▸ Summary and Case Study

Hour 15 commences Part IV, "Delivering Value," where we focus on Phase 3 of our Design Thinking Model for Tech (see Figure 15.1). Phase 3 takes us on a journey exploring how to deliver value early by using prototyping methods that help us learn to rapidly create our initial solutions. Afterward we cover techniques for starting fast by prototyping and solutioning in small ways, and later we cover how to deliver value more quickly. Here in Hour 15, however, we need to further cement our ability to work within and across other teams through techniques for collaborating, cross-teaming, and communicating more effectively. In this context, we cover four Design Thinking techniques for working across teams and another three techniques for working through communications challenges. A "What Not to Do" focused on exclusively using words when a picture is desperately needed concludes this hour.

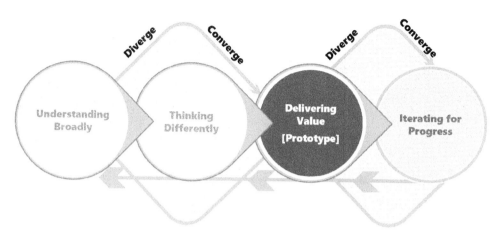

FIGURE 15.1
Phase 3 of our Design Thinking Model for Tech.

Cross-Boundary Teaming for Collaboration

Very few things worthwhile or enduring can be successfully completed solo, particularly in the world of complex tech initiatives and business transformations. Such work requires collaborative *cross-boundary teaming*, or simply *cross-teaming*, to deliver against a difficult-to-achieve set of committed benefits and other valuable outcomes. Project teams, product development teams, workplace initiatives, and so on can rarely be successful without effective cross-teaming.

But what makes an effective project or product team? How might we effectively connect multiple teams to one another in a way that promotes collaboration without stifling innovation and killing progress? And how might we create a healthy work climate across the entirety of a project or initiative wherein people bring out the best in one another within and across their individual teams while getting the job done?

As we will cover in the following pages, effective cross-teaming requires talented individuals who are not only capable of *doing* the work but are happy *operating* in the following kinds of ways:

▶ By embracing a growth mindset that acknowledges learning requires trying and doing and occasionally failing on the way to achievement

▶ By practicing strong initiative and enduring motivation, even when things inevitably get tough

▶ By exercising situationally aware leadership and equally adept and consistent follower-ship

▶ By practicing and improving on a set of inclusive communications and conflict management skills

- By exercising self-awareness and self-management

- By sharing courageous perspectives through respectful person-to-person communications

- By regularly pulling in the perspectives of less-vocal team members

- By demonstrating the ability to work with anyone and everyone while helping one another learn and grow

Teams that look back at their performance and apply feedback to improve their processes are effective teams. This "reflective" mode of team evolution unsurprisingly models the best of Design Thinking's principles of feedback loops, thoughtful iteration, and continuous improvement.

Finally, as we explored in Hour 6 and the dimensions of the Culture Cube, effective cross-teaming requires the time, care, and attention necessary to create and maintain a supportive culture. Such a culture reflects and promotes a healthy environment, work climate, and diverse work styles. Let us turn our attention now to several techniques that establish or accelerate such a culture of cross-teaming.

Techniques for Working Across Teams

While there are hundreds of techniques for working well across a diverse body of people and teams, four Design Thinking techniques in particular help us create a culture of teamwork and effective communications between our team and other teams supporting our work. These cross-teaming techniques include

- Framing Governance for Collaboration

- Concentric Communications

- Inclusive Communications

- Creating a Shared Identity

Let's take a look at each of these Design Thinking techniques next.

Design Thinking in Action: Framing Governance for Collaboration

Working within our own team has its challenges but is simple in the sense that we tend to have a specific set of tasks to complete and have our own team cadences for meetings and working together. Easy!

But when our team is asked to solve a tough problem or develop a product or solution for another organization, and we need to partner with other organizations in the process, our connections and communications grow exponentially complex. As we add additional teams into the mix—teams that we absolutely count on to help all of us make progress against that problem or solution—we need to consider the connections between those teams and how to foster and govern those connections. Consider the number of teams and connections we might need to navigate for a conventional product development initiative, as depicted in Figure 15.2.

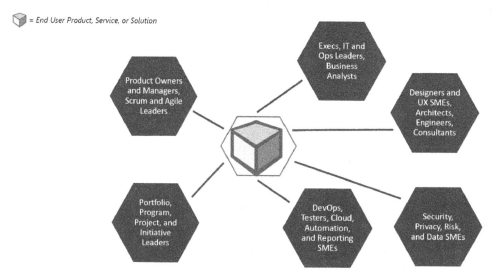

FIGURE 15.2
A typical initiative or project cross-teaming environment.

In these cases, we need to overlay a governance structure atop our broad collection of teams. What is governance? Simply put, governance is oversight. It's the work of administering or overseeing an endeavor to help ensure that the endeavor delivers a set of expected outcomes. The endeavor might be a project, or it might be a simpler initiative or a broader program.

Such a governance structure in the context of projects or initiatives is always virtual in nature, composed of people who will wear specific hats and play specific personas supporting a collection of organizations who cross-team and work together to create value. In this sense, while governance itself is not considered a Design Thinking technique in its own right, Framing Governance for Collaboration creates the virtual structure, in the form of a framework or matrix, and specifies the organizational bodies necessary for completing complex endeavors.

Framing Governance for Collaboration drives clarity by organizing people around a number of virtual governance bodies—committees, councils, and boards—each tasked with a charter and specific set of responsibilities. A good governance framework or matrix makes hierarchies visible while establishing clear lines of communication and escalation (Furino, 2016). For most tech projects and initiatives, these virtual governance bodies include

▶ An Executive-Level Steering Committee, which includes a team of people who make key decisions, who serve as the final point of escalation for issues, and who track planned benefits from initiation through to realization, including the quality and timing of those benefits.

▶ A Product Council or working-level Operational Steering Committee, which meets regularly to review progress and make both strategic and tactical decisions to achieve a set of planned benefits.

▶ An Architecture Review Board, instantiated to govern strategic technology decisions and direction, ensuring the decisions made today are supportable and aligned with tomorrow's future.

▶ A Change Control Board, to govern project or initiative scope changes including strategies, user implications, financial repercussions, and other matters related to the "gaps" that a particular solution represents to the organization's overall solution and technology footprint.

▶ A traditional Project Management Office (PMO) or an Agile Product (SCRUM) Management Office, to own the high-level plan including project standards, financials, resources, schedules, reporting, and so forth.

▶ An Internal Stakeholder Council representing the virtual team responsible for establishing and maintaining the overall governance framework.

We may decide we need to spin up other governance bodies, or conversely merge one or more of them together. Regardless, membership in these virtual committees, councils, and boards spans different teams and creates its own frame or matrix atop our physical organizations. In this way, *Framing Governance for Collaboration* makes governance visible and visual, as we see in Figure 15.3.

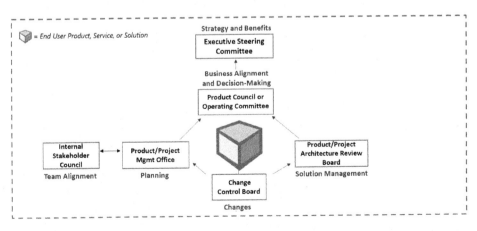

FIGURE 15.3
Note how the process of framing governance draws people from underlying physical organizations to create a virtual framework or matrix of committees, councils, and boards needed to support a project or initiative.

Figure 15.4 illustrates what it looks like to overlay our virtual governance framework atop our physical organizational structure.

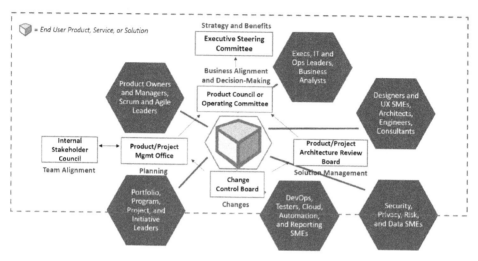

FIGURE 15.4
The virtual governance framework sits atop our physical organizational structure. Together, they provide visibility into the stakeholders spanning our project or initiative.

Design Thinking in Action: Concentric Communications

Concentric Communications is a technique for keeping all of the right people informed at the right time with the right set of information using the appropriate communications channel—the who, when, what, and how. The idea is to visually organize a team, project, and its group of stakeholders with related goals into a set of concentric circles or rings laid atop a grid (we can reuse the Bullseye Prioritization template for this purpose). Each circle or ring represents both a priority and a cadence for communications, and the grid itself reflects up to four channels of communication used for each stakeholder, governance body, or other group.

▶ Determine the four primary communications channels and map them to the four quadrants of the grid. Common channels include email, group meetings, one-on-one meetings (1:1s), and Instant Messenger (IM). Add others, such as newsletters, portal updates, website updates, blog postings, and so on (and convert the four grids into six or eight sections like we did with the Possible Futures wheel in Hour 13).

▶ The inner circle, or ring #1, is the "project leadership team," or core team of people who must always remain aware of and control the project or initiative. This circle should include the day-to-day leadership team composed of the project manager or product manager or SCRUM master, the enterprise architect, the primary solution architect, the chief business analyst or functional leader, the development leader, and the test leader. The core team needs real-time information concerning the project or initiative. This ring of leaders should be getting and sharing real-time updates several times a day through meetings, email or IM updates, and so forth.

▶ Create a second circle or ring around the core team. This is circle or ring #2 and consists of the broader team who need to know some but not all of the information known and shared by the core team. Alternatively, they might need to know everything the core team knows but don't need to be informed as frequently (the ideal cadence might be every few days or once a week rather than daily, for example). Tie specific people and governance bodies to this ring. Use the quadrants to organize by channel of communication, including traditional email status reporting, regular calendared weekly calls, and so on.

▶ Surround the broader team with a third circle and label this circle or ring #3. In this circle sits an even broader subset of people who perhaps have a regular need for basic awareness without all the detail. Alternatively, they might need to know everything but can wait a few weeks or a month or more. Tie specific people and governance bodies to this ring too.

▶ A fourth circle or ring might include our executive sponsor and other executive stakeholders who have a need for biweekly updates under normal circumstances; organize these communications by channel in the appropriate quadrant of the grid.

▶ Build in as many concentric circles as needed to comprise the entire ecosystem of stakeholders, governance bodies, user communities, specialty contributors, partners, service providers, friendly followers, and so on. See Figure 15.5 for a worked example of a Concentric Communications visual.

As we can see from the figure, the value of Concentric Communications is threefold:

▶ It gives us another way to organize our stakeholders, in this case around their communications needs (the "what") and communications cadences (the "when").

▶ It helps us identify missing stakeholders (the "who") and insufficient communications or communications gaps.

▶ It helps us see and adjust both the timing and channel (the "how") of communications as they fan out from the core team to the outer reaches of the people tied to the project or initiative.

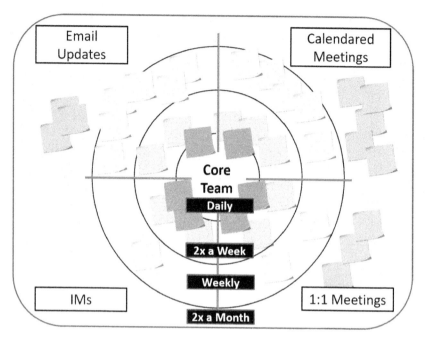

FIGURE 15.5
Concentric Communications helps us visualize not only our stakeholders but also the communication cadences and channels associated with each stakeholder.

Use Forcing Functions (covered in Hour 16) to ensure communications are indeed shared in a timely kind of way with each concentric circle of stakeholders. Basic small team and project communications, along with stakeholder engagement and expectation management, are improved through good concentric communications practices.

Strive for consistent communications, too. The people and groups in each concentric circle need to be able to depend on the frequency and accuracy of communications. In cases where strategy and follow-on messaging and direction changes, be sure to share the updated "why" and the "when" at the right time with the right audience.

Design Thinking in Action: Inclusive Communications

With our governance framework intact and our concentric communications channels established, this next focus area is about giving everyone a voice. Inclusive Communications underpins healthy cross-teaming in that it helps ensure we include and listen to the whole of our teams, believing that each person has ideas and thoughts worth surfacing and considering. Inclusive Communications starts with choosing words that unite and include. Use *we* rather than *I* or *my*. Doing so creates a sense of teamwork and even family.

Notice how Inclusive Communications squarely focuses on the "how." Concentric Communications covered the who, when, and what of communications, but Inclusive Communications guides us in how we communicate. Intentional consideration to inclusion helps us avoid silos of misunderstanding and chasms of ignorance, both of which drive frustration and confusion and usually just drive people away, further excluding the precise people we need to draw in.

Inclusive Communications is also about accessibility as much as it is about including everyone, and accessibility often boils down to the channels of communication we choose. Ensure our messages land well by using the communications channels that different people require or prefer (consider how executive communications differ from development team communications, and how the channels for millennials versus baby boomers fundamentally differ). Consider also how to communicate in inclusive ways with people holding different roles. Communicating in the morning with a person who is not a morning person requires a different approach than sharing that same news later in the day. And for urgent messages, we may need to communicate in a way that is sensitive to timing as well (consider time zones, early risers, weekend workers, and midnight candle burners). Our communications approach and style need to vary accordingly.

Consider how to inclusively communicate with people of different abilities. People who are colorblind, people with dyslexia, people with hearing impairments, and people with mobility constraints likely communicate best in ways that differ from one another. We must therefore know our teams and our colleagues so as to avoid largely avoidable missteps. Again, inclusion is as much about the channel of communication as it is about the message itself.

How we use language and ability etiquette to practice inclusion is a big part of how we communicate well across our colleagues and teams too. For example, think about how "people-first language" describes a person with a disability by putting the person before the disability. People-first describes what a person has, not who a person is. When communicating with those with disabilities, ask how they describe themselves. Examples of good person-first language include

▶ A colleague with blindness

▶ Our initiative leader with autism

▶ My product manager, who is deaf

Note how this is different than saying a "blind person" or "our autistic leader" or "my deaf product manager." Think of Inclusive Communications through the lens of how a person would like to receive communication rather than how we might prefer to send it. Finally, try adapting these Guiding Principles for healthy and inclusive stakeholder and team communications:

▶ Individual credibility, accuracy, and respect for others by our leaders set the bar for how the rest of the team and extended project or initiative's stakeholders trust and respect one another.

▶ Regardless of the communications channel, be timely and accurate with our communications because others need to be able to rely on when we are expected to share updates and what we are actually sharing.

▶ Argue respectfully and listen as though we are *wrong*, as if we may have missed or misunderstood something.

▶ Know when to share time-consuming stories and when to be concise.

▶ Consider and share the information that various team members need rather than the information that we might wish to share. Consider a special Concentric Communications circle as we identify new stakeholders with new communications or channel needs.

▶ In the absence of hearing from us the why and the when, uninformed people will fill a communications void with their own ideas, worries, and fears. Minimize communications voids.

▶ Know enough about our specific and varied audiences to strike the right balance between too little and too much information shared at once. Consider Time Pacing (covered in Hour 16) to balance frequency and quantity.

▶ The right people need to deliver the right messages; for example, technology or architecture matters need to be delivered by technology or architecture experts, not project managers.

▶ Know when face-to-face communication is needed and when other channels are acceptable, and then choose these channels wisely.

▶ Repeat key messages, and for urgent or critical communications, use more than one communications channel that the receivers actually listen to so as to ensure the message is received.

Leaders need to be seen actively communicating to their stakeholders and teams. It's in the visibility and effort of this communication that effective relationships and healthy cultures are reinforced. And it's worth reiterating that by communicating in a way that demonstrates respect, we will more naturally practice and set the bar for Inclusive Communications.

Design Thinking in Action: Creating a Shared Identity

Increasing and reinforcing a team's shared identity are among the most important activities that a team leader can take upon themselves. Going beyond a single team, however, and creating a shared identity across multiple teams is even more important. Doing so can be the difference maker between a collection of teams that think about themselves and a unified team that thinks about their collective goals and commitments.

Think of Creating a Shared Identity as the natural but *accelerated* process of finding common ground, developing cross-team relationships, and creating common threads or themes between people and teams.

Upon first meeting or connecting with our colleagues from another team, we should do introductions, explain our roles, use icebreakers such as the following "Fun Facts" exercise to reduce tension. An easy Fun Facts icebreaker might include customizing the following questions. We have included sample responses that a leader might provide to each question as well—responses that humanize and therefore set the stage for authentic connecting and learning:

- **What is my dream job?** Writing and consulting while rotating between homes in Paris, Singapore, and the Bahamas.

- **What is my favorite team?** Whatever team my child is playing on.

- **What was my first car?** An orange Ford Torino.

- **What is my proudest accomplishment?** Completing my MBA while serving full-time active duty in the Marines.

- **What is at the top of my bucket list?** To skydive exactly one time. And live.

- **What music or podcast am I listening to?** Olivia Rodrigo—with my kids. Brutal.

- **How did I spend last weekend?** Since it rained nearly all weekend, my family and I sat around watching all of the Harry Potter movies (again) while living on popcorn and home delivery.

We need to be ourselves, be vulnerable, and share who we are with others! Turn to Creating a Shared Identity to learn more about one another. Play the *Rating Game*, for example, or walk through a *This Is Me* exercise when getting to know one another (look to the two Try It Yourself sidebars for examples of each).

And don't just do these things when we are introduced to new teams. Use this kind of accelerated relationship building when we onboard new team members too. Outside of face-to-face coffee breaks, lunches, and other shared meals, there are few better ways of accelerating how we connect with and learn about one another.

▼ TRY IT YOURSELF

The Rating Game

An easy and fun way of accelerating getting to know one another is to play the Rating Game. This game is a simple icebreaker played as a group. Have a leader or other facilitator share each of the following questions, one at a time, after which each person, including the facilitator, weighs in with which is "better" or preferred. Modify the list to fit our culture, geography, and so on:

- ▶ Dogs or cats? What about a bird?
- ▶ Boredom or busyness?
- ▶ Coke or Pepsi?
- ▶ Monster or Mountain Dew?
- ▶ Steak or fish? Or swamp rat!
- ▶ Comedy or action movie?
- ▶ iPhone or Android? Blackberry anyone? :)
- ▶ The cold or the heat?
- ▶ Vacation in the mountains or at the beach?
- ▶ Boeing or Airbus? Would an RV be better?
- ▶ Hiking or running? Walking?

Add other questions to the list to personalize it for our situation or for the team playing the Rating Game. Be careful to stay respectful and inclusive and have fun with this while we learn more about one another in the process.

▼ TRY IT YOURSELF

This Is Me

A great way to learn more about one another is to sprinkle in This Is Me dimensions across a series of stand-ups or other regular meetings. Avoid bombarding a new team or new team member with too many of these at one time! Weave maybe 5 or 10 of these dimensions into an initial discussion, and later have fun exploring another 5 or 10. Above all, keep this informal, optional, and inclusive!

- ▶ Our name (yes, everyone needs to hear how we say our name!)
- ▶ The coolest job we have ever had
- ▶ The thing that brings us the most joy or pride
- ▶ The thing for which we are most grateful

- Our current-day aspirations and goals

- Our childhood dreams

- Our favorite music, book, food, movie (genre, band, song, whatever)

- Our favorite TV or streaming series (or one we are thinking about watching next)

- Our industry experience and qualifications

- Our birth month and why it's tough (or conversely, why we love this month)

- A person in this world who might be our twin—or should be!

- Our work location or geography or time zone

- Any family or pet information we think would be fun to share

- Any hobbies we think would be fun to share

- Our college major or focus area, including what we may have first pursued!

- Our last vacation we took, where we traveled, and with whom!

While the intention here is to learn about one another in a fun and informal kind of way, be careful not to pursue or call out differences in a way that divides or polarizes. Participation in any of these types of exercises or events should always be strictly optional, with zero pressure to share anything that makes someone uncomfortable. After all, when we are trying to build relationships faster than usual, privacy and respect still surpass everything else.

As we continue to work with one another, additional opportunities will arise to go deeper. Use icebreakers and other such exercises to not only get to know new people but also get to know our existing team better. Use them as a way to learn more about others and find new ways to cement and Create a Shared Identity. For example:

- Add new questions to the Rating Game or This Is Me exercises and share this new material to connect in new ways with one another.

- Look for and create opportunities for shared experiences—team meals, after-work events, weekend get-togethers, planned downtime for relaxing together, morning coffee with our extended team, regular lunches with our core team, and so on.

- Work to create common threads or connections between new people and teams and in-place people and teams. These threads and connections will help replace differences with similarities, all of which are useful to create and sustain shared visions, drive stronger relationships and collaboration, and further shape how the team works and collaborates with one another.

If *we* are the new person on a team, or the new leader for a cross-team initiative or project, consider how *we* can draw others in and quickly build relationships faster than organically possible. How? By sharing Fun Facts about ourselves, driving a This Is Me series of questioning, or running a Rating Game or another icebreaker.

And remember the goal of these games and exercises goes beyond learning about one another. We are really after where we are similar and where we are unique, with an eye toward building connections, increasing our Shared Identity, and evolving our shared culture.

Techniques for Communications Challenges

Across many of these hours, we have highlighted the need for creating healthy teams and enabling cross-boundary or cross-team collaboration and communication by giving our teams a safe space for ideating, problem solving, and working together. However, when we run into inevitable communications and collaboration challenges, beyond the usual techniques we may need at our disposal another set of Design Thinking techniques for getting us through the rough spots. In the pages that follow, let's explore three such situations and the communications techniques that may prove helpful:

- ▶ Black Box Illumination

- ▶ Storytelling for Deeper Understanding

- ▶ Structured Text for Rapid Comprehension

Each of these Design Thinking techniques for making communications visible or consumable is covered next.

Design Thinking in Action: Black Box Illumination

When the facts or the truth are hidden, it's easy for schedules to slip and milestones to be missed. And in the absence of understanding the "why" behind schedule and milestone misses, untold numbers of people may start jumping in to help understand root causes while others ponder and share their unfounded opinions. In the same way, when we are faced with a "black box" of unknown processes or status, and we have lost confidence in the progress being made within that black box, we need to shine a light into that black box lest people start making up their own reasons for the delays. We need a way to communicate that illuminates the reality and opportunities for progress underpinning our challenges. In conjunction with several other techniques, a recipe that uses the umbrella technique called Black Box Illumination can provide the necessary light.

- ▶ If we are running into problems related to progress, validate how well we are already using Time Boxing and other time management techniques covered in Hour 16 to turn a development black box, for example, into a series of planned sprints with inputs, dependencies, and outputs.

▶ If we continue to miss milestones, dig deeper into the black box to uncover, identify, and regularly communicate through our DevOps tools the real-time status and the specific people who need to complete tasks X, Y, and Z, including the dependencies for each task. Employ Forcing Functions as needed to drive predictable progress.

▶ If we find ourselves unable to meet the date for a full commitment, turn to Black Box Illumination to light up, reorganize, and recommunicate the commitment into smaller components or chunks of work so we can be planful at a more granular level.

To this last point, let's say we have a large body of development customizations to complete. If we miss our dev-complete milestone, the downstream effect on process and performance testing, bug remediation, end user training, and so on is tremendous. If we shine a light into our development process and reorganize and refocus it by functional areas as soon as we know the dev-complete milestone is at risk, though, we can salvage our schedule a bit by focusing on completing individual functional areas first, second, and third so that they're ready for testing and training sooner rather than later. In Figure 15.6 note that if we focus our developers on the two remaining developments pending for functional area one, we will be ready to hand over that functional area to our testing team. Yes, some of the work will be delivered late. But by keeping our testing and training colleagues busy (rather than sitting around waiting for the whole body of development work to be completed), we have a better chance of meeting our uber goals related to testing and go-live.

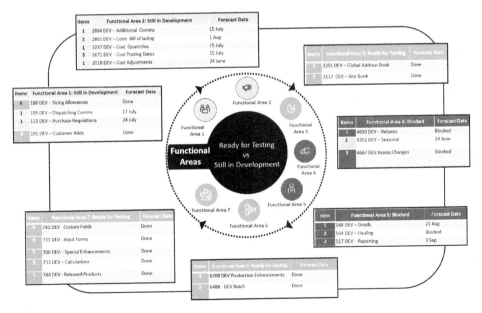

FIGURE 15.6
Use Black Box Illumination to shine a light into the black boxes of Tech. We might do so, for example, to refocus our custom development work so as to allow follow-on work (such as testing) to be started for specific areas while development for lagging areas continues.

Design Thinking in Action: Storytelling for Deeper Understanding

Storytelling is a universal way of helping others learn, understand, think differently or deeply, and find inspiration and courage. It's a method of communicating and empathizing in a way that's emotionally sticky. Why does this matter? How does this help us from a cross-boundary or cross-teaming perspective?

- ▶ Good stories drive understanding.

- ▶ Good stories connect with us and stay with us.

- ▶ Good stories change perceptions and remold biases.

- ▶ Good stories ultimately shape work groups and cultures.

We lean on stories of courage when times are tough, and we look to stories from our leaders and colleagues in uncertain times. Stories comfort us and give us self-confidence. And good stories resonate long after they're shared. In these ways, good stories influence the smallest of teams just as they do the largest of organizations and their corporate cultures.

NOTE

Parables

Parables are a special form of story that help us communicate complex or abstract situations through the intersection of a person and a metaphor. Use them to land a universal truth or gain broader understanding and deeper empathy.

All of us have heard examples of parables, fables, and similar storytelling techniques that build on a story of a person and a simple metaphor to explain a more complex situation. Consider old Greek parables such as Hercules at the Crossroads, the old Persian parable about Akhfash's goat, and the Quranic parable of the good and evil tree. In the New Testament, Jesus used parables and similar storytelling techniques to communicate abstract ideas in simple ways. For example, the stories of the prodigal son, the lost sheep, and the lost coin are all parables focused on redemption and the value of people. When the message matters, such stories help us land abstract ideas in ways that are "sticky" and enduring long after the message is shared.

We can mold stories for themes that can ultimately be summarized in a single word such as truth, courage, or love. It's the theme that continues to resonate in an audience's minds and hearts long after the words are read or spoken; it's usually the theme that drives the stickiness of the story. Use stories when we

- ▶ Need to be inspired to start something new

- ▶ Need additional courage to persevere and continue

▶ Need to teach something complex through a simple theme

▶ Need to share a hard lesson without specifics and details

▶ Need to land the seed of an idea, influencing and informing future decisions in the most subtle of ways

Stories have power. However, be sure to use this power appropriately and sparingly enough to retain our audience's attention long enough, so we can reap the power of storytelling when we need it most.

Design Thinking in Action: Structured Text for Rapid Comprehension

Sometimes words are indeed more effective in communicating than pictures, especially if a brief written update is required and the context of a picture is less intuitive. In these cases, use Structured Text to quickly communicate when pictures or figures aren't appropriate or just take too long to create or update. A well-structured and appropriately formatted email, text, or IM can be read and understood more quickly than an unstructured paragraph reflecting the same content.

Structured Text considers how we use formatting, physical placement, margins, and other whitespace (literally the space around words), along with text highlighting and color to help those words be understood and absorbed by another.

▶ **Bullets.** Create a set of bulleted items to help consolidate thinking or themes and to draw attention to the most important items.

▶ **Numbering.** Use a numbered list to walk through a process or sequence of activities step by step (1, 2, 3…).

▶ **Whitespace.** Place key words in a format that naturally draws the eye to them; writers need to employ their best System 2 (deep and slow) thinking to illicit a reader's System 1 (fast or automatic) response (Kahneman, 2011).

▶ **Consistency.** Start each bullet in the same way with verbs (Perform, Execute, Review…) or gerunds (Performing, Executing, Reviewing…). End each bullet consistently as well; variety distracts readers and, worse, may cause them to pause and consider if there is intention buried in that variety.

▶ **Style.** Use a single font that is easily read and understood. Apply bold to that font sparingly and only as a way to either organize the overall message (as we have done here) or to draw attention to next steps or key risks when color is not inclusive or appropriate.

> ▶ **Color.** Use color sparingly to draw attention to a few key words in a paragraph or sea of bullets when color is inclusive and appropriate for an audience. For example, highlight the few words necessary to draw a reader's attention to next steps or key risks.

With these formatting and readability tips in mind, many of the attributes we appreciate about a good picture can be built into an email or a text document. Lean on pictures and visuals when needed, but otherwise use Structured Text to land our messages accurately and quickly.

What Not to Do: Using Words When a Picture Is Needed

All of us have reached a point where verbal communication eventually fails us. Consider how we misuse words, use words with different meanings, or try to describe a complex situation with lots and lots of words. In these cases, words may be insufficient. Communicating with a picture might be exactly what's needed.

One project manager insistent on verbose and detailed communications found he simply could not impart the complexity of the work in front of him, his team, and his customer's technology and business teams. He tried for months to communicate what was happening and what needed to happen. He used meetings and status reports. In retrospect, his replacement found that all of the words of his predecessor only served to confuse the broader teams. People lost interest and would quit listening as the barrage of words went on and on. The new project manager communicated complexity with a simple project roadmap and by using the Black Box Illumination technique to help everyone see the need and rally around a set of next steps.

Summary

This hour we explored the kinds of Design Thinking techniques that help us communicate and collaborate cross-team. We set the stage for effective cross-teaming by typing together teams through a virtual governance overlay called Framing Governance for Collaboration. Then we turned to the many tips and activities we can use for organizing Concentric Communications, operating through Inclusive Communications, and Creating (and increasing) a Shared Identity to foster an inclusive team and shared culture. Afterward, we covered three techniques for addressing communications challenges, including Black Box Illumination for communicating complexity, Storytelling for deeper understanding, and Structured Text for rapid written comprehension. Hour 15 concluded with a "What Not to Do," highlighting the problem with communicating exclusively through oral or written words.

Workshop

Case Study

Consider the following case study and questions. You can find the answers to the questions related to this case study in Appendix A, "Case Study Quiz Answers."

Situation

Satish is concerned that several of his OneBank initiative leaders are not creating the kinds of environments where people can bring their authentic selves to work and do their best work. As some of the initiatives have sprawled across organizational lines and in some cases needed to pull in partner organizations, workplace culture has stagnated at exactly the same time when many new people are onboarding weekly. Some of these new team members have shared that they feel as though they're working in silos, whereas others have shared that they feel as though they're working among a loose collection of initiatives rather than across a unified OneBank team.

Satish has asked you to share some of your learnings and techniques for working effectively cross-team, including techniques for creating a more inclusive and connected workplace and for addressing communications challenges.

Quiz

1. What kinds of activities or steps can the OneBank initiative leaders perform to create a shared identity?

2. Which technique will help create an overlay or matrix of governance across the collection of OneBank initiatives?

3. Which Design Thinking technique takes into consideration how communications may be visualized in terms of radiating circles that call out the specific cadences and channels for different people and teams?

4. Which technique can be useful for visually simplifying heavy word-based communications?

5. When a visual or picture is not appropriate, which technique is useful to create concise written communication?

Prototyping and Solutioning by Doing

What You'll Learn in This Hour:

▶ The Prototyping and Solutioning Mindset
▶ Making Progress versus Solving the Entire Problem
▶ Techniques for Making Planned Progress
▶ What Not to Do: Ignoring the Inverse Power Law
▶ Summary and Case Study

In this hour, we turn our attention to prototyping and solutioning as a way to arrive at the first makings of a solution. As we noted earlier, sometimes we need to do something or draw something or build something to help us get our minds around a challenge or situation. The act of doing solidifies our thoughts, and the act of externalizing our thoughts makes it possible to enlist the aid of others to create a shared understanding and get on the road to progress. As we learn this hour, from Process Flows to various forms of Prototyping, Building to Think, and more, we have many techniques available to help us make progress quickly. And through Forcing Functions, Time Boxing and Pacing, and applying the Inverse Power Law for change, we can create a roadmap for progress that is both planful and predictable. Hour 16 concludes with a "What Not to Do" focused on an oft-repeated real-world example of what happens when we ignore the Inverse Power Law.

The Prototyping and Solutioning Mindset

Prototyping is a broad-based term for getting what's in our heads down on paper, or in our hands, or up on a screen so others can see it, consider it, learn from it, iterate on it, and improve it. Like so many other techniques and exercises we have already covered, prototyping helps us externalize our thinking and create a shared understanding. And it's a great example of a transformational change agent. Prototyping helps us make the really big leaps from today to next year. Iterating, on the other hand, is a great example of an incremental change agent. Iterating helps us make the smaller day-to-day jumps that improve on the transformational (until we eventually need to transform again). We iterate to refine (our solution) and add (new capabilities and features) and subtract (complexity and that which is unnecessary).

Thus, the goals of prototyping and solutioning, followed by iterating, are threefold:

1. To externalize our ideas into potential solutions

2. To drive greater insights while achieving a shared understanding

3. To capture early feedback from our own teams and from the people who will ultimately use what we're designing, building, and deploying

In this hour, we consider the various ways we can learn and "solution" by prototyping and executing other forms of "doing." Remember that our goal is to simply make progress rather than completely solve a complex problem or deliver a fully baked solution.

NOTE

Let's Prototype First...

Before we invest time and energy in developing and deploying a full-fledged solution, we need to ensure we are directionally heading in the right direction. Prototyping in all of its forms, as we will see here, helps us validate that direction. Fear not, though, as in Hour 21, we will spend a full hour exploring the ways of doing and iterating that help us deliver with confidence as we finally deploy our work for others to use.

Making Progress versus Solving the Entire Problem

In the name of making progress through iterative feedback and other learnings from our own teams and from a subset of those people who will one day use our solution in some form or fashion, consider the following techniques:

▶ Cover Story Mockup for creating a shared vision

▶ Process Flows for Clarity

▶ Building to Think

▶ Rough and Ready Prototyping

We explore each of these Design Thinking techniques next.

NOTE

The Design Mindset

Designing and prototyping naturally benefit from what is called a *Design Mindset*. This way of approaching a situation is centered around how something works. Thus, this is a solution-focused rather than a problem-focused mindset, and as such requires a balance of cognitive analysis skills and imagination. Consider using the warm-ups, tips, and techniques we covered previously for Divergent Thinking in Hour 12 to create a Design Mindset.

Design Thinking in Action: Cover Story Mockup for a Shared Vision

When we explored Simple Rules in Hour 4, we mentioned how important it was to establish the legacy that the team wished to leave behind. In the same way, we also need to think with the end in mind regarding our projects, initiatives, products, services, and solutions. What do we want people to say and think about our work when that day finally arrives and our work is available for others to use? What can we learn today as we pull together resources and build sponsorship for our product or service?

Developing the cover of a magazine, newspaper, or online news story a la the LUMA Institute's Cover Story Mockup method is a powerful way to create alignment and generate excitement *today* for a day in the future when our products and services will finally become a part of others' lives. Our cover story serves several purposes:

▶ It creates a foundation for our future solution and promotes a shared understanding of that future in the context of the work we're doing.

▶ It gives us a format and forum for a powerful unifying visual or other image.

▶ It forces us to summarize our final end product or service into several succinct bullets, like an elevator pitch captured in words.

▶ It allows us the chance to explain the need or benefit of our product or service through the lenses of future users and future perspectives.

▶ It helps align, rally, and engage our own team as we work to realize that product or service and future.

Use Microsoft Word's newspaper template or an online fake-magazine cover generator to quickly create a Cover Story Mockup. In these ways, by painting a successful vision of our work and showing its impact among a future community of users, we can also drive stronger buy-in, excitement, and support from sponsors and other stakeholders who today might be on the fence or simply unaware of the impact we intend to make with our work. Consider how the mocked-up magazine cover depicted in Figure 16.1 showcases what our fictional case study organization, BigBank, seeks to accomplish through one of its many OneBank initiatives.

NOTE

Ongoing Vision, Please

Communicating vision is not a one-time event. Sustaining such clarity must be an ongoing activity of any project or initiative that spans more than a couple of months. People quickly forget otherwise! Sustaining clarity of vision creates and helps maintain alignment when competing priorities and conflicts naturally arise over time.

FIGURE 16.1
When we think ahead about the positive impact we wish to leave behind in our work, we can create a vision for the future that a team can rally around.

Design Thinking in Action: Process Flows for Clarity

Process flows have been used for years to provide clarity. Think of a process flow as a highway system connecting our potential solution together. If we understand how data flows from one place to another, and in which direction, and under what condition, then we can model a set of functions and capabilities. Process flows create the structure upon which the rest of our potential solution depends. Poor process flows help us find areas in our solution that require more thought, be it architecture, design, or functionality. In this way, process flows provide for us the shared understanding outlined so often in this book and needed so desperately by the very people seeking to solve tough problems.

Visual process flows and process diagrams provide insight into how a process works, including its inputs, dependencies, tasks, and outputs. The real value in visually documenting these flows spans the following:

- ▶ A shared understanding realized through making the complex visual and visible

- ▶ A broad appreciation for the people involved and the people being served by the process

- ▶ A shared vocabulary

To this last point, in tech we often use acronyms, words, and phrases that mean different things to different people and different disciplines. Visualization is the great equalizer, driving everyone to a single shared place of understanding. Visualization gives us context. It drives questioning, making terms and acronyms clearer. And it connects the people who execute the work of the process with the people connected in various ways to the process (and its inputs, dependencies, tasks, and outputs!). Once we understand a process, we can intelligently make changes or otherwise improve that process.

As a Design Thinking technique, explore and experiment with the flow of data through a proposed system. Consider where the data is housed, how it is surfaced, and where it is used as an input and an output. Create drawings and schematics to help drive discussions and close the gaps in prototypes. Use process flows to help close the gap between potential solution and production solution.

Design Thinking in Action: Building to Think

When we set out to solve a problem, we first spend time learning about the problem's surface area—what it touches, what it affects, its ecosystem, and so on. And then we usually do some planning. And then we probably talk about the plan, refine it and squeeze it, and plan some more. We talk and plan and talk and plan, and these things are good in moderation. But the longer we spend doing the planning and putting off the "doing," the longer we risk misunderstanding the problem in the first place. Imagine planning six months and then taking the plunge into "doing" and finding that nothing works as planned. It happens. We need to get out of planning and get to the doing!

At this point, Building to Think comes into play. Building to Think is about jumping in and "doing" as a way of learning and thinking so we can more effectively plan and do and deploy. View this Design Thinking technique as a way of "thinking with our hands."

In the world of technology and software development, developers build mock-ups or engage in system prototyping as a natural way to Build to Think. We can apply Building to Think outside of the specific tasks associated with software development too; wherever we have a tough problem and need to validate that we're heading down the right path, we have a case for Building to Think. Consider the following:

▶ Draw! This includes all forms of mapping, including Stakeholder Mapping, Mind Mapping, Journey Mapping, Empathy Mapping, and so on. As we covered in Hour 5, making our ideas and prototypes visual and visible aids in context setting and creating a shared understanding. Use any number of tools, from old-fashioned paper and pen and whiteboards to Adobe Photoshop, Microsoft PowerPoint, Paint, Klaxoon, and more.

▶ Create mock-ups of ideas and prototypes using sticky notes and simple step-by-step process flows.

▶ Mock up sample reports or other outcomes using Microsoft PowerPoint, Word, or Excel. If we consider the outputs that need to come out of a process flow (in the form or reports or cubes or other outcomes), we can easily work backward and consider how to get the data for those reports.

▶ Sketch out or whiteboard how the data flows through a system, how "work" flows through a system (a la time and motion studies), what a person might interact or interface with, and what that interface might need to include.

▶ Animate static figures and pictures to illustrate a process flow step by step. Microsoft PowerPoint is still one of the easiest tools for quickly animating designs and storyboards.

NOTE

Storyboarding!

Storyboards are created through Storyboarding, the work of organizing in a stepwise fashion a set of rough sketches or drawings used to illustrate a sequence or set of steps in a process. Each sketch or drawing represents a step, and the overall Storyboard provides a powerful visual for creating a shared understanding.

As we can see, Building to Think is about drawing, modeling, prototyping, and so on, using many of the techniques and ideas from Hour 5. Sometimes the best models are completed in super low-cost ways with markers and a whiteboard to sketch out simple processes or models (where A leads to B leads to C, with outputs from A, B, and C). If we can model in three dimensions or create something tangible, something we can hold and manipulate, that's even better. The sooner we can get our thoughts out of our heads and out into the open world, the faster we can find gaps and iterate on our ideas to improve them (see Figure 16.2).

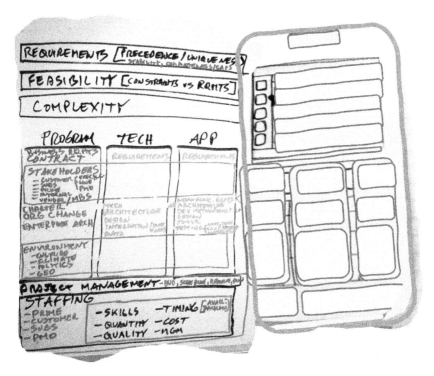

FIGURE 16.2
We arrive at our destination faster when we replace extensive planning with Building to Think (in this case, turning a whiteboard drawing into a mobile interface for tracking the health of a project or initiative).

Remember that Building to Think is framed around the notion that we can do our best thinking and arrive at solutions faster when we simply jump in. Don't think too much beforehand; the opportunity for thinking smarter arrives quickly in the wake of jumping in!

NOTE

Planning to Think? Eventually, Yes.

When we plan too early and too long, many of our learnings will come later in execution when changes become time-consuming and expensive, and where ill-conceived designs need to be reworked perhaps all the way back to the drawing board. We need to plan, sure. But there's a time and a place for planning, and there's a time and a place for failing early and failing cheaply...or that is, learning early and learning cheaply. Build to Think and *then* consider the kind of planning necessary to realize longer-term value.

Some final thoughts include the following:

▶ Remember to accommodate the Rule of Threes when Building to Think. Set expectations that it will probably take at least three iterations to really get something directionally right.

▶ Build Feedback Loops into our Building to Think work-in-progress.

▶ Consider Silent Design feedback as a way to meaningfully rethink and improve a solution.

▶ Use Forcing Functions to review and refresh our solutions on a regular cadence; if the time is not intentionally set aside, the refresh might never occur.

Above all, when we're tempted to enter a long cycle of planning, just remember what Tim Brown tells us: "Rather than thinking to build, build to think." (Brown, 2019)

Design Thinking in Action: Rough and Ready Prototyping

Another way to make real progress rather than wasting time in complex situations trying to solve the whole problem is to engage in Rough and Ready Prototyping, another term for thinking with our hands to create rough prototypes. Create a rough prototype, something users can see and touch, to visualize a shared vision of the future, which in turn can help us

▶ More quickly test our ideas

▶ Validate features and interface ideas early

▶ Iterate through development and test faster than otherwise possible

Rough and Ready Prototyping is intended to create concept models and interface designs quickly, using low-cost methods and readily available materials. The sooner we can put something tangible in front of our prospective user community, the faster we can obtain useful feedback. Rough and Ready Prototypes help us validate what's directionally correct and what's not (and therefore where we need to spend more time prototyping and fine-tuning). Rough and Ready Prototype examples include mocking up solutions, wireframing designs on whiteboards, creating paper sketches, and assembling two-dimensional artifacts. We may also create three-dimensional models out of low-cost materials, including clay, foam, and paper products, to better understand how an idea might look and feel (while noting prototype weaknesses earlier than later).

QUOTE: As the famous architect Frank Lloyd Wright said, "You can use an eraser on the drafting table or a sledgehammer on the construction site."

Techniques for Making Planned Progress

After we have directionally made some progress against our goals using prototyping and solutioning techniques such as Building to Think and Rough and Ready Prototyping, we can begin planning the work in front of us. The first bit of work benefits from some structure so as to learn and iterate more quickly than otherwise possible. And with a lightweight and structured plan in place, and a backlog or body of work from which to draw upon, we can finally begin making real progress. Our Design Thinking tool bag provides a number of techniques that have proven useful over the years in driving this kind of progress, which we will continue to use even as our solution grows more mature:

- ▶ Forcing Functions

- ▶ Time Boxing

- ▶ The Inverse Power Law

- ▶ Time Pacing

Let's explore each of these Design Thinking planned-progress-maker techniques next.

Design Thinking in Action: Forcing Functions for Progress

All of us use deadlines as a way to help us or make us get things done, especially the kinds of hard things that don't naturally get done without a bit of focus. Deadlines *work* for us; they bring us visibility and usually come with consequences that help us get the tactical work done that we *have* to get done. How might we use deadlines to ensure we complete the really important long-term tasks we absolutely need to get done? How might we use deadlines to make planned progress with regard to completing tasks that don't include any intrinsic motivators?

And who's to say that a deadline needs to be assigned by our manager or another leader? Instead, try giving ourselves our own deadlines, even artificial deadlines, to drive progress. Such manufactured deadlines are called Forcing Functions, and they are incredibly useful for getting both the important tasks and the mundane tasks done at work and in our projects and initiatives.

A long-time scheduling and calendaring technique, Forcing Functions help us achieve a schedule or help us meet a set of planned milestones and deadlines. And Forcing Functions can be used to drive preparation and readiness too. Most importantly, Forcing Functions help us make progress. That progress might very well include a bit of failure too, but the progress is undeniable. Consider a case where we schedule a date in the near future to complete a technology certification exam. The date serves as a Forcing Function for studying. Even if we fail the exam the first time, the Forcing Function served its purpose by driving us to prepare earlier than we might otherwise have prepared. And like many technology specialists know firsthand, we will pass the certification exam sooner by taking it, failing it, and taking it again rather than never actually attempting the exam in the first place. Forcing Functions drive us to try.

And in the workplace, Forcing Functions drive us to try too. Our managers, colleagues, and user communities will appreciate that we jump in and try rather than never try at all. They will appreciate our work as we Build to Think, even when we fail; failure quickly fades away in the wake of success.

There are many other examples of manufacturing Forcing Functions to help us get things done and make real progress:

▶ Schedule completion of key tasks a week before they are actually due, as a way of achieving if not overachieving our deadlines (a twist on Mission Impossible Thinking outlined in Hour 11).

▶ Use other guardrails and techniques for thinking differently in our day-to-day work as Forcing Functions for gaining experience in those techniques prior to needing to use them on our tech projects and initiatives.

▶ Assign new tasks to newer team members rather than the more senior ones we already know can deliver; doing so pushes the new person while returning bandwidth to the senior person (consider how this approach is a twist on Buddy System Pairing and Slaying the Hero, both covered later in Hour 22).

▶ Pursue a new role as a Forcing Function for our current employer to either promote us or let us go.

▶ Use replanning exercises and other tough situations in the wake of failure as Forcing Functions to bring together people and groups who might not normally connect.

▶ Apply a "no quitting allowed" mindset to a situation to eliminate quitting or turning back as an option, which then becomes a Forcing Function for finding a way through our current challenge (as we see in the Failing Forward technique covered in Hour 17).

▶ Divide a large body of work into smaller time-boxed sprints to serve as a Forcing Function for faster engagement and to uncover challenges sooner rather than later (called Time Boxing, explored next).

Forcing a goal or condition to occur is as much about paying attention to a calendar or schedule as it is about pursuing the things that are important enough to warrant respecting that calendar or schedule.

Design Thinking in Action: Time Boxing for Speed and Feedback

In 1955, Cyril Parkinson explained that "work expands so as to fill the time available for its completion" (Scott, 2018). and most of us know by experience that Parkinson's Law, while informal, remains true today. If we give ourselves two months to test an application, human nature says we will surely not complete our testing any earlier. If we plan for a three-month development cycle, we will surely not wrap up development sooner. The work just tends to fill the time we've allotted.

Parkinson's Law is a problem for two reasons. First, without a sense of urgency, we tend to start slowly. So by the time we run into the inevitable challenges, we have less time to solve them, potentially destroying our schedule. Second, operating inside a large unstructured black box of time doesn't give us a set of targets to hit along the way.

One solution? Try Time Boxing, a simple Agile technique for time management developed by James Martin (1991). Time Boxing (or some prefer timeboxing) an activity helps drive great progress if not outright completion of that activity. The idea is simple. Give ourselves and our teams not only a deadline but the maximum amount of time that they can work on something. This creates healthy tension in the form of a "box" of time, driving a sense of urgency alongside a bit of Good Enough Thinking (covered in Hour 11). Why has this technique proven itself so effective over the years? Consider:

▸ When we give a team unlimited time, with less urgency often comes less progress.

▸ When we give a team no deadline, with less definition comes more uncertainty and less progress.

▸ If we Time Box a task on a calendar, however, we will get something done that in the worst case needs a bit of iteration or refinement through planned feedback cycles (which we should be planning for regardless).

So when we are faced with many tasks to complete, stagger and time-box those tasks to accomplish everything in front of us. Time-box our preparation time, time-box the important dependencies we need to complete to make progress, and time-box the mundane work on our desks to give us more bandwidth for tackling the truly important work awaiting us. As we see in Figure 16.3, through Time Boxing, we can get more done with greater predictability and less wasted time.

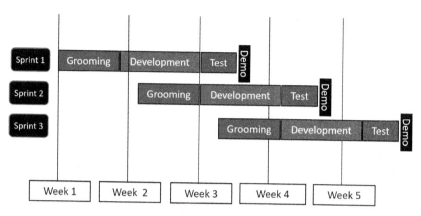

FIGURE 16.3
Use Time Boxing to organize the work in front of us and our teams, balancing Forcing Functions with Good Enough Thinking to make speedier and more predictable progress.

Design Thinking in Action: The Inverse Power Law for Loading

Nature has a natural way of distributing the large, medium, and small events of life. When we turn to Mother Nature and statistics, we find an interesting distribution of such events. Whether we're looking at weather patterns such as tornadoes, hurricanes, and dust storms, or geologic events such as earthquakes and volcanic eruptions, we find

▶ A high number of small-sized events

▶ A fewer number of medium-sized events

▶ Even fewer large or major events

The inverse relationship here is one of size versus frequency; the larger the event, the fewer times it typically occurs. This relationship is called the Inverse Power Law, and such distributions of events are also widely observed in biology, astronomy, and in the world around us. For our purposes, we use the Inverse Power Law as a constraint for task loading, for learning, and for considering the ability of a community to absorb change, as noted in Figure 16.4.

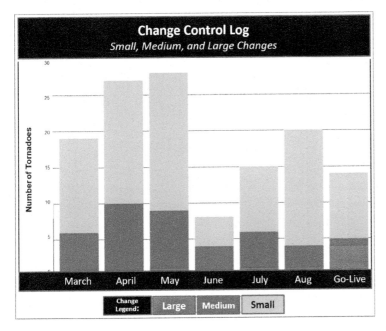

FIGURE 16.4
Consider the Inverse Power Law to determine the number of small, medium, and large-scale changes that a community can absorb over a period of time.

Apply this Design Thinking technique for organizing and tackling the large changes in a project's or initiative's lifecycle whether we are driving the changes or dealing reactively with changes around us. By seeing and accommodating the size and frequency of the changes occurring within and around our projects and initiatives, we can make smarter decisions as we grapple with typical scenarios such as these:

▶ Should we take on another set of sprints while we are in the middle of deploying the latest release to our user community?

▶ Where should we insert time for user testing when those same users are closing out the quarter's financials or dealing with one of their industry's peak seasons?

▶ How might we break up two medium-sized changes into four or smaller changes that our stakeholders can better accommodate?

▶ Can we employ Modular Thinking or another guardrail from Hour 11 to restructure our upcoming changes into more consumable chunks?

▶ How might we work around the dramatic change we are seeing in our industry as we seek to transform our business at the same time?

▶ In what ways should we rebalance our upcoming tasks, changes, and events to make predictable progress?

Consider how our upcoming schedule, changes, and goals come together over time and look for the opportunities, the gaps, where little change or fewer events are occurring. Where we have gaps, we might also have the necessary bandwidth to accommodate task loading or changes or new events. Of course, the real key lies in the size of the tasks or changes. The larger the task or change or other event, the more impact it has on our timeline and the less time we therefore have for other tasks, changes, or other events.

Design Thinking in Action: Time Pacing for Interdependencies

While the Inverse Power Law is about accommodating the varying size and frequency of a set of tasks, events, or changes, turn to Time Pacing to consider the repeatable and predictable rhythms of a business, project, industry, and so forth. Time Pacing is about making progress *around* a user community's already-scheduled or regular events by slowing down or working around those rhythmic peaks and speeding up or loading up changes in the business-as-usual valleys.

Time Pacing can also be used to drive predictability within a user community or project team. Kathleen M. Eisenhardt and Shona L. Brown described time pacing in a 1998 *Harvard Business Review* article as a way of "competing in fast-changing, unpredictable markets by scheduling change at predictable time intervals." In this way, our work *becomes* the rhythm of the business, something others should expect to see and accommodate on a regular basis. Consider how an organization's mandatory training might be expected to be completed every month; it becomes part of the rhythm of that organization's business.

In the world of software deployment, Time Pacing gives us a way of thoughtfully structuring the staffing models and implementation methods necessary to deploy a piece of software to different user communities over time. For big tech companies, it's also about scheduling product launches and other changes into the fabric of their operations as a way of staying both predictable and relevant.

QUOTE: "If you don't have time for things that matter, stop doing things that don't." —Courtney Carver

Consider how Time Pacing can be applied to help project and initiative teams schedule work and deliver value or other outcomes when it makes the most sense:

▶ Organize the project's regular set of financial outlays, such as monthly consulting and cloud consumption costs, across time and against the project's incoming budget to proactively see gaps in funding or opportunities to tackle more work.

▶ Alongside the project's roadmap, call out the regular project-external cadences and workstreams we have no control over that might affect us and our teams, and consider these external items as "bandwidth" constraints or dependencies.

- ▶ Combine what we know about the peaks of our work (a la the Inverse Power Law), including the size and frequency of our planned milestones, with the valleys of downtime we can use to either accelerate or recharge and regroup.

- ▶ Combine Time Pacing with Time Boxing to better organize how and what we will focus on during the valleys to accelerate our schedule or the cadence of our deliverables.

Time Pacing is best implemented visually against a calendar, wall clock, or series of other regular events. For example, in the image depicted in Figure 16.5, we can see a mock organization's "business as usual" peaks and valleys, and the durations of those peaks and valleys, as they span a typical week. Given the greater intensity of activities during Thursday and Friday, we might be well served to avoid introducing new changes, meetings, and so on during these days.

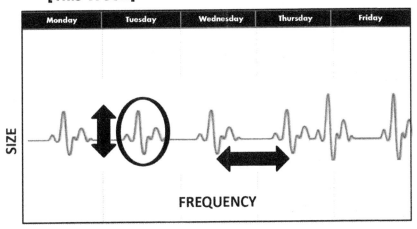

FIGURE 16.5
Use Time Pacing to consider the size and frequency of an organization's "business as usual" calendar so we can introduce new changes where those changes may be most easily absorbed or accommodated.

What Not to Do: Ignoring the Inverse Power Law

Most individuals and organizations have learned over time that we cannot force too much change on our people in too short a time, including our user communities, tech teams, business leaders, and executive leadership teams. People can only absorb so much change before they push back or revolt entirely. Yet for some unknown reason, an experienced program manager for a global automotive manufacturer thought he knew better.

Ignoring the advice of his highly paid consultants and even his own executive committee, the program manager leading a series of global application rollouts created an aggressive development and onboarding schedule. His program-level roadmap and more detailed rollout plan for a series of new application development and deployment projects did not consider the large size and frequency of changes he was asking an already-strapped user community to absorb.

Time-consuming sprint planning, testing, and training tasks overlapped previously planned business activities and a major cycle of the automobile manufacturer's product launches. Fortunately for the company's user communities, the program manager's roadmap was wiped clean at a monthly Steering Committee meeting. A new person was assigned to review and lead the program, this time considering how the Inverse Power Law and Time Pacing would affect the overall roadmap and schedule. While the program still encountered many other challenges, at least the respective user communities around the world were prepped, trained, and provided the time and space necessary to absorb these key changes in how they worked.

Summary

In this hour, we explored four techniques for incrementally learning by doing, including Cover Story Mockup, Process Flows, Building to Think, and Rough and Ready Prototyping. Next, we reviewed another four techniques for making planful progress while we're executing. From Forcing Functions and Time Boxing to the Inverse Power Law and Time Pacing, we reviewed how to organize and plan for progress given the breadth, size, and frequency of tasks, events, and changes we're asking a community to absorb. Hour 16 concluded with a "What Not to Do" focused on what happens when we ignore the Inverse Power Law.

Workshop

Case Study

Consider the following case study and questions. You can find the answers to the questions related to this case study in Appendix A, "Case Study Quiz Answers."

Situation

BigBank's Executive Committee (EC) is curious how each OneBank initiative leader should execute, and they heard you talking with Satish about a collection of techniques for learning by doing followed by another collection of techniques for making more predictable progress. As several of the initiatives span multiple countries and user communities, the EC is concerned about their organization's ability to consume change with so much activity in flight. They would like you to chat with their teams about these techniques and how they might accommodate the massive changes on the horizon.

Quiz

1. Which four techniques can help a team benefit from user feedback and other learnings through "learning by doing"?

2. What technique helps us by painting a successful vision of our work and showing its impact among a future community of users?

3. What technique creates structure by understanding how data moves from one place to another, and in which direction, and under what condition?

4. What are four techniques that can help us make planful and predictable progress?

5. Which informal law is reflected in Time Boxing?

HOUR 17
Solutioning Small and Fast

What You'll Learn in This Hour:

▶ The Progress Mindset: Showing Up and Starting Small

▶ Realizing Value Through Objectives and Key Results

▶ Starting Small and Delivering Fast

▶ Techniques for Delivering and Executing to Think

▶ For a Limited Time Only...

▶ What Not to Do: The Forever MVP

▶ Summary and Case Study

Hour 17 outlines the Design Thinking mindset surrounding what it means to make progress, including the techniques and other practices useful in solutioning when our users' needs, or the path ahead, are unclear. We then explore the notion of value, followed by the steps necessary to define and measure value through the use of Objectives and Key Results. To deliver value early, we explore four techniques that can help us bridge the gap between the problem solving and prototyping we have completed and the final solution we need to deliver. The four techniques include executing a Proof of Concept (POC), deploying a Minimum Viable Solution (MVP), deploying a fully featured Pilot to a subset of our community, and using the Failing Forward for Progress technique to focus our teams on the future rather than the past. Our "What Not to Do" this hour illustrates what can happen when, after traveling the path of the unknown, we finally reach a place of certainty and comfort and wind up stagnating there rather than delivering a full solution to a community desperately waiting for it.

The Progress Mindset: Showing Up and Starting Small

Learning and thinking and prototyping are all useful practices when faced with uncertainty and ambiguity, but eventually we need to make real progress against the Objectives and Key Results we've laid out. We need to do, create, and deliver outcomes. After all, it's in the doing and finishing that we deliver value.

The first step toward crossing the finish line? Showing up. Carl Jung (1980) said years ago, "You are what you do, not what you say you'll do." Nothing of planned value has any potential until we actually show up. "I am going to do this" and "We will work to finish that" mean nothing until we show up as individuals and as teams ready to work together on the tasks in front of us. Showing up is step one of finishing.

While showing up sets us to get the work done, as we have seen in previous hours the work is made easier and imminently more achievable by starting small, moving fast, and accumulating little wins along the way. Starting small and delivering fast let us learn quickly through doing, and they let us course-correct without wasting too much time. And we will need to course-correct! Uncertain paths and ambiguous surroundings will naturally lead us down paths where we need to double back. That's the nature of uncertainty and ambiguity. Design Thinking helps us arrive at those conclusions—that we indeed need to learn more or validate our understanding or indeed double back—sooner rather than later.

Fortunately, there are many Design Thinking techniques and exercises for helping us better understand and empathize along the way, learn and fail fast, think to course-correct, prototype to learn, course-correct again, and so on. It's in this way of working that we can deliver value even in the midst of uncertainty and ambiguity.

But what is value? And how might we measure it? Let's explore these questions next.

Realizing Value Through Objectives and Key Results

Also referred to as benefits or business outcomes or realized goals, *value* is anything that contributes to the outcomes we've been asked to deliver as part of a technology project or initiative. Value comprises the benefits, improvements, assets, and other outcomes realized by a community on the receiving side of our work; it's the difference makers between where the community is today and where we are trying to take it. And value is measured exclusively from that community's perspective. After all, they are the intended beneficiaries.

As we have seen in previous hours, value isn't exclusively delivered at the end of a project or initiative. In fact, the premise of this hour is that we need to deliver value *early*, as early as possible, if only to get a bit of feedback. And we need to continue delivering value throughout our work, bite-sized chunks of usefulness that help us not only get to the finish line but (through feedback again) help us validate along the way that we are still on the right track.

Defining and Measuring Value

Sometimes value is easy to "see." When we deliver products or services, they are tangible examples of value. When our user community or intended beneficiaries acknowledge that we have delivered value, we can take that at face value too. But how might we identify and measure value early so that later we can return to validate it has indeed been delivered in full? How do we know we delivered 100 percent of the value intended by our product or service? How can we be sure that we haven't come up short?

It's for these reasons that value must be inherently measurable. And to that end, we need a set of *Objectives,* and we need to tie to each Objective to a quantifiable measure. A good measure is typically reflected in a verb or gerund or another action word that indicates directionally that we have, for example, increased X, or reduced Y, or improved Z. Real-world examples of value expressed in common and measurable ways include

- Increase sales revenue by R percent

- Reduce the average number of bugs per sprint by S percent

- Improve the average support center hold time by T percent

Such measurable results or outcomes are called *Key Results.* They need to be easily measurable, which assumes we have instrumented our systems to not only be measurable but to allow measures to be taken. How else might we measure value? Value can be measured in terms of

- Direct financial benefits, including top-line revenue increases, bottom line cost reductions, and other outcomes that are directly measurable from a financial perspective.

- Direct nonfinancial benefits, which include outcomes that can be quantified but are oftentimes hard to quantify financially. Examples might include productivity gains, fewer customer complaints, improved processes leading to better support team responsiveness, improved staff turnover and other people-retention measures, and so on.

- Indirect benefits, which are benefits or outcomes that can be seen but are often more difficult to quantify or subject to bias. Consider how improved end user satisfaction, better customer service, higher team morale, and other such measures can be measured through surveys, for example.

There are other classes of value and benefits, but for our purposes, these ways of measuring value are a good start. Ensuring value is measurable, and tying that value to direct financial, direct nonfinancial, or indirect benefits is easy to keep top-of-mind. We want these notions of value in the front of our mind as we work to "solution small and fast" on the journey to delivering something worthwhile, something of value.

Objectives and Key Results

Ensuring value is measurable is key to ensuring we actually deliver something of value. But how might we go about organizing a stepwise view of value?

1. Consider what we learned through ideation and problem solving about a user community and their needs.

2. Determine what a "good" solution looks like to that user community.

3. Convert "good" into a set of high-level directional *Objectives*.

4. Map each Objective to one or more measurable *Key Results*.

With these underpinnings, we can measure at any point in our project or initiative just how well our Objectives are being realized. *Objectives and Key Results*, or OKRs, connect a project's or initiative's strategic goals with the day-to-day activities executed by a delivery team to achieve those goals. OKRs therefore reflect a goal-setting or value-focused framework designed to connect strategic goals set by a community with the activities that others execute to deliver those goals. With the completion of these goals comes value; the two become synonymous. OKRs therefore create clarity around what value looks like and how we know we have achieved it.

▶ The Objective in OKR is the *what*. The Objective should inspire and motivate (reflecting, for example, what we created using the Cover Story Mockup technique explained in Hour 16). The Objective states what we are going to accomplish or what we are going to achieve through our work. It can be big picture and strategic, or it can be something less grand.

▶ The Key Result in OKR is the *how*. Key Results are measurable as we have said, and in this way they quantify what "good" looks like. We should state how often we will measure our Key Results (monthly or quarterly, for example), and we need to tie these Key Results to the activities or sprints that we will execute to deliver those Key Results. We might even tie a range of "good enough" to our expected outcomes. Regardless, they must be measurable.

As we can see, for technology projects, OKRs map well to epics (Objectives) and features (Key Results). OKRs also map well to those who think in business terms. It's for these reasons that OKRs provide just the kind of value framework we need to measure our progress as we transition from prototyping to solutioning and delivering.

SMART Thinking

When it comes to *Key Results*, don't forget to think SMART! SMART is an acronym for specific, measurable, attainable, relevant (some prefer realistic), and timebound. This acronym is credited to Peter Drucker and his book *The Practice of Management* published in 1954. And SMART Thinking is a great approach for helping us create measurable Key Results. How? By ensuring that each Key Result is specific, measurable, attainable, relevant or realistic, and bound by time (such as two months, or 11 sprints, and so on). The more we can support our Key Results with data-derived or plan-based measures, the easier it will be to track our progress over time.

Starting Small and Delivering Fast

Oftentimes the best way to learn and understand is to do something or build something. As we covered last hour, prototyping and Building to Think are fundamental to Design Thinking both from a problem-solving perspective and, more to the point of this hour, from a broader solutioning perspective. So, too, are a myriad of Design Thinking techniques intended to help us gain better end-to-end solution clarity and learn along the way. Remember all of the techniques and methods we covered previously? In this hour, we build upon those mock-ups, wireframes, process flows, and a host of Rough and Ready Prototyping methods to make the next level of progress, as we see in Figure 17.1

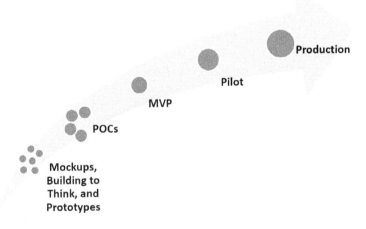

FIGURE 17.1
Note the natural left-to-right progression of value as we bridge the gap from the earliest of prototypes to various Proof of Concept exercises and ultimately to a full production solution.

In the next section we explore four long-time Design Thinking techniques that help us bridge the gap from our earliest prototyping and Building to Think efforts to developing full solutions as we Execute to Think, including

▶ The Proof of Concept (POC)

▶ The Minimum Viable Product (MVP)

▶ The Pilot

▶ Failing Forward for Progress

Techniques for Delivering and Executing to Think

With Building to Think behind us, we can turn our attention to a new twist on thinking with purpose coined Executing to Think. The difference hinges a bit on scope and a bit on the audience. In the first case, with regard to scope, Executing to Think helps us build on the work we've already completed and to learn more for our own benefit, if only to validate we're directionally on the right path. As we move into Design Thinking exercises for delivering small wins, though, we turn our focus even more to the second bit, where we learn more about what our audience needs, how they need it, when they need it, and so on.

Design Thinking in Action: The Proof of Concept

Coined by Bruce Carsten (1989), a Proof of Concept, or POC, exercise sets out to prove if a big idea or activity is actually possible. A POC is all about doing something small as a way of demonstrating feasibility for something much larger or more complex. In this way, it's similar to prototyping but in a more solution-oriented (albeit partial) kind of way, as illustrated in Figure 17.2. Consider the following examples:

▶ We might want to demonstrate through a POC how an out-of-the-box ERP or CRM configuration meets an end user community's requirement.

▶ We will want to prove that a new type of user interface is snappier and more performant than the current interface *before* we make that new interface the standard for the broader user community.

▶ We might like to prove that our cloud provider's new technology for securing access keys works for us in a way that will still pass our regulatory and compliance audits prior to adopting that new technology.

▶ We might wish to show key decision makers how a low code/no code reporting solution gives nontechnical users the ability to do the kind of business reporting previously requiring three months of expensive customization or the need for a "reporting expert."

Proof of Concept (POC) examples:
- Demo how well an out-of-the-box configuration meets an end user community's requirement.
- Validate that a new type of user interface is snappier.
- Prove that a cloud provider's new technology for securing access keys works perfectly.
- Show key decision makers a low code/no code reporting solution.

FIGURE 17.2
The Proof of Concept (POC) builds on our earlier work of prototyping and Building to Think to validate that a particular approach or technology is indeed feasible.

Each of these examples is a popular use case for POCs. The more we can demonstrate in a small way that something is indeed feasible, the more confidence we'll create and the more time we'll save. And perhaps more importantly, if we try and fail in a small and intentional way without disrupting our users, we will not only maintain their confidence in us but also pave the way for trying and learning again.

Design Thinking in Action: The MVP

An MVP, or Minimum Viable Product, reflects the minimum functionality or capability useful to a subset of a targeted audience. The key here is that the targeted audience uses the MVP to get real work done; the MVP is a small-scale production solution, as we see in Figure 17.3. It's not complete, and it's not a solution for everyone across the user community, but it works and provides real, albeit limited, value to a small group within that community.

Thus, in the same way that we Build to Think by prototyping and running POC exercises, we improve our understanding of a solution by Executing to Think or Refining to Think as we build out an MVP. This practice lets us course-correct to refine not only the value we deliver but also how quickly it's delivered. Once that MVP is iterated upon and fleshed out, it can support the role of a Pilot, covered next.

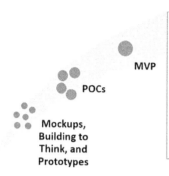

The MVP:
- An incomplete but functional solution supporting a subset of the user community.
- Builds on the work of prototyping, Building to Think, and POCs.
- Provides real and measurable value to that community.

FIGURE 17.3
The Minimum Viable Product (MVP) builds on our prototyping, Building to Think, and any number of POCs to provide value to a subset of a community.

Design Thinking in Action: The Pilot

It's prudent to Pilot a full-featured solution to a small user audience before rolling it out more broadly. This notion of putting forth an early version of a solution for a subset of users is all about gaining early feedback to tweak and tune the Pilot after it's released, in the same way that a television series might issue a pilot and then modify the storyline or characters in the wake of feedback.

As we see in Figure 17.4, Pilots are therefore functionally complete, unlike the tactical or partial functionality associated with a POC or the bare-bones functional capabilities available for only a subset of users reflected in an MVP. Like prototypes, POCs, and MVPs, though, a Pilot reduces risk by collecting important feedback prior to investing time and budget rolling out the piloted solution to a broad audience for productive use.

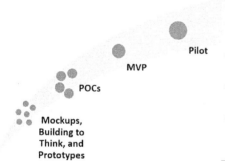

The Pilot:
- A functionally complete solution for a subset of the user community.
- Builds on the work of prototyping, Building to Think, POCs, and MVP.
- Provides real and measurable value to a reasonably broad community.
- The final step on the journey to releasing the system for production use by the full user community.

FIGURE 17.4
The Pilot builds on our MVP to create a full-featured solution validated by a subset of a community.

Design Thinking in Action: Failing Forward for Progress

Failing Forward is an important technique and Forcing Function (as we covered in Hour 16) used to encourage if not force forward progress. The idea is simply to remove the option of falling back in the wake of difficulties to a previous state or version. This technique has many other names, including Burning the Ships and Blowing the Bridges, but in tech we tend to call this Failing Forward. Failing Forward forces us to fight for progress rather than give up and return to the old and insufficient status quo.

NOTE

Burn the Ships!

In 1519 and the days of sailing ships, the Spanish Conquistador Hernando Cortez traveled from Spain and landed on the shores of the Yucatan. It is said that he and his team of 11 ships and more than 600 men were there to conquer, reap the spoils of war, and claim the riches of the land. At some point his men grew less committed to going to war, though, so the story goes on to say that Cortez gave the order to "Burn the Ships!" Why? To eliminate the possibility of retreat or falling back. Without the ships necessary to physically return back home to Spain, Cortez's men had no choice but to go to war; win or lose, they were destined to fight and fail and fight again for as long as it took to be successful and win.

We should consider employing Cortez's perspective as we read in the sidenote to drive individual and team progress after setbacks or even in the wake of catastrophe. Eliminate the option of going back to old products and no-longer-relevant solutions by taking those past products and solutions off the table. The practice of Failing Forward increases a team's motivation and commitment to move forward by literally removing the option to turn back. No turning back allowed! And with no other choice, we are that much more inclined to push forward and work on the current problems and issues. Failing Forward sets the stage for running toward a presumably brighter future.

For a Limited Time Only...

As we have seen, POCs, MVPs, and Pilots allow us to Execute to Think in the same way that we Build to Think as we prototype new ideas. However, we need to be careful not to lose our audience by "thinking" too long! After all, the pursuit of perfection is the enemy of progress. Instead, consider the following questions that can help us move forward and even push forward when we might be tempted to relax and iterate inside a comfortable sphere of POCs and the like:

▶ Do we really understand the Minimum Viable Product necessary for the broader audience to benefit from a piece of work? Have we documented the attributes of our MVP and gotten agreement on it?

▶ What about timing? Can we achieve an MVP through a small set of time-boxed sprints or iterations, or will it take more cycles or releases? How does this timing fit in with the team's and organization's need to validate and deliver value?

▶ Are there external realities, such as the need to retire an existing solution, which might prohibit us from pushing out our time-to-value? Can these realities be used as healthy Forcing Functions for making progress as we outlined in Hour 16?

▶ In the absence of hard external Forcing Function dates, can we align on a good set of artificial or other dates that can also act as Forcing Functions for driving progress?

▶ Do we understand the trade-offs between delivering an MVP and waiting to deliver a full-featured solution? Are we keeping 90 percent of the user community waiting while 10 percent are served? Should we expand the scope of our MVP or, conversely, decrease its duration?

▶ Can our users execute a part of their job in the new solution and a part of their job in the current solution? Or would this "swivel chairing" be too confusing or too expensive to orchestrate from a business and tech perspective?

As we circle through iterations of POCs and build out our MVPs and Pilots, we need to remain vigilant of the tension between improving our work for a small audience and delivering something of value to our broader audience. Throughout our work, we must remember that the broader audience is waiting!

And in nearly all cases, making progress is more important than achieving perfection. Do we understand what is Good Enough to be deployed? Has our user community confirmed enough of what we need to know? Do we recognize when our solutioning for a short-term horizon needs to finally give way to a solution that satisfies the longer-term horizon? Do the rewards outweigh the risks? Do we need to orchestrate our own version of Failing Forward for Progress? Gain alignment on these important questions early. And stay focused on the broader audience and our value delivery plan.

What Not to Do: The Forever MVP

In small tech initiatives and large business transformations alike, it is common and encouraged to use Design Thinking techniques such as prototypes, POCs, MVPs, and Pilots to learn, adapt, and refine our solutions. But we cannot iterate and circle around these pre-production solutions forever. POCs and MVPs are meant for a season, not for a lifetime, as an IT organization of a small consumer goods company learned the hard way.

Remaining in the grip of paralysis analysis, the organization iterated on too few features for too long with no benefit in sight for the fully intended audience. The development team and many others surrounding and supporting it wasted months and months of precious time delivering too little and with no velocity. Eventually, the combined team grew complacent, delivering something like 10 to 25 percent of its planned features each sprint. Meanwhile, the small user community tasked with developing user stories and grooming sprints busied itself seeking perfection in the few delivered features it was actually able to test.

With no sense of urgency and no measurable or timebound value, the executive sponsor grew weary of her "Forever MVP" project and pulled her sponsorship. Leaders were shuffled as the project went on "pause" for what was intended to be a short time. Eventually, the project was shut down because the intended user community lost patience and looked inward for its own solutions.

Summary

In this hour we explored the Design Thinking mindset surrounding what it means to make progress, including a set of techniques and practices useful in solutioning and making progress when our needs (or the path) are unclear. We explored the notion of value and steps necessary to define and measure value through the use of Objectives and Key Results (OKRs). Then we tied this notion of measuring value to four "Executing to Think" techniques useful for bridging the gap between problem solving and prototyping and the final solution we need to deliver to our broad user communities. The four techniques included executing a Proof of Concept (POC), deploying a Minimum Viable Solution (MVP), deploying a fully featured Pilot to a subset of our community, and using the Failing Forward for Progress technique to focus our teams on the future rather than the past. Hour 17 concluded with a "What Not to Do" highlighting what can happen when we run MVPs and other such pre-production exercises too long rather than deploying a solution to our broader community of users.

Workshop

Case Study

Consider the following case study and questions. You can find the answers to the questions related to this case study in Appendix A, "Case Study Quiz Answers."

Situation

Satish and the Executive Committee (EC) of BigBank are pleased with how the initiative teams seem to be working smarter and faster thanks to improved cross-teaming and prototyping techniques. But the teams are still under pressure to deliver value, any value, as quickly as possible. Some of BigBank's stakeholders and sponsors are growing restless with investments in people and budget and prototyping that only deliver incremental value. Others have even suggested that these investments are now going nowhere.

The Executive Committee has a number of questions pertaining to techniques you have seen and used that will help the Bank deliver small and quick wins on the journey to the planned big wins. They need to see outcomes; they need to see results. And they trust you can help get this work in motion.

Quiz

1. What are the three techniques outlined in this hour that help a team "Execute to Think" and ultimately deliver something small and of value?

2. As discussed this hour, how might a team define and refine the notion of value?

3. What does it mean to "Fail Forward" and how is this useful to a team?

4. How does a Pilot differ from a Proof of Concept or an MVP?

5. In what way does the "Progress Mindset" establish a way for making progress when the path is uncertain or the needs of a community are unclear?

HOUR 18

Delivering Value at Velocity

What You'll Learn in This Hour:

▶ Delivery Techniques for Increasing Value Velocity

▶ Team Considerations for Velocity

▶ Change Control Considerations for Velocity

▶ What Not to Do: Shrink Sprints to Speed Up

▶ Summary and Case Study

Hour 18 builds on the ways of starting small to deliver value sooner rather than later as we previously covered in Hour 17. In this hour we focus on techniques for delivering value with velocity and another set of techniques that teams may use to deliver faster. We also review a set of change control considerations that can greatly affect velocity. We conclude Hour 18 with a real-world "What Not to Do" focused on misunderstanding the implications of shrinking or shortening design and development sprints with the hopes of increasing speed or agility.

Delivery Techniques for Increasing Value Velocity

As mentioned before, some of the same techniques for simply making progress are also ideal for making that progress quickly or responsibly. We've already covered popular Design Thinking techniques such as Time Boxing, Time Pacing, and the Inverse Power Law. Here, let's explore Release and Sprint Planning, considerations for Operating Small to Deliver Big, and the role that Smart IP Reuse plays in achieving velocity.

Design Thinking in Action: Release and Sprint Planning

Only briefly mentioned in Hour 13, Release Planning is the process of identifying, prioritizing, and selecting the high-level capabilities and user stories (needs) to be reflected in our solution, built over a period of time, and delivered at the conclusion of that time in the form of a time-boxed "release." We tend to think about releases as spanning months rather than weeks. Given that Agile sprint planning and grooming are well adopted and considered standard operating procedure by the Project Management Institute (PMI), we have not covered them in any depth here other than using techniques to make sprints and releases visible and visual.

To actually organize, prioritize, and consider the dependencies between items, we divide each large release-level time box into multiple smaller time boxes called *sprints*. Each sprint within a release is typically executed sequentially and reflects the work necessary to configure or develop the code necessary to deliver the planned set of capabilities and user stories. Sprints are typically one to four weeks long. For context around this hierarchy of releases and sprints, see Figure 18.1.

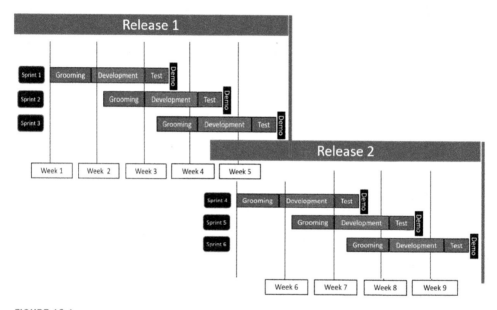

FIGURE 18.1
Note how sprints run sequentially to form a release, a release plan, and ultimately an important component of the overall project or initiative plan.

Thinking about and planning for the specific sprints and larger releases associated with our solution helps us create a plan and see the big picture. Doing so doesn't naturally help us increase velocity, however. But with the big picture clear and our schedule aligned, we can then think ahead and think more deeply about the next best step that *can* help us achieve greater velocity.

▶ What is our three Horizon Plan (as we covered in Hour 13), and how well does our Release Plan and its underlying sprints align with these horizons? Is there room to deliver early? Are there opportunities to run certain sprints or other work in parallel? Might we actually run two or more *releases* in parallel?

▶ Can we better identify and assess the value and impact of the benefits we expect to achieve? How well are we tracking against our planned benefits realization? Are we overstepping what we learned about Good Enough Thinking, or do we have an opportunity to apply another guardrail for thinking to increase velocity as we covered in Hour 11?

▶ How might we improve sprint grooming and planning to deliver more predictably? Why are we underdelivering, for example, and how can we apply the Five Whys, Problem Framing, Problem Tree Analysis, or Problem Stating outlined in Hour 9 to improve our velocity?

▶ Are we monitoring the delivery of our outputs well? Where might we move faster and deliver more? Do we need to better instrument how we operate so as to highlight how our expected benefits and other outcomes are slow to be realized? Do we really understand how all of this work contributes to the bigger picture or our Horizon Plan?

▶ How might we better analyze the potential impact of planned changes on our expected benefits and outcomes? Is there an opportunity to engage our users again and reimagine a set of sprints, for example?

▶ How well are our expected benefits aligned against our goals, objectives, and key results. What's missing or misaligned?

We need to consider also how we might optimize our processes and personas as we consider responsibility and accountability surrounding benefits realization. As we will cover in later hours, the better we understand how well we are delivering value and our expected benefits today, the better we can ensure in the future that those expected benefits can be sustained.

Design Thinking in Action: Operating Small to Deliver Big

As most people understand, it is more important to focus on outcomes rather than outputs. Being busy doesn't equate to delivering value. When it comes to sprints and our other work in flight, we need to remember to establish those sprints and time boxes in ways that contain a body of work that can actually be completed within the sprint. The idea is to deliver something of use, something that can be tested, something of value (keeping in mind that sometimes value will require more than one sprint, of course). It is through the small pieces of work we deliver that big changes and impact are delivered. Consider the following:

▶ Size user stories using story points, T-shirt sizing, or similar approximation approaches to estimate the time and effort or development capacity necessary to create a feature or process. User Story Sizing is key to creating better sprints, releases, and schedules.

▶ Employ User Story Mapping to bring together the steps necessary to deliver a user story, from identifying goals and user journey to solutioning, organizing work into time boxes or sprints, and publishing a release plan.

▶ Focus on understanding and delivering key dependencies and core underpinnings first. To be sure, we will need to explain the value of delivering these items, but the explanation should reflect the fact that future impact depends on this first bit of work.

▶ Focus next on delivering the right features at the right time (rather than delivering a collection of features that may or may not actually be useful in the short term).

▶ In parallel, use techniques such as POCs and MVPs outlined in Hour 17 as a way to deliver fast while obtaining the feedback necessary to deliver well in a directionally accurate kind of way.

▶ Organize the remaining work to accommodate dependencies on other work, especially work external to the bit that we're focused on.

▶ When we need to divide large bodies of work across multiple sprints (because one discrete component builds on another), work in parallel on landing the reasoning as well as highlighting and demonstrating the value in these discrete components.

▶ Conversely, organize work in parallel when such work can be accommodated within the same sprint and we have onboarded the necessary resources (and resource bandwidth) to accommodate running in parallel.

In these ways, we should be able to demonstrate value early and demonstrate it throughout each sprint and across each release.

Design Thinking in Action: Smart IP Reuse

Our world is filled with accelerators in various shapes and sizes that can help us start faster or move with greater velocity. Though overused in the tech realm, the term *intellectual property (IP)* represents a broad source of accelerators. For our purposes, IP is the work that others have completed before us that may be reused (or adapted and reused) to help us make better progress today. Consider the following list and illustration depicted in Figure 18.2:

▶ **Document deliverables.** How might we reuse functional and solution design documents, technical blueprints, and the like as a form of template for more quickly creating our own documents?

▶ **Planning deliverables.** How might we adapt previously used Release and Sprint Planning documents, Horizon Plans, roadmaps, and project plans for our benefit?

▶ **Checklists.** How might we leverage existing checklists to help ensure we don't miss something important as we design, develop, deploy, and operate our solutions?

▶ **Test plans.** How might we adapt a well-designed test plan to accelerate our understanding and preparation for testing?

▶ **Preconfigured templates.** How might some of our work already be reflected in the previous work of others such that we can lift and reuse them as a literal or figurative template to accelerate our own work?

▶ **Design Thinking templates.** In the same way we might adopt solution-oriented IP, how might we borrow the templates, worked examples, tools, and other artifacts used in our Design Thinking exercises to accelerate how we prepare and deliver those exercises?

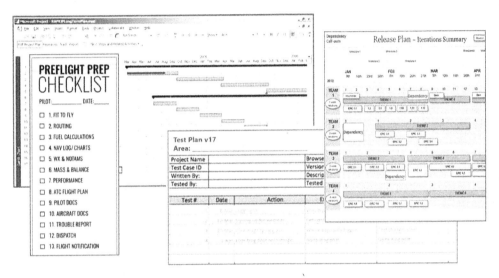

FIGURE 18.2
Reusable artifacts and other IP are natural kick-starters for velocity.

The idea is simple enough. Avoid the temptation to create what doesn't need to be created. Save our time and energy for thinking through and creating what hasn't been done before. Adapt and reuse what we can to help us make progress faster than otherwise possible.

NOTE

The Standardized Template

Another common form of IP is the Standardized Template, which is a content-empty document outlining and organizing (in an empathy-aligned and structured way) content for a set of well-understood users. Templates help us understand the "what" of a document by understanding its structure. Standardized templates are intended for repeatable purposes; use them to build artifacts with consistency and speed, ensuring nothing contentwise is missed in the process.

Team Considerations for Velocity

As our teams go about their work learning, empathizing, problem solving, and so forth, we face natural challenges to moving with some level of velocity. And as most of us know, those challenges typically slow us down. But we can turn to three Design Thinking techniques to help us reclaim lost time or speed up: Smart Multitasking, Gamification, and Shortcut or Wormhole Thinking, each of which is covered next. Consider stringing all three together in the form of a recipe for considering and validating velocity.

Design Thinking in Action: Smart Multitasking

The notion of multitasking or performing two or more tasks simultaneously is nothing new. The idea was popularized in the 1960s by IBM's computer engineers, but most of us have since come to realize that multitasking is not nearly as effective in increasing productivity or saving time as we once believed. True multitasking is more of a conundrum, in fact; instead of getting twice as much done, multitasking often leaves us with less than half of either task completed. Why? Because the task switching that our brain does as we move from one task to the other and back again creates too much of a burden. Getting ourselves back into the context of the new task takes too long, wasting time as we retread old ground to pick up again where we left off.

Of course, the reality for all of us is this: We need to multitask in some capacity because we simply don't have a choice. We still have a hundred things to get done each day and something like 16 hours to get it all done. Thus, we have to find a way to get things done and fight the inertia that pulls us toward stalling in between tasks. We need to avoid overload and strike a sustainable balance. How? Consider these questions:

▶ How might we reduce the number of tasks on our plates? That is, how might we say no or delegate tasks to others, so that 100 tasks become 80?

▶ How might we use Forcing Functions, Time Boxing, and other techniques to help us focus and prioritize our multitasking?

▶ How might we automate some of these tasks so that we spend a bit of time monitoring and verifying tasks that have been completed rather than spending all of our time *doing*?

▶ How might we reduce or eliminate the distractions around us that shatter the glass house of cards we mentally build as we think about a task?

▶ How might we better give our full attention to what's in front of us so that we actually complete our tasks faster than typically done?

The two greatest techniques for smarter multitasking include

▶ Do what gives us the most energy at the time; follow our passion.

▶ Make sure we make time for the most important *big rocks*; if the big and important tasks aren't accounted for first, it's oftentimes impossible to add them in later.

These are simple techniques, but they are powerful. Do the thing that gives us the most energy at the time, and then move on to the next thing that gives us the most energy. And make progress on the big rocks (the most important items) lest we run out of room or bandwidth or energy to get these done at all. Use Time Box and use Forcing Functions as necessary to help us complete the mandatory work that doesn't give us energy. And for lasting change, consider how personal productivity apps and coaching such as that available from BillionMinds can help us discover and embed the specific mindset and techniques that personally work best for us and for our situations (see https://billionminds.com).

To this last point, when we focus on the tasks that give us the most energy:

▶ We get things done, and generally get them done quickly.

▶ We naturally create more bandwidth for other tasks.

▶ We get the endorphin rush that comes from checking off an item on our to-do list, which in turn gives us energy to tackle the next task.

▶ Our brain gets primed to tackle a similar task with relative ease, giving us more bandwidth for such tasks.

When we follow our energy and our passion, we get more done. And when we thoughtfully inject Forcing Functions and similar Design Thinking techniques into our less-than-energizing tasks, we might get the rest of our work done. For those most elusive tasks, we might even consider Gamification, too, covered next.

Design Thinking in Action: Gamification for Engagement

We might try our hand at Smart Multitasking or Time Boxing to get work completed, and we might even use a Forcing Function to help us make progress when tasks simply need to be completed. But what if we are still having trouble finding the self-discipline to just get a set of tasks done? What else might we try?

Consider how Gamification can be used to drive progress and check off tasks. Gamification, a term coined in 2002 by Nick Pelling, a computer programmer and inventor, helps us by increasing our engagement and our motivation (Wood & Reiners, 2015). To help us engage in the work ahead of us and finish the necessary but mundane work we dread, consider making a game out of those tasks by building a reward system around them.

Video game manufacturers have long used the notion of ribbons and badges and other such accolades as a way to incentivize people to spend time playing their games. Car manufacturers have more recently done the same, using green economy leaf visuals when we drive economically as a way to reward us (and improve our perception of the vehicle's mileage). Training vendors and new-language apps use Gamification to reward students with new features, awards, certificates, levels, and more to those who complete a training section or make progress in a program or curriculum.

In the same way, apply Gamification to the low-passion and low-energy tasks awaiting us. Instead of solely earning video game badges or points or new levels, though, reward ourselves and our team with little but meaningful trinkets or prizes. Gift cards, coffee breaks, half-day Fridays, free lunches, and so on can serve as grand prizes too, for those who mightily achieve.

Design Thinking in Action: Shortcuts and Wormholes

Sometimes the fastest path between two points is not a straight line. Also called Shortcut Thinking or Finding the Wormhole, this technique is about finding not-so-obvious shortcuts between where we are today and where we need to go. The key lies in this: navigating everything between us and our destination without allowing ourselves to get caught up in the detours and side routes. The obvious paths aren't necessarily the best paths for our specific situation, after all.

To find shortcuts, we need to know something about the map that describes where we are and where we want to go. We should lay out a traditional route for starters, if only to help us understand that route more deeply (in the same way that we might employ Journey Mapping, covered briefly in Hour 3 and in more detail in Hour 8).

Let's consider the route that a student might follow to complete a traditional four-year college degree (see Figure 18.3). What if we don't have the funds to pay as we go? Or we don't want to invest in college loans? Is there a shorter path? There may be! Map the route to make it visible, and the makings of a shorter path may begin to become self-evident.

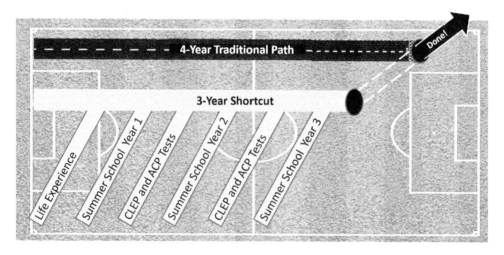

FIGURE 18.3
Shortcuts and wormholes abound if we simply make the playing field visible. Alternatively, we may be able to actually *change* the playing field itself to finish faster.

▶ Avoid the long breaks over the summer and in between semesters. The route should visually show us these breaks. Instead, attend school year-round and this single shortcut will allow us to complete a four-year degree in three years or less.

▶ Avoid the traditional four-year degree curriculum, which is usually something like 120 to 132 credit hours (or 40 to 44 courses). Instead, find a degree program that requires 110 credit hours or less, which will help us reduce the four-year time commitment a bit.

▶ Most universities award at least some college credit for life experience or for certificates we completed (such as that gained in military training, technology certification programs, and the like). Instead of assuming we must complete every course, work with the counselor to reduce the number of required courses, which will also help us reduce the four-year time commitment a bit more.

▶ Finally, most universities also extend college credit for earning minimum scores on Advanced Placement (AP) exams and College Level Examination Program (CLEP) tests. Study for and take some of these tests in parallel to avoid the courses that bring us no energy or passion, and we shave even more time off our regular four-year journey.

Again, the key may lie in changing the playing field so we can change the route. Thus, it's important to really understand that playing field, or the lay of the land, and how we might change it. There are plenty of ways to complete a four-year degree in three years. Know our goal and know what we are willing to trade off to achieve that goal. Truth be told, there are typically many ways to get from Point A to Point B if we are more focused on the speed of the trip rather than the experience. So consider the trade-offs and map new routes. The shortcuts and wormholes are just waiting to be found.

Change Control Considerations for Velocity

Though some might debate this premise, executing with velocity does not mean we throw *change control* out the window. Managing change to schedule, scope, resourcing, and so on is an important part of thinking ahead to maintain velocity (or alternatively, to accept the trade-offs for another good reason such as higher quality or regulatory and audit requirements).

NOTE

Not Change Management but Rather Change Control

What is Change Control? As we briefly outlined in Framing Governance for Collaboration in Hour 15, it is the formal process we follow in tech to ensure that changes to our solution, its business case, its technical underpinnings, and the resources and schedule associated with all of this are considered in light of change. Such change is often measured in terms of impact to the final solution, including how and when value is delivered. The Change Control process helps us consider, document, and apply change in a controlled and coordinated manner.

Change Control takes foresight and time. But the process helps us sustain a strong and resilient link to our solution delivery and deployment goals. And thoughtful change control forces us to consider new opportunities for creating value and driving velocity.

Events that should invoke the change control process in a way that might positively affect velocity include

▶ New technologies or services that might slow us down as we consider their effect on our as-is design or solution, but offer new ways to deliver business outcomes or improve velocity in the longer term.

▶ Existing technology updates that typically slow us down but could offer new features, capabilities, and other opportunities that might improve velocity in the longer term.

▶ Changing market conditions that might slow us down but help us refine what value looks like in the wake of those changes.

▶ Resourcing additions that may allow us to enhance our solution's quality, time-to-market, or ability to deliver value sooner than later.

When change presents itself and we are required to react, consider how that change might be converted into a difference maker or velocity enabler.

What Not to Do: Shrink Sprints to Speed Up

In software development and platform configuration, we can spend a lot of time thinking about how long the ideal sprint should be. Two-week sprints, three-week sprints, and even four-week sprints are pretty common.

When the inevitable challenges occur and we wind up pushing out or "snow plowing" too much of our uncompleted work into future sprints, we can be tempted to remediate this problem by changing the sprint cadence. A product consultant in a financial services firm ran into this temptation first-hand. He thought moving the team from three-week sprints to two-week sprints would give the team better agility and more time to make up lost ground. But he was "solving" the wrong problem. The real problem had something to do with poorly executed grooming, late user stories, and new and unclear user stories being added to sprints without proper planning and grooming. Shrinking the sprint cycle time only *reduced* the amount of time the team had for development.

How was this so? Shrinking sprint cycles gave the team less time to get the work done and less time to test that work because, as a percentage of overall time, they were spending even more time executing all of the typical sprint ceremonies. Grooming, show-and-tell demonstrations, retrospectives, and so on continued to consume the same amount of time regardless of the sprint cycle time. So the ratio of work-to-ceremony-overhead only suffered when the consultant moved the team to two-week sprints.

Sometimes too much of a good thing is a bad thing. Too many demos and retrospectives stuffed into a two-week time period, as our consultant found here, drove quite a bit more overhead as a percentage of effort. Fortunately, he was able to return to his original cycle time, and more importantly was able to work with the team to investigate the real problems that needed attention.

Summary

In Hour 18, we explored three techniques for increasing value velocity, including Release and Sprint Planning, Operating Small to Deliver Big, and Smart IP Reuse. Then we covered another three techniques for increasing the velocity of our teams, from Smart Multitasking to Gamification and Shortcut or Wormhole Thinking. After outlining change control considerations, the hour concluded with a "What Not to Do" focused on shrinking sprint lengths with the mistaken idea that such a move could improve both agility and velocity.

Workshop

Case Study

Consider the following case study and questions. You can find the answers to the questions related to this case study in Appendix A, "Case Study Quiz Answers."

Situation

Satish needs your help to drive greater velocity across a number of the OneBank initiatives. He has observed way too much wasted time as various initiative architects and consultants tend to re-create the wheel over and over again. In other cases, Satish has also observed how different teams tend to randomize themselves and their work. He is sure you have some ideas for responsibly increasing focus and velocity and has asked you to sit down with several initiative leaders to discuss techniques for delivering value at greater velocity.

Quiz

1. What is the hierarchy of releases to sprints, and how do they map to one another?

2. What technique considers how the initiative leaders might adapt existing templates and artifacts to improve velocity?

3. In what cases does multitasking make sense and actually prove useful?

4. What technique might be employed to use ribbons, badges, and other rewards to encourage initiative testers to complete their test cases?

5. Which technique sets the stage for reinventing the playing field to find a faster or more effective route between two points?

HOUR 19
Testing for Validation

Hour 19 commences the final six hours in Part V, "Iterating for Progress," where we focus on Phase 4 of our Design Thinking Model for Tech, including testing and the feedback loops between phases (see Figure 19.1). Here in Hour 19, we look at the Testing Mindset, set the stage with traditional types of testing, and then detail five Design Thinking testing techniques for learning more about and validating user needs. We conclude with a look at two feedback testing tools and a "What Not to Do" focused on negative ROI from automating too much regression testing.

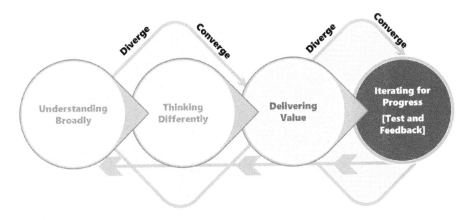

FIGURE 19.1
Phase 4 of our Design Thinking Model for Tech.

The Testing Mindset

It has been said that the flip side of thinking is testing. We test to prove our theories and ideas. This kind of Testing Mindset is integral to problem solving as we validate what we *think* we know, discover gaps as we uncover what we don't know, and generally learn more throughout the testing process. In the context of prototyping and building a solution, testing is central as well. We prototype to test our theories and learn in the process, and we execute POCs to validate our own thinking. And we run MVPs (Minimum Viable Products) and Pilots to validate with our users that a proposed solution is directionally on track (as we covered in Hour 17).

Testing is also an early form of *doing* in the sense that we have a first-hand chance to quickly learn so we can avoid the wasted time associated with incorrectly designing, developing, or building. Done early enough, testing helps us avoid dead-end ideas and theories too. Finally, testing gives us the early feedback we desperately need from others and through what we observe and learn.

And it is this feedback that helps us refine how we are empathizing, thinking, prototyping, retesting, and building our solutions. The Testing Mindset gives us new insights we can bake into how we work through problems and situations to realize value. Testing therefore gets us closer and closer to something that truly solves our problems. We might Build to Think, but we test to learn, do, and solve.

Traditional Types of Testing

There are many types of testing as we see illustrated in Figure 19.2, and most of these types are focused on validating that what we have designed or prototyped or built does what we expect. While outside of the scope of this book, these types of testing span the prototyping and solutioning lifecycle. We run some of these tests very early and others much later and with a subset of our users. Let us set the stage with these traditional testing approaches:

▶ **Unit Testing.** We need to test that a specific Proof of Concept or atomic user transaction or bit of customized code that we have developed does what we expect it to do.

▶ **Process Testing.** We need to build on Unit Testing to validate that a string of developed code or string of previously tested user transactions works together as expected in the form of a process (oftentimes synonymous with a business process).

▶ **End-to-End Testing.** We need to build on Process Testing to ensure that a collection of related processes works together to deliver an end-to-end business capability or feature, such as Order-to-Cash or Procure-to-Pay.

▶ **System Integration Testing.** We need to test that our collection of capabilities and features—our solution—holistically works together as a fully integrated system. In particular, we need to ensure that one process doesn't break another and that all processes receive their inputs as expected, execute as expected, and deliver their outputs as expected.

▶ **User Acceptance Testing (UAT).** Finally, we need to give a subset of our users the chance to exercise and test our solutions before those solutions are finally *promoted to production* and made available to the whole of the community. Properly executed UAT validates not only that the system works as expected (a la *happy path testing*), but that it also reacts as expected when users use the system in unconventional or unexpected ways.

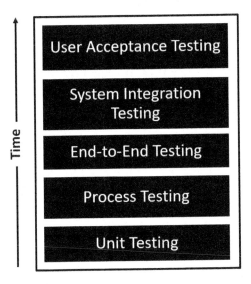

FIGURE 19.2
Traditional testing comprises Unit Testing, Process Testing, End-to-End Testing, System Integration Testing, and User Acceptance Testing.

User Acceptance Testing does not represent the final form of traditional testing, however. As our solution is *hardened* or made ready for production, we also need to consider how that solution will perform under the weight of many users concurrently accessing the system, or reports being generated, or long-running batch processes or jobs being run behind the scenes. How will the system perform under these loads? Where are the system's weak spots? What are the user community's expectations around performance and availability? How might these expectations need to be reset to accommodate business or seasonal peaks or simply the capabilities of the system? How might we test and validate performance and scalability under different loads or conditions?

With so many questions to answer, it is paramount to consider three more performance-related types of testing and the questions posed here for each:

▶ **Performance Testing.** How well does a single user transaction or a single process perform with no other load on the system? How does that single user transaction's performance degrade as additional transactions are placed on the system?

▶ **Scalability Testing.** Also called *usability testing at scale*, how well does the system perform when the full user community is using the system as intended?

▶ **Load and Stress Testing.** How well does the system perform under load or stress? What level of performance degradation might the user community experience at peak times in their season or business calendar? How might we set expectations with the community regarding performance in light of varying loads or various points in time?

Note that performance, scalability, and load and stress testing are prepped for as early as practical and actually performed once the solution is stabilized and ready for that particular type of testing. These final three performance-related testing approaches (along with others related to specific attributes of performance as well as security testing, user profile testing, and more) complete what we call our Traditional Testing Framework, as illustrated in Figure 19.3. Again, none of this is necessarily Design Thinking–inspired but rather simply a good set of user-centric practices for responsibly testing products and solutions prior to deploying those products and solutions for productive use.

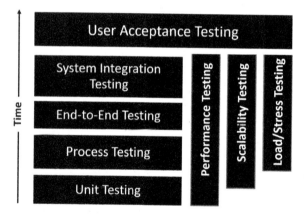

FIGURE 19.3
The Traditional Testing Framework represents all seven traditional testing types (and others not specifically outlined here).

Finally, to validate and quantitatively measure our system's performance, we need to *instrument* our system for performance and availability monitoring (which is yet again out of the scope of this book but important to share in the context of testing). What kinds of performance monitors and thresholds should we establish as part of *Service Reliability Engineering* to help us understand and manage our solution day to day and under load? What do we need to carefully watch, and what can we potentially automate so that we're alerted *before* our solution runs into major performance problems?

NOTE

What Is SRE?

SRE, or Service Reliability Engineering, comprises the engineering, technical, and change control methodologies and procedures necessary to manage the reliability of a system and resolve reliability operations and infrastructure issues (often in an automated or *self-healing* kind of way). Synonymous with a culture or mindset of service reliability, service reliability engineers work to automate what can be responsibly automated as a way to avoid manually introduced issues (in the same way that we seek to automate perhaps 80 percent of our system's *regression testing* as we make changes to that system, covered later this hour).

With our Traditional Testing Framework and the notion of Service Reliability Engineering in place, let us turn our attention to the Design Thinking techniques and tools that build on and add value to these long-standing mainstays of testing and monitoring.

Testing Techniques for Learning and Validating

Beyond the many types of traditional testing outlined previously, we also can lean on several Design Thinking-inspired testing techniques. Of course, Prototyping in all of its forms (covered in Hour 16) is one of our earliest testing methods. We prototype to test our ideas and test our partial solutions, after all. Beyond prototyping, we also test and validate our ideas and solutions through POCs, MVPs, and Pilots, too, as we covered in Hour 17.

But how might we better engage our users to prototype and test more deeply? What can we do differently to better ensure our solution meets their spoken and perhaps even unspoken needs? How might we learn those unspoken needs before our solution is ever even turned into an MVP or Pilot?

The answer to these questions lies with several techniques outlined next. Most of these Design Thinking techniques are associated with the iterative testing we do surrounding prototyping, but indeed every one of these techniques is useful throughout solutioning and even afterward when we find ourselves iterating on a solution already in production.

Design Thinking in Action: A/B Testing

A/B Testing is one of the simplest and yet most valuable testing techniques at our disposal. When we want to validate a preference around two features, or two aspects of an interface, or perhaps two different approaches to solving a problem, we can turn to A/B Testing. As the name implies, the idea is to test one alternative against another alternative, as we see in Figure 19.4. Users sometimes prefer this approach of comparing one feature to another feature, for example, rather than trying to explain why they don't like a particular feature.

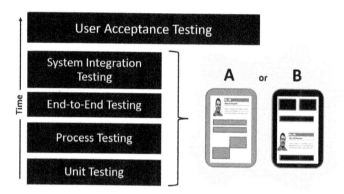

FIGURE 19.4
Consider how A/B Testing may be employed alongside traditional testing to determine a user community's preference for one alternative over another.

Because it can be easily structured and rapidly executed, A/B Testing lends itself to quantitative evaluation. That is, from a user community of tens or hundreds or thousands, we can quickly determine where to next spend our time based on the likes and other feedback from the community. Use this technique early in prototyping and continue using this technique throughout testing and well after a product or solution has been deployed to production. A/B Testing is great for evaluating minor proposed changes to our production solution—for example, in the name of continuous feature testing and improvement.

Design Thinking in Action: Experience Testing

When we need valuable prototype insights from the only people who really matter—prospective users—turn to Experience Testing. This type of testing often overlaps with Structured Usability Testing (covered next), and it may be used as part of traditional End-to-End and System Integration Testing to assess a user's experience with our prototype or proposed product or solution. Wireframes, rough and ready prototypes, and even simple line drawings can also serve as a source for Experience Testing.

Again, the idea is to gain early feedback from the very people who will presumably use our product or solution one day. Encourage these people to vocalize their likes, dislikes, and what they might change. Good products and solutions are generally viewed as intuitive to use. Confirm the extent this intuitiveness to be true, and capture what has been missed in design or the implementation of that design.

Practice Experience Testing early on. A product's or solution's intuitiveness can often be assessed very early in the design and development phases. As a product or solution matures, other modalities and methods can be used to gather such feedback too, ranging from traditional post-sprint or post-release User Acceptance Testing to the other Design Thinking techniques outlined this hour and techniques such as Silent Design outlined later in Hour 20.

Design Thinking in Action: Structured Usability Testing

To test and validate our prototypes early on with our users, turn to Structured Usability Testing. The idea is to confirm that a product or solution works effectively and is indeed *usable*. The difference between this kind of testing and traditional User Acceptance Testing is in the timing; Structured Usability Testing occurs well beforehand, when we have time to make fundamental product and solution changes.

The key to Structured Usability Testing lies in creating a uniform and repeatable environment for this testing. By establishing a plan that includes level-setting each user about the test's purpose and goals, along with a sequenced set of test cases or scenarios to execute, our earliest users can help us accomplish a number of objectives:

- ▶ Gain an early perspective from the very people who will use our product or solution one day, including how well the different personas interact with our early prototypes. Do some personas naturally understand our prototype better than others?

- ▶ Validate our assumptions and early direction about the product or solution. Are we on the right track?

- ▶ Validate the effectiveness of the inputs, processing, and outputs required by the product or solution. Are we missing something?

- ▶ Confirm how intuitive our interface or design is based on questions asked or time spent by our users to navigate our product or solution. Did our users have to ask a lot of questions to actually use our prototype?

- ▶ Consider product or solution performance including individual users' thoughts and expectations. Is the system snappy, slow, or somewhere in between? Are certain aspects of the experience faster or slower than others?

- ▶ Rate each user's overall experience on a scale of 1 (deeply intuitive and satisfied) to 10 (unclear and unsatisfied), for example. Would additional context, user preparation, or training be effective?

In these ways, we can quickly pivot and change our design, our interface, the underlying technology, or even the fundamental nature of the product or solution based on quasi real-world experiences and feedback. Doing so earlier rather than later saves cost and time while creating much-needed clarity early on. The test lead or a test facilitator should consider videoing or in some other way recording these structured usability tests too so that the whole team can benefit from these early learnings. Such learnings constitute a portion of our user engagement metrics too.

NOTE
___

What Are User Engagement Metrics?

As we work through testing our products and solutions (and eventually deploying and operationalizing them), we need to track from our users how well *they* believe we are engaging them. Called User Engagement Metrics, this direct feedback and knowledge help us understand what we might need to do differently to make our testing more user-centric and effective.
___

Design Thinking in Action: Solution Interviewing

After we conclude traditional User Acceptance Testing, which is oftentimes the final type of testing we conduct prior to promoting a product or solution to production status, we need to confirm in another important way that our product or solution is truly "accepted." We can accomplish this final checkpoint through Solution Interviewing.

Solution Interviewing builds on the static pass/fail results we tend to get from UAT. Users validating pass/fail for the transactions and business processes they will execute as part of their "Day in the Life of" is important feedback, to be sure. But it's dry feedback. On the other hand, Solution Interviewing gives us the rich feedback we need to make smart updates to our products and solutions even if they *are* accepted.

Be sure to interview a breadth of users, and group or apply Affinity Clustering to key subsets or personas within the user community. Our goal is to determine first-hand and verbally what a user likes, dislikes, would like to be changed, and so on. Create a list of such questions organized around product features, solution capabilities, and so on.

Above all, ensure we *listen* much more than we talk. Lean on our listening and understanding skills acquired in Hour 6, using Active Listening, Silence by Design, Supervillain Monologuing, and Probing for Better Understanding techniques. Ideally, we should be able to create a backlog of new ideas and features that the team can consider, prototype, and iterate against.

One final point: Solution Interviewing is ideal for providing confirmation for soon-to-become production systems, but we should seek this confirmation prior to deploying MVPs and Pilots too. Use Solution Interviewing to build on the feedback obtained not just from preproduction UAT but from our earlier testing conducted prior to releasing MVPs and Pilots. In these ways we can learn and iterate earlier.

Design Thinking in Action: Automating for Regression Velocity

Automation is about velocity. We need to automate what we can, especially repetitive complex business processes subject to manual testing errors. Much has been written in blogs and other books about the need to automate something like 80 to 90 percent of our regression tests. The upfront investment in tools and scripting pays dividends when we're 10 sprints into a release and need to quickly test changes and validate that bug fixes haven't broken yet another part of our system.

NOTE
What Is Regression Testing?
After we make any kind of substantive change (and some would rightly argue *any* change) to a proto-type, MVP, Pilot, or production system, we should run a series of functional and nonfunctional tests to validate that our new change didn't break our existing system or any of our existing functionality. Such tests are combined together and labeled Regression Testing, as we are testing our system to validate that it still works as expected and has not *regressed*. If an existing feature "breaks" in light of our change, we say it has experienced a regression. To be clear, the problem might lie with our change, but it might also reflect a deficiency in our existing feature or code. Either way, something needs to be remediated.

It sounds tempting to fully automate a regression test. But we need to take care not to automate every regression test case. The diminishing returns come quickly as we exceed 80 to 90 percent of our test surface area. Beyond this range of 80 to 90 percent, where each new sprint requires script maintenance and each bug fix potentially breaks our scripts (sometimes erroneously if the bug fix fails to actually remediate what it was intended to fix), we eventually wind up doing more manual script maintenance than regression testing. Automate the easy test cases, automate the test cases especially prone to manual human error, and seek to automate complex test cases as much as feasible.

Testing Tools for Feedback

Though we cover feedback in detail in the next hour, two user feedback capture tools are worth exploring here. These Design Thinking tools are used in the context of testing and can be useful across both traditional and Design Thinking-inspired types of testing.

▶ **The Testing Sheet.** As the name implies, this is typically a one-page template useful for consistently gathering the kind of feedback we need to iterate on a prototype, MVP, or product or solution as is. We are looking for the learnings and insights our users have as they interact with our work-in-progress. Use this tool in conjunction with any of the traditional or Design Thinking–inspired techniques covered this hour. See Figure 19.5 for a sample Testing Sheet.

▶ **The Feedback Capture Grid.** This simple 2×2 matrix tool provides the structure necessary for users to quickly test and record our findings, observations, and other learnings. Because it is pretty general in nature, the Feedback Capture Grid can also be used by attendees to capture their feedback after concluding a meeting, workshop, Design Thinking exercise, and so on. See Figure 19.6 for a sample Feedback Capture Grid.

Test Case #_____		Tester _____	
Description of this test case		**Test pass/fail criteria**	
Objective/Process		**Persona/Roles**	
Results		**Learnings**	
Verbatims/Documented Outcomes			

FIGURE 19.5
Consider this sample template to create and customize a Testing Sheet for our prototype, MVP, Pilot, or other product or solution.

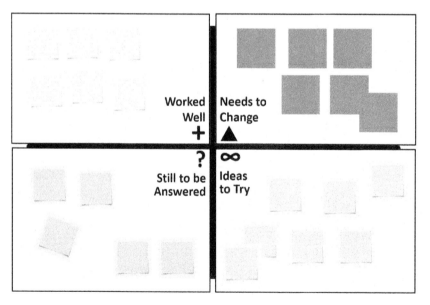

Worked Well +

Needs to Change ▲

? Still to be Answered

∞ Ideas to Try

FIGURE 19.6
Use a simple 2×2 Feedback Capture Grid to quickly record test feedback organized by what worked well, needs to change, still needs to be answered, and ideas to try.

Remember to capture customer and user verbatims and other feedback as accurately as possible. If we find it necessary to add our own details and comments alongside our users' feedback, make it clear *who* exactly provided *what* feedback.

What Not to Do: Automate Everything

We might be tempted to fully automate our regression tests as time goes on and we see the repercussions from poorly executed manual testing. In the wake of a series of regression "misses" in their complex ERP (Enterprise Resource Planning) and web landscape, a well-known petrochemical company invested heavily in automated regression testing. The company intended to find bugs and validate the functionality of its existing features in the wake of regularly introduced updates well before its user community found issues in production.

But there's a fine line between automating too little and automating too much, and this petrochemical company learned the hard way the cost of trying to automate everything.

First, its automation test tool didn't support all of the user interface actions in the primary UI and provided even worse coverage on the mobile interface. So the time invested in automating perhaps 10 percent of the overall regression test cases was wasted. Second, as the UI technology itself was updated several times a year, the automation scripts would break. Each instance required time to troubleshoot and remediate another 10 percent of the scripts that didn't survive those UI updates. The company found that the test tool provider's annual update broke another subset of the scripts as well. These were easy fixes but required combing through the full regression test suite and making another round of script updates. And finally, as everyone fully expected, the regular feature updates and bug fixes coming every four weeks as scheduled required the team to do a good amount of script maintenance as well. The expected time and cost in this case were not a surprise, but combined with the other issues noted here, the expected return on investment in automated regression testing would be impossible to realize.

Summary

In Hour 19, we explored the Testing Mindset, eight traditional types of testing, and Service Reliability Engineering. With this foundation in place, we then turned our attention to five Design Thinking testing techniques for learning more about and validating our users' needs. These techniques included Structured Usability Testing, A/B Testing, Experience Testing, Solution Interviewing, and Automating for Regression Velocity. Next, we explored the Testing Sheet and the Feedback Capture Grid, two tools for gathering richer feedback during testing. We concluded the hour with a "What Not to Do" focused on the misconception that automating everything is actually possible or financially prudent.

Workshop

Case Study

Consider the following case study and questions. You can find the answers to the questions related to this case study in Appendix A, "Case Study Quiz Answers."

Situation

As each OneBank initiative engages its respective users in testing, Satish has noticed little consistency in how feedback is given or documented. Worse, he is seeing no consistency in how the testing is conducted and has asked you to look into this matter. Satish sees opportunities to bring people and teams together more effectively across the business and the technology organizations to test smarter. For starters, though, you have pulled together the test leads from most of the initiatives to level-set as well as share new approaches.

Quiz

1. What are the five traditional types of testing and the three performance-related types of testing that should be organized by every initiative's test leads?

2. How would you explain the Testing Mindset?

3. What are the five Design Thinking testing techniques covered in this hour?

4. How is Structured Usability Testing similar to or different from a traditional type of testing?

5. What are the two Design Thinking testing tools we might use for capturing user feedback?

6. In terms of overall percentage of regression test cases, what number should the test leads target for Automated Regression Testing?

Feedback for Continuous Improvement

What You'll Learn in This Hour:

- ▶ Simple Feedback Techniques
- ▶ Strategic Feedback and Reflection Techniques
- ▶ What Not to Do: Wait for Late Feedback
- ▶ Summary and Case Study

In this hour, we focus on three simple techniques and two more strategic techniques useful for collecting and learning from the feedback necessary for continuous product and solution improvement. From Looking Back and Testing Feedback, to Gathering Silent Design Feedback, to running Context Mapping and instrumenting our products and solutions for continuous feedback, we have many opportunities throughout the Design Thinking Cycle for Progress to learn and iterate. A "What Not to Do" reflecting the impact of waiting on late feedback concludes Hour 20.

Simple Feedback Techniques

In life and at work, no matter the source or frequency, feedback helps us learn. Feedback helps us improve who we are, how our teams deliver, what we deliver, and how we can improve what we deliver. From general big-picture feedback to the feedback we instrument across our Design Thinking Model for Tech, feedback keeps us on the road to ongoing reflection, continuous improvement, and fewer surprises.

NOTE

The Principle of No Surprises

Consider what it means to delight users and stakeholders. When it comes to designs, user interfaces, artifacts, standard documents, status reports, feedback mechanisms, and other outcomes, we should not have to struggle with how to use, read, or otherwise consume them. Design should inspire, delight, be intuitive, and drive clarity rather than surprise.

Design Thinking in Action: Looking Back

Consider the analogy of driving a car, where we must check the rearview mirror now and then to see what has happened and what might be catching up with us. It's important to look back occasionally, though of course we cannot drive for long and make progress while looking back.

The most general and big-picture technique for acquiring feedback is to simply look back at what's taken place in the recent past. What have we done well? What should we stop doing? What might we do differently and better? These questions are fundamental to Looking Back, an umbrella technique that comprises numerous other techniques and exercises. Common techniques under the umbrella of Looking Back include

▶ **The Retrospective.** Run a classic Retrospective with a team at the conclusion of a sprint or release using the Good, the Bad, and the Ugly approach. Discuss what the team accomplished and what still remains to be accomplished.

  ▶ Think about why things aren't moving fast enough and in other cases why we have achieved a reasonable velocity. What are the difference makers, and where can we repeat the good, improve the bad, and totally eliminate the ugly?

  ▶ Perform a twist on the classic Retrospective by using the Retrospective Board, a 2×2 matrix organized into four quadrants for discussion and reflection. The four quadrants include

    ▶ Things we will continue doing

    ▶ Things we will do differently next time

    ▶ Things we want to try out

    ▶ Things that are no longer relevant

▶ **Lessons Learned.** Run a Lessons Learned session organized around the broad-based successes, opportunities for improvement, failures that resulted in learnings, and the misses or missteps of a project, initiative, or significant period of time (such as a six-month stretch of prototyping, testing, and iterating). To be of later use to others, ensure these learnings are captured regularly in a Lessons Learned *register* or *knowledgebase* throughout (rather than exclusively at the end of) a project or initiative.

▶ **Postmortem.** Run a deeper Postmortem on the misses or outright failures regardless of where they exist within the project or initiative lifecycle. View these through the lens of both a Growth Mindset and what we would do differently if we had a do-over. Remember that Postmortems do not need to be exclusively dedicated to dead things! Consider running a Postmortem on our greatest victories and accomplishments too. Identify and celebrate the things we did right—and therefore absolutely need to keep doing—which led to these victories.

Consider how each of these feedback mechanisms tends to occupy a different part of the timeline (see Figure 20.1). Our place in the Design Thinking process is less important in these cases than our place in a project's or initiative's lifecycle.

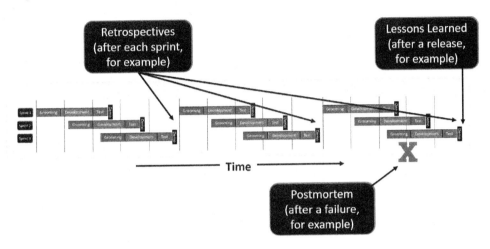

FIGURE 20.1
Looking Back naturally occurs at different phases or stages within the project or initiative lifecycle.

To ensure we actually do the work of Looking Back, use a Forcing Function (as covered in Hour 16) and *calendar* these Retrospectives, Lessons Learned sessions, and Postmortems. Reserve 30 minutes on our calendars each month. Include others who can help us see what went well and not so well. And document these findings and insights. Reviewing the lessons we learn along the way is critical to understanding and not repeating how and where we ran into problems. Look back to learn and reflect and consider.

Design Thinking in Action: Testing Feedback

As we covered extensively in Hour 19, testing is intended to provide us with feedback. Each of the various forms of testing, spanning traditional as well as our Design Thinking-inspired testing types, gives us a particular form of feedback. For starters, consider the feedback gained through the five traditional testing types:

▶ Unit Testing, which provides feedback on code quality and how well we understand our users' requirements, their use cases, or their user scenarios

▶ Process Testing, which provides feedback on how well our developers and testers are adhering to standards, talking to one another (in cases where different developers code different components of a process), and so on

▶ End-to-End Testing, which provides feedback on how well we understand key functional areas and their mega-processes

- ▶ System Integration Testing, which provides feedback on how well we have considered external endpoints, integrations to other systems, and orchestrated regression testing

- ▶ User Acceptance Testing, which provides us feedback from our users along the lines of fit-for-use, directional status, and acceptance

Additionally, the three types of traditional performance testing provide feedback in the following ways:

- ▶ Performance Testing, which provides good data around the performance and user experience of a transaction or process

- ▶ Scalability Testing, which provides feedback for the technology and architecture teams

- ▶ Load and Stress Testing, which provides feedback around where our system will break under load and which components are likely to break first, second, and third

Finally, the five types of Design Thinking test approaches help us fill in gaps in the feedback we receive through traditional testing:

- ▶ A/B Testing provides user feedback on two alternatives.

- ▶ Experience Testing provides user experience feedback.

- ▶ Structured Usability Testing provides user feedback across a breadth of functional areas, user experience, and more.

- ▶ Solution Interviewing provides a final bit of valuable user feedback prior to promoting a product or solution into production.

- ▶ Velocity-inspired Automated Regression Testing provides the functional teams, developers, and testers with insights related to their work and in particular the quality and understanding of proposed bug fixes.

All of the aforementioned feedback capabilities are useful prior to promoting a product or solution to production. How might we benefit from our users after our product or solution is already in productive use, though? Let us turn our attention to another technique for gathering feedback called Silent Design.

Design Thinking in Action: Gathering Silent Design Feedback

Silent Design is an important aspect of feedback we can obtain from our users of products and services that are already in production (and therefore already being used). Based on research by Peter Gorb and Angela Dumas in the 1980s, Silent Design reflects the changes that end users make to our products and services after we deploy them to production (see Figure 20.2). These *user augmentations* represent valuable sources of feedback.

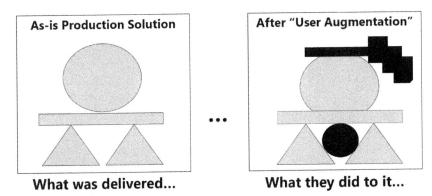

FIGURE 20.2
Consider how the changes that our user communities make to our production systems represent yet another opportunity to collect and use their feedback for the continuous improvement and sustainment of our products and solutions.

Learning from Silent Design can make the products and solutions we already have deployed even more usable. Therefore, we need to treat user-derived changes to our products and solution like user feedback—because such changes are indeed feedback. Further, we need to regularly and repeatably pursue these kinds of insights. After all, the easiest addition we can make to our backlog is to incorporate proposed changes coming out of the user community that is already using and has found ways to improve our products and services.

Strategic Feedback and Reflection Techniques

While the previous techniques are simple, they are effective. If we have a bit more time and budget, though, or simply wish to approach feedback and reflection differently and more deeply than we might be accustomed to, then consider Context Mapping and Instrumenting for Continuous Feedback. Each of these techniques is covered next.

Design Thinking in Action: Context Building and Mapping

Another way to gather feedback is to flip this reflection method on its head. Instead of asking a group of end users for their thoughts on how they work and what they do, physically or virtually *travel* to where they work today. Then passively watch and learn how they use their current product or service (or alternatively how they use our prototype or MVP we may be targeting as a replacement for their current product or solution). Pay attention to the surroundings and context by which they get their work done, building and mapping context along the way.

Organize this context into various Affinity Clusters or groups. Some like to use the STEEP acronym used by the Futures Wheel and Possible Futures Thinking (Hour 13) or the AEIOU for Questioning warm-up technique and taxonomy (covered in Hour 10). Still others might prefer to create a custom context taxonomy composed of the Design Thinking phases or a set of dimensions such as environment, challenges, economy, politics and systems, uncertainties, needs, and so on. Consider organizing these into a circle or daisy with five or eight sections or petals, respectively (a la the Golden Ratio Thinking explored in Hour 12).

This Design Thinking feedback technique is a bit like rolling Journey Mapping, "Day in the Life of" Analysis, and Empathy Immersion all together. Context Building and Mapping reflects research, observation, understanding, and empathy. Of course, in this case our learnings and empathy come through passively watching others rather than actively and personally doing. Still, it's a powerful tool for retrospectively learning and truly understanding why people want what they say they want.

Design Thinking in Action: Instrumenting for Continuous Feedback

Borrowed from the worlds of engineering and electronics, instrumenting our systems and solutions for continuous feedback is also known as creating a closed-loop or feedback control system. The premise is simple: build feedback mechanisms into our technology and/or our system's functionality so we and our systems learn over time and make smarter user experience-based or satisfaction-based decisions.

▶ **Technology-instrumented feedback loop:** The easier of the two options, the idea is to establish smart thresholds within our technology stack through systems management tooling and automated cloud Dev/Ops. In this way, if our technology stack experiences high demand, for example, it will automatically provision additional compute, memory, or storage as needed. This kind of feedback is intended to preserve user experience from a performance or throughput perspective despite the peaks and valleys of demand.

▶ **Functionality-instrumented feedback loop:** The more difficult of the two options, the idea is to build artificial intelligence (AI) or machine learning (ML) into the functionality itself. In this way, if we see that a particular type of user or persona tends to follow a proscribed user journey, we can onboard users who begin to meet the attributes of that persona profile earlier into that user journey, presumably to drive greater user or customer satisfaction. And if another type of user tends to need or purchase Y after obtaining X, the system can be instrumented to look for such trends and more quickly offer Y to our X customers, again to improve the user's satisfaction and experience.

Combinations of instrumented technology and functionality can help automate repetitive end user tasks so those users benefit from greater process throughput or get to the right "place" within our systems faster than otherwise possible. We might automate how emails sent from a user to a customer-service function, for example, are automatically routed to achieve the best functionality or greatest end user responsiveness to a particular class of users or personas.

Other forms of automation can be used to drive mini-surveys of users navigating our systems so we can learn more about why those users are making particular choices. We might also inject A/B Testing (as we covered in Hour 19) into our workflows, for example, to derive a sampling while in production. Similarly, we can inject user experience–related AI into different aspects of a user's customer journey, or automate a subset of Structured Usability Testing within our systems, or configure our survey mechanism to auto-survey every 100th user trying a new feature.

Instrumenting our platforms and solutions from a technical as well as a functional perspective therefore provides us with a steady stream of feedback upon which to make subsequent decisions and derive other insights (see Figure 20.3).

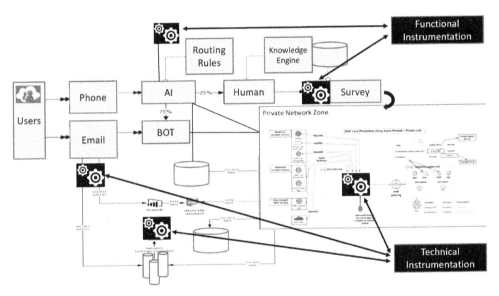

FIGURE 20.3
Note how we might instrument our solution from a technical as well as functional perspective to provide us with a steady stream of feedback and other insights.

The more we understand our users and their needs, the better and faster we can service them, all with an eye toward improving their user experience and ultimate satisfaction. In turn, greater satisfaction helps organizations achieve the kinds of improved revenue flows, profitability, and other financial and value-based outcomes tied to the organization's Objectives and Key Results (OKRs), as we outlined in Hour 17.

What Not to Do: Wait for Late Feedback

While feedback in any form and at any time is useful, waiting for weeks on feedback prior to deploying a prototype or updating an MVP isn't a good idea. But a financial services firm did just that. The firm waited to update its bare-bones MVP while feedback from an early round of Structured Usability Testing was being collected and analyzed. Then the firm waited for a sprint that promised new capability to be completed...and waited on sprint feedback from its product owner and consulting manager...and waited a bit longer for yet another sprint promising even more capabilities to be completed.

In the meantime, the firm's bare-bones MVP just sat there, static, serving the needs of a few users but doing nothing to help an even broader community of additional users waiting in the wings for the chance to weigh in.

By keeping the broader community on ice, waiting on something to get their hands on, the firm missed three months' worth of opportunities to learn early on that the prototype was still missing some pretty important additional features that would take another few months to develop. The firm missed the chance to introduce new users to its work-in-progress too, which would later hurt the MVP's adoption.

The lesson is simple. Wait for feedback when that feedback loop runs in parallel to other work we're completing. But when we are ready to deploy something, be it a prototype or MVP or updates to our MVP, just deploy. There will be time for more feedback soon enough. Don't let perfection be the enemy of learning, of progress. And don't let the fear of a bit of rework keep us from moving forward either. Rework is just another word for iterating, and that's the key as we apply Design Thinking and its techniques and exercises to our design, development, and deployment work.

If we ever intend to maintain any kind of velocity or stick to a plan, we need to leave late feedback behind, to be used for the next round of feature updates. Treat it like an unexpected gift for the product or solution backlog and move ahead!

Summary

In this hour, we focused on three simple techniques for collecting feedback, including the umbrella technique called Looking Back, various forms of Testing Feedback, and Gathering Silent Design Feedback for continuous improvement. Then we turned our attention to two strategic techniques for regular feedback and reflection, including Context Building and Mapping and Instrumenting for Continuous Feedback our products and solutions. A "What Not to Do" reflecting the impact of waiting around for feedback concluded Hour 20.

Workshop

Case Study

Consider the following case study and questions. You can find the answers to the questions related to this case study in Appendix A, "Case Study Quiz Answers."

Situation

BigBank's Chief Digital Officer, Satish, has always been a huge fan of feedback. He built his career around meaningful feedback and deployed quite a few transformational business programs and large systems well before joining BigBank.

So when Satish asked for your assistance to improve how the bank was obtaining and using feedback in support of the dozen OneBank initiatives and the velocity of some of those initiatives, you knew there must be a pretty big problem. As it turns out, Satish needs new tools in his tool bag of feedback techniques. He has questions, too, and needs your fresh perspective.

Quiz

1. What is the name of the technique covered in this hour that reflects feedback gained from users and how they may have made changes to a product or solution *after* it has been in production?

2. Which broad-based technique reflects feedback and other learnings from the breadth of traditional and newer Design Thinking testing techniques?

3. What are the three specific feedback techniques or methods underneath the umbrella of the Looking Back technique?

4. Which technique reflects an ongoing review we should conduct with our design and development teams or other sprint teams on a regular cadence?

5. What might we tell Satish about the timing of feedback, including how to treat late feedback?

HOUR 21
Deploying for Progress

What You'll Learn in This Hour:

▶ Avoiding Perfection Traps

▶ Novel Techniques for Making Progress

▶ Edge Case Techniques for Deploying and Realizing Value

▶ What Not to Do: Deploying Too Soon

▶ Summary and Case Study

In previous hours, we tested, subsequently improved, and continued to iterate on our product or solution, oftentimes for a small audience as a way to learn and refine. In this hour, we go beyond the basics of deployment and consider what it means to deploy products and solutions when we find ourselves stuck. After briefly discussing perfection traps, we turn to three novel techniques for regaining velocity in the wake of stalled deployments. Then we cover two edge case techniques that may be useful when product or solution complexity affects deployment velocity. We conclude Hour 21 with a "What Not to Do" case study focused on the real-world lessons of deploying too soon.

Avoiding Perfection Traps

As we know from previous hours, we cannot simply iterate and iterate again until we have a perfect solution. Perfection does not exist; there is always more work to do, more features to develop and deliver, and new needs to understand and surface in the solution.

▶ Design is never fully complete. We need to draw a line in the sand, however, and claim that design is complete from a release perspective. Subsequent design change requests need to be placed into the backlog for the next release.

▶ Development is therefore never fully complete either. But we still need that line in the sand that claims feature development *for now at least* is complete from a release perspective. New requested features need to be pushed to the next release.

▶ Testing of a release in all of its required forms can be tempting to continue ad infinitum too. But we eventually need to claim that testing is good enough.

▶ End user training and other responsibilities related to solution readiness and adoption are similarly affected by the desire to be 100 percent ready and the need for just-in-time training and readiness and access to help that allow for something less than 100 percent readiness.

The key to avoiding perfection traps lies in setting and managing expectations. Having the right conversations at the right time with the right people will set us up for success. Nearly always, people prefer that we make progress, and they generally buy in to that perspective when we've had the right discussions and talked through the trade-offs. While perfection is the enemy of progress, good enough is its ally.

Novel Techniques for Making Progress

Earlier in Hour 17 we explored the Progress Mindset and a host of techniques for making progress focused on starting small, delivering small bits of value quickly, and organizing the notion of value around a set of Objectives and measurable Key Results.

But what if there are fundamental challenges to delivering at all? What if we need to step back and do something different before we can become the progress makers we're hoping to become? In these cases, we might wish to first try a set of precursor techniques, explored next. String these three techniques together to create a recipe for making progress when other methods seem insufficient or have proven ineffective.

Design Thinking in Action: Fixing Broken Windows

Before we can make progress, we might need to first slow down and fix the "broken windows" surrounding our teams and our users. Based on criminology and social theory, the *Broken Windows Theory* states that visible signs of unresolved neglect or bad behavior promote greater neglect and worse behavior. Conversely, as criminologists James Q. Wilson and George L. Kelling shared in *The Atlantic Monthly* in 1982, if we address the small transgressions and evidence of neglect around us, the likelihood for greater transgressions and neglect nearly disappears. Bad behavior begets worse behavior, and good behavior begets better behavior.

So when it comes to making progress, step one for our tech teams might be as simple as setting the project or initiative aside and first cleaning up and organizing the workplace…or fixing the site's broken internet…or restoring the free-coffee-at-work-for-everyone benefit that naturally dried up during the pandemic. And for our user communities, the team that comes in and literally fixes the broken workspaces and cleans up the shared spaces before moving in has a better chance of building positive sentiment and buy-in. When we invest in becoming part of the solution early on—when we employ the Fixing Broken Windows technique—others will remember and respond to that.

Design Thinking in Action: Avoiding the Abilene Paradox

In 1974, Jerry B. Harvey wrote an article called "The Abilene Paradox: The Management of Agreement" where he shared a story about a family of four comfortably sitting around in the hot Texas heat playing the game of dominoes. One of the family members, concerned the others were growing bored of the game, suggested they all drive an hour to the nearest city, Abilene, for dinner. One by one, the remaining family members agreed, operating under the belief that the others probably also wanted to drive an hour or more in the heat to go to dinner.

As it turned out, no one actually wanted to go to Abilene. The family wasted several hours driving there and driving back. Worse, they had an awful dinner that left no one satisfied. And four hours after leaving they found themselves in the same place as before, as we see in Figure 21.1, having made no progress whatsoever.

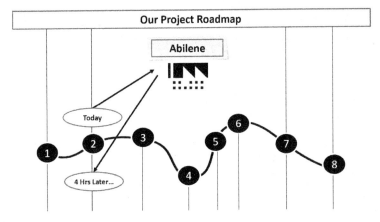

FIGURE 21.1
When we fail to poll others and vocalize our own true wants and needs, we risk consuming precious time and energy yet going absolutely nowhere a la the Abilene Paradox.

The lesson or takeaway is simple: We need to draw out people's true wants and needs before making decisions that cost the group time and progress. When we are faced with taking a journey that may or may not be necessary, consider how to poll the group in a discreet or anonymous manner to validate their true wants and needs. We need to vocalize our own true wants and needs too! And we might be surprised at what we find. More importantly, like taking an unnecessary trip to Abilene, we may avoid the kinds of detours and anti-shortcuts that kill progress.

Design Thinking in Action: Reducing Cognitive Load

Sometimes we fail to make progress simply because we are overwhelmed with too much to consider and think through. Too much cognitive load undermines or slows down people and teams that otherwise know what they need to do next. Excessive cognitive load can rob us of the ability to take the Next Best Step as we understand it today, and instead think and consider about x and think and consider about y.

The Reducing Cognitive Load technique is simply about recognizing and reducing the extraneous load that we are placing on ourselves and others. Once we have completed our thinking and ideation, what can we do to turn the corner from *thinking* to *doing*? How might we focus afresh and begin to execute? How might we need to think or operate differently to kick-start the *doing*?

For example, we might find it useful to Time Box our cognitive activities to create a clear stopping point or Forcing Function for moving forward and getting the work done. These are important considerations and questions to answer when we find ourselves stalled or stuck. Remember the power of "doing" and take the steps necessary to turn that corner!

Edge Case Techniques for Deploying and Realizing Value

Just as we read in the previous section, we have techniques at our disposal to help us preserve or regain velocity. Two such edge case techniques may be useful when deployment itself of a complex product or solution proves too challenging.

Design Thinking in Action: Backward Invention

Sometimes the weight of complexity holds us back from deploying value. As we have seen in numerous examples and case studies throughout the book, our desire to bring maximum value to our users and customers can keep us in limbo. We might wait for more sprints to be completed, or for a user interface to be perfected, or for data loads to complete without error, or for our MVP to get a collection of last-minute features. Surely, there are cases when this kind of waiting is warranted.

In many cases, however, it's the waiting that keeps us from deploying and realizing value. It might be time in those cases to practice Backward Invention as a way to again make progress. Backward Invention calls for us to strip out features and complexity as a way to simplify a design, prototype, or MVP, as we see in Figure 21.2. Such an exercise targets the features or capabilities that we continue to struggle with, features and capabilities that our A/B Testing, Structured Usability Testing, and other early testing reveal we still don't have right. When a user shares with us in a Solution Interview that a particular feature is irritating and should be removed, do it. Follow their advice, if only for the short term. And continue refining and iterating with the smaller community those irritating and questionable items so that one day we can again build atop our stripped-down design, prototype, or MVP.

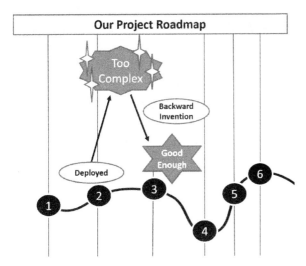

FIGURE 21.2
When deployments are stalled, Backward Invention can take us to a place where we can at least make some progress while we work out complexity and other details that are holding us back.

Design Thinking in Action: Balancing the Essential and the Accidental

Sometimes in our deployments we find that complexity is interfering with value realization. Truly, we should have discovered this type of situation earlier through feedback gathered from prototyping, testing, MVPs, and Pilots. But these things happen, and when they do, it is important to be able to step back and consider:

▶ From where does the complexity come?

▶ Is this complexity absolutely essential?

▶ Is the complexity accidental, the outcome of another decision or an oversight?

▶ Is there a lighter-weight design, interface, or deliverable we can quickly turn around while we solve this complexity problem properly?

The value of the Balancing the Essential and the Accidental technique lies in helping us think through what is truly required from the complexity in front of us. As we consider a complex idea, design, interface, deliverable, deployment process, onboarding method, and so on, it is important to understand the *complexity that can be removed versus the complexity that is necessary.*

There is often a vague line that separates the value found in an idea, design, or interface, for example, and the loss of that value. This line separates the essential from the accidental, the required from the unrequired or optional, as we see in Figure 21.3

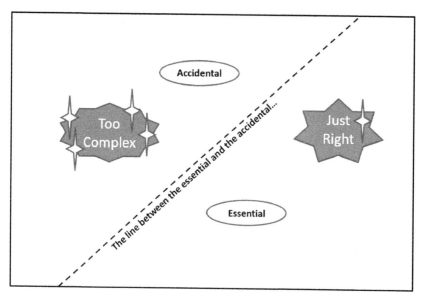

FIGURE 21.3
Identifying the fine line separating what is essential from what is accidental can help us find unnecessary complexity and strip it out to make progress again.

Based in philosophy, how might we apply the Balancing the Essential and the Accidental technique to our work products? How might we learn to recognize this thin line separating the essential from the accidental?

▶ Some features are more essential than other features. Do we have traceability back to those features deemed essential early on by a user community?

▶ Forced ranking can help us find the line between the essential and the accidental. Can we use the Buy a Feature technique outlined in Hour 13 to force users to "put their money where their mouth is" and thus create a line between what is "funded" and therefore essential and what is not?

▶ Evaluations and discussions can also illuminate the line between the must-haves and the nice-to-haves. Can we find that line through an anonymously administered survey?

To be clear, we oftentimes find the accidental to be useful. We may even depend on such accidental items. Consider how certain ways of displaying data in reports, for example, can be accidentally introduced in a sprint. Our users might find such an accidental approach to reporting useful and capitalize upon it. Weeks or months later, after removing such an accidental feature in a subsequent sprint, we might suffer backlash from those who came to count on that feature. Regardless, as we come to better know our users through their production feedback (consider again Gathering Silent Design Feedback from Hour 20), we might include those newfound or newly understood needs into our sprint backlogs and release plans.

What Not to Do: Deploying Too Soon

We have frequently highlighted the need to avoid perfection. But the reality is that people and teams are often more inclined to deliver something—anything—than nothing at all. Teams want to prove their worth after all, and business executives and sponsors naturally tend to push (rightly so) for value realization. In the world of prototypes, MVPs, and Pilots, deploying early and often is absolutely the right mindset.

When it comes to deploying our product or solution for our broader user communities, however, deploying too soon presents another problem: user perception and adoption. That is, if the product or solution is not fully tested and "baked" and we have not properly set such expectations around our poor baking skills, then our end users will quickly reflect perception and sentiment problems with our work on day one. And within several more days, if nothing changes, we might risk losing our users as they fight against adopting our product or solution at all.

Such examples are all too common, and they typically reflect a waterfall approach to development and deployment. Consider the story of a large pharmaceutical company that worked on its Enterprise Resource Planning (ERP) solution for over three years. After spending $60 million on consulting and licensing fees and introducing the solution to a small team of senior and presumably influential users, the company finally deployed the solution to its broader community. And it found out on day one that this huge investment failed to meet many users' expectations in terms of look and feel, functionality, and performance. Why? Because the ERP project and business teams failed to do the kinds of Design Thinking–inspired activities that help us circumvent such outcomes.

There was little prototyping, for example, and zero demonstrations beyond a small subset of friends and family. The company declined to run an MVP for fear of revealing a fully functional system, and it decided against a Pilot under the mistaken belief that its show-and-tell demonstrations were nearly as effective and much less costly. In the end, the pharmaceutical company spent well beyond what it budgeted to simply remediate the gaps between what was built and what its end users expected.

Summary

In Hour 21, we assume we can finally deploy our product or solution for broader use. After briefly discussing perfection traps, we covered three novel techniques for making progress when progress stalled or we got stuck: Fixing Broken Windows, Avoiding the Abilene Paradox, and Reducing Cognitive Load. Each technique covered a unique challenge related to deployment progress. Then we outlined two edge case techniques useful when deployment of a complex product or solution proves too challenging, including Backward Invention and Balancing the Essential and the Accidental. We concluded Hour 21 with a "What Not to Do" case study focused on the lessons of deploying our products and solutions to production too soon.

Workshop

Case Study

Consider the following case study and questions. You can find the answers to the questions related to this case study in Appendix A, "Case Study Quiz Answers."

Situation

Your sponsor and the Bank's Chief Digital Officer, Satish, has been concerned about deployment slips and surprises. Some of the excuses have him concerned that two of the initiative leaders may have overengineered their solutions. In other cases, Satish is worried about the pursuit of perfect testing and training. You reminded him that there are many techniques and exercises for thinking through deployment issues and restoring progress.

In response, Satish has organized a workshop with all of the deployment specialists who float across the Bank's OneBank initiatives. He would like you to cover new techniques or methods beyond deployment itself, novel techniques that really focus on recovering stalled deployments and regaining lost velocity.

Quiz

1. What are four examples of areas that many organizations struggle with when it comes to avoiding perfection traps?

2. Which technique reflects the premise that bad behavior begets worse behavior?

3. What is the moral of the Abilene Paradox story?

4. Which Design Thinking technique presumes that simplifying a product, solution, or service can help adoption?

5. What does it mean in philosophy or Design Thinking to work at Balancing the Essential and the Accidental?

HOUR 22
Operating at Scale

What You'll Learn in This Hour:

▶ Techniques and Exercises for Effective Scaling

▶ Operational Resiliency Techniques

▶ Techniques for Sustaining Systems and Value

▶ What Not to Do: The Scale versus Features Mandate

▶ Summary and Case Study

In this hour, we go beyond what it means to simply deploy a solution and focus instead on what it means to scale that solution and the team behind it. We explore the operational and sustainment changes necessary behind the scenes to improve operational resiliency as our user base grows. Finally, we explore three additional techniques for sustaining our newly scaled systems. A "What Not to Do" related to addressing the "Should we scale to satisfy more users, or should we build more features to satisfy our current users?" question concludes Hour 23.

Techniques and Exercises for Effective Scaling

In the world of business and citizen-enabling solutions, scaling those solutions for more people to use and benefit from them eventually trumps the need for developing new features for an MVP or Pilot audience. And scaling our solutions means scaling the skillsets and number of our people and support teams. However, if our people-scaling strategies are not sound, we may not be able to responsibly deploy our prized solution to the broader community for which it was intended.

Fortunately, there are several Design Thinking–inspired strategies for scaling people and teams effectively. In the pages that follow, we consider how to expand our teams through Scaling by Fives. We also explore how to refine our team's effectiveness and velocity through the Subtraction Game. Afterward, we consider how AntiFragile Validation can be used to confirm individual strength or resiliency while positioning our teams for greater longevity. Use these techniques and methods together to create a powerful recipe for scaling.

Design Thinking in Action: Scaling by Fives

When we look around the workplace, we find many different sizes of teams and workgroups. Some are very large, with a span of control between leaders and workers of 1:20 to 1:50. In other cases, smaller teams are often led by individuals who both manage and participate in the day-to-day workplace tasks. Such managing directors, managing architects, managing consultants, and so on might run 1:5 to 1:10. In yet other cases, project managers might run virtual teams composed of 5 to 50 people who still have direct line managers. And in still other cases, some organizations employ self-managed teams where management and leadership are collectively decided and spread across smaller 3- to 10-person feature teams or other self-managed and semi-autonomous teams.

What is the best approach if we're concerned about growth and scalability? Experts, experience, and research surprisingly agree that the magic number is somewhere between four and six people, which in turn led to the rise of the Scaling by Fives technique.

The point of Scaling by Fives isn't so much about span of control or the type of management structure as it is about the *size* of the most productive teams. Research shows the optimal team size is five, with team dysfunction and other performance problems increasing exponentially as team size reaches double digits. The U.S. Navy Seals and Marine Corps fire teams organize in groups of four. So, too, does McKinsey's engagement teams. Typical surgical teams are composed of six people, and studies have shown that the optimal size for innovation teams is between four and six people.

As we see in Figure 22.1, the larger our teams become, the greater the need for, and therefore overhead of, additional point-to-point communications and collaboration. The weight of these connections ultimately consumes valuable bandwidth, robbing the team of its effectiveness and ability to drive consensus building, decision-making, and velocity.

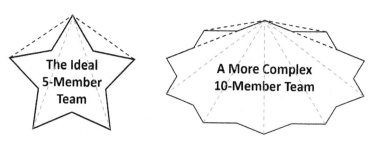

FIGURE 22.1
Scale organizations through the growth of teams composed of four to six team members; additional team members require point-to-point complexity that drives overhead and robs teams of their valuable bandwidth.

NOTE

The Two Pizza Rule!

Jeff Bezos of Amazon fame used to talk of the "Two Pizza Rule." His perspective on the ideal team size? Teams should consist of no more than the number of people who can be fed by two pizzas, or about four to six people.

Design Thinking in Action: The Subtraction Game

As we scale our teams to numbers that potentially exceed five or six people, we need to consider what might be *removed* from those teams. What is hindering the team as it grows, what is no longer effective today, and what should therefore be eliminated? One way to consider these questions is to play the Subtraction Game.

TIME AND PEOPLE: A Subtraction Game exercise requires a full team (likely 4–10 people) for 20 minutes total.

The Subtraction Game is a hyper-focused timed exercise reflecting a combination of Divergent Thinking and Brainstorming. It comprises three timed steps spanning a mere 10 minutes, with another 10 minutes earmarked afterward for sharing and discussing what to eliminate and how to do so:

1. For the first *three* minutes, each team member brainstorms solo about how the team or workgroup operates today. What aspects of the team (or factors immediately external to the team) serve as constraints? What was once useful but today is an impediment to progress or to velocity? What is adding needless friction or randomizing our team and our individual attention? True to Divergent Thinking, the goal is quantity; the longer the list of ideas and *subtraction targets*, the better.

2. For the next *four* minutes, in pairs or in groups of three, share our lists with one another. Identify and add new *subtraction targets* to a group list.

3. For the next *three* minutes, in these same two- to three-person groups, converge around a single subtraction target. How might the group envision eliminating this one item off all the combined lists? Given the small two- to three-person group size, three minutes is sufficient. Take care not to overthink this elimination exercise. A group as small and therefore as close to the challenges should quickly arrive at what to eliminate and how to eliminate it.

With the 10 minutes expired, round-robin through the broader team to share and discuss our single subtraction target with other groups of two to three people. Present to others as needed to further discuss, prioritize, and make these changes necessary to preserve the team's effectiveness and velocity.

Design Thinking in Action: AntiFragile Validation for Longevity

Rooted in psychology and medicine, and popularized recently by Nassim Taleb (2012), the notion behind antifragility is to recognize our individual stresses and struggles through the lens of strength. How are we growing stronger from our challenges, from what opposes us? Not just surviving or coping, but actually growing stronger, the opposite of fragile. Consider how a broken bone heals faster and grows back stronger in the wake of external stress on that bone. Those who are antifragile don't just recover from adversity; they grow stronger. The antifragile reflect more than resilience; they come out of tough situations better and stronger.

AntiFragile Validation seeks to confirm how well we are converting the stress of life into tools and experiences for newfound strength and adaptability. How might we validate antifragility?

▶ Look for an attitude of perseverance, an attitude that says we will outlast the hardship. This attitude embodies antifragile. We have all endured tough work situations and near-impossible relationships. If we told ourselves that we would survive those situations and relationships, and we indeed did so, we were showing off our antifragile skills.

▶ Look for the outward signs of stress and its internal manifestations. Are we getting through and letting go? If we are giving ourselves permission to view stresses and struggles as something that simply needs our attention for a season, then we are reflecting an antifragile perspective. The antifragile embrace the fact that hardship ends one day.

▶ Understand the position our colleagues and teams occupy on the continuum of antifragile recognition. How well are they coping? How well are they growing and adapting? Consider how the team's culture or workplace climate reflects an antifragility attitude. Does the team operate and respond in healthy ways to the inevitable stresses surrounding teamwork, projects, and schedules?

Validating antifragility is about checking in with our teams and ourselves, exploring how we and our teams cope and respond to hardship and trauma. Self-medication is not antifragile, nor is ignoring stress. The antifragile recognize, confront, and take steps to manage it. Help is found in connecting with others a la Mesh Networking (Hour 4), leaning on our Shared Identities (Hour 15), Actively Listening to one another (Hour 6), and more. The most visible signs of antifragility are found in individual and team track records of effectively coping, growing, and progressing.

QUOTE: "A wind extinguishes a candle but fuels a fire."

—Nassim Taleb

Operational Resiliency Techniques

With a nod toward Service Reliability Engineering mentioned in Hour 19, we need to harden and automate not only our solution but our team as well. AntiFragile Validation helps us go beyond resiliency as we covered, but there are also practical techniques to increase team resiliency. Design Thinking in particular gives us an interesting arsenal of helpful techniques, including two borrowed directly from the worlds of disaster recoverability and risk management. In this next section we explore Buddy System Pairing and Slaying the Hero. Together, they form a time-tested duo and recipe for increasing team resiliency.

Design Thinking in Action: Buddy System Pairing for Risk

It is common practice to pair team members together, including pairing a new team member together with a veteran team member. The newer team member benefits from the wisdom and experience of the more senior peer, and interestingly the veteran tends to learn new ways of thinking and operating as well. Called Buddy System Pairing, it is one of the strongest and oldest techniques for shadowing, ensuring redundancy, and performing knowledge transfer as quickly as possible while safeguarding and preserving operations. And again, through this intentional redundancy, Buddy System Pairing not only provides operational resiliency but also serves as a risk management and disaster recovery best practice.

There are other benefits to Buddy System Pairing too. We can learn and put much into practice from the other well-intentioned and positive people to whom we are connected. Step one is simply to show up, to connect.

Step two, *who* we connect with, is just as important. For example, if we or our leaders are really interested in growing and executing smarter, we need to buddy-up in a way that reflects intentional diversity. Consider the following:

▶ We should connect with someone who looks different or sounds different than ourselves or our team members.

▶ We should consider how "buddying" would play out; watching, learning, and considering another person's "Day in the Life of" (DILO) would be an ideal step prior to confirming a pair.

▶ We should also consider connecting with a variety of different people for shorter periods of time to get exposed to more ways of thinking and executing.

As pairs are formed, we need to consider our buddy's track record of past successes and learnings or failures to help us plug into lessons and learnings that we can personally use today. For example:

▶ Connect with a buddy who has a history of completing difficult projects and initiatives.

▶ Connect with those who might hold a senior role (if that is indeed possible), again to learn from a broader base of experiences.

▶ Connect with a buddy who has a reputation for navigating through ambiguity and uncertainty. Such a buddy can help us with the "what" of a role as well as the "how" to navigate complexity.

Again, remember that partnering and buddying with others does not only help our new or junior member. Buddying helps the other half of the partnership too. And buddying will naturally help other colleagues and our entire team as well. Pairing intentionally and leaning on one another has an interesting way of making everyone stronger. It is fundamental to why we buddy in the first place.

Design Thinking in Action: Slaying the Hero for System Resiliency

Our next technique, Slaying the Hero, is a long-time staple of disaster recovery planning and exercises. The idea is both simple and brilliant, and for our purposes akin to "human prototyping and testing." We use Slay the Hero to test our systems and processes for human resiliency.

At work, we might consider Faizel our superstar production support expert and all-around subject matter expert for our solution. We count on Faizel day to day and even more so when the system is undergoing monthly system updates and the annual disaster recovery exercise. We don't know what we would do *without* Faizel. And this is exactly why we need to figuratively slay Faizel on occasion: to see how the team "steps up" and covers his responsibilities in his absence.

Why else is Slaying the Hero important? People casually say that everyone can be replaced, but we're not so sure when it comes to Faizel's skills, calm demeanor, and ability to work through seemingly *any* problem. Just like a good system, though, we cannot allow a single person to become a single point of failure (SPOF). And Faizel is indeed a SPOF; he is our only network hub tech on the team, for example. We need "people redundancy," just as we have technology and facilities redundancy built into our cloud infrastructures and new generation of cloud apps.

What happens when Faizel takes an unexpected holiday? What if he needs to stay home to take care of sick loved ones? What if he simply disappears one day? What are our workarounds? More to the point, "who" are our workarounds? Before these scenarios ever play out in reality, we need to play them out mentally (and typically through a tangible exercise as well). Do this by imagining that our key person, team, or process—Faizel in this case, our hero—is removed from the picture for a period of time. What would happen if our lone network hub tech, Faizel, disappeared from Figure 22.2? Do we have a backup?

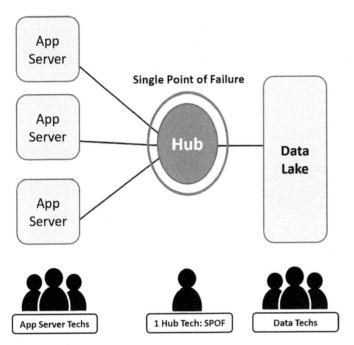

FIGURE 22.2
Use the Slaying the Hero technique to prototype and test our human single points of failure (SPOFs).

Use Slay the Hero to prototype and test our team's resiliency and our personal ability to recover from everything from slight system hiccups to major disasters. Are we too dependent on a specific person or system or process? Do we have the right skills distributed across enough people? Do we have fallback people and partners we may lean on in an emergency? Knowing these options in advance—and thinking through and testing how we would operate without the benefit of our heroes—will help us survive such conditions when they inevitably occur in the real world.

Techniques for Sustaining Systems and Value

Once a solution begins delivering its expected benefits and other outcomes, we need to focus even more on sustainability. Value and other benefits are only sustained via a prescriptive strategy for operating, monitoring, upgrading, evolving, and extending our solutions in alignment with our people and teams.

Design Thinking in Action: Operating Structures for Scale

As we move through deployments and begin operating at scale, there is the need to plan for, deploy, and over time optimize our Operating Structures for Scale. Though outside the scope of this book, we need to prototype, test, and harden our support organization in the same way that we do our products, services, and solutions, so they can help us maintain an available, scalable, and resilient solution. There are many implications, but some of the most overlooked include

▶ **Timing.** Establish the initial support organization as soon as we have deployed an MVP or Pilot or other production-like solution supporting a cast of end users.

▶ **Evolution.** Remember that our support organization needs to grow with our solution as it is developed and deployed; consider this need as just another requirement for iterating as we fine-tune our support structure and their connections to the user community.

▶ **Onboarding.** Onboard key support personnel as early into a solution's lifecycle as possible, again to create a record of institutional knowledge and experience.

Consider the breadth of support required too. Readying our Operating Structures for Scale means putting people at the center of the particular problems and situations we may encounter. For systems that run at scale:

▶ Our solution team will need access and help from an internal or contracted team of developers and testers tasked with maintenance and updates.

▶ Our global user community will need a Level 1 Help Desk that is available in some form 24 hours a day.

▶ Our Level 1 Help Desk will need knowledge management capabilities and a second level of support for escalations (sometimes called an L2, or Level 2, Support Organization).

▶ Our Level 2 Support Organization will require liaisons to work with our hardware and infrastructure providers, cloud providers, application and software providers, security and third-party app vendors, and so on (typically the responsibility of an L3, or Level 3, Application Support Team).

Additional teams and people will need to be employed along the lines of support as well (again, outside the scope of this book). Practice our Design Thinking process to understand and empathize with the myriad of people and teams connected to our products and solutions. Through creating intentional partnerships and building support organizations early, we can intentionally sustain our solution's usefulness and its value and other benefits to our end users and stakeholders.

Design Thinking in Action: Validating OKRs and Value

Once a solution is deployed to production—regardless of whether this means as an MVP or Pilot or full production systems—we need to sustain its benefits over time. To do so, it is common to create an intentional and ongoing benefits or value *workstream*. To be clear, we should have been validating and thinking about measures for value earlier as we ideated, problem-solved, prototyped, and tested. But once users and customers begin realizing value from the time spent in the Design Thinking process, we owe it to ourselves and our stakeholders to actively and regularly validate that we

- ▶ Are delivering and realizing value as identified in our solution's objectives

- ▶ Can measure that value in the form of a set of objective-specific key results

- ▶ Are aligning our people and teams to the value creation and sustainment process

- ▶ Are taking the necessary steps to sustain and grow that value

This imperative to realize and measure value needs to be captured in the organizations' Sustainment Plan. A good Sustainment Plan maps back to the organization's vision, mission, evolving strategies, products and solutions used to realize value, and the various objectives and key results established to realize and measure the effectiveness of the organization's strategies, products, and solutions—all of which serves as a wonderful feedback loop for further growth and transformation.

NOTE

Aligning People to Value

Value realization is predicated on team members who understand, respect, and hold themselves accountable for delivering value and other expected outcomes. This alignment between individual people and the outcomes they are expected and accountable to deliver is required for realizing value and therefore success. Be sure to align our people and teams to the value their products and solutions are expected to provide!

Design Thinking in Action: Silent Design for Sustainment

As previously outlined in Hour 20, we must not forget to bake in learnings gleaned from the Silent Design choices that our users are already making to our products and services in production. Remember that the modifications and additions our user communities make to our production systems represent yet another opportunity to collect and use their feedback for the continuous improvement and sustainment of our products and solutions.

As design leaders and thinkers, we need to learn from our users who are working around our unknown and known product gaps and processes. And we need to be proactive as we learn, baking those learnings into our product and solution backlogs. Anything we might do sooner rather than later to make our products and solutions more useful will return time back to everyone who adopts and adapts them today.

What Not to Do: The Scale versus Features Mandate

As we arrive at the point in time when we absolutely must deliver measurable value, we need to eventually decide when scale trumps new features; that is, when the many needs of a community outweigh the "eyes closed" wishful needs of a handful of super users. For a 100-year-old insurance company, a CRM project's business liaison finally needed to make that decision unilaterally. Her technology leadership counterpart seemed happy to continue improving on the features and capabilities of a successful MVP (as we discussed in Hour 17). The MVP started life with 40 elated users, and six months later this MVP was much improved in terms of capabilities but was only servicing 50 elated users.

In the meantime, the business was screaming for its long-promised solution. The company had grown weary of the mixed bag of partial solutions strung together with nightly interface updates and a swivel chair to pivot between different systems and screens. It had grown equally weary of the "next quarter" promises made over the course of nine months by the slow-to-deploy-value technology leader.

The company's business liaison had to eventually step in and demand that the current solution, as is, be turned over to the remainder of the business. She rightly explained that the solution was Good Enough (as we covered in Hour 11). The time had come for scale to trump the desire to deploy new features. In increments of 500 and 1,000 users, different parts of the business were onboarded every two to three weeks over the next three months. As most of the team expected, the new users were also elated with their new solution. The solution's business liaison helped the entire organization sidestep a major landmine on the journey to deploying and realizing value.

Summary

In Hour 22, we explored how to scale and refine the team underpinning our solution through Scaling by Fives, the Subtraction Game, and AntiFragile Validation for Longevity. We then outlined two operational and sustainment techniques useful for improving operational resiliency as our user base grows, including Buddy System Pairing and Slaying the Hero. Later, we explored three additional techniques for sustaining our newly scaled systems using Operating Structures for Scale, Validating OKRs and Value, and considering Silent Design for Sustainment. A "What Not to Do" related to avoiding the "Scale versus New Features" decision concluded Hour 22.

Workshop

Case Study

Consider the following case study and questions. You can find the answers to the questions related to this case study in Appendix A, "Case Study Quiz Answers."

Situation

Satish and the Executive Committee (EC) of BigBank have been happy with your support of their initiative leaders, executives, and other stakeholders. They are now enlisting your aid to help BigBank scale several of its **OneBank** initiatives on their journey to reimagining the Bank's future and reinventing how the Bank delivers its new business capabilities and outcomes with velocity. Satish has asked you to host a Q&A session to answer several of the committee's questions surrounding scale methods, solution scalability approaches, operational considerations, and more.

Quiz

1. While several methods exist, which two have we explored that can give organizations such as BigBank a way of thinking about and scaling the teams underpinning the Bank's various projects and initiatives, especially as they become productive and grow quickly?

2. Which technique forces us to consider value measures and how the notion of value might have changed throughout a project's lifecycle?

3. What are two techniques for bolstering operational resiliency?

4. What role does Silent Design play in the overall pursuit of solution and system sustainability?

5. Which technique might help BigBank consider the fragility of its teams as well as its people?

HOUR 23
Making Change Sticky

In Hour 23, we review a number of simple change management and solution adoption techniques and exercises with the idea of making our new solutions "sticky" and enduring within their user communities. To organize these Design Thinking techniques and exercises, we connect them to a simple four-phase model for change management and adoption. Several popular Design Thinking methods are tagged to each phase as we walk through methods for creating awareness, providing purpose, driving readiness, and doing the work necessary for adoption. We conclude Hour 23 with an important "What Not to Do" related to addressing change management too late in the solution design, development, and deployment cycle.

Change Management and Adoption

In the broadest sense, change management and adoption reflect the processes and techniques necessary to land and accept change. Attention to these matters is critical but often diminished; managing change is time-consuming and hard work. In light of this, we expect the techniques and exercises shared in this hour will prove helpful for even the most experienced change management experts.

Change Management versus Change Control

For our purposes, change management and change control satisfy two very different objectives. Change management focuses squarely on managing the changes that a person will need to navigate in the face of that change. Change management therefore applies to user communities that will be asked to use a new product or business solution. Change management also applies to the technical teams that must learn and adopt new technologies in the course of designing, developing, and deploying new business-enabling products and solutions. However, as we covered in previous hours, change *control* is focused squarely on tracking and recording the changes to an initiative or a project rather than the people delivering or being served by that initiative or project.

What is change management? Think of it as the steps a user community and their supporting tech teams must navigate to learn about, understand, prepare for, and embrace a change in how they operate. This process for change seems easy enough, as we see in Figure 23.1.

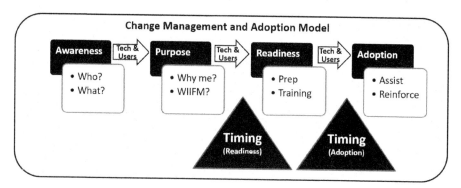

FIGURE 23.1
The Change Management and Adoption process reflects the steps necessary for both a user community and the tech team that works with that user community to navigate the change process.

Adoption, in particular, speaks to the final phase or step in the change management process illustrated in Figure 23.1, where a user community actually uses or adopts a change, or a tech team actually interacts with and deploys technology that will support a user community. Such changes could include new ways of operating, along with new or updated technologies and solutions that enable those new ways of operating.

As all of us know from experience, adoption is arguably the most difficult leap for people to make. We like to hang onto our old ways of operating. In a complex ever-changing world, we often treasure the few things that remain static for a while—such things give us comfort and indeed act as an anchor when everything around us is changing.

NOTE

People and Change

Change takes time, as it is adopted a person at a time and a day at a time. Remember that *people* adopt change, not teams or organizations.

But everything eventually changes. And when those things that give us comfort eventually succumb to change, the process for understanding and adopting what's next becomes paramount to successfully changing.

The Four-Phase Change Process

There are numerous models and methods that help people and organizations navigate and think about change. Burke-Litwin's detailed 10-component change model and Kotter's well-known 8-step model for change are two of the long-time heavyweights for change. PROSCI's model for change is a simpler and highly effective 3-phase process for change, along with their 5-step methodology for individual change.

For our purposes here and as illustrated previously in Figure 23.1, we have organized the change process into four phases that generally align to most of these popular change management models. The phases include creating awareness, providing purpose, driving readiness, and adopting change. These four phases are covered next.

Methods for Creating Awareness

Nearly all change management experts agree that awareness is a key and early action for landing change. In our case, awareness is synonymous with understanding *who* will use or be affected by an upcoming change and *what* that change entails. Helpful techniques or exercises for awareness are illustrated in Figure 23.2 and include the following:

▶ Big Picture Understanding can help us understand the broader community that will use our new product or solution or in some other way be affected by the change. In these ways, we can craft more targeted awareness campaigns and collateral.

▶ Fractal Thinking can give us a sense of what is echoing down to us from higher up in the organization, company, industry, or broader ecosystem. With this understanding, we can create awareness campaigns and initiatives that resonate with different levels of the organization.

▶ Stakeholder+ Mapping is useful for mapping the user community's key leaders, sponsors, mentors, coaches, and other such enablers. Including what these people say and what we believe they are thinking can give us another level of insight too.

▶ Persona Profiling and grouping can help us better understand whom to target for a particular change. Don't forget to include both the affected user communities and the various tech team roles and personas who support the product or solution.

▶ Use a Cover Story Mockup to drive excitement and connect a user community or tech team to a new tech-enabled business vision.

▶ Consider the Snaking the Drain and Sacrificing the Calf techniques to influence awareness, work through past missteps, and reduce resistance.

▶ Finally, Make Our "Awareness" Ideas and Collateral Visible and Visual to drive a faster shared understanding and connect on multiple levels with the communities and tech teams involved in the change.

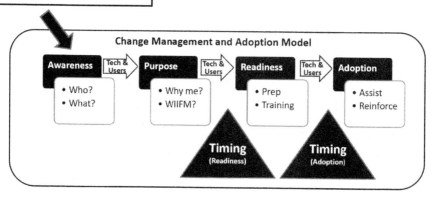

- Big Picture Understanding
- Fractal Thinking
- Stakeholder+ Mapping
- Persona Profiling
- Cover Story Mockup
- Snaking the Drain
- Sacrificing the Calf
- Making Ideas Visible and Visual
- Problem Tree Analysis
- Problem Framing
- Problem Stating

Change Management and Adoption Model

Awareness — Tech & Users → **Purpose** — Tech & Users → **Readiness** — Tech & Users → **Adoption**

- Who?
- What?

- Why me?
- WIIFM?

- Prep
- Training

- Assist
- Reinforce

Timing (Readiness)

Timing (Adoption)

FIGURE 23.2
Many Design Thinking methods are available to help us create awareness.

For some audiences, we might even explore the underlying problems or situations to connect and obtain deeper buy-in. Techniques and exercises we used in Hour 9 that could prove useful in creating such awareness include Problem Tree Analysis, Problem Framing, and Problem Stating.

As we generally conclude our work of Creating Awareness, we may move into the next change management phase where we are tasked with providing purpose and answering the often unspoken question "What's in it for me?"

Techniques for Providing Purpose

As we consider change management at an individual level, we eventually arrive at the place of purpose and WIIFM, or "what's in it for me?" WIIFM is perhaps the key component to the entire change management process since it directly reflects how change occurs: a person at a time and a day at a time. People without a good sense of purpose or WIIFM will rarely support an upcoming change. Worse, these people might passively avoid the change or actively rally against it, sabotaging good change management practices along the way.

Helpful Design Thinking techniques for providing purpose help us answer another question too: "Why me?" Illustrated in Figure 23.3, consider the following:

▶ Map the change to the user's "Day in the Life of" (DILO) analysis or Journey Map in such a way as to create excitement through problem solving, improving the user journey, simplifying key DILO tasks, and so forth.

▶ Use Verbatim Mapping to showcase the kinds of issues, problems, or opportunities that have been shared that highlight the problems underpinning the need for change.

▶ Publicize Looking Back feedback and other learnings from early prototypes and testing that validate the usefulness of an upcoming change.

▶ Work through the visual Force Field Analysis "for and against a proposed change" exercise with the community or tech team that would be affected by an upcoming change initiative. Then use the resulting for-change analysis as a way to objectively promote and support the WIIFM for change.

▶ Use the Force Field Analysis exercise's "against-change" analysis as feedback for influencing the business case, OKRs (objectives and key results), design, prototyping, testing, and so on of an upcoming change initiative.

▶ Apply the Fixing Broken Windows technique alongside other change management techniques as a way to proactively remediate problem areas today that will help us be more successful tomorrow.

With a better understanding of the "Why me?" and WIIFM, user communities and their supporting tech teams need to begin thinking through the kinds of readiness-related items and techniques that need to be addressed before change can truly land or be adopted. We call this third phase Readiness, and it's the topic of our next section.

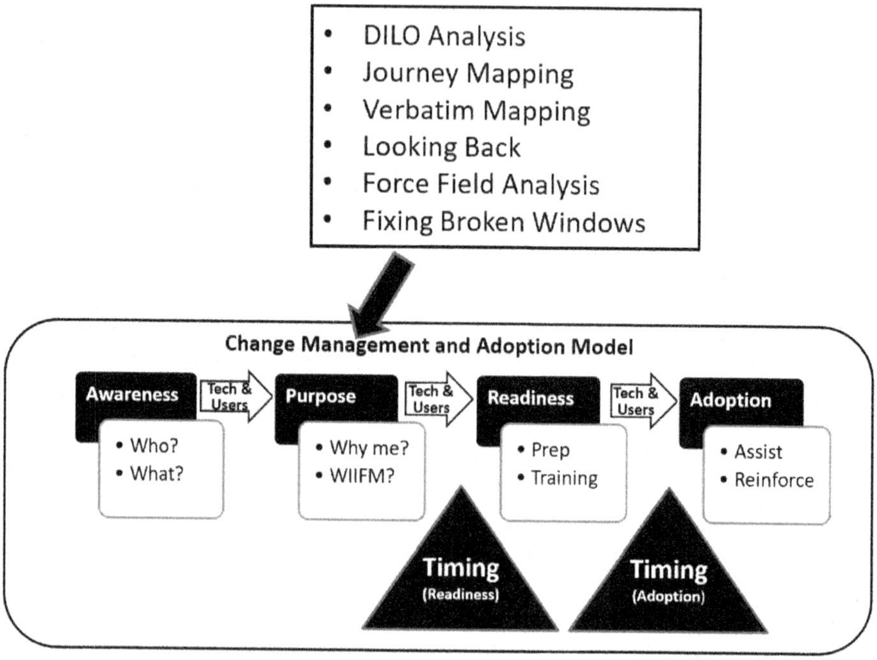

FIGURE 23.3
Note the diversity in Design Thinking techniques useful for providing purpose and addressing the question "What's in it for me?"

Driving Readiness Through Design Thinking

Beyond creating awareness and providing purpose, change management also reflects an organization's *readiness for and ability* to change. We need to understand how prepared for change a user community is so we can then engage in a set of activities intended to bolster that preparedness. Steps include understanding the size or magnitude of the change and gaining an understanding of the *business organization's* readiness for the change.

In a parallel sense, change management also speaks to the *tech team's* ability to support the change from an underlying technology and process perspective. New solutions nearly always mean new technology solutions and infrastructure, data technologies, application and integration platforms, user experience tech, and so on.

Design Thinking techniques and exercises we can use to help us drive readiness, as illustrated in Figure 23.4, include the following:

▶ Consider how Analogy and Metaphor Thinking can help us align around a shared understanding of the change, the process for changing, and therefore the gaps that organizations and teams will face.

▸ Prototypes and Mockups can help us see and interact with upcoming changes in an early and safe kind of manner where we not only know what to expect but have an opportunity to influence the design and implementation of that change.

▸ Testing in all its forms, especially SIT and UAT and Design Thinking–inspired Structured Usability Testing and Solution Interviewing (covered in Hour 19) helps organizations and teams highlight readiness gaps.

▸ Training delivered in a just-in-time manner is paramount too. Training needs to be accessible to the entire community, consumable by the entire community, presented in different video and written forms and formats as needed, available offline for reference later (and for future community users and tech team members not in the role today), and delivered not too early but not too late.

▸ Tools and similar enablers are also an important aspect to driving readiness. Consider the role that wikis, frequently asked questions (FAQs), support organizations, Buddy System Pairing (outlined in Hour 22), community leads and mentors, power users and user groups, and so on play to help the overall community work through questions, resolve issues, and onboard future users and tech team members.

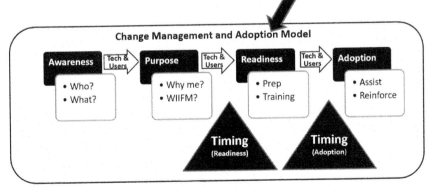

FIGURE 23.4
Note the breadth of change management techniques for driving readiness.

Change needs to be planned so it lands well within its user and tech communities. And as we have mentioned, the change itself must be consumable by each respective community. General preparation and readiness questions include the following:

▶ Does the community truly understand how the new product or solution aligns to the organization's or team's overall organizational vision?

▶ Have we asked the community its perspective on readiness and the gaps that need to be addressed prior to adopting a planned change?

▶ Have we evaluated readiness for changes to existing business or tech-related processes?

▶ How will existing organizational structures, roles, and specific teams be impacted, and therefore what needs to occur from a tactical readiness perspective?

▶ Have we considered how *other* systems and technologies may be impacted by our change initiative and therefore what might need to be accommodated from a broader readiness perspective?

▶ Do we have a set of defined and measurable objectives and key results (OKRs, discussed in Hour 17) that we can lean on specific to readiness?

Remember that readiness is the final step prior to adoption. Any changes that need to be made to enable adoption, including incentivizing new behaviors, are ideally made in this phase. The earlier we think about the upcoming change, the better off we will be when that day finally comes to adopt the change, discussed next.

Four Techniques for Adopting Change

When it finally comes time to help our user community or tech teams adopt a change, we use the following techniques, the first three of which have been outlined previously and together create a repeatable recipe for driving adoption:

▶ Forcing Functions for Adoption

▶ Gamification for Adoption

▶ Context Building and Mapping

▶ Making Change Consumable

Let's briefly look at each of these adoption-related techniques next, illustrated in Figure 23.5.

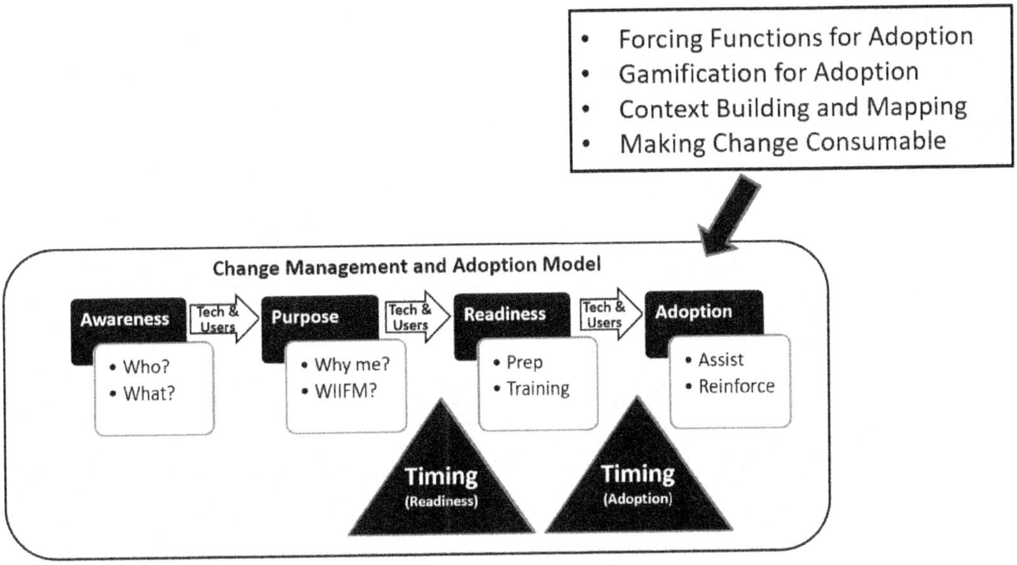

FIGURE 23.5
Consider how these Design Thinking techniques serve us well when it comes to driving adoption of a change by a user community or a tech team.

Design Thinking in Action: Forcing Functions for Adoption

We know that Forcing Functions are useful to help us make progress and get hard things done. When it comes to adopting a new system, we need to consider the Forcing Functions we may have available.

▶ Do our current systems need to be retired for high maintenance cost reasons?

▶ Are our current systems subject to new licensing that will make them prohibitively more expensive?

▶ Do our current systems no longer comply with regulatory or compliance mandates?

▶ Are our current systems at their end-of-life from a support perspective?

Surely some of these Forcing Functions are more palatable than others. All of these reflect reasons to run away from the current state too, rather than run toward a better product or solution.

Design Thinking in Action: Gamification for Adoption

As we covered briefly in Hour 3 and in more detail in Hour 18, the Gamification technique can help us increase engagement, motivation, and feedback, and incentivize new behaviors.

▶ We should use Gamification in our earliest testing workstreams as outlined in Hour 19. Early feedback promotes healthy solutioning and user community buy-in.

- ▶ Employ Gamification in our training workstream by awarding badges, points, or tangible rewards to those individuals who complete the required training (especially those who complete it early or on-time).

- ▶ Gamify healthy competition between teams to drive better and faster training outcomes across the board.

- ▶ As we get closer to go-live, gamify other activities by awarding meaningful prizes and gift cards or by conducting a drawing for a single more expensive gift such as a $500 gift card, an Apple iWatch, or Microsoft Surface Go (in this last stretch toward adopting change, we need to get the attention of *everyone*).

Use Gamification to help us create more energy and excitement as we work through the entire change management and adoption process.

Design Thinking in Action: Context Building and Mapping

As outlined in Hour 20, physically or virtually traveling to where our end users and tech teams work today can help us in several ways. Run training sessions onsite and be there to not only help but walk away with new ideas for the pending go-live or the backlog. Observe how they use the training system. Pay attention to areas of confusion and discussions of shortcomings or perceived necessary workarounds. All of these insights act as context that we can organize and use today and in future product or solution releases.

Design Thinking in Action: Making Change Consumable

New for Hour 23, Making Change Consumable is an oft-used collection of tips and techniques for landing change, driving energy, creating more effective training, and more.

- ▶ Provide early communications into upcoming changes.

- ▶ Make change visible and visual using pictures and figures.

- ▶ Share early vision surrounding upcoming changes, using techniques such as the Cover Story Mockup to paint a picture of the future.

- ▶ Share the "difference makers" and WIIFM data points that also get people excited about the future.

- ▶ Release bite-sized awareness videos of three to five minutes to drive another level of excitement about the future.

- ▶ Pull in key users and influencers into the prototyping and testing phases and ensure their feedback is heard and echoed throughout the organization.

- ▶ Ensure the organization's executives and other leaders talk about upcoming changes in terms that get others excited about the possibilities.

▶ Also ensure that training videos and other collateral are easy to access, easy to use, detailed enough to address the need, and short enough to keep people's attention.

The more we think about change in terms of how palatable, accessible, and consumable we can make it, the more easily adopted our changes will be.

Techniques for Timing Change

In previous hours, we covered techniques for timing change including Time Pacing and the Inverse Power Law. These and other techniques covered here can help us determine when a user community or tech team is primed for change based on its readiness, its preparedness for adoption, and most importantly its bandwidth to consume or adopt the change. After all, a ready and prepared business community, for example, may not have the time to accommodate a change until a particular period within its business cycle.

Historical context is important too. We need to consider the organization's or team's track record when it comes to managing, handling, and adopting change. Key questions include

▶ Is there a dedicated change management team assigned to most projects or initiatives?

▶ Does the organization or team follow a structured change management and adoption methodology?

▶ In the recent past, have changes been viewed as negative or positive experiences?

▶ Does the current change initiative reflect a shared vision and understanding across the organization or team?

▶ More tactically, does the current change initiative reflect a strong WIIFM or other reasons to change?

▶ To what extent do employee behaviors or operational processes need to change to achieve the desired outcomes?

▶ Is the organization or team capable of changing its behaviors to the extent necessary?

▶ Does the organization or team have the bandwidth and capacity to accommodate this change given other changes in flight?

▶ Are there competing priorities that might interfere with this particular change initiative?

▶ Does this change initiative change the organization's or team's structure or required roles?

In light of the preceding questions, we can then turn next to several Design Thinking techniques covered in previous hours that affect the timing of change and are illustrated in Figure 23.6:

▶ How might the Culture Snail for Pace of Change illuminate past difficulties or rough spots as the organization or team changed a person at a time a day at a time?

► In what ways might Bias Recognition and Validation help the organization or team be more planful or careful on the change journey?

► How is the community currently handling stress or recent organizational or team traumas? To what extent does the team embody AntiFragile behaviors?

► As an organization or team, do we need to go about Fixing Broken Windows to showcase to our community that we understand their needs? Or in some way show how we are all in this together?

► Does it make sense to Time Box any remaining critical items to ensure they are planned for and completed?

► If we look at the organization or team through the lens of the Inverse Power Law, are there high-magnitude changes or forces on the horizon that must be accommodated?

► Finally, with regard to Time Pacing, are there frequency or duration matters at play that we must better understand before we commit to the timing for this latest change initiative?

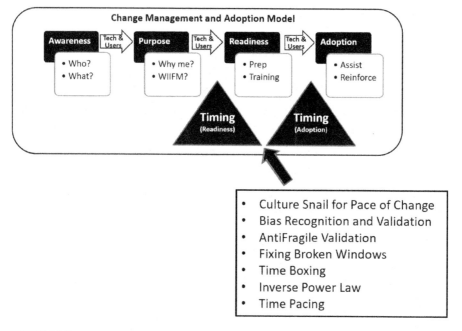

FIGURE 23.6
Covered previously in various contexts, consider how this cross section of proven Design Thinking techniques can help us when it comes to landing and "timing" when change should land or can be absorbed by a user community or tech team.

Surely other timing factors may be at play. Consider the recent past and what the communities have recently navigated. Review today's priorities and changes currently in flight. Finally, look ahead at what is coming. Within these horizons using the preceding techniques, identify the required block of time necessary to successfully integrate the current change initiative.

What Not to Do: Change Management Can Wait

We cannot leave the work of change management and adoption until the days before a new product or solution is introduced to its users. A large government agency did just that, though. In response to an early awareness campaign revealing a reluctant user community, the agency did much of the work designing a new employee-enabling portal solo. It prototyped solo, working through portal options provided by two different portal vendors. After selecting a portal platform, the agency developed and tested the solution solo, using project team members to develop and execute test cases.

The government agency also pushed change management far into the project plan. To be sure, there was little attention ever paid again to creating awareness. The project was practically a top secret mandate after the initial round of awareness feedback showed no one in one of the agency's organizations wanted to change. The agency never formally shared with its other organizations that the project existed. No vision was painted, no WIIFM was ever formulated and shared. The agency skimped over awareness and failed to share the purpose of the new employee portal too.

Late into the project, the agency commenced a bit of work to facilitate readiness. A team was asked to pull together a set of videos and training collateral to help prospective users become familiar with the portal's interface. Project team members created the videos, demonstrating poorly understood use cases. Upon seeing these videos, user community employees would snicker at how poorly the project team even understood the real purpose of the portal.

A subset of the user community was asked to engage in User Acceptance testing using the test cases built by a team who would never actually use the portal. The few who showed up also snickered as they executed high-level UAT test cases. And several weeks before the portal was to replace an old collection of websites and online checklists, training was scheduled for the breadth of the portal's intended users.

The portal project team used two of the oldest forms of Forcing Functions on the prospective user community. First, the team shared that if users failed to show up to training, their managers would be notified. Second, they offered the half-day training over the course of a single calendar week; if users missed the training, there would be no other chance to attend it again.

The portal training team reinforced during training that the old websites and online resources would be retired when the new portal was released. There would be no parallel testing, and there would be no other communications related to retiring the legacy systems and resources. The high number of employees who ignored the training mandate or happened to be sick or on vacation that week never had the official opportunity to hear about the forced retirement of their favorite tools.

A few managers held meetings to ensure their teams knew that the portal was coming and that the old tools would be retired. Other managers sent emails the weekend before. When the fateful day finally arrived for the portal to be released, it was met by its new users with everything from discontent to impartiality, resignation, and contempt. The agency missed its opportunities to create excitement, to deliver something of value, and to put into the hands of its employees something that could truly help the citizens for which the agency existed. Instead, the portal became just another example of botched change management and missed opportunities to drive adoption and realize value.

Summary

In Hour 23, we reviewed a simple four-phase change management and adoption model focused on creating awareness, providing purpose, driving readiness, and adopting change. For each of these phases, we then outlined a number of Design Thinking techniques and exercises shown to be useful in making our new solutions "sticky" and enduring. We concluded Hour 23 with an important "What Not to Do" related to what happens when we push change management out to sometime later in the future and miss our opportunities to socialize and land change early in solution design, development, or well before deployment.

Workshop

Case Study

Consider the following case study and questions. You can find the answers to the questions related to this case study in Appendix A, "Case Study Quiz Answers."

Situation

Satish has been talking about the change process lately and has connected the dots between antifragile teams, digital perseverance, and the ability to thrive even in the toughest and most uncertain times. He is concerned, however, with how the bank will thrive if its **OneBank** initiative leaders don't land their changes well. These landing challenges are further complicated by the bank's diverse user communities, geographic and remote implications, lack of a consistent approach to managing change and adoption, and several poorly formulated change awareness campaigns. Satish knows that he needs some help, and he assumes that his initiative leaders probably need new ways of thinking about change management.

With these challenges and needs in mind, Satish has asked you to host a workshop with five of the initiative leaders and their respective business and tech team members. He cited the ongoing theme of helping the bank reimagine its future and rallying its people and teams around a new set of business capabilities and value drivers. You have concluded that a walk-through of what it means to think about and manage change is necessary, along with a discussion around techniques for change management and adoption.

Quiz

1. What are the four phases to the change process outlined in this hour?

2. Which Design Thinking techniques covered in this hour may be useful to create *awareness* of a change?

3. Which Design Thinking techniques outlined in this hour might be employed as we drive *readiness* for an upcoming change?

4. Which four techniques outlined in this hour can help organizations and teams *adopt* change?

5. What are a number of Design Thinking techniques outlined in this hour that can help organizations and teams consider the *timing* of a change include?

HOUR 24
Design Thinking for Project Velocity

What You'll Learn in This Hour:

▶ Project Management Velocity

▶ Leadership and Governance

▶ Stakeholders and Expectations

▶ Development Approach

▶ Risk Management

▶ Schedule Management

▶ Managing Scope

▶ Delivery and Quality

▶ Communications and Collaboration

▶ What Not to Do: No Courage, No Future

▶ Summary and Case Study

In our final hour together, we do not introduce new Design Thinking exercises or techniques but rather recast what we have previously covered through the lens of project management velocity. Our goal this hour is twofold: to provide a single source of methods and to loosely organize those methods around how the Project Management Institute (PMI) views select project management knowledge areas, performance domains, and guiding principles. While every PMI knowledge area, project performance domain, and guiding principle is important, through the lens of velocity, some are more impactful or critical than others. We conclude this hour with a familiar "What Not to Do" theme reflecting the need for courage to drive value when faced with the unknown.

Project Management Velocity

Though not always the case, tech projects and initiatives tend to be professionally managed or in some other way led by a project manager, product manager, initiative leader, workstream lead, or feature team lead. Even self-managed teams still need to organize their work and execute in ways that lead to outcomes. And surely everyone needs to give some thought to how to achieve expected outcomes more quickly.

As we view PMI's knowledge areas, performance domains, and guiding principles through the lens of velocity, it is important to reflect on our Design Thinking Cycle for Progress covered in Hour 1 (see Figure 24.1). Consider how the cycle starts with understanding the situation, followed by diagnosing the problem, selecting and executing Design Thinking techniques and exercises, selecting follow-on techniques and exercises as needed, solving the problem in whole or in part, looping back to learn, and realizing value as we iterate. This entire process can be applied to each PMI project management knowledge area, performance domain, and guiding principle.

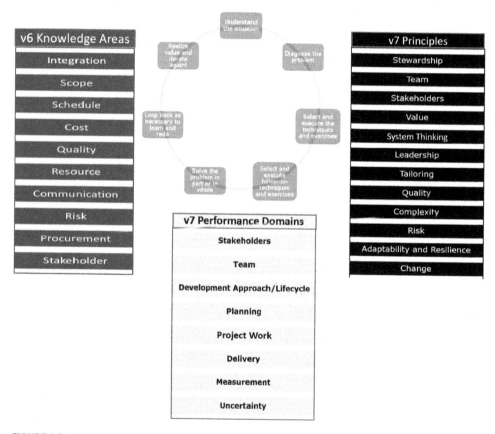

FIGURE 24.1
Apply the Design Thinking Cycle for Progress to consider and select exercises and techniques useful for each project management knowledge area, performance domain, or principle.

Using the Design Thinking Cycle for Progress, project and initiative leaders can think about how they might use specific techniques or exercises to augment how they already operate when it comes to managing risks, communications, stakeholders, and so on. Figure 24.2 helps us visualize PMI's knowledge areas (outlined in the sixth version of the popular Project Management Body of Knowledge, or PMBOK) in this context.

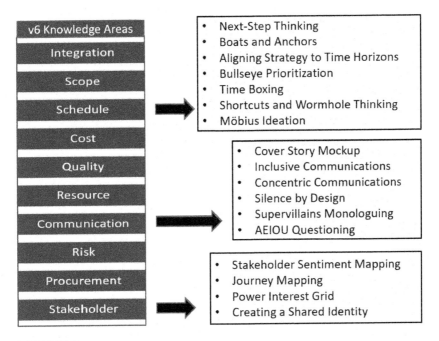

FIGURE 24.2
Note how the Design Thinking Cycle for Progress can help us map PMI's 10 project management Legacy Knowledge Areas to a set of area-specific Design Thinking techniques and exercises.

Turning to a set of Design Thinking–inspired exercises and techniques can help us move with greater speed—or make progress again—when the traditional methods and approaches fail us. In this way, value may be delivered with greater velocity.

Similarly, we can apply the Design Thinking Cycle for Progress to the performance domains and principles shared in PMI's more recent guidance, the seventh edition of the PMBOK Guide. Note the similarities between legacy PMI guidance reflected in Figure 24.2 and PMI's newer guidance in Figure 24.3.

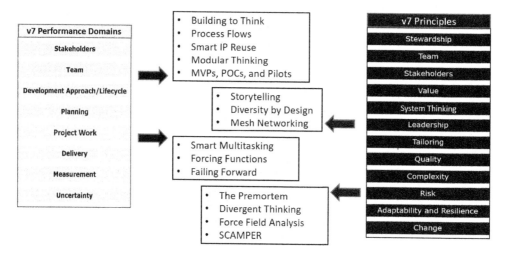

FIGURE 24.3
The Design Thinking Cycle for Progress can also help us map PMI's 8 Project Performance Domains and 12 Principles to a set of area-specific Design Thinking techniques and exercises.

For the remainder of this hour, we have organized a set of Design Thinking techniques around an amalgamation of project management Principles, Performance Domains, and Knowledge Areas spanning PMI's guidance over the last decade:

- Leadership and Governance

- Stakeholders and Expectations

- Development Approach

- Risk Management

- Schedule Management

- Managing Scope

- Delivery and Quality

- Communications and Collaboration

Each area is covered next through the lens of pursuing, maintaining, or increasing velocity. Remember that beyond these eight amalgamations, quite a few other project management principles, domains, and knowledge areas were covered in detail throughout previous hours!

Leadership and Governance

To be effective, leadership must be visible and visual. Leaders must show up and lead from the front—be seen and be heard—and demonstrate the kind of empathetic leadership necessary for change and progress (Tyler, 2019). For many years, the Project Management Institute has shared guidance and a set of traditional techniques for leading and managing resources. More recently, PMI has shared its thoughts on leadership styles and behaviors including how such styles and behaviors may be tailored for specific situations. A subset of these foundational techniques that help us move with velocity includes the following:

▶ Coaching and exercising specific leadership styles based on situations, choices, and actions to drive outcomes

▶ Evolving leadership through competence and commitment

▶ Using video conferencing in lieu of face-to-face meetings

▶ Developing virtual teams spanning remote and geographic boundaries

▶ Solving problems through brainstorming and other fundamental ideation techniques

If we seek to lead and govern our projects and initiatives more effectively and with greater speed, we can also turn to Design Thinking methods, including

▶ Simple Rules and Guiding Principles to establish clarity among our teams in terms of what we do, when we do it, and how we execute (Hour 4)

▶ Stakeholder+ and Stakeholder Sentiment Mapping for understanding and tracking key relationships (Hour 7)

▶ The Power/Interest Grid for prioritizing key relationships (Hour 7)

▶ Framing Governance for collaborating and driving key stakeholder connections with clarity and regularity (Hour 15)

From a team leadership perspective, use the following techniques and exercises to build relationships and shared understanding faster, all of which lead to greater velocity long term:

▶ Diversity by Design to build high-performing connected teams capable of ideating more creatively (Hour 4)

▶ Mesh Networking for connecting and preserving the health of our islands of remote workers and avoiding the Archipelago Effect (Hour 4)

▶ AntiFragile Validation for verifying that our individuals and teams are growing stronger even in the wake of hardship (Hour 22)

▶ Growth Mindset for learning and teaming by creating learn-it-all work climates and extending grace to one another in the face of inevitable failures (Hour 4)

▶ Visual Thinking for more quickly creating a shared understanding (Hour 5)

▶ Analogy and Metaphor Thinking for team alignment and for simplifying the complex (Hour 11)

▶ Creating a Shared Identity to connect our people with one another, with other teams, and with our user communities (Hour 15)

▶ Storytelling for sharing and reinforcing the organization's vision (Hour 15)

Surely there are many more techniques and exercises to help us lead more effectively, but the preceding list serves as a solid Design Thinking–inspired foundation for achieving and maintaining velocity. Let's turn our attention now to techniques and exercises for engaging stakeholders and managing their expectations.

Stakeholders and Expectations

As outlined in Hour 7, sometime after publishing the sixth edition of the PMBOK (2017), the Project Management Institute changed its stance on stakeholders from *managing* them to engaging them and managing their expectations. Traditional techniques for "managing stakeholders" or their expectations include stakeholder analysis, classic stakeholder mapping, prioritizing and ranking techniques, the engagement assessment matrix, conflict management skills, and team skills for improving political and cultural awareness.

When the traditional methods are incomplete or simply insufficient, turn to the Design Thinking techniques and exercises outlined here for creating a better understanding, connecting with stakeholders while better engaging them, and managing their expectations:

▶ Big Picture Understanding for insights into an organization's broader industry and ecosystem (Hour 6)

▶ The Culture Snail and Culture Cube for exploring an organization's recent journey and current state (Hour 6)

▶ Recognizing and Validating Bias (Hour 6)

▶ Stakeholder+ Mapping for understanding hierarchies and monitoring key relationships (Hour 7)

▶ Stakeholder Sentiment Mapping for tracking stakeholder satisfaction over time (Hour 7)

▶ Power/Interest Grid for understanding priority relationships (Hour 7)

▶ Empathy Mapping for empathizing and connecting most effectively with others in light of the different types of empathy (Hour 8)

▶ Inclusive and Concentric Communications, Storytelling, Structured Text, and other communications techniques (Hour 15)

- ▶ Creating a Shared Identity to create a single virtual team regardless of the number of physical teams involved (Hour 15)

- ▶ Various visualization techniques for connecting more deeply and arriving at a shared understanding more quickly (Hours 5 and 12)

- ▶ The Waterfall Analogy and Analogy and Metaphor Thinking for simplifying the complex (Hours 4 and 11)

With leadership, governance, and stakeholders accounted for, let's take a look at how a chosen development approach may be further influenced through a set of Design Thinking techniques and exercises.

Development Approach

In the world of tech deployment and software development projects, the notion of a development approach often boils down to two polar opposites: an adaptive or Agile approach on one end, and a more sequential Waterfall approach on the other. Truth be told, nearly all organizations operate somewhere in between, borrowing what's needed from each extreme to move as quickly and responsibly as they believe they can.

A chosen development approach can vary too, based on the phase or needs of a project or initiative. Adaptive approaches may vary in terms of iterative or incremental development. External realities, including the need for regulatory audits or governance gates, also may influence the approach.

Regardless of the specific development approach, though, a set of Design Thinking–influenced exercises and techniques can oftentimes help organizations think, test, and move a bit faster:

- ▶ Building to Think to get started and learn faster (Hour 16)

- ▶ Rough and Ready Prototyping to obtain early feedback (including mockups, wireframes, and other methods outlined in Hour 16)

- ▶ Process Flows for driving clarity (Hour 16)

- ▶ Aligning Strategy to Time Horizons for smart release and sprint planning (Hour 13)

- ▶ Time Boxing, Pacing, and the Inverse Power Law for planning, organizing, and executing work (Hour 16)

- ▶ Shortcut and Wormhole Thinking for changing the landscape to increase velocity (Hour 18)

- ▶ Smart IP Reuse to get started faster (Hour 18)

- ▶ Modular Thinking to build smarter and faster (Hours 3 and 11)

- ▶ MVPs, POCs, and Pilots for meaningful user community feedback (Hour 17)

- ▶ Automating for Regression Velocity to manage changes faster (Hour 19)

Let's turn our attention next to what many consider the most important project management knowledge area or performance domain: managing risk.

Risk Management

Risk management is arguably second only to communications when it comes to the job of project and initiative leaders. A mature discipline, even risk management benefits strongly from a set of Design Thinking exercises and techniques that fundamentally improve how we identify potential risks, bake them into our Risk Register, and manage and mitigate risks over the lifecycle of a project or initiative.

Traditional techniques for managing project risk include these and more:

- ▶ Executing enterprise-level risk management planning

- ▶ Conducting risk breakdown exercises

- ▶ Conducting brainstorming for risk identification

- ▶ Performing contingency reserve analysis and related techniques

- ▶ Running postmortem exercises for threat planning, risk identification, and smarter risk remediation

- ▶ Performing root cause analysis (RCA) and similar data analysis techniques in the face of problems

- ▶ Performing risk reviews and other auditing and risk planning exercises to continuously refine a project's risk profile and mitigate newly identified risks

In addition to these traditional risk management methods, we may turn to a myriad of Design Thinking exercises and techniques for planning, identifying, analyzing, mitigating, responding to, and monitoring project risks. Some of these Design Thinking-inspired methods include

- ▶ Trend Analysis for predicting risks (Hour 6)

- ▶ Divergent Thinking for identifying previously uncovered risks (Hour 10)

- ▶ Guardrails for Thinking Differently and ideating more effectively (Hour 11)

▶ Pattern Matching and Fractal Thinking for considering and predicting potential risks (Hour 12)

▶ SCAMPER, Reverse Brainstorming, and Worst and Best Ideation for innovative twists on Brainstorming to identify and mitigate risks more deeply (Hour 14)

▶ The Premortem for thinking ahead to mitigate and plan for possible risks (Hour 11)

▶ Boats and Anchors for identifying schedule risks (Hour 11)

▶ Inverse Power Law to avoid scheduling changes at the worst times for a particular community or team (Hour 16)

▶ Time Pacing to consider schedule changes in terms of task frequency and duration (Hour 16)

▶ Force Field Analysis to quickly consider risks for and against a proposed change (Hours 14 and 23)

▶ Rose, Thorn, Bud (RTB) exercises for organizing risks (Hour 13)

▶ Affinity Clustering to identify risk themes (Hour 13)

▶ Structured Usability Testing to reduce solution misses (Hour 19)

▶ Silent Design for uncovering user community risks associated with missed expectations (Hours 20 and 22)

We should also consider team-based Design Thinking techniques for minimizing risks and therefore preserving velocity:

▶ Diversity by Design to reduce the risks of homogeneous thinking (Hour 4)

▶ Simple Rules and Guiding Principles to avoid team misalignment (Hour 4)

▶ Mesh Networking to avoid the Archipelago Effect (Hour 4)

▶ Looking Back (includes the Retrospective, Lessons Learned, and the Postmortem) to learn and avoid repeating the same mistakes (Hour 20)

Of all the project management knowledge areas or principles, risk management arguably benefits most from a wide cross section of Design Thinking techniques and exercises.

Schedule Management

Like risk management, managing to a plan and a schedule is another staple of project management. PMI provides an abundance of guidance for schedule management. Traditional techniques include these and more:

▶ Precedence diagramming or sequencing tasks in light of dependencies

▶ Using the Critical Path Method (CPM) for determining the minimum project duration

▶ Resource optimization practices to balance resource availability against time

▶ Building leads and lags into schedules to control or manage timing

▶ Performing Agile release planning as we organize large bodies of work into smaller bodies such as user stories and features across a timeline

▶ Practicing various forms of schedule compression including fast-tracking and schedule crashing

In addition to the traditional methods, we may turn to Design Thinking techniques and exercises for planning, defining, sequencing, estimating, developing, and controlling a project schedule. Some of these methods include

▶ Boats and Anchors, one of the most useful exercises for considering and mitigating potential impact on our schedule (Hour 11)

▶ Next-Step Thinking to design an effective near-term schedule (Hour 13)

▶ Aligning Strategy to Time Horizons to create a longer-term roadmap (Hour 13)

▶ Time Boxing for creating a predictable schedule (Hour 16)

▶ Inverse Power Law and Time Pacing for preserving our schedule once it's formalized (Hour 16)

▶ "What, So What, Now What?" for reshaping a schedule in the wake of a problem or situation (Hour 13)

▶ Journey Mapping to consider an underlying path or schedule (Hour 8)

▶ Bullseye Prioritization to prioritize and make smarter stepwise choices (Hour 13)

▶ Shortcuts and Wormhole Thinking to reshape or recast the landscape for speed (Hour 18)

▶ Smart Multitasking for avoiding unnecessary context switching (Hour 18)

▶ Forcing Functions for driving forward progress (Hour 16)

▶ Fractal Thinking and Pattern Matching to think ahead about potential schedule implications (Hour 12)

▶ Inclusive and Accessible Thinking to minimize future rework (Hour 11)

▶ Good Enough Thinking to move forward (Hour 11)

▶ Mission Impossible Ideation for compressing the schedule (Hour 11)

▶ Möbius Ideation to minimize or avoid waiting on additional resources (Hour 11)

With our schedule preserved, optimized, and potentially accelerated, let us turn next to managing our scope of work spanning this schedule.

Managing Scope

The Project Management Institute has long provided guidance for managing our scope of work. A subset of the traditional techniques we often turn to for managing project scope include the following:

▶ Expert judgment

▶ Inspection

▶ Affinity and various relationship-based diagrams

▶ Facilitation skills

▶ Brainstorming

▶ Voting

Alongside PMI's traditional methods, we can turn to Design Thinking techniques for planning, collecting, defining, creating, validating, and controlling project scope. Remember to link OKRs to our scope, creating a direct connection between the tactical features and business value we are delivering and an organization's strategic vision. Some of these techniques include

▶ Time Boxing and Time Pacing to organize and distribute scope (Hour 16)

▶ Journey Mapping to consider scope in a stepwise user-centric manner (Hour 8)

▶ Balancing the Essential and the Accidental to identify scope that is more essential than other scope (Hour 21).

▶ Buy a Feature to reduce scope uncertainty and gain consensus in sprint and release planning (Hour 13)

▶ Bullseye Prioritization to make prioritized scope choices (Hour 13)

▶ Affinity Clustering to organize scope into themes, stories, features, and so on (Hour 13)

▶ Verbatim Mapping to directionally confirm scope or user needs and priorities (Hour 9)

▶ Five Whys to validate scope timing or priority (Hour 9)

▶ Golden Ratio Analysis to assess scope "fit" (Hour 12)

▶ "What, So What, Now What?" to rebalance scope in the wake of a problem or situation (Hour 13)

▶ Rough and Ready Prototyping and various forms of Building to Think as a way to directionally validate scope (Hours 16 and 17)

As the Project Management Institute shares, managing scope goes hand in hand with delivery and quality, covered next.

Delivery and Quality

Delivery is synonymous with execution. PMI tells us that delivery is about delivering a particular scope of work at the expected quality. Thus we have combined delivery and quality as we consider what it means to deliver with quality our scope of work. PMI's most recent guidance and techniques include the following:

▶ Executing to achieve contracted outcomes

▶ Realizing project value and other benefits on schedule

▶ Managing stakeholder expectations in the wake of delivery and quality missteps

▶ Meeting requirements by delivering scope at the expected quality to drive the intended outcomes

▶ Using requirements management systems to provide traceability between outcomes and the requirements that must be delivered to realize such value

▶ Instrumenting delivery through validation and control-related policies, procedures, and other guidance

▶ Accommodating industry-specific quality standards or metrics

▶ Methods for identifying and stabilizing unstable or "moving" requirements

▶ Factoring in sustainability and other company or industrywide standards as part of responsible delivery

Applying Design Thinking to increase delivery velocity includes the following exercises and techniques, many of which tie back to schedules or timelines, organizing scope, and prioritizing our work to achieve value and other intended outcomes:

- Bullseye Prioritization to prioritize delivery choices or impasses (Hour 13)

- Adjacent Spaces Technique to consider low-impact delivery paths (Hour 13)

- Rose, Thorn, Bud (RTB) exercises for organizing delivery and quality matters (Hour 13)

- Affinity Clustering to identify themes in delivery (Hour 13)

- Smart Multitasking to deliver faster (Hour 18)

- Next-Step Thinking to select the next best step (Hour 13)

- Good Enough Thinking to deliver what is needed rather than what might be desired (Hour 11)

- Shortcut or Wormhole Thinking to recast a landscape for greater delivery velocity (Hour 18)

- Mission Impossible Thinking to uncover or target extreme delivery solutions (Hour 11)

- Forcing Functions to drive delivery (Hours 16 and 23)

- Failing Forward to stay future-focused and make delivery progress (Hour 17)

- Fixing Broken Windows to get delivery back on track (Hour 21)

- Avoiding the Abilene Paradox to minimize unnecessary delivery detours (Hour 21)

While PMI values delivery, PMI reflects an even richer track record of quality management, or what it means to deliver with quality. Traditional techniques for managing quality include the following and more:

- Flowcharts and models for visual planning

- Various types of testing (for validating features and evaluating fit through the traditional techniques covered in Hour 19)

- Test and inspection planning

- Inspection methods for validating conformance to a standard

- Cause-and-Effect for problem solving through data and diagramming methods

- Root Cause Analysis for problem solving

Alongside PMI's traditional quality methods, we can turn to numerous Design Thinking techniques helpful for planning, managing, and controlling quality in ways that preserve if not improve velocity. Some of these quality-enhancing techniques include

▶ Snaking the Drain for thinking with a clean slate (Hour 10)

▶ Premortem Exercise for planning ahead (Hour 11)

▶ Worst and Best Ideation for planning (Hour 14)

▶ Rule of Threes for managing expectations (Hour 4)

▶ "How Might We?" Questioning for exploring what's next in an inclusive and positive manner (Hour 4)

▶ Slay the Hero to improve operational quality (Hour 22)

▶ Silent Design to populate our backlog with what might have amounted to quality misses (Hour 22)

▶ Running the Swamp for extreme quality thinking (Hour 12)

▶ Golden Ratio Analysis for evaluating quality fit (Hour 12)

Note that many of the techniques and exercises related to understanding and solving problems are helpful when it comes to managing quality. Refer to Hours 9 and 14 to think through how to use additional delivery and quality techniques.

Communications and Collaboration

Always a top priority but not always executed well, communication demands special attention to be executed well. The Project Management Institute (2017) shares that communication is the "process of planning, collecting, storing, and updating project information...to ensure that the information needs of the project and its stakeholders are met through development of artifacts and implementation of activities designed to achieve effective information exchange." Traditional techniques for managing project communications include these and more:

▶ Tending to cross-cultural communication realities

▶ Analyzing communication requirements to determine the types and channels of communication

▶ Considering the effectiveness of channels for specific needs or situations

▶ Using the Encode-Transmit-Decode communication model

▶ Employing push-and-pull communications methods as needed

▶ Learning the role of nonverbal communications and the skills necessary to use and pivot to nonverbal communications

▶ Expanding individual observation and conversation skills, including team listening and communication skills, to be more effective communicators

In conjunction with our traditional communications management methods, we may also turn to Design Thinking techniques for communicating more effectively, inclusively, and with greater clarity. Some of these techniques include

▶ Simple Rules and Guiding Principles for communicating internally what and when and how our teams execute (Hour 4)

▶ Cover Story Mockup for communicating vision and generating buy-in and excitement (Hours 3 and 16)

▶ Active Listening to learn and therefore communicate faster in a meaningful way (Hour 6)

▶ Probing for Understanding to learn and therefore communicate faster and with greater clarity (Hour 6)

▶ Silence by Design to learn and therefore communicate faster in a meaningful way (Hour 6)

▶ Supervillain Monologuing for quickly collecting information that might not otherwise be proffered in formal discussions (Hour 6)

▶ Concentric Communications for communicating with the right people at the right time (Hour 15)

▶ Inclusive Communications to ensure everyone has a voice and is drawn into team communications (Hour 15)

▶ Storytelling for deeper understanding and to share vision and purpose (Hour 15)

▶ AEIOU Questioning for verbally and rapidly assessing situations and taking better-informed next steps (Hour 9)

▶ Structured Text so receivers may more quickly comprehend complex written communications (Hour 15)

▶ Mesh Networking to create a more effective communications network linking our teams to one another and to other resources (Hour 4)

For additional communications tips and techniques, consider the material and techniques throughout Hours 4 and 15 for leading healthy teams and effectively communicating and collaborating cross-boundary.

Beyond the eight areas covered here—spanning leadership and governance, stakeholders and their expectations, development approaches, risk management, schedule management, scope management, attention to delivery and quality, and communications and collaboration—PMI has recently outlined additional areas where Design Thinking techniques may be helpful. Consider, for example, how the following areas were also covered throughout the previous 23 hours.

- ▶ Value (Hours 1, 2, 4, 6, 17, 18, 21, 22, and more)

- ▶ Complexity (Hours 1, 9, 21, and more)

- ▶ Uncertainty (Hours 1, 3, 13, and more)

- ▶ Adaptability and Resilience (Hours 4, 13, 16, 22, and more)

- ▶ Change (Hours 3, 6, 11, 12, 13, 16, 18, 19, and, of course, 23)

As we go about the work of understanding people and situations to solve complex problems, let's look for those opportunities where we can drive clarity and velocity through Design Thinking. As we have seen in every case study and "What Not to Do" real-world example throughout this book, the opportunities are all around us!

What Not to Do: No Courage, No Future

As we have seen in several previous "What Not to Do" case studies, an unwillingness to move forward in light of the risks of the unknown only serves to keep our teams and our solution from realizing their intended value. It takes courage, but we must eventually quit iterating and refining our work—and actually deploy something of value. After all, our value hangs in the balance in the same way that velocity hinges on delivering value.

For a global wealth management firm, a nervous Product Owner eventually only found a world of missed expectations and the unemployment line. The Product Owner missed early opportunities to pull in her user community's feedback. Demonstrations were cancelled more often than actually held, and the idea for an MVP never materialized despite the firm's positive experiences with other such MVPs.

Instead, the firm's Product Owner continued to have her team groom and iterate to perfection several admittedly important feature sets. Together with her Product Manager and a frustrated consulting partner, the Product Owner created a beautiful but incomplete case management system. But like a pearl stuck in mud, the system would never be enough to wow her users; they never even got the opportunity to provide feedback in a meaningful kind of way. In the end, a new Product Owner and tech leader were given the opportunity to create with the team a more user-inclusive release and sprint plan to complete their predecessor's work.

Summary

In Hour 24, we reviewed a host of Design Thinking exercises and techniques cast through the lens of project management velocity. We organized these methods around a number of PMI knowledge areas, performance domains, and principles. While every PMI knowledge area, performance domain, and principle is important, through the lens of *velocity*, we identified eight focus areas that strongly benefited from new Design Thinking–inspired ways of thinking and executing. These eight focus areas included leadership and governance, stakeholders and their expectations, development approach, risk management, schedule management, managing scope, delivery and quality, and communications and collaboration. We concluded this hour with a "What Not to Do" reflecting the need to deliver value despite ever-present uncertainty and other unknowns that can trap us into iterating endlessly.

Workshop

Case Study

Consider the following case study and questions. You can find the answers to the questions related to this case study in Appendix A, "Case Study Quiz Answers."

Situation

As your time with Satish is finally wrapping up, he has called you again, this time concerned about velocity. It seems that a number of the OneBank initiatives are progressing slower than expected. The initiative leaders are generally employing good project management techniques, but when their initiatives stall or seem to get stuck, some of the leaders are at a loss for what to do next. You have been asked to share Design Thinking techniques useful in restarting and accelerating the bank's initiatives.

To help the initiative leaders, you have organized a virtual workshop where you can demonstrate some of these techniques and exercises and answer their questions. Your initial review of each initiative has highlighted gaps in governance, schedule management, delivery and quality, communications and collaboration, and more.

Quiz

1. How might the initiative leaders improve governance across their respective initiatives through Design Thinking?

2. When the traditional methods of managing an initiative's scope fail to deliver results, which scope-related Design Thinking techniques may prove useful?

3. The initiative leaders are looking for a new way to think more deeply and visually about potential schedule impact. Which Design Thinking exercise is probably the most useful to start with in this regard?

4. Which quality-related Design Thinking techniques might prove interesting to the initiative leaders alongside the standard approaches for thinking about and managing quality?

5. Which set of Design Thinking techniques or exercises are especially useful for initiative leaders looking for new ways to connect and communicate with their respective stakeholders or teams?

Case Study Quiz Answers

The answers to each case study quiz provided at the conclusion of each Hour follow:

Hour 1

1. Design Thinking is about slowing down and taking the time to deeply understand, think, and iterate on solutions to the toughest problems as a way of delivering value. We slow down our thinking and problem solving so we can speed up solutioning and iterating on that solution.

2. Techniques are simple precepts, axioms, or principles that are in many ways self-evident and simply need to be followed. On the other hand, exercises reflect a series of activities executed stepwise, one after the other, to arrive at some kind of understanding or output.

3. Our primary enemy when it comes to making progress in the midst of the toughest, most ambiguous, and most complex problems is time.

4. Design Thinking provides us with the foundation for solving problems and creating and realizing value. From Design Thinking comes a set of point-in-time best practices and later a set of common practices that typically suffice—until it is time to revisit the problem by applying Design Thinking.

Hour 2

1. Beyond the traditional ways of organizing projects or initiatives, we might also consider where they sit within the Design Thinking process and its four phases.

2. In the context of learning or empathizing, "Understanding Broadly" relates to understanding the broader ecosystem and situation, the people caught in the middle of the situation, and the problems associated with the situation and its people.

3. Traditional thinking tends to focus less on the problem and much more on the solution. On the other hand, Design Thinking arms us with techniques and exercises that help us think and ideate differently to approach OneBank's initiatives in new ways.

4. Phase 3, "Delivering Value," is the place where primary value is initially delivered through the Design Thinking process and its techniques and exercises. More importantly, though, value is also delivered incrementally throughout the process, particularly as we recursively learn, iterate, and refine our solution.

5. While the Design Thinking process follows a stepwise phase-based approach, the real value in Design Thinking is found in the power to recursively circle back to better understand, circle back to think more deeply or differently, and circle back to deliver new manifestations of value along the way.

Hour 3

1. One of the easiest ways of organizing Design Thinking techniques and exercises for individual and small team use is by learning more quickly, thinking differently and deeply, coping with ambiguity, prioritizing next best steps for uncertainty, and executing more effectively.

2. Ambiguity reflects the unknowns of the situation and problem, whereas uncertainty ties back to the choices or priorities facing the people in the midst of that situation or problem.

3. Design Thinking techniques or exercises useful for coping with ambiguity include Modular Thinking, Building to Think, MVP Thinking, Cover Story Mockup, and the Premortem.

4. Design Thinking techniques or exercises that can help individuals or small teams think differently include Visual Thinking, Pattern Matching, Fractal Thinking, Divergent Thinking, and Opposite Thinking or Reverse Brainstorming.

5. Design Thinking techniques or exercises useful for prioritizing "next best steps" in the face of uncertainty include Bullseye Prioritization; the Adjacent Spaces Exploration technique; the Rose, Thorn, Bud (RTB) exercise; and Affinity Clustering.

Hour 4

1. To make decisions more quickly and stay aligned from a strategy and operational perspective, teams should consider establishing a set of 6 to 10 Simple Rules (and probably develop a set of Guiding Principles for each of those Simple Rules or similar focus areas).

2. "How Might We?" questioning sets the stage for teams to optimistically approach a situation together, considering ideas that might not otherwise be shared.

3. Turn to Diversity by Design to help homogeneous teams improve how they ideate and problem solve. The greater diversity in terms of experience, ways of thinking, background, culture, time in role, positions held, beliefs, color, gender, lifestyle, and more, the greater the ability of a team to ideate and problem solve.

4. Teams that seem to be excluding others in discussions, meetings, and workshops would benefit from creating as a team a set of Guiding Principles for inclusive communications, along with adopting Inclusive and Effective Meeting techniques.

5. Briefly, the Archipelago Effect occurs when people and teams work too long in isolation and unconnected from others. Once people have become islands or collections of islands without benefit of connection and relationship, they become less productive, lose interest, and oftentimes leave for no other reason than to pursue something different that hopefully fills this relationship and connectedness hole in their lives.

Hour 5

1. Visual Thinking is nothing more than turning words into pictures and figures to help arrive at a shared understanding.

2. There are dozens of examples of Visual Collaboration exercises, including Stakeholder Mapping, the Power/Interest Grid, Journey Mapping, Problem Tree Analysis, Boats and Anchors, Metaphor and Analogy Thinking, Mission Impossible Thinking, Möbius Ideation, Pattern Matching and Fractal Thinking, Affinity Clustering, Running the Swamp, Cover Story Mockup, Culture Cube, Golden Ratio Analysis, Bullseye Prioritization, Force Field Analysis, Mind Mapping, 2×2 Matrix Thinking, Adjacent Space Exploration, RTB, Mockups, the Inverse Power Law, Concentric Communications, Structured Text, Process Flows, and many more.

3. In cases where a team cannot physically meet to run a Design Thinking exercise or session, consider using Klaxoon or Microsoft Whiteboard.

4. The three-stage process for running a Design Thinking exercise includes preparing for the exercise, running the exercise, and concluding the exercise.

Hour 6

1. Beyond good active listening skills, the three "listening and understanding" techniques that might help Satish encourage the organization's business stakeholders to talk more freely and openly include Silence by Design, Supervillain Monologuing, and Probing for Understanding.

2. The Culture Snail for Pace of Change helps explain how various parts of the business got to where they are today by mapping key events, inflection points, decisions, successes, failures, and more as a way to describe the organization's culture journey and its ability to absorb that particular pace of change.

3. Use the Culture Cube to view a team's culture in terms of three dimensions and eight perspectives.

4. When it comes to researching and arriving at a Big Picture Understanding of a company or organization, consider the following environmental dimensions that start broad but help us narrow down and understand the organization more deeply: the macroeconomic environment and industry, the company or entity within its industry and environment, and finally the organization or business unit within the company or entity.

Hour 7

1. Each initiative leader should perform a Stakeholder Mapping exercise to identify and map their respective stakeholders to their initiative.

2. An easy way to reflect stakeholder sentiment is to color-code (using red, amber, and green, for example) an existing Stakeholder Map. Revisit this color coding monthly and use non-color-based markings to accommodate inclusive design and accessibility needs.

3. The Power/Interest Grid reflects power or influence on one axis and stakeholder interest on the other axis. Satish should pay attention to the two quadrants where power is the highest, as stakeholders in these two quadrants have the greatest ability to help or hinder the OneBank transformation and its initiatives.

4. Satish has at his disposal a number of techniques and exercises that might help him engage more deeply with his most important or influential stakeholders, including Empathy Mapping, Analogy and Metaphor Thinking, various forms of brainstorming and visualization techniques, methods for Creating or Increasing a Shared Identity, numerous communications techniques including Inclusive and Concentric Communications, Story Telling, Structured Text, and more, and promoting the positive changes that the teams have already successfully implemented as a way to drive stakeholder Empathy through Realized Changes.

Hour 8

1. A persona is an amalgamation of fictional characters (such as "finance user," "sales user," "executives," and so on) of a community who share common needs and will use specific artifacts or features of a solution or deliverables in similar ways.

2. The Persona Profiling Design Thinking exercise is especially useful in organizing and helping a Design Thinking team connect with different personas.

3. The three types of empathy discussed here include cognitive, emotional, and compassionate empathy. While all three would be useful in understanding why consumers choose to bank elsewhere, the Moonshot team should consider "getting in the hole with non-BigBank users" to really understand their situation, why they are stuck in that hole or choose to stay in that hole, and therefore what BigBank might do differently to draw users out of that hole.

4. Empathy Mapping is the kind of work done from the safety of a desk as we identify and document what a user or persons thinks and feels; what they see and hear; what they say and do; what seems to be their biggest pain points; and what seems to be their top goals, gains, or objectives. Empathy Immersion, on the other hand, requires us to don the clothes and safety gear and "skin" of another person and actually "walk a mile in their shoes."

5. A "Day in the Life of," or DILO, analysis builds on Journey Mapping in three important ways. First, it extends the "journey" to consider the full day versus a portion of the day. Second, it adds context about how our user feels as they navigate their daily journey. And, finally, in a DILO we include the user's thoughts and weigh in with our own thoughts as to how effectively or efficiently the time is being spent and tasks are being completed.

Hour 9

1. While we covered three Design Thinking exercises for identifying problems, the two that are known for creating good problem statements include the Problem Framing Exercise and the Problem Stating exercise.

2. A Problem Tree Analysis provides clarity by separating a problem's root causes from its effects or outcomes, using a tree metaphor to share this perspective visually and visibly.

3. The four different Design Thinking techniques or exercises useful in validating a particular problem include Verbatim Mapping, AEIOU Questioning, the Five Whys, and Pattern Matching.

4. The Executive Committee seems to be confusing the power of Design Thinking to start and fail and learn fast when it comes to ideating, thinking, prototyping, and solutioning in general; the EC is trying to incorrectly apply this principle to problem identification and validating.

Hour 10

1. Without knowing more, the team's execution model may indeed be fundamentally flawed. But it seems that the team members are spending all of their time "doing" and probably need to step back and spend a lot more time "thinking" in the short term. They cannot possibly solve their continuing challenges with the same thinking that failed to restore velocity previously. And they'll need some help to think differently and deeply.

2. For the short term, the initiative's leadership team probably needs to flip the amount of time they are thinking and the amount of time they are executing, The need to practice more divergent thinking in particular, and afterward converge on a few ideas to make progress and restore confidence in the team and their work.

3. The danger of changing how a team thinks and executes in the short-term falls back on velocity. Team members will need to go slower before they can go faster, a bit like the adage of the tortoise and the hare. So we will need executive leadership support to slow down and deeply think through what needs to change before we can hope to go faster and operate more predictably against an updated plan.

4. There are quite a few tips for individuals and teams to "warm up" their brains for thinking differently, such as walking or exercising, dreaming, drawing, building something, listening to music, praying, and meditating, Even taking a warm shower has been shown to open our minds for ideating and thinking differently. And we might also use popular taxonomies as a way to help a team think through areas more broadly, including STEEP, AEIOU, a standard Risk Register, and even the Agile Manifesto's 4 values and 12 principles.

5. Two easy ways to help people who are stuck in their old ways of thinking think anew include Snaking the Drain and Sacrificing the Calf.

Hour 11

1. In addition to a Postmortem, the team should also run a Premortem after it solidifies its plans for the second upgrade attempt. A combined Premortem and traditional Postmortem will help the team identify more what-ifs and flesh out the Risk Register with a fresh set of risks to consider and mitigate.

2. A Mission Impossible exercise should be run to push the team to think about how zero downtime might be achieved.

3. The team should think through the plan from a Good Enough Thinking perspective. The team needs to ask itself what "good" looks like, so it knows when to stop working through aspects of the plan that are adequate and instead turn its attention to those aspects that truly require more time.

4. Use a Boats and Anchors exercise to think more deeply about schedule risks as it lays out the next multiweek upgrade plan. Consider each phase of the plan in terms of anchors that might slow down progress, sharks that need to be identified and mitigated or eliminated, shoals and rocks that might cause the plan to run aground, major hurricanes and other issues on the horizon, and so forth.

5. The Möbius Ideation technique asks us to view a problem or situation through the lens of efficiency.

Hour 12

1. The Visual Thinking technique is really focused on getting thoughts out of the head and onto paper or a whiteboard as a way to increase shared understanding among a group.

2. Divergent Thinking comprises many different tips and techniques that help us think deeply and differently.

3. While Running the Swamp is a great way to drive new ideas, it also helps a team empathize with the people (rather than a faceless product or a project) trying to cross the swamp.

4. Use Fractal Thinking to help us seek out and see otherwise invisible self-similar patterns playing out at scale below, around, and beyond us.

5. Fibonacci's Sequence forms the basis of the Golden Ratio, which gives us a measuring stick for analyzing the natural fit or dimensions of a particular solution (or problem, team, process, and so on).

6. The workshop's participants should view this collection of creative thinking techniques and exercises as "bolt-ons" to be used atop other methods. For example, classic brainstorming is incomplete with concluding such an exercise with a follow-on Reverse Brainstorming exercise.

Hour 13

1. The difference between uncertainty and ambiguity can be briefly described in the sense that people face uncertainty, but situations reflect ambiguity.

2. Use Possible Futures Thinking and a six- to eight-section wheel organized by Social, Technology, Economic, Environmental, Political (and potentially other) areas to look out into the future and assess that future broadly.

3. If an organization wants to capitalize on what it already knows and what it already does but still transform itself incrementally, it may turn to Adjacent Space Exploration to capitalize on those areas that are least risky to tackle next.

4. Bullseye Prioritization serves two distinct purposes. First, it helps a team organize a broad set of options or choices across just a few areas (quadrants). Second, it allows for those options and choices to be prioritized against one another given that only one choice for each quadrant can occupy the bullseye.

5. It's often said that the middle or mid-term horizon is the most difficult to envision or achieve because it occupies the space between what we know/who we are and what we aspire to know or be.

6. Run a Buy a Feature exercise to create consensus among a team that shifts and changes its opinions. Let the exercise's use of imaginary money make each team member put their money where their mouth is (let the money do the talking).

Hour 14

1. To select and prepare the Executive Committee's participants for Brainstorming, it's recommended to employ Diversity by Design as a way to ensure diversity in thought, experience, background, education, culture, and more. The EC should give its participants plenty of advance notice to allow for preparation and share the Problem Statement as well as any recent findings or research with the participants.

2. Each Brainstorming session should begin with the facilitator stating aloud to the team that curiosity is the goal, and no idea is too crazy to be considered. Before starting the actual Brainstorming exercise, the facilitator should also consider running a creative warm-up to get the team thinking; examples might include sharing a taxonomy that reflects the problem area or practicing some of the divergent tips and techniques shared previously with the EC. Finally, to commence the actual Brainstorming exercise, the facilitator should use the "How Might We?" questioning technique to set the stage for thinking optimistically and inclusively.

3. When a Brainstorming session seems stalled or derailed, the Executive Committee could reinvigorate the team's ability to focus or think by clearing or unclogging the mind through Snaking the Drain or Sacrificing the Calf, use a mix of solo and group-level Brainstorming, reminding the committee throughout the session that no idea is a bad idea, making sure that all voices are being heard and considered, and using keywords and guardrails for thinking differently.

4. SCAMPER is a stepwise method and acronym to improve a team's brainstorming ability, using the following keywords in a "How Might We?" structure to consider a problem or situation in terms of (S) how might we substitute...?, (C) how might we combine...?, (A) how might we adapt...?, (M) how might we modify or magnify...?, (P) how might we repurpose or put to another use...?, (E) how might we eliminate or minimize...?, and finally (R) how might we reverse or rearrange...?. Each of these keywords opens the door to thinking differently and deeply.

5. To help ensure breadth and depth in the exercise, the Executive Committee and indeed every Brainstorming facilitator across BigBank should conclude its Brainstorming sessions with an opposite-thinking exercise such as SCAMPER (the R includes reverse thinking), Worst and Best, or Reverse Brainstorming.

Hour 15

1. The OneBank initiative leaders can take many different steps to create a shared identity, all of which revolve around accelerating relationship building by finding common ground, developing cross-team relationships, and creating common threads or themes between people and teams. Some of these steps and methods include icebreakers and relationship builders, such as the Rating Game, Fun Facts, and This Is Me.

2. Use the Framing Governance for Collaboration technique to help create an overlay or matrix of governance across the collection of OneBank initiatives,

3. Concentric Communications is a Design Thinking technique that takes into consideration how communications may be visualized through radiating circles that call out the specific cadences and channels for different people and teams.

4. Black Box Illumination is a good technique for visually simplifying heavy word-based communications.

5. When a visual or picture is not appropriate, use the Structured Text for Rapid Comprehension technique to create concise and easily consumable written communication.

Hour 16

1. Four techniques that can help a team benefit from user feedback and other learnings through "learning by doing" include Cover Story Mockup for creating a shared vision, Process Flows for creating clarity, Building to Think to make progress when the path is unclear, and Rough and Ready Prototyping for thinking with our hands.

2. The Cover Story Mockup technique helps us paint a successful vision of our work in the future so we can visualize how that work would impact a community of users.

3. Use Process Flows to create structure by understanding and documenting how data moves from one place to another, and in which direction, and under what conditions.

4. The four techniques that can help us make planful and predictable progress include Forcing Functions, Time Boxing, the Inverse Power Law, and Time Pacing.

5. Parkinson's Law is reflected in Time Boxing, which is based on Cyril Parkinson's answer to the problem of work naturally expanding "so as to fill the time available for its completion."

Hour 17

1. The three techniques outlined in this hour that help a team "Execute to Think" and deliver something small and of value include the Proof of Concept, the MVP (Minimum Viable Product), and the Pilot.

2. To define and refine the notion of value, a team might use Objectives and Key Results.

3. When we choose to "Fail Forward," we employ a Forcing Function that says there's no turning back. This kind of focus and reality is useful because it aligns a team toward the future rather than spending time trying to return to an old and insufficient state or situation.

4. A pilot differs from a POC or MVP in that Pilots are functionally complete, unlike the tactical or partial functionality associated with a POC or the bare-bones functional capabilities available for only a subset of users reflected in an MVP.

5. The "Progress Mindset" is about small wins as we deliver value fast. Doing so establishes a way for making progress when the path is uncertain or the needs of a community are unclear.

Hour 18

1. Releases are higher in terms of hierarchy than sprints; many sprints are assigned to a single release.

2. Initiative leaders should consider the Smart IP Reuse technique, which includes using and adapting existing templates, documents, checklists, plans, and other artifacts to improve velocity.

3. Multitasking is a normal part of life, but if we follow our passion or our energy, we can get more done more quickly. And for the tasks that remain, use Forcing Functions and Gamification to drive progress.

4. The Gamification technique employs ribbons, badges, and other rewards (including tangible ones) to encourage and motivate people to complete their work faster than they might otherwise be inclined to do.

5. Shortcut Thinking (or Finding the Wormhole) sets the stage for reinventing a playing field, rather than resigning oneself to that playing field, to find a faster or more effective route between two points.

Hour 19

1. The five traditional types of testing include Unit Testing, Process Testing, End-to-End Testing, System Integration Testing, and User Acceptance Testing. In addition, the three performance-related testing types include Performance Testing, Scalability Testing, and Load and Stress Testing.

2. The Testing Mindset is integral to problem solving as we validate what we think we know, discover gaps as we uncover what we don't know, and learn more throughout the testing process.

3. The five Design Thinking testing techniques outlined in this hour include Structured Usability Testing, A/B Testing, Experience Testing, Solution Interviewing, and Automating for Regression Velocity.

4. Structured Usability Testing is similar to traditional User Acceptance Testing in that users are validating our product or solution, but Structured Usability Testing is done much earlier than UAT, giving us much more time to pivot or change the direction of our product or solution.

5. The two Design Thinking testing tools we might use for capturing user feedback include the Testing Sheet and the Feedback Capture Grid.

6. Test leads should target 80 to 90 percent of test cases to be automated for Regression Testing.

Hour 20

1. A special technique called Silent Design reflects feedback gained from users and how they make changes to our products and solutions after they have been deployed to production.

2. The Testing Feedback technique is the broad-based technique reflecting feedback and other learnings from the breadth of traditional and newer Design Thinking testing techniques.

3. The three specific feedback techniques or methods underneath the umbrella of the Looking Back technique include running a Retrospective, running a Lessons Learned session, and running a Postmortem.

4. The Retrospective is an ongoing review we should conduct with our design and development teams or other sprint teams on a regular cadence (typically tied to the conclusion of a sprint or release).

5. To avoid waiting too long for feedback, we might share with Satish to deploy the work we are concluding. Design Thinking is about progress through iteration and learning, and we will have plenty of time to iterate and learn as long as we are making progress. Treat late feedback like a gift for the backlog and keep moving ahead.

Hour 21

1. The four examples of areas that many organizations struggle with when it comes to avoiding perfection traps include design, development, testing, and training or other end user readiness goals.

2. Consider applying the Fixing Broken Windows technique to flip "bad behavior begets worse behavior" into "good behavior begets better behavior"!

3. The moral of the Abilene Paradox story relates back to assumptions and their ability to derail us. We need to draw out people's true wants and needs before making decisions that cost the group time and progress. We need to consider how to poll the group in a discreet or anonymous manner to validate their true wants and needs while honestly vocalizing our own true wants and needs too.

4. Turn to the Backward Invention Design Thinking technique to simplify a product, solution, or service that has grown excessively complex or unwieldy to deploy or adopt.

5. The long-time philosophy-based Design Thinking technique called Balancing the Essential and the Accidental gives us a way of thinking about complexity in terms of what is truly necessary and what is optional or unneeded. There is oftentimes a vague line that separates true value from lost value, for example. This line separates the essential from the accidental, the required from the unrequired.

Hour 22

1. Though several scalability methods are available to support BigBank's transformation initiatives, Scaling and Subtracting by Fives and AntiFragile Validation for Longevity are a good initial lens for team scalability.

2. The Validating OKRs and Value technique forces us to consider value measures and how the notion of value might have changed throughout a project's lifecycle.

3. Two techniques for bolstering operational resiliency include Buddy System Pairing to reduce risks and Slaying the Hero for disaster recoverability and overall operational resiliency.

4. Attention to Silent Design helps organizations such as BigBank plan, backlog, and implement sustainable changes to the system over time.

5. AntiFragile Validation can help BigBank consider and validate the fragility of its teams as well as of its people. Turn to AntiFragile Validation to assess individual and team health and expected longevity.

Hour 23

1. The four phases to the change process include awareness, purpose, readiness, and adoption.

2. A number of Design Thinking techniques covered in this hour may be useful to create awareness of a change, including Big Picture Understanding, Fractal Thinking, Stakeholder+ Mapping, Persona Profiling, Cover Story Mockup, Snaking the Drain, Sacrificing the Calf, Making (Our Awareness Collateral) Visible and Visual, and for some audiences problem-related techniques including Problem Tree Analysis, Problem Framing, and Problem Stating.

3. Design Thinking techniques covered this hour and useful for driving readiness include Analogy and Metaphor Thinking, Prototypes and Mockups, Design Thinking–inspired Structured Usability Testing and Solution Interviewing, and Buddy System Pairing.

4. The four techniques outlined in this hour that can help organizations and teams adopt change include Forcing Functions, Gamification, Context Building and Mapping, and Making Change Consumable.

5. Design Thinking techniques outlined in this hour that can help organizations and teams consider the timing of a change include the Culture Snail for Pace of Change, Bias Recognition and Validation, AntiFragile Validation, Fixing Broken Windows, Time Boxing, the Inverse Power Law, and Time Pacing.

Hour 24

1. The OneBank initiative leaders could improve governance across their respective initiatives by creating a set of Simple Rules and Guiding Principles for execution alignment and clarity, Framing Governance for stakeholder connections, using Stakeholder+ and Stakeholder Sentiment Mapping for understanding and tracking key relationships, and using the Power/Interest Grid for prioritizing key relationships.

2. When the traditional methods of managing an initiative's scope fail to deliver results, the initiative leaders should turn to Time Boxing and Time Pacing, Journey Mapping, Balancing the Essential and the Accidental, Buy a Feature, Bullseye Prioritization, Affinity Clustering, Verbatim Mapping, the Five Whys, Golden Ratio Analysis, Rough and Ready Prototyping and other forms of Building to Think, and the "What, So What, Now What?" Design Thinking technique.

3. One of the most effective ways for the initiative leaders to think more deeply and visually about potential schedule impact includes running a Boats and Anchors exercise viewed through the lens of schedule management.

4. Interesting quality-enhancing Design Thinking techniques include Snaking the Drain, the Premortem Exercise, Worst and Best Ideation, Rule of Threes, "How Might We?" Questioning, Slay the Hero, Silent Design, Running the Swamp, and Golden Ratio Analysis.

5. The initiative leaders should turn to Simple Rules and Guiding Principles, Cover Story Mockup, Active Listening, Probing for Understanding, Silence by Design, Supervillain Monologuing, Storytelling, Concentric Communications, Inclusive Communications, AEIOU Questioning, Structured Text, and Mesh Networking to better connect and communicate with their respective stakeholders and teams.

Summary of Design Thinking Techniques and Exercises

The Design Thinking techniques and exercises summarized here are covered in one or more of the hours of this book. Each technique and exercise is arranged alphabetically here (and further organized by hour in Appendix C).

2×2 Matrix Thinking This technique is used to help people and teams evaluate a number of options across two dimensions and four quadrants. Considering options in this way helps us uncover the best choice or the ideal path forward.

A/B Testing This technique is used to compare one alternative against another alternative, which can be easier or more useful than trying to explain why any one single alterative might fail to meet a person's needs.

Active Listening In this technique, we show up, are present, listen like we are wrong, and learn. There's arguably no better way to learn and empathize with one another than through listening to their experiences, stories, and unsolicited challenges and pain.

Adjacent Spaces Thinking As we change our goals and consider what might be next, consider how we can incrementally ease into the "white space," or conceptual adjacent space, surrounding our current processes, methods, tools, and so on, with the idea that such change is more easily adopted or consumed because it is similar to what is currently in place. Said another way, use what we know today including our current strengths and capabilities to move into (or learn, or adopt) a new adjacent space. Such spaces could be technology-related, or reflect new business or application features, or new areas to master, new markets to dominate, new processes to better understand, and so on.

Affinity Clustering In this exercise popularized by the LUMA Institute, we organize data into themes, logical groups, or clusters of options to help make smarter choices and determine next best steps. Use Affinity Clustering with RTB and other prioritization or grouping exercises to naturally reduce some of the uncertainty or ambiguity surrounding complex situations.

Agile Practices These are the methodology, process, techniques, and other practices often used to operate in an iterative and collaborative way. They include practices and ceremonies that go well beyond this book but nonetheless often reflect a Design Thinking mindset, practices, techniques, and exercises. Consider how working in an Agile way means working in close collaboration with others to provide progressive and incremental value to end users.

Aligning People to Value   Value realization is predicated on project or initiative team members who understand, respect, and hold themselves accountable for delivering value and other expected outcomes. This alignment between individual people and the outcomes they are expected and accountable to deliver is required for realizing value and therefore success.

Aligning Strategy to Time Horizons   We need to think about today, the short term, the mid-term, and the long term, recognizing that our long-term vision must be prioritized to be realized (which, in turn, means that our short-term vision needs to blend the new with the current). Popular research suggests that the *mid-term* Time Horizon can be the most important, as it is often overlooked yet integral to achieving the long term.

AntiFragile Validation   Rooted in psychology and medicine, and popularized more recently by Nassim Taleb, this life hack is about recognizing our own stresses and struggles and how we're growing stronger from them. Not just surviving or coping, but actually growing stronger, or the opposite of fragile. AntiFragile Validation seeks to confirm that we are converting the hard things of life into tools and experiences for newfound strength and increased abilities to adapt and overcome.

Avoiding the Abilene Paradox   With this technique, we draw out people's true wants and needs before making decisions that cost the group time and progress. When we are faced with taking a journey that is perhaps unnecessary, consider how to poll the group in a discreet or anonymous manner to validate their true wants and needs.

Backporting into the Past   In this technique, we consider how current innovations can be "backported" into current processes or businesses or organizations to give them new life. Get to the future faster by building on what has already been built in a way that affords greater time-to-value at less cost and risk.

Backward Invention   This technique involves stripping out features to simplify a design, prototype, or MVP (often reflecting features that our users do not want, find irritating, or simply do not need).

Balancing the Essential and the Accidental   With regard to complexity of an idea, design, interface, or deliverable, it is important to understand the complexity that can be removed versus the complexity that is necessary, lest the idea, design, interface, prototype, MVP, or other deliverable or outcome lose its value. That is, we must find that thin vague line that separates the essential (required) from the accidental (optional or not required at all).

Bias Recognition and Validation   This is the process of understanding in-place biases across an organization or team.

Big Picture Understanding   This technique entails researching and understanding a number of environmental dimensions that start with a broad pursuit and drive deeper and deeper to better understand the macroeconomic environment and industry, the company or entity within its industry and environment, and finally the organization or business unit within the company or entity.

Billboard Design Thinking   Created by Sean McGuire, this technique for organizing content, engaging stakeholders, driving discussions, and delivering Design Thinking workshops is based on the visual analogy of a billboard.

Black Box Illumination   When we are faced with a "black box" of unknown processes or status, and we've lost confidence in the progress being made within that black box, we need to "shine a light" into the box lest people start making up stuff.

Boats and Anchors   In this visual method of Reverse Brainstorming, the brainstorming participants assign problems, or *anchors*, to a situation, or *boat*, with the intention of identifying what will slow down the boat as it moves toward its destination. The exercise can be expanded to include sharks and rocks in the water, storms and hurricanes on the horizon, and so forth. After the initial exercise, "flip" the logic to consider how to eliminate or minimize the anchors or transform them into speed enablers.

Brainstorming   In perhaps our most germinal ideation technique, we set the stage with others and frame a question or issue to be considered, prepare the team to "embrace a mindset of curiosity," facilitate the brainstorming process through techniques such as a creative warm-up or guardrail for thinking, up-level for individual brainstorming, gather feedback, and share the resulting ideas.

Brainstorming in Reverse   Instead of trying to answer a question or think about a problem head on, we reverse the question or problem and have the team consider what would make things *worse*. Afterward, "flip" the team's answers to think through answering the original question/problem (similar to the **Boats and Anchors** exercise where users assign problems, or "anchors," to a situation, or "boat").

Buddy System Pairing   In this practice, a new team member is paired with a veteran team member for a period of time (such as the first month the new team member is on the Program or Project) to help answer onboarding questions, provide background data, and allow the new team member the chance to ease into their new role, the team's work climate, and the organization's overall culture. Though team-internal, the Buddy System shares similarities with user Shadowing.

Building to Consider and Converge   This technique involves engaging in freeform drawing, outlining, building, organizing, considering, or discussing, in any order and recursively as the need arises, to help us move from divergent thinking to convergent solutioning (and perhaps back and forth as we crystallize our problem solving around a potential solution).

Building to Think   This technique employs the notion that we may do our best ideation and thinking, and therefore arrive at solutions faster, when we simply jump in and start building or "doing." In contrast, for complex endeavors, "planning to think" takes more time and will push many of our learnings late into the solutioning or testing process where changes are expensive and ill-conceived designs must head back to the drawing board.

Bullseye Prioritization   This exercise helps a team organize a broad set of options or choices across four areas (quadrants) and then allows for those options and choices to be prioritized against one another, given that only one choice for each quadrant can occupy the bullseye.

Buy a Feature   This exercise, popularized by the LUMA Institute for creating consensus among a divided team, uses the concept of imaginary money that each team member assigns to their go-forward choice (such that each team member can "put their money where their mouth is" or "let the money do the talking").

Co-Innovation   In this technique, we develop solutions and deliverables together with users, partners, team members, or others in real time side by side, rather than going back and forth between iterative defining, ideating, prototyping, demonstrating and testing, ideating again, eventually building the solution or deliverable, and so on.

Collaboration   This technique involves working with others to arrive at outcomes or execute in ways that would be difficult or impossible alone, with the understanding that no one does their best work, nor can difficult problems be solved, solo.

Concentric Communications   This technique and exercise keeps all of the right people informed at the right time with the right set of information by visually organizing stakeholders into a set of concentric circles laid atop a grid. Each circle represents a priority and a cadence for communications, while the grid reflects a number of key communications channels.

Context Building and Mapping   In this technique we physically or virtually travel to where a community works today, and passively watch and learn how they use their current product or service (or alternatively how they use our prototype or MVP).

Cover Story Mockup   Developing the cover of a magazine, newspaper, or online news story a la the LUMA Institute's Cover Story Mockup method is a powerful way to create alignment and generate excitement today for a day in the future when our products and services will finally become a part of others' lives. This technique casts a vision that answers the question "What do we want people to say and think about our work when the day finally comes, and our work is available for others to use?"

Creating or Increasing a Shared Identity   This is the process of finding or creating common threads or themes between people and teams; increasing Shared Identity is useful for creating and sustaining shared visions, driving stronger collaboration, and intentional culture shaping.

Culture Cube   The Culture Cube reflects three dimensions: an organization's or team's environment, its work climate, and its work style. Use these dimensions to better understand an organization's current-state culture.

Culture Snail for Pace of Change   In this technique, we map how an organization's or team's culture has morphed and changed over time, a person and event at a time. The technique comes from the path a snail takes; like a snail, culture change is organic and alive, slow to move and change, and sometimes amorphous and messy.

Customer Journey Map   This map is an illustration of the various touchpoints from beginning to end that together describe how a customer "flows" through their interaction with a product or service (Kelley & Kelley, 2013). Each touchpoint represents an opportunity to satisfy or disappoint a customer.

"Day in the Life of" Analysis   This technique involves observing or recording the activities of a single representative user to understand the tasks and nature of their work. The more repetitive the work, the more immediately useful this DILO analysis; nonrepetitive edge cases typically represent only 10 to 20 percent of the typical day.

Demonstrations   In this technique, we show mock-ups, prototypes, and other "demos" or ideas to others (team members and especially users) for the purpose of learning and course correcting and iterating.

Design Mindset   This way of approaching a situation is centered around how something works. The Design Mindset is therefore a solution-focused rather than a problem-focused mindset, and as such requires a balance of cognitive analysis skills and imagination.

Design Thinking   This technique is a "human-centered approach to innovation that draws from the designer's toolkit to integrate the needs of people, the possibilities of technology, and the requirements for business success" (Brown, n.d.).

Divergent Thinking   Rather than trying to find the "right" idea or answer to a problem, Divergent Thinking is about getting our mind prepared to creatively find many possible ideas and potential answers. We do this by using tips for getting into a divergent mindset, by applying different thinking and ideation techniques and exercises, and by challenging current thinking (or ideas or designs) as a way to explore the surrounding situation.

Diversity by Design   In this technique, we build teams from the ground up with diversity in mind; consider how the availability and location of skills and capabilities, geographic and time zone implications, communications norms and human capabilities, and a myriad of cultural and other factors can aid or hinder creating balanced and diverse teams.

Edge Case Thinking   While edge cases are, by definition, rare in that they occur at extremes or boundaries, thinking through inevitable edge cases early helps provides insights into users who think, do, and consume systems and solutions differently than the majority. Such insights help us create smarter designs and solutions in the long run, and they may help us build smarter solutions faster for everyone.

Empathy Immersion   Empathy Immersion, or "Walk a mile in another's shoes" as outlined by the LUMA Institute, takes empathy mapping to a deeper level as we personally "walk" another person's journey and experience their joys, conflicts, and weariness along the way. Such immersion helps us feel and connect more deeply with another person and their needs.

Empathy Mapping   This type of mapping is a process for learning about a specific Persona (a community or group of people who perform similar activities) by documenting how a user thinks and feels, what a user sees and hears or says and does, their biggest pain point, and their top one or two goals.

Empathy Through Realized Changes   In Design Thinking, teams usually spend their time empathizing with users. In this case, however, we see users or other stakeholders empathizing with the team seeking to help the users or stakeholders; the empathy comes as a result of realized changes and seeing real progress (no matter how small that progress might be). Thus, *empathy through realized changes* flips the user/team source/target relationship and flow of empathy from team→users to users→team.

Experience Testing   Through this technique, we gain early feedback from the very people who will presumably use our product or solution one day. As we expose them to our products and services, we need to encourage these users to vocalize their likes, dislikes, and what they might change. As Experience Testing is performed early, a portion of Structured Usability Testing performed later will naturally overlap and confirm any changes made in light of previous Experience Testing.

Failing Forward   This important technique (and a type of Forcing Function) is used to force forward progress by removing the option of falling back in the wake of difficulties to a previous state or version. Also called Burning the Ships and Blowing the Bridges, Failing Forward forces us to fight for progress rather than give up and return to the old and presumably insufficient status quo.

Feedback Loop   In one of the fundamentals of Design Thinking, the idea is to create and employ feedback loops as ways to learn and apply those learnings back into the initial problem, an idea, a design, a prototype, a test, and more.

Five Whys   This important method is used for discovering the root cause or reasons behind a particular situation, line of thinking, decision, and other matters. This technique helps us understand user motivations, values, and biases as well. Ask "why" again and again to go beyond the obvious and explore the hidden.

Fixing Broken Windows   Before we can make progress, we might need to first slow down and fix the "broken windows" surrounding our teams and our users. Based on criminology and social theory, the broken windows theory states that visible signs of unresolved neglect or bad behavior promote greater neglect and even worse behavior.

Force Field Analysis   Created by Kurt Lewin in the 1940s as a tool for the social sciences, a Force Field Analysis, or FFA, helps us visualize a situation and the pressure for and against changing that situation.

Forcing Functions   This technique involves using upcoming events or scheduling and calendaring to create very real or completely artificial deadlines for driving progress.

Fractal Thinking   This form of vertical thinking is based on recognizing and using the relationship between the small and the large to learn and think differently. Consider how small team behaviors and practices are reflected or echoed upward into businesses and industries, and how the trends and themes we see at a country level are reflected downward into our economies, industries, businesses, and teams.

Framing Governance for Collaboration   This technique is based on overlaying a virtual governance or oversight structure atop our broad collection of teams and stakeholders. Through this virtual structure, Framing Governance for Collaboration specifies the organizational bodies necessary for overseeing and completing complex endeavors.

Gamification   In this technique, we build game design techniques such as badges and rewards into a prototype, pilot, solution, testing, or training to drive deeper or earlier engagement, incentivize new behaviors, and collect richer feedback.

Golden Ratio Analysis   Using the ratio 1.6:1.0 found in the Fibonacci Sequence, we can turn to the Golden Ratio to explain why a design, product, user interface, or situation does not look or feel right.

Good Enough Thinking   This is the notion that going beyond a design's, deliverable's, or solution's requirements is not only unnecessary but incredibly expensive from a diminishing returns perspective; increasing a deliverable's quality from 95 to 96 percent might double its cost or time-to-value, for example. Common practices (rather than best practices) are often executed to deliver "good enough" outcomes or other results.

Growth Mindset   This technique is about operating and thinking in a way that acknowledges learning requires trying and doing and also failing, and that failing is an important step on the journey to achievement. A growth mindset is incomplete without the ability to extend grace to others who are also learning and occasionally failing on their own knowledge journeys.

Guardrails for Thinking   Guardrails are synonymous with any of the many ways of thinking outlined here that help us ideate differently and therefore focus our thinking in new ways.

Guiding Principles   In this technique, we establish a lightweight set of foundational beliefs, rules, or behaviors that describe and explain "how" an organization or team should operate.

Heatmapping   This is the process of creating heatmaps or visualizations of data or concepts to simplify a complex landscape. Heatmaps depend on the use of color (such as red, yellow, green) or other identifying marks (for accessibility and inclusive design purposes) to highlight attention areas. The variety and gradation of color or other markings help illustrate status or changes, for example, and therefore draw attention to those changes.

"How Might We?" Questioning   This Socratic-inspired Design Thinking staple creates an inclusive, optimistic, and safe place for team ideation, team problem solving, collaboration, and teamwork. HMW Questioning implies that many solutions are possible, and that the team will tackle a problem or situation together, as a team.

Ideate   This is the general process or mindset for thinking, imagining, learning, and ultimately identifying potential answers to questions. Ideation can be performed singularly or as part of a broader collaboration. Common ideation techniques include Brainstorming, Reverse Brainstorming, Good Enough Thinking, Visual Thinking, and Modular Thinking.

Inclusive Communications   This technique underpins healthy cross-teaming in that it helps ensure we include and listen to the whole of our teams, regardless of abilities, believing that each person has a voice, ideas, and thoughts worth surfacing and considering.

Inclusive and Accessible Thinking   In this technique, we consider user community abilities, challenges, culture, values, lifestyles, and preferences; we allow this knowledge to influence with whom we empathize and how and what we design and deliver. Compare this to Edge Case Thinking where the focus is on identifying and delivering the capabilities required versus how those capabilities are accessed.

Instrumenting for Continuous Feedback   Also known as creating a closed-loop or feedback control system, this technique is about building feedback mechanisms into our technology and/ or our system's functionality so we and our systems learn over time and make smarter user experience-based or satisfaction-based decisions.

Inverse Power Law   In this technique, we consider the distribution of changes (small, medium, and large) in terms of how they can be accommodated by a community and in a schedule. A community may be able to absorb a high number of little changes, but fewer numbers of medium changes, and only very few major changes (just as we observe in biology and nature in terms of earthquake and hurricane frequencies and sizes). If the frequency of our planned changes fails to map well to the Inverse Power Law, it is likely we are taking on too much change at once (which might be necessary but should then influence how we plan, think, prepare, execute, or otherwise operate in light of the number and size of these changes).

Iterating   Perhaps the greatest value found in Design Thinking is to build on, refine, or otherwise iterate on something already built. The process of iterating takes our idea, prototype, solution, or understanding to another level of capability or usability.

Lessons Learned   This technique is a form of Looking Back and a core Design Thinking method for surfacing learnings and feedback to be injected into future work. To be of use, learnings and knowledge must be captured regularly rather than exclusively at the end of a project or initiative.

Making Ideas Visible and Visual   The best way to get what is trapped in our heads *out* of our heads is to do so visually. Do so by creating and together refining pictures, figures, charts, models, and so on to help us create a shared understanding between our team members and others we might invite to help us think through and solve problems.

Mesh Networking   Also called Archipelago Networking, as in connecting islands of people and teams, Mesh Networking is about the caring and feeding of teams through intentional connections and a mesh of informal and formal communications. Through an overlay of these connections, we can increase belonging, community, social capital, and social cohesion across our teams, which in turn will positively affect the team's culture and work climate.

Mind Mapping   This common technique is used across business and elsewhere to brainstorm, think, drive clarity, and eventually create a shared understanding of a problem or idea. Created by Tony Buzan in the 1970s, the resulting Mind Map from a Mind Mapping exercise gives us a visual representation as we explore and better understand a central problem or idea by linking a second tier of other ideas or attributes or dependencies to it, followed by linking additional ideas to the second tier, and so on. As we branch out from the central idea, the mind map reveals a hierarchy or set of dependencies and other considerations illuminating that central idea. Mind maps are useful to better understand ideas, concepts, problems, prototype features, potential solution challenges, stakeholder relationships, deliverables structure, and required content.

Minimum Viable Product (MVP) Thinking   In this technique, we engage in thought to understand the minimum level of functionality or capability that delivers value to users, with the understanding that such an MVP must continue evolving through additional iterations to become the full-fledged solution envisioned or required by a community in the first place. MVP Thinking helps us determine next best steps. This technique is also referred to as "seed thinking," in the sense that an MVP, like a seed, grows into much more as it is nurtured and cared for.

Möbius Ideation   In this technique, we maximize our resources by rethinking or reassembling our resources to maximize their usefulness. Consider how a Möbius strip can be fully used, front and back, to provide potentially twice the value we might otherwise realize.

Mocking Up   This is the practice of creating a lightweight prototype of a conceptual solution or design created for experimentation and visualization purposes. Mockups are often simple drawings or arrangements of diagrams and pictures, or a partial replica of a larger whole, created for our purposes here using commonly available tools such as a physical or virtual whiteboard or a tool such as Klaxoon, Figma, PowerPoint, and others.

Modular Thinking and Building   Whether a design, prototype, plan, organizational structure, or career, the idea is to build and think in terms of modules that can be incrementally added or recombined with other modules to create new capabilities, artifacts, or value.

Next Best Step Thinking   When faced with uncertainty, in this technique we consider how to ascertain the next single best step versus trying to map out the entirety of a full journey or plan.

Objectives and Key Results (OKRs)   These are essential to the Progress Mindset, where we execute to deliver value. OKRs connect a project's or initiative's strategic goals with the day-to-day activities executed by a delivery team to achieve those goals. OKRs therefore reflect a goal-setting or value-focused framework designed to connect strategic goals set by a community with the activities that others execute to deliver those goals. With the completion of goals comes value; the two become synonymous. OKRs therefore also create clarity around what value looks like and how we know we have achieved it.

Pattern   This is a high-level blueprint or design useful as a guide for future work; the conceptual version of a (standardized or other) template.

Persona Profiling   This long-time exercise is used to create abstracted fictional characters (such as "finance user," "sales user," PMO users, specific document or artifact users, and other such amalgamations) who represent types or subsets of a real user community. Each persona profile shares common needs and uses specific artifacts or features of a solution or deliverable in similar ways.

Piloting   The idea is to put forth an early version of a solution for (typically) a subset of users to utilize for feedback purposes as well as productive use; pilots are more functionally complete than prototypes.

Possible Futures Thinking   Based on the Futures Wheel created by Jerome C. Glenn in 1971, through this exercise we visually model different versions of the future based on current-day trends or events and the possible consequences of those trends or events using a wheel analogy and the acronym STEEP (Social, Technology, Economic, Environmental, and Political).

Postmortem   A form of Looking Back, this practice involves looking back in time to examine and dissect how a situation or problem arose, progressed, and concluded; sometimes synonymous with lessons learned though the postmortem connotation typically implies a one-time examination at the end of a project or initiative.

Power/Interest Grid   This visual prioritization exercise forces us to map the power (or influence) and interest that each stakeholder holds in our IT project or initiative as a way to determine who holds the most power or influence over decision-making, who has the highest interest in our work and therefore needs to be kept informed, who needs to simply be kept satisfied, and who only needs to be monitored.

Premortem   The "pre" version of a postmortem or backbrief, this exercise is performed to purposely think ahead about what might fail or occur and why, *before such failures occur*. Premortems include building in mitigations or additional user involvement to avoid these failure scenarios. Premortems can help us identify and subsequently avoid the kind of fantastic failures that otherwise surprise and shut down projects and initiatives while also helping us see biases at work (that is, confirmation bias or group think).

Probing for (Better) Understanding   This technique involves investigating and asking questions of users and others that cannot be answered without some thought. The goal of Probing is to bring clarity to a situation (whether current or potential) to avoid mistakes that have been made before and to find a way through the ambiguity ahead of us. Probing questions must also go beyond those questions that only clarify, though, and seek to understand the *edges* through open-ended "Why?" and similar lines of questioning.

Problem Framing   Based on the work performed by Getzels and Csikszentmihalyi regarding the need to understand problems as a precursor to creativity, a Problem Framing exercise provides context and helps us understand and prioritize a particular problem over a set of other potential problems. Problem Framing also gives us the seeds for creating a definitive problem statement.

Problem Stating   This is the process or exercise of turning a potential problem into a problem statement, which, in turn, provides a crisp and shared understanding of the problem to help a team rally around what is needed to solve that problem.

Problem Tree Analysis   Based on Paulo Freire's work in education in the early 1970s, this exercise helps us to separate the causes of a problem from the effects or implications of that problem. This simple method is based on a tree metaphor. Draw the trunk to represent the problem, the roots below to represent root causes, and the branches above to capture the effects and other outcomes stemming from that problem.

Process Flows   Useful in prototyping, process flows provide clarity through visualizing how a sequence of events unfolds. Explore and experiment with the flow of data through a proposed system to understand where the data is housed, how it is surfaced, where it is used as an input and an output, its dependencies, and more. Process flows made visual through drawings and schematics help us drive discussions and close the gaps in our prototypes.

Proof of Concept   This limited prototype or exercise is used to demonstrate that a particular approach, capability, or feature set is directionally aligned with user needs. A Proof of Concept exercise demonstrates feasibility.

Prototyping   This is the process of "building to think" by creating a solution (or partial solution) to a problem that may then be shared with users, tested, and iteratively refined (or tossed out); the idea is to learn fast, fail fast, iterate, and therefore make meaningful progress while learning and failing cheaply.

Rapid or "Rough and Ready" Prototyping   This is the process of quickly putting together a visualization of a potential solution to determine if the prototype is directionally accurate. Examples could be as simple as a whiteboard diagram, animated PowerPoint, or software-based wireframe.

Reducing Cognitive Load   This technique is about recognizing and reducing the extraneous load we place on ourselves and others when we fail to stop thinking and start doing. After a period of thinking and ideation, we may need to find ways to focus afresh and kick-start execution.

Release Planning   The process involves identifying, prioritizing, and selecting the high-level capabilities and user stories (needs) to be reflected in our solution, built over a period of time, and delivered at the conclusion of that time in the form of a time-boxed "release."

Retrospective   This technique is a form of Looking Back, where, at the conclusion of a sprint or release, we discuss what the team accomplished and what still remains to be accomplished. We also think about why work isn't moving fast enough and in other cases why we have achieved a reasonable velocity. We consider the difference makers, and we discuss how we can repeat the good, improve the bad, and totally eliminate the ugly.

Rose, Thorn, Bud (RTB) Exercise   This exercise, popularized by the LUMA Institute, is used for exploring an option or choice by organizing the positive, the negative, and the opportunities associated with the option or choice. Roses are those aspects of an option or choice that are positive, healthy, or working well. Thorns are those outcomes or consequences that are not healthy or positive. Finally, buds are areas of potential insights or opportunities for improvement. Note that buds are often the difference makers in choosing one option over another.

Rough and Ready Prototyping   A long-time method popularized more recently by the LUMA Institute, this umbrella technique for "thinking with our hands" is used to quickly create low-cost models and designs. The sooner we can put something tangible in front of our prospective user community, the faster we can obtain useful feedback. Such prototypes help us validate if we are directionally correct in our thinking and designing. Examples of rough and ready prototyping include creating mockups, wireframes, sketches, and inexpensive three-dimensional models.

Running the Swamp   This time pressure exercise is intended to help us think fast to generate the kinds of fantastically exacting ideas necessary to survive or escape a terrible situation.

Sacrificing the Calf   This technique is a way to work through the tired old ideas or solutions floating in our heads by taking those dead-end ideas off the table and calling them what they are for us at this particular time and with this particular problem: dead. This untimely death serves as a Forcing Function for trying new ideas or learning new skills.

Scaling by Fives   This technique involves sizing the most productive teams using the optimal team size of five, which has been shown through research and vast experience to represent the number of people who can connect and work most effectively together.

SCAMPER Ideation   Using this stepwise method and acronym, we can improve a team's brainstorming ability using the following keywords in a "How Might We?" structure to consider a problem of situation in terms of (S) how might we substitute…?, (C) how might we combine…?, (A) how might we adapt…?, (M) how might we modify or magnify…?, (P) how might we repurpose or put to another use…?, (E) how might we eliminate or minimize…?, and finally (R) how might we reverse or rearrange?

Service Reliability Engineering (SRE)   This technique comprises the engineering, technical, and change control methodologies and procedures necessary to manage the reliability of a system and resolve reliability operations and infrastructure issues (often in an automated or self-healing kind of way). Synonymous with a culture or mindset of service reliability, service reliability engineers work to automate what can be responsibly automated as a way to avoid manually introduced issues.

Silent Design   In this technique, we learn and gather feedback by observing the changes that users (not designers!) make to a product, service, or solution to increase its effectiveness or usability after it has been deployed.

Simple Rules   This set of six or fewer Rules describe who and what you are as a team or organization; they may include what you do and don't do, outputs, priorities, boundaries; stop and start parameters, and more.

Shadowing   This is the process of following or working side by side with a user or another person to either understand or learn their work first-hand. Shadowing can be extended (and made much more repeatable) by recording standard processes or step-by-step instructions.

Shortcut or Wormhole Thinking   This technique is about finding not-so-obvious shortcuts between where we are today and where we need to go. The key lies in two areas: navigating everything between us and our destination without allowing ourselves to get caught up in the detours and side routes, and fundamentally changing the playing field to find a shorter route. The straight lines and obvious paths aren't necessarily the best paths for our specific situation.

Slay the Hero   This technique is a long-time staple of disaster recovery planning and exercises. The idea is both simple and brilliant, and for our purposes akin to "human prototyping and testing." We use Slay the Hero to test our systems and processes for human resiliency.

Smart IP Reuse   In this technique, we use templates, previous deliverables, accelerators, and other IP to help us start faster or move with greater velocity.

Smart Multitasking   This technique builds on the classic multitasking method where we perform two or more tasks simultaneously in several ways: Do the thing that gives us the most energy at the time, and then move on to the next thing that gives us the most energy; make progress on the big rocks (the most important items) early so we still have time and energy to get these done at all; and use Time Boxing and Forcing Functions when the tasks to complete fail to give us the natural energy to get them done.

Snaking the Drain   This lightweight discussion technique or exercise is used to reset our minds when the old solutions or quick fixes tend to creep back into our heads, holding us back from thinking differently. With little emotion, talk through the old way of doing things. Discuss its advantages and disadvantages one final time, and either adopt the old solution or rule it out so we can restart our thinking with a clean slate. Snake the Drain to refresh, reset, and rethink.

Solution Interviewing   After we conclude traditional User Acceptance Testing, we confirm our product or solution is truly "accepted" using Solution Interviewing, which builds on the static pass/fail results and dry results obtained through UAT. Solution Interviewing gives us the rich feedback we need to make smart updates to our products and solutions even if they have been "accepted" for the time being.

Stakeholder Mapping   This is the process of creating a visual or graphic representation of the stakeholder register, including specific people, roles, and groups that have a stake or interest in Program/Project outcomes. The map and register are organized around users, sponsors, leaders, partners, and the various teams required to design, develop, test, deploy, and operate a solution or product, and they include contact information, engagement dates, assessments of power and influence, and classifications and interests of each stakeholder. Maps and registers are not precisely interchangeable, but they both reflect similar data.

Stakeholder+ Mapping   This exercise adds a useful Design Thinking element to a traditional stakeholder map by including thought bubbles and speech bubbles to each stakeholder identified on the map. Thought bubbles reflect what we believe each stakeholder is thinking, and speech bubbles reflect what each stakeholder is telling us or sharing with others.

Stakeholder Sentiment Mapping   In this technique, we apply color or icons to a traditional stakeholder map to visually communicate, or "visualize," stakeholder sentiment. The RAG (red, amber, green) method for color-coding is common, where unsatisfied stakeholders are coded red, neutral are coded amber or yellow, and satisfied stakeholders are coded green. In cases where color differentiation is impractical for accessibility or other reasons, use happy/neutral/unhappy emojis to communicate status.

Storytelling   This communication and change management method yields emotionally sticky and memorable outcomes by uniting the right (creative) side of the brain with the left (logic) side. Stories help messages resonate in ways that other communications mediums cannot. Good stories educate and change people and their attitudes, biases, and thinking, ultimately influencing work climate and culture.

Structured Text   In this technique, we use words rather than pictures; this technique considers how formatting, physical placement, margins and other whitespace, and text highlighting and color are used to drive consumability and elicit meaning.

Structured Usability Testing   This technique is used to test and validate our prototypes early on with our users by creating and using a uniform and repeatable environment for this testing, including sharing with each user the test's purpose and goals across a sequenced set of test cases or scenarios to execute.

Subtraction Game   This hyper-focused timed exercise reflects a combination of Divergent Thinking and Brainstorming. It comprises three timed steps spanning 10 minutes, with a follow-on 10 minutes earmarked afterward for sharing and discussing what to eliminate and how to do so.

Supervillain Monologuing   This technique is used for engaging and learning from others by encouraging people with knowledge of our situation and the landscape to monologue about their perspectives—like an evil supervillain! Lead them where they want to go, get them to talk, and then simply listen and learn.

Taxonomy Kick-starters   When our minds are too tired or too cluttered to think in new ways, we use the structure of a common taxonomy to kick-start our thinking processes and reinvigorate our creativity. Examples include SCAMPER's 7-step process for brainstorming, the Agile Manifesto's 4 values and 12 principles, Heuristic Analysis and its 10 usability heuristics, the STEED acronym used in Possible Futures exercises to help us think across 5 or more dimensions, a standard Risk Register, the AEIOU mnemonic for problem validation, and so on.

The Rule of Threes   A prototype, new design, solution, deliverable, or other work product is rarely successful out of the gate; set expectations that it often takes three iterations to meet minimum requirements.

Time Boxing   This simple Agile technique for time management was developed by James Martin. The idea is to create a "box" of time in which to complete a task or body of work. The box serves as a deadline and provides healthy tension that drives a sense of urgency and Good Enough Thinking.

Time Pacing   Businesses, processes, nature, and more exhibit rhythms in how they naturally unfold. In this technique, we strive to understand the peaks and valleys of these existing rhythms to thoughtfully structure other activities in and around them to create the most effective schedule or strategy.

Trend Analysis   This technique is used to assess the broader environment rooted in observation, research, and analysis. It is usually associated with end user and user community trends, but can be applied more broadly to teams, business units, companies, industries, and other sources. Trend Analysis requires collecting and analyzing data from the source in question to determine if there is a correlation or relationship present in the data over time. We might assess similarities and differences based on groups of users or other sources and correlate these similarities or differences (deltas) based on the time or day (or week, month, or season), geography, industry, organization, education, language, age, gender, effectiveness, performance, number of errors, choices offered, default decisions made, and so on. Use Trend Analysis to draw high-level conclusions about a situation's big picture, an organization's culture, and a team's work climate and biases.

User-Centric (or User-Centered or Human-Centered) Thinking   This general term is synonymous with Design Thinking, where understanding the needs of a user or user community in the context of a specific environment, situation, and problem drives empathy and ultimately better problem definition and solutioning.

User Story Mapping   In this technique, a process or recipe is used to bring together the steps necessary to deliver a user story, from identifying goals and user journey to solutioning, organizing work into time boxes or sprints, and publishing a release plan.

User Story Sizing   In this technique, we use story points, T-shirt sizing, or similar estimation approaches to estimate the time and effort or development capacity necessary to create a feature or process.

Visual Thinking   When we turn our ideas and plans and solutions into pictures and figures, thus making them visible and visual, we arrive at a shared understanding more quickly. Visual thinking is about transforming the shapeless and invisible thoughts in our heads into figures and maps and images that help us understand and think, which in turn allows us to communicate and collaborate with others.

"Wakanda Forever!"   This technique is used for connecting an individual to a team or organization with a legacy of purpose and achievement. Doing so can help motivate an individual to deliver at a higher level of performance than they would have been capable of delivering solo.

"What, So What, Now What?"   This game-based exercise helps us learn enough to break free of indecision. The idea is to work through a recent event and view it through the questions and lenses of "What?" "So what?" and "Now what?" This exercise opens the door to determining the next best step while having healthy conversations about how to effectively tackle similar situations in the future.

Wireframing   This is the process of illustrating a process, flow, interface, or view (typically in the context of a user interface). A good wireframe focuses on functionality and accessibility through a well-designed layout and intuitive navigation. Wireframes serve as the basis for prototyping.

Worst and Best Ideation   This lighthearted thinking-in-reverse exercise is useful with people and groups who are unfamiliar with one another and may be uncomfortable thinking so "differently." The Worst and Best exercise is drawn from the Worst Possible Idea method shared by Interaction-Design.org. Instead of putting people on the spot to solve a problem, each participant is given a situation or problem and simply asked to answer what would make this situation or problem even worse. Afterward we can "flip" this answer like we do with Reverse Brainstorming to generate a potential solution worth considering.

APPENDIX C

Design Thinking in Action (by the Hour)

The Design Thinking terms, techniques, and exercises summarized here are organized by the Hour in which they appeared (note that each technique and exercise is also arranged alphabetically in Appendix B).

Hour 1: Design Thinking Explained

Techniques versus Exercises

The Design Thinking Cycle for Progress

Hour 2: A Design Thinking Model for Tech

Human-Centered Thinking

Understanding Broadly

Thinking Differently

Delivering Value

Iterating for Progress

Hour 3: Design Thinking for Small Audiences

Learning More Quickly   Stakeholder Mapping

Persona Profiling

Stakeholder+ Mapping

Journey Mapping

"Day in the Life of" Analysis

Thinking and Problem Solving   Visual Thinking

Pattern Matching

Fractal Thinking

Divergent Thinking

Problem Tree Analysis

The Five Whys

Opposite Thinking or Reverse Brainstorming

Coping with Ambiguity	Modular Thinking
	Building to Think
	MVP Thinking
	Cover Story Mockup
	The Premortem
Prioritizing Next Best Steps for Uncertainty	Bullseye Prioritization
	Adjacent Spaces Technique
	Rose, Thorn, Bud (RTB) Exercise
	Affinity Clustering
Executing More Effectively	Forcing Functions
	Time Boxing
	Gamification
	"Wakanda Forever!"

Hour 4: Resilient and Sustainable Teams

Simple Rules for Healthy Alignment

Guiding Principles for Operating Consistency

"How Might We?" for Inclusive Teamwork

Diversity by Design for Smarter Ideation

Growth Mindset for Learning and Teaming

The Rule of Threes for Iterating

Inclusive and Effective Meetings

Mesh Networking for Resiliency

Hour 5: Visible and Visual Teamwork

Making Ideas Visible and Visual

Visual Thinking for Understanding

Exercises for Visual Collaboration

Billboard Design Thinking

Icebreakers for Exercise Preparation

Warm-ups for Thinking Differently

Guardrails for Reinvigorating Thought

Hour 6: Understanding the Lay of the Land

Active Listening

Silence by Design

Hour 11: Guardrails for Thinking Creatively

Analogy and Metaphor Thinking

Good Enough Thinking

Edge Case Thinking

Inclusive and Accessible Thinking

Modular Thinking and Building

The Premortem

Boats and Anchors

Mission Impossible Thinking

Möbius Ideation

Hour 12: Exercises for Increasing Creativity

Visual Thinking

Heatmapping

Divergent Thinking

Running the Swamp

Fractal Thinking

Golden Ratio Analysis

Hour 13: Exercises for Reducing Uncertainty

Next Step Thinking

Possible Futures Thinking

Aligning Strategy to Time Horizons

Backporting into the Past

Adjacent Space Exploration for Lower Risks

"What, So What, Now What?"

MVP Thinking

2×2 Matrix Thinking for What's Next

Bullseye Prioritization

Rose, Thorn, and Bud

Affinity Clustering

Buy a Feature

Hour 14: Thinking for Problem Solving

"How Might We?" for Problem Solving

Brainstorming

SCAMPER for Better Brainstorming

Co-innovation

Worst and Best Ideation

Reverse Brainstorming

Building to Consider and Converge

Force Field Analysis

Mind Mapping

Hour 15: Cross-Teaming and Communicating for Outcomes

Framing Governance for Collaboration

Concentric Communications

Inclusive Communications

Creating a Shared Identity

Black Box Illumination

Storytelling for Deeper Understanding

Structured Text for Rapid Comprehension

Hour 16: Prototyping and Solutioning by Doing

Cover Story Mockup for a Shared Vision

Process Flows for Clarity

Rough and Ready Prototyping (including Mocking Up, Wireframing, etc.)

Building to Think

Forcing Functions for Progress

Time Boxing for Speed and Feedback

The Inverse Power Law

Time Pacing for Interdependencies

Hour 17: Solutioning Small and Fast

Objectives and Key Results

The Proof of Concept (POC)

The Minimum Viable Product (MVP)

The Pilot

Failing Forward for Progress

Hour 18: Delivering Value at Velocity

Release and Sprint Planning

Smart IP Reuse

Operating Small to Deliver Big

User Story Sizing

User Story Mapping

Smart Multitasking

Gamification

Shortcut or Wormhole Thinking

Hour 19: Testing for Validation

Structured Usability Testing

A/B Testing

Experience Testing

Solution Interviewing

Automating for Regression Velocity

Hour 20: Feedback for Continuous Improvement

Looking Back (includes the Retrospective, Lessons Learned, and the Postmortem)

Testing Feedback

Gathering Silent Design Feedback

Context Building and Mapping

Instrumenting for Continuous Feedback

Hour 21: Deploying for Progress

Fixing Broken Windows

Avoiding the Abilene Paradox

Reducing Cognitive Load

Backward Invention

Balancing the Essential and the Accidental

Hour 22: Operating at Scale

Scaling by Fives

The Subtraction Game

AntiFragile Validation

Buddy System Pairing

Slaying the Hero for System Resiliency

Operating Structures at Scale

Validating OKRs and Value

Aligning People to Value

Silent Design for Sustainment

Hour 23: Making Change Sticky

Creating Awareness	Big Picture Understanding
	Fractal Thinking
	Stakeholder+ Mapping
	Persona Profiling
	Cover Story Mockup
	Snaking the Drain
	Sacrificing the Calf
	Make Ideas Visible and Visual
	Problem Tree Analysis
	Problem Framing
	Problem Stating
Providing Purpose	"Day in the Life of" Analysis
	Journey Mapping
	Verbatim Mapping
	Feedback from Prototyping and Testing
	Force Field Analysis
	Fixing Broken Windows
Driving Readiness	Analogy and Metaphor Thinking
	Prototypes and Mockups
	Structured Usability Testing
	Solution Interviewing
	Buddy System Pairing
Adopting Change	Forcing Functions for Adoption
	Gamification
	Context Building and Mapping
	Making Change Consumable

Timing Change	Culture Snail for Pace of Change
	Bias Recognition and Validation
	AntiFragile Validation
	Fixing Broken Windows
	Inverse Power Law
	Time Pacing

Hour 24: Design Thinking for Project Velocity

Methods for Leadership and Governance

Methods for Stakeholders and Expectations

Methods for Development Approach

Methods for Risk Management

Methods for Schedule Management

Methods for Managing Scope

Methods for Delivery and Quality

Methods for Communications and Collaboration

References

Argyris, C., & Senge, P. (1990). "Ladder of Inference." Retrieved August 13, 2022, from https://www.toolshero.com/decision-making/ladder-of-inference/.

Besant, H. (2016). "The Journey of Brainstorming." *Journal of Transformative Innovation*, Issue: 1, Vol 2

Brown, T. (n.d.). "Why Design Thinking." Retrieved May 6, 2019, from https://www.ideou.com/pages/design-thinking.

Brown, T. (2019). *Change by Design: How Design Thinking Transforms Organizations and Inspires Innovation*. NY, NY: HarperBusiness.

Buzan, T. (2017). *Mind Maps*. Tony Buzan Learning Centre. Retrieved May 6, 2022, from https://www.tonybuzan.edu.sg/about/mind-maps/.

Carsten, B. (1989). Carsten's Corner. *Power Conversion and Intelligent Motion*. November 1989, 38.

CrowdStrike. (2022). "What Is Backporting?" Retrieved June 3, 2022, from https://www.crowdstrike.com/cybersecurity-101/backporting/.

Debevoise, N. D. (2021). "The Third Critical Step in Problem Solving That Einstein Missed." Retrieved May 13, 2022, from https://bthechange.com/the-third-critical-step-in-problem-solving-that-einstein-missed-4c0dc0c1a96d.

Drucker, P. (1954). *The Practice of Management*. New York, NY: Harper & Row.

Dweck, C. (2006). *Mindset: The New Psychology of Success*. New York, NY: Random House.

Eberle, B. (2008). *Scamper: Creative Games and Activities for Imagination Development*. Oxfordshire, GB: Routledge.

Eisenhardt, K. M., and Brown, S. L. (1998). "Time Pacing: Competing in Markets That Won't Stand Still." *Harvard Business Review*. Retrieved June 8, 2022, from https://hbr.org/1998/03/time-pacing-competing-in-markets-that-wont-stand-still.

Forbes. (2011, July). "Global Diversity and Inclusion: Fostering Innovation Through a Diverse Workforce." *Forbes Insight Report*. Retrieved April 19, 2019, from https://i.forbesimg.com/forbesinsights/StudyPDFs /Innovation_Through_Diversity.pdf.

Freire Institute (2022). "Paulo Freire." Retrieved Aug 20, 2022, from https://www.freire.org/paulo-freire/.

Furino, R. (2016). *Stakeholder Engagement: A Very Human Endeavor.* Paper presented at PMI® North America Congress—San Diego, CA: Project Management Institute (September 25–28).

Gay. B. (2016). "Design Thinking and Project Management." Retrieved July 1, 2022, from https://www.slideshare.net/brussik3/design-thinking-project-management-june-2016.

Getzels, J. W., & Csikszentmihalyi, M. (1976). *Perspectives in Creativity. From Problem Solving to Problem Finding.* Oxfordshire, GB: Routledge.

Glenn, J. C. (1972). *Futurizing Teaching vs Futures Course.* Social Science Record, Syracuse University, Volume IX, No. 3.

Gorb, P., & Dumas, A. (1987). "Silent Design." Retrieved February 8, 2022, from https://www.sciencedirect.com/science/article/abs/pii/0142694X87900378.

Gray, D., Brown, S., & Macanufo, J. (2010). *Gamestorming: A Playbook for Innovators, Rulebreakers, and Changemakers.* Sebastopol, CA: O'Reilly Media.

Greer, L. L., de Jong, B. A., Schouten, M. E. & Dannals, J. E. (2018). "Why and When Hierarchy Impacts Team Effectiveness: A Meta-Analytic Integration," *Journal of Applied Psychology*, 103, 591-613.

Harvey, J. B. (1974). "The Abilene Paradox: The Management of Agreement." Retrieved July 17, 2022, from http://web.mit.edu/curhan/www/docs/Articles/15341_Readings/Group_Dynamics/Harvey_Abilene_Paradox.pdf.

IDEO. (2022). "Brainstorming." Retrieved June 29, 2022, from https://www.ideou.com/pages/brainstorming.

Interaction-Design.org (2022). "What is Worst Possible Idea?" Retrieved June 1, 2022, from https://www.interaction-design.org/literature/topics/worst-possible-idea.

Jung, C. G. (1980). *Psychology and Alchemy* (Collected Works of C.G. Jung Vol.12). Princeton, NJ: Princeton University Press.

Kahneman, D. (2011). *Thinking, Fast and Slow.* NY, NY: Farrar, Straus and Giroux.

Kauffman, S. A. (2002). *Investigations.* Oxfordshire, GB: Oxford University Press.

Kelley, D., & Kelley, T. (2013). *Creative Confidence: Unleashing the Creative Potential within us All.* NY, NY: Crown Business.

Klein, G. (2007). "Performing a Project Premortem." *Harvard Business Review.* Retrieved January 2, 2022, from https://hbr.org/2007/09/performing-a-project-premortem.

Lewin, K. (1951). *Field Theory in Social Science.* New York, NY: Harper and Row.

Lowy, A., & Hood, P. (2004). *The Power of the 2 x 2 Matrix: Using 2 x 2 Thinking to Solve Business Problems and Make Better Decisions.* Hoboken, NJ: Jossey-Bass.

LUMA Institute. (2012). "Methods." Retrieved July 5, 2022, from https://www.lumaworkplace.com/methods/

Martin, J. (1991). *Rapid Application Development.* New York, NY: Macmillan Publishers.

McGuire, S. (2021). *Billboard Design Thinking Moderator Training: How to Start a Career as a Design Thinking Moderator.* Amazon Independent. Paperback. Retrieved April 25, 2022, from https://www.amazon.com/Billboard-Design-Thinking-Moderator-Training/dp/B09FRR76BC/ref=sr_1_1?crid= 1W5LN9YV4VIR1&keywords=billboard+design+thinking&qid=1661233011&s=books&sprefix=billboard+design+thinking%2Cstripbooks%2C95&sr=1-1.

Mittal, P. (2021). *The Theory of Creativity.* Amazon Independent. Paperback. Retrieved May 6, 2022, from https://www.amazon.com/Theory-Creativity-Prashant-Mittal/dp/B09CKPGCCY/ref=tmm_pap_swatch_0?_encoding=UTF8&qid=&sr=.

Patnaik, D. (2022). "Innovation Starts with Empathy." Retrieved June 28, 2022, from http://www.jumpassociates.com/learning-posts/innovation-starts-with-empathy/.

Pink, D. H. (2009). *Drive: The Surprising Truth About What Motivates Us.* NY, NY: Riverhead Hardcover.

Project Management Institute. (2017). *A Guide to the Project Management Body of Knowledge (PMBOK® Guide)—Sixth Edition.* Newtown Square, PA: Project Management Institute.

Project Management Institute. (2017). *The Standard for Program Management—Fourth Edition.* Newtown Square, PA: Project Management Institute.

Project Management Institute. (2021). *A Guide to the Project Management Body of Knowledge (PMBOK® Guide)—Seventh Edition and The Standard for Project Management.* Newtown Square, PA: Project Management Institute.

Rittel, Horst W. J.; Webber, Melvin M. (1973). "Dilemmas in a General Theory of Planning." *Policy Sciences.* 4 (2): 155–169.

Robinson, R. E. (2015). "Building a Useful Research Tool: An Origin Story of AEIOU." Retrieved June 8, 2022, from https://www.epicpeople.org/building-a-useful-research-tool/.

Scott, S. J. (2018), "What is Parkinson's Law? (and 7 Ways to Use Time Constraints to Your Advantage)." Retrieved May 4, 2022, from https://www.developgoodhabits.com/parkinsons-law/.

Sheedy, K. V. (2021). "Nurturing Nature: Leadership, Fractal Thinking and the Myth of Creativity." Retrieved May 6, 2022, from https://nebhe.org/journal/nurturing-nature-leadership-fractal-thinking-and-the-myth-of-creativity/.

Straker, D. (n.d.). "Reverse Brainstorming." Retrieved July 1, 2022, from http://creatingminds.org/tools/reverse_brainstorming.htm.

Sull, D., & Eisenhardt, K.M. (2015). *Simple Rules: How to Thrive in a Complex World.* Mariner Books.

Taleb, N. (2012). *Antifragile: Things That Gain from Disorder.* New York, NY: Random House.

Toyoda, S. (2022). "5 Whys Analysis." https://www.toolshero.com/problem-solving/5-whys-analysis/.

Tyler, C. F. (2019). "The Rise Of Empathetic Leadership." *Leadership Excellence,* 36(5), 8-9.

Wilson, J. Q., & Kelling, G. L. (1982). "Broken Windows." *The Atlantic Monthly.* Retrieved June 1, 2022, from https://www.theatlantic.com/magazine/archive/1982/03/broken-windows/304465/.

Wood, L. C., & Reiners, T. (2015). "Gamification." In M. Khosrow-Pour (Ed.), *Encyclopedia of Information Science and Technology* (3rd ed., pp. 3039-3047). Hershey, PA: Information Science Reference. DOI: 10.4018/978-1-4666-5888-2.ch297.

Zeigler, K. (2022). "Five Ways Leaders can Design a Culture of Belonging." Retrieved May 4, 2022, from https://www.linkedin.com/pulse/5-ways-leaders-can-design-culture-belonging-karen-zeigler/?trackingId=LrhImFOWSw23VrO%2BIJeIPg%3D%3D.

Index